To

A sampling of young
Leuvense theologians.

With thanks for your
scholarship and
friendship.
                    Terrence

THEOLOGY AND THE QUEST FOR TRUTH

BIBLIOTHECA
EPHEMERIDUM THEOLOGICARUM LOVANIENSIUM

UNIVERSITÉ CATHOLIQUE DE LOUVAIN
LOUVAIN-LA-NEUVE

KATHOLIEKE UNIVERSITEIT LEUVEN
LEUVEN

BIBLIOTHECA EPHEMERIDUM THEOLOGICARUM LOVANIENSIUM

CCII

THEOLOGY AND THE QUEST FOR TRUTH

HISTORICAL- AND SYSTEMATIC-THEOLOGICAL STUDIES

EDITED BY

M. LAMBERIGTS – L. BOEVE – T. MERRIGAN

in collaboration with

D. CLAES

LEUVEN
UNIVERSITY PRESS

UITGEVERIJ PEETERS
LEUVEN - PARIS - DUDLEY, MA

2006

ISBN 90-5867-576-9 (Leuven University Press)
ISBN 978-90-5867-576-7
D/2006/1869/60
ISBN-10: 90-429-1873-X (Peeters Leuven)
ISBN-13: 978-90-429-1873-3
D/2007/0602/26

Library of Congress Cataloging-in-Publication Data

Theology and the quest for truth: historical- and systematic-theological studies / edited by
M. Lamberigts, L. Boeve, T. Merrigan in collaboration with D. Claes.
    p. cm. -- (Bibliotheca Ephemeridum theologicarum Lovaniensium ; 202)
Based on a Symposium held Sept. 12-14, 2004 in Westmalle, Belgium.
Includes bibliographical references and index.
ISBN 978-90-429-1873-3 (alk. paper)
    1. Truth -- Religious Aspects -- Christianity. 2. Theology. I. Title. II. Series.

BT50.T475 2007
230.01--dc22
                                                                            2006050878

Leuven University Press / Presses Universitaires de Louvain
Universitaire Pers Leuven
Blijde Inkomststraat 5, B-3000 Leuven-Louvain (Belgium)

© 2006, Peeters, Bondgenotenlaan 153, B-3000 Leuven (Belgium)

PREFACE

In 2001, three research groups from the field of systematic theology and church history at the Faculty of Theology, K.U.Leuven, decided to join forces in an interdisciplinary theological project, entitled: "Orthodoxy: Process and Product". The main aim of this project consists of a "church-historical and systematic-theological study of the determination of truth in church and theology". Senior and junior scholars from the three groups agreed to take this theme as the starting point and leading question from which the many research projects they are engaged in, could be brought into relationship and – as far as possible – integrated. On a competitive basis, the Research Fund of the K.U.Leuven assigned this joined project a considerable grant for five years (2003-2007).

Although the question for theological truth already structured the research being conducted in the three groups to a significant degree, joining forces promised the realisation of a surplus-value, and this both through the gathering of a considerable critical mass (in total more than thirty junior and senior researchers) and the interdisciplinary design of the project. In view of the integrating question leading this research (i.e., the nature and determination of theological truth), and the divergent methodologies employed by church historians and systematic theologians, a twofold methodological concern comes to the fore. In the first place, the project involves explicitly church-historical and systematic-theological research into the process by which theological truth claims emerge. Secondly, this inquiry into the problematic addressed by this project is always conducted against the background of the methodological 'meta-question' regarding the precise relationship between church-historical research and systematic-theological reflection on that research. Finally, it is the same theological-epistemological research hypothesis which underlies both methodological concerns: radical and irreducible particularity does not preclude theological truth, but may well be seen as a condition of possibility of its disclosure, both historically and theologically.

In this volume a first collection of contributions to this project, from a diversity of angles and research subjects, is presented. Preliminary versions of these papers were presented and discussed at a research symposium in Westmalle, September 12-14, 2004. In these contributions scholars from the participating research groups investigate the implications of the overall research question for their particular line of research and research methodologies, and suggest how from this specific research the overall question may be refined and elements of answering it can be provided.

This first exercise clearly shows the productive force of the research design of "Orthodoxy: Process and Product", and of the encounter of scholars from different theological fields discussing the theme of theology and truth. With this collection, however, the work has only started. In due time, we hope to publish the more elaborate results of our project. But as for now, the present contributions bear witness to a surely fruitful and promising endeavour.

Lieven BOEVE
Mathijs LAMBERIGTS
Terrence MERRIGAN

CONTENTS

INTRODUCTION

As already mentioned in the Preface, this collection of essays consists of a number of studies investigating how the question for theological truth can be dealt with from a variety of particular historical-theological and/or systematic-theological research projects. In this introduction we first present the main lines of the research design of "Orthodoxy: Process and Product", and afterwards we shortly introduce the contributions to this volume.

I. THEOLOGY AND THE QUESTION OF TRUTH
MAIN LINES OF AN INTERDISCIPLINARY PROJECT[1]

The question of truth and the way in which it is determined is as pertinent as ever. This problematic permeates contemporary theological discussions, and is quite prominent in the following areas: the so-called 'borderline' questions shared between philosophy and theology; the reflection on the development of tradition and the hermeneutics of tradition; the relationship between the world religions. The problematic of theological truth (orthodoxy) can be said to involve two major issues, namely, the question of *the nature of theological truth*, and the question of *the determination of theological truth*. The former question concerns the characteristics of (theological) truth, with particular attention being devoted to the issue of its normative character. The latter concerns the criteria of theological truth, that is to say, the way in which theological truth is identified and legitimated. The overall 'Orthodoxy: Process and Product'-project is devoted to these questions, and seeks to address them in view of a *twofold methodological concern*.

In the first place, the project involves explicitly *church-historical and systematic-theological research into the process by which theological truth claims emerge*. The project takes as its point of departure paradigmatic moments in the history of theology, including the contemporary scene. The aim here is to provide insight into the process by which theological truth has emerged in the past (church-historical component), and,

---

1. For a presentation of this project and the research groups involved in it, see: http://www.theo.kuleuven.be/goa, or http://www.orthodoxy.be.

using this research, to develop a responsible and intellectually-defensible position with respect to its emergence in the present and the future (systematic-theological component). The *research-hypothesis* underpinning this inquiry is that the (postmodern) rediscovery of the importance of particularity for understanding the nature of theological truth, and the way in which it is determined, provides a key to re-conceptualize both the history of theological truth, and systematic theological reflection on such truth. This same hermeneutical key will be operative with regard to both the 'meta-question' which is generated by this research, and the methodology employed in the research.

The horizon against which this research is undertaken is the *methodological 'meta-question'* regarding the precise relationship between church-historical research and systematic-theological reflection on that research. Indeed, one of the main concerns of this project is to inquire into the feasibility of interdisciplinary cooperation between church-historical and systematic-theological research. The point of departure for such an inquiry is the recognition that both disciplines are united in their attention to the particular and the contingent. The question is whether – despite the differences between them, and the real possibility of methodological conflicts – the attention to particularity cannot contribute to a renewed and fruitful encounter between these disciplines.

Taking as the starting point the expertise available in the existing research-groups, the following three avenues of research are pursued:

- *Augustine and the reception of Augustine* in the history of theology, including contemporary theology, i.e., from the Pelagian controversy to the neo-Augustinianism of 'Radical Orthodoxy'.
- *Theology in confrontation with modernity*, with particular attention being devoted to the development and reception of the thought of John Henry Newman, and the study of Vatican II.
- *The role of particularity in theological epistemology*, with particular attention being devoted to the project's foundational research-hypothesis by means of the test-case of the contemporary theology of religions.

The third avenue of research in particular, especially when supplemented by the findings emerging from the first and second avenues, will provide an occasion for the critical testing of, and reflection on, the methodological meta-question.

II. THEOLOGY AND THE QUESTION OF TRUTH
HISTORICAL AND SYSTEMATIC STUDIES

One of the first exercises undertaken by the Orthodoxy-project group consisted of confronting the overall research questions and the many specific research projects going on in the three research groups. A mutual critical-productive interaction was called for. The fruits resulting from such interaction are gathered here.

In the section dealing with "Augustine and the reception of Augustine in the history of theology", the four papers related to this overall theme are put together. The first two essays start from a historical-theological perspective; the following two share a systematic-theological approach.

Jonathan YATES investigates into the way how Augustine reconciled two at first sight opposing views on orthodoxy; namely the fact that to Augustine, orthodoxy could be mediated in a 'particular' contextual way of a Christian community, as well as in a universally given *regula fidei* and a universal church, guided 'into all truth' by God the Holy Spirit. Also his use of the Bible in order to establish orthodoxy as opposed to the Manichaeans, is examined.

Wim FRANÇOIS describes how Luther and the sixteenth century reformers advanced the thesis that only Scripture was needed and sufficient to gain access to divine truth. According to catholic theologians as e.g. the Louvain master John Driedo, however, Scripture needed to be interpreted and supplemented by ecclesiastical tradition(s). François points out that Church history clearly shows that politics was at least as influential on the rapid spread of Luther's positions in Germany and the preserving of Catholicism in the southern part of the Low Countries, as was the 'veracity' of the antagonists' theological positions.

Also in the contemporary theological scene, Augustinianist approaches are forwarded to profile the specificity of Christianity vis-à-vis the late-modern and/or postmodern context. Tom JACOBS both analyses and critiques the idea that only a tradition-related rationality would be capable to present a solution in the debate between Christianity and context. To this purpose, Jacobs examines two variants of such epistemologies by Alasdair MacIntyre and John Milbank. The former holds on to a dialectics between various traditions, both to avoid relativism and not to give up the notion of objectivity. However, since such dialectics presupposes a transcendental element, contradicting MacIntyre's own premises, this approach ultimately fails. Milbank on the other hand, presents a more coherent version of a tradition-dependent epistemology, based upon his reading of Augustine. Instead of dialectics, Milbank calls upon rhetoric:

strong and persuasive narratives. Unfortunately, Milbank's rhetorical turn leads to excluding schemes of opposition. Where MacIntyre's model appears to be incoherent, Milbank's would seem to be undesirable, because it leads to the complacency of one's own narrative.

Yves DE MAESENEER questions the Orthodoxy-project's underlying notion of truth in the light of the context of epistemological aestheticisation. In particular, he demonstrates how Hans Urs von Balthasar and Theodor W. Adorno, both pioneers of the aesthetic turn in today's theology and philosophy, offer a framework to conceptualise the irreducible relation between universality and particularity, or truth and embodiment. As such they illustrate the ruling aesthetic-epistemological paradigm and, at the same time, expose its problematic features.

The second section, "Theology in confrontation with Modernity" consists of five essays, ranging from the way in which Newman, Schelling and Baader dealt with the modern challenges over the discussion between modernism and anti-modernism to Schillebeeckx' redefinition of theological truth in terms of orthopraxis rather than orthodoxy.

Denis ROBINSON's paper reflects on Newman and orthodoxy by way of a critical examination of Newman's theological method. In particular he focuses on the innovative way in which Newman incorporates systematic theological problems with historical analysis. Some conclusions are drawn regarding Newman as a historian, a systematic theologian, and a Victorian sage. Newman's approach to questions of history and doctrine take the form of what has been described as a "parabolic imperative" as the designation for defining orthodoxy.

In his essay "'Truth' according to the Later Schelling and Baader: An Attempt at Transcending Modernity" Joris GELDHOF argues that a theologically relevant concept of truth was developed in the philosophies of Baader and the later Schelling. Crucial in this regard was their critique of modern philosophy and its stubborn emphasis on subjectivity as the only legitimate source of truth. Schelling and Baader inversely insisted on the ontological anteriority and the totality of truth, and, at the same time, convincingly defended the intrinsic connection between truth and (historical) reality. These are all important reasons why their thought should be taken into account in contemporary debates about 'truth' and 'Christianity'.

Jürgen METTEPENNINGEN considers the question of truth as crucial to understand the conflict which aroused concerning the 'nouvelle théologie'. After having outlined this moment of crisis both in its historical and theological context, the different positions and frictions related to the discussion are charted, in particular regarding the question of 'truth'. Using the position of protagonist R. Garrigou-Lagrange on "the 'nouvelle théologie's modernist nature" (i.e. retro-contextualisation), Mettepenningen discusses the perspective on truth of the so-called modernists, followed by a short review of reactions against Garrigou-Lagrange's position. In his concluding remarks, he suggests that, from the point of view of the question on truth, the 'nouvelle théologie' must not be understood as a return to the modernist crisis, but as a further reflection on this debate. The notion of 'truth' as unvarying, untouchable and a-historic (i.e. de-contextualisation), mostly adhered by the Dominicans and Roman theologians, strongly contrasts with the vision as advocated especially by the French Jesuits: for the latter 'truth' is historical, subjective and continuously developing (i.e. re-contextualisation).

The study presented by Karim SCHELKENS focuses on the so-called 'neo-modernist controversy' between the *Biblicum* and the Lateran university. In the late 1950s, both institutions challenged each others views on the historicity of Scripture and its 'correct' or 'orthodox' hermeneutics. To this purpose, both parties used (identical) authoritative sources in order to proof and safeguard their 'own orthodoxy'. The underlying issue – i.e. the clash between a rigid historiographic-scientific reading, and a dogmatic reading of Scripture – relates to the heart of the 'Orthodoxy-project'. A possible way to reconcile both hermeneutics, can be found in the notion of *analogia fidei*: in this 'particular' context, both hermeneutics are no longer incompatible, but complementary.

Finally, Annekatrien DEPOORTER relates the question concerning the determination of theological truth to her research into the work of Edward Schillebeeckx, with a special focus on his concept of *orthopraxis*. For Schillebeeckx there is no orthodoxy without *orthopraxis*. In his view the major hermeneutical question of Christian faith is that of the relation between theory and practice. Schillebeeckx concludes that only those articulations related to human experiences can count as true affirmations. Therefore, doctrinal pronouncements are only true when situated in the context of experience in which they were formulated. In his method of correlation, (human) experience figures as the bridge between tradition and culture. However, Schillebeeckx' appeal to experience as the basis for theological truth also raises some problems when confronted with post-modern reality. Therefore, Depoorter elaborates on the relation between universality and particularity in this context.

With this last essay, the connection is made to the final section on the role of particularity in the determination of theological truth.

The third section indeed collects six essays dealing with the rediscovery of the role of particularity in theological epistemology. They range from cultural-theological to philosophical-theological approaches.

In his discussion of the history of religious experience, Hans GEYBELS shows how the mere conceptualisation of the category of religious experience gives evidence for the irreducible contextual embeddedness of such exercise. The history of this conceptualisation clearly shows how the definition and role of religious experience are transformed under the influence of religious, psycho-social, cultural contextual factors, relating to each other in a dialectical process. According to Geybels, because of such dynamics of action and reaction conceptualisations have moved throughout history between intellectual and sensitive fields of meaning.

In "Truth, Rock Music and Christianity", Johan ARDUI explores the question of truth by focussing on the cultural-theological dialogue between rock music and theology. Since rock stands for a truth without redemption, the question is how the Christian redemptive notion of truth should be related to this kind of music. Ardui confronts two different approaches which – each in the name of the truth of Christianity – deal with this question. Whereas this confrontation refers the impasse of the debate, Ardui shows how a contemporary reading of "Gaudium et Spes" offers a way out of this impasse.

Frederik GLORIEUX investigates John Hick's search for truth and meaningfulness of theology and theological language. In Hick's quest for truth one can distinguish two major periods. First, Hick went to battle against so-called non-cognitive conceptions of religion, reducing theological claims for truth to human emotions, spiritual *chimeras* and moral ideals. Hick therefore elaborated an experience-based religious epistemology, as a result of which he was able to hold on to the conviction that religions can make pronouncements on 'what is' and 'how things are'. In his second period, Hick attempts to defend religious truth in light of religious pluralism. In this effort, Hick criticises the universality claims of particular religious discourse on truth, and introduces a pragmatic criterion, to which all (universality) claims of the different religions are subdued. Glorieux then concludes, that Hick in his second period reduces the cognitive level of religious truth claims, by introducing these claims in a philosophical system with which these claims have no affinity.

In traditional Christian theology, to a large extent, the discussion on the doctrine of Incarnation remains limited to its internal logic or its meaning for the development of the Trinitarian doctrine. According to Christophe MOONEN, British theology constitutes an exception. Such British approach includes both an effort to mediate this idea of the Incarnation philosophically, and to reflect upon the doctrine's ethical implications. In his essay Moonen particularly focuses on the specific nature of philosophical mediation going on in a theological reflection on the doctrine of incarnation; and relies hereto on the work of D.M. MacKinnon (1913-1994), an outstanding representative of this British tradition. In the course of his reflection, Moonen critically evaluates the opportunities as well as the limitations of philosophical registers and theological correctives in a postmodern, pluralist context. In particular, Moonen tries to shed light on the compelling question whether theologians, in their search for the truth-bearing structure of orthodoxy, are able to deny a fundamental philosophical mode of research that also exceeds the Christian narrative's particularity.

The contribution of Frederiek DEPOORTERE consists of three parts. First, Depoortere discusses Gianni Vattimo's thoughts on truth. The point of departure hereto is Vattimo's understanding of Nietzsche's proclamation of the dead of God, and of Heidegger's announcing of the end of metaphysics. According to Vattimo, both philosophers treat the same phenomenon, i.e. the end of 'foundations', or the end of reality as an objective given. For Vattimo, such nihilism implies that all (use of) language should be qualified metaphorical (it is no longer possible to distinguish between 'objective' and 'metaphorical' language), which implies that also religious discourse can be taken serious again. In a second part, Depoortere discusses Vattimo's efforts to avoid a complete relativism, resulting from this nihilism. By way of conclusion, Depoortere enters into the tensions, present in Vattimo's work, to illustrate the contemporary situation of the faithful.

"'And there shall be no more boredom': Metaphysics and Particularity in Contemporary Philosophy (Heidegger, Levinas and Marion)" is the last essay of this collection, authored by Joeri SCHRIJVERS. Schrijvers meditates upon the theme of 'overcoming metaphysics' so abundantly present in contemporary philosophy. Heidegger, Levinas, and Marion all argue that philosophy has preferred present-to-hand objects. For Heidegger, however, this metaphysical theory already presupposes existence's particular being-in-the-world. Nevertheless, when Heidegger proposed 'Angst' as the instance that reveals being-in-the-world, one wonders why 'Angst' is qualified again by a correspondence theory: when anxious, that what is being disclosed, coincides with the disclosing itself. Schrijvers argues that in Levinas and Marion a similar mode of procedure is used. He concludes with some reflection on the problematic nature of these (and any) attempts of 'overcoming metaphysics'.

In his concluding remarks, Dirk CLAES describes the acceptance throughout the essays of the role of particularity as a hermeneutical key in determining and articulating theological truth. This can be expressed in three summarising catchwords: context, ranging from biographical to ecclesiastical-political factors influencing institutions and persons in their truth claims; community, or the influence the Church, both as a centralised institution and its centrifugal forces in local churches, has exerted on defining and articulating truth; and text, or how the definition of an authoritative text has contributed to defining orthodoxy. Also some future research scopes are presented.

Lieven BOEVE
Mathijs LAMBERIGTS
Terrence MERRIGAN

PART ONE

THE FIRST AVENUE OF RESEARCH

AUGUSTINE AND THE RECEPTION OF AUGUSTINE IN THE HISTORY OF THEOLOGY

AUGUSTINE AND THE MANICHAEANS ON SCRIPTURE, THE CANON, AND TRUTH

INTRODUCTION

In this paper, I plan to demonstrate, by means of one very particular example, the way in which actions Augustine took in direct response to his own particular context profoundly affected his relationship to "truth". More specifically, I will show how historical and theological/exegetical circumstances converged in order to compel Augustine and his fellow North African bishops to delimit the canon of Scripture during the 390's, thus establishing an ultimate source of truth and of theological authority both for themselves and for (western) Christendom at large. In my view, this episode serves as an excellent example of how an influential individual's "radically particular" historical and chronological context – as well as actions directly resulting from that context – profoundly impacted his truth claims and, by extension, his understanding of both theological orthodoxy and ultimate reality[1].

I. BIOGRAPHY AS CONTEXT[2]

As Augustine himself tells us, from a very early age he was deeply concerned to discover a reliable source of truth. In fact, Augustine's quest was so acute that his search profoundly marked two of the first three

---

1. As those who are more conversant with the complexities of Augustine's views on truth and authority and/or with the issues surrounding the history of the canon can testify, this is only a part of the bigger picture. On many levels, Augustine's religious epistemology was more simultaneously complex and more mystical than just directly appealing to the Bible. It is an equally grave mistake to believe that the entire story of the West's biblical canon, much less its entire theological tradition, can be boiled down to the will of one North African bishop – no matter how charismatic and influential he may have been.

2. Given the vast amount of biographical material available for Augustine, it is unnecessary here to go into much detail or to offer many of the primary references for the following story. While biographical details are to be found *passim* in his oeuvre, much of what we know comes straight out his *Confessiones*. A very readable English translation is that of H. CHADWICK, *Saint Augustine Confessions*, Oxford, Oxford University Press, 1991. Generally solid biographies have been supplied by both Bonner and Brown. See, respectively, G. BONNER, *St. Augustine of Hippo Life and Controversies*, Norwich, Canterbury Press, ³2002; and P. BROWN, *Augustine of Hippo*, Berkeley, CA – Los Angeles, CA, University of California Press, ²2000.

decades of his life, i.e., from about 373 to 386. Although it was triggered by his reading of Cicero's *Hortensius* – something which caused him to resonate with the true philosopher's thirst for truth and life wisdom while also pushing him to become more of a rationalist – before he was done, his pilgrimage would take him to the feet of many and various masters[3].

This drift toward rationalism in turn paved the way for the Manichaeans whom he found attractive for several reasons, not the least of which was their claim to offer a pure and enlightened form of Christianity that rendered the illogical and plebian faith of his childhood obsolete[4]. Also important was their rejection of many of the difficulties that Augustine had encountered in his very frustrating attempts to read the enigmatic and literarily uncouth catholic Scriptures. The Manichaeans taught Augustine that it was not only proper, it was also necessary to reject many of these books outright. Even those books they did choose to retain were radically edited and re-interpreted. Although never a full-blown member, Augustine remained affiliated with them for nine or ten years convinced that, in their fellowship, he had hit upon the proper balance between rationality and revelation.

His drift away from them was slow, spurred on by his continued study of the arts and (Platonic) philosophy. Once their system had been thoroughly discredited in his eyes – an event which took place during 383[5],

---

3. While it must be remembered that it was produced both as part of a polemic and several years after the fact, in *c. ep. Man.* 12,14, we can find Augustine's explanation of why he became a Manichaean, viz. to find "truth … without uncertainty". Cf. CSEL 25, p. 208: "Hoc est, quod dicebam, sic mihi demonstrari debere ueritatem, ut ad eandem sine ulla ambiguitate perueniam. […] Me tamen hoc exigere et flagitare oportebat, ut tanta mercede cognitionis euidentissimae atque certissimae ex catholico Christiano quibuslibet contradicentibus Manichaeum me fieri non puderet".

4. Especially apropos is the summary remark of J.K. Coyle: "In adhering to Manicheism, … [Augustine] thought he was ascribing to an improved version of the Christianity he had known in his childhood". For this, see A. FITZGERALD, et al. (eds.), *Augustine through the Ages: An Encyclopedia*, Grand Rapids, MI, Eerdmans, 1999. S.v. "Anti-Manichaean Works".

5. While many have documented both this event and its chronology, few have captured the gradual and inherently ambiguous nature of the process as well as has J. RIES. See his *La Bible chez saint Augustin et chez les manichéens*, in *Revue des Études Augustiniennes* 7 (1961) 231: "En automne de l'année 383, Augustin gagne Rome, puis Milan. Aux yeux de la secte, il reste un auditeur, mais dans son intelligence et dans son cœur, Augustin n'est plus manichéen". Closely connected to this is the plausible, if somewhat overly-psychologized, observation of Lieu that it was the Manichaeans' dualism (on both the metaphysical and the anthropological levels) that "was the umbilical cord which held him to the sect after he had begun to reject intellectually some of its tenets". See S.N.C. LIEU, *Manichaeism in the Later Roman Empire and Medieval China: A Historical Survey*, Manchester, Manchester University Press, 1985, repr. 1988, p. 147. Ries' article represents the first installment of a three part series that Ries published between 1961 and 1964 (*Revue des Études Augustiniennes* 7 (1961) 231-243; 9 (1963) 201-215; and 10 (1964) 309-329,

Augustine retreated again to rationalism. This time it was even more extreme since he no longer harbored the more pure curiosity of a teenager looking for wisdom but, rather, the frustration and disillusionment of a mature adult who believed no other course remained open to him beyond that of an ultra-critical Skeptic.

This much shorter season of skepticism was brought to a dramatic – not to say supernatural – end in Milan in 386. Unquestionably, the future Bishop of Hippo's return to the Catholic faith was, from a human standpoint, inaugurated and superintended by Ambrose, that city's Catholic bishop. Ambrose baptized Augustine into the Catholic Church during the Easter feast of 387.

While it may, at least in some sense, be true that "the rest is history", it should *not* be assumed that life, either practically or intellectually, became immediately easier for Augustine. Practically, he soon had to bury his beloved, if somewhat meddlesome, mother. Intellectually, the Manichaeans, complete with their seemingly logical but also (at least partially) Gnostic worldview, were still on the scene. By any measure, the loss of someone as gifted as was Augustine would be a major blow to any cause: it certainly was for the Manichaeans. However, they were far from defeated. For his part, it is clear that, in order to squelch both personal and professional demons, Augustine needed to engage them. This he did in increasingly intense and increasingly public stages[6]. The brand-new Catholic seems to have been well aware that, until they were properly defeated, he could expect little internal peace and even less external respect.

II. THE MANICHAEANS, THE CANON, AND THE TRUTH

Although it was excessively optimistic to believe that the theory serving as both the impetus for the research on this topic and the core of this essay was new[7], given its implications, it does bear repeating. Briefly put,

---

respectively. Henceforth, they will be referred to by J. RIES, *La Bible*, followed by a Roman numeral I, II, or III and the appropriate page number(s). Although the entire series has been brought together and reprinted in J. RIES, *Les études manichéennes: Des controverses de la Réforme aux découvertes du XXe siècle* (Collection Cerfaux-Lefort, 1), Louvain-la-Neuve, Centre d'histoire des religions, 1988, pp. 125-207, it is likely that the original publication remains the most widely accessible and, hence, is the one referenced here.

6. Augustine's first formal engagement vs. the Manichaeans is the *De moribus ecclesiae Catholicae et de moribus Manicheorum*, which he began the same year he was baptized, i.e., 387 and completed in 389.

7. Here I in no way intend to imply that I was surprised to find that my thunder, as it were, had been stolen. On the contrary, my real point is to illustrate how easy it is for inter-

this theory is that the North African Catholic Church generally, and Augustine specifically, was compelled to define their canon of Scripture as a direct result of their conflicts with the Christian sect known as the Manichaeans and that both the timing and the content of this definition were specifically impacted[8].

In fact, the link between the timing of the first two North African councils which decreed on the issue of the canon and the influence of the Manichaeans in North Africa has been noted by scholars for decades. No less than seventy-five years ago, A. Allgeier published a study in which such a link is plainly asserted[9]. His words make plain that the drive for a definitive canon in North Africa lay in Augustine's battle with the Manichaeans:

> Man geht nicht fehl, wenn man annimmt, daß also auch die kanonkritischen Ausführungen, die sich da und dort zerstreut finden, durch die anti-manichäische Kritik veranlaßt worden sind. Das ist um beachtenswerter, als die ersten abendländischen Synoden, welche sich mit dem Kanon der Bibel beschäftigt haben, ja die ersten Synoden überhaupt, auf deren Tagesord-

esting observations and connections to become lost within the vast spaces of *Augustiniana*. It is also intend to point out that, for whatever reasons, this detail has not often been seized upon by scholars of the history of the canon.

8. Cf. this more contextually sensitive – if certainly more complex – explanation to statements one often finds in general histories of the Church or in survey articles regarding the Bible and the canon in the West. See, e.g., J.N.D. KELLY, *The Bible and the Latin Fathers*, in D.E. NINEHAM (ed.), *The Church's Use of the Bible Past and Present*, London, SPCK, 1963, p. 44: "... recognition was accorded to [all the books of the present NT] towards the end of the fourth century, but it needed the strenuous efforts of popes supported by theologians like Jerome and Augustine to secure this; and it is plain that the governing motive was the desire not to be out of step with the Greek Church". Of course, it would be wrong to suggest that the western authorities were *unconcerned* to keep in step with the eastern churches. The fact is that the western rationale was multifaceted and, all else being equal, the timing can more plausibly be traced to pressures that were coming to bear during the same period that the decision was taken. If the West had been governed primarily by a desire to keep in step with the East, it seems much more likely that there would have been multiple local councils called to make proclamations regarding the canon as soon as the various churches got wind of the eastern decisions such as Athanasius' famous 39th Festal Letter of 367. For an excellently-argued article which shows that the contextual particularity of even Athanasius' decision to delimit the canon and then to promulgate that decision, see D. BRAKKE, *Canon Formation and Social Conflict in Fourth-Century Egypt: Athanasius of Alexandria's Thirty-Ninth Festal Letter*, in *HTR* 87 (1994) 395-414, esp. 405 and 418. Cf. also n.1.

9. A. ALLGEIER, *Der Einfluß des Manichäismus auf die exegetische Fragestellung bei Augustin*, in M. GRABMANN – J. MAUSBACH (eds.), *Aurelius Augustinus: Die Festschrift der Görres-Gesellschaft zum 1500. Todestage des Heiligen Augustinus*, Köln, J.P. Bachem, 1930, 1-13. Note this is *not* a claim that Allgeier was the first to make this link. To establish that would require perusal of several interesting-looking older studies such as F. TRECHSEL, *Ueber den Kanon, die Kritik und Exegese der Manichäer: Ein historisch-kritischer Versuch*, Bern, 1832, a work currently unavailable to me.

nung, so viel man Weiß, die Frage des Kanons stand, die Synode von Hippo 393 und die zwei Synoden von Karthago 397 und 419 waren[10].

Probably the most contextually sensitive statement of which I am aware is one that was made by F. Decret in an opinion published in 1970[11]. Here, he linked several of the important historical, ecclesiastical, and – certainly not least – psychological factors that the leaders of the North African Catholic Church in the period of ca. 390-405[12] must have had to deal with as they tried to "nail down" the links between Scripture and truth for their Church. We can fairly assume, as Decret does, that Augustine was also challenged by these factors and that the pressures they generated increased proportionally as his stature and leadership responsibilities increased. Decret deserves to be quoted in full:

> Il faut bien reconnaître d'ailleurs que la position d'Augustin n'est guère confortable. L'histoire du canon des textes reçus par la *Catholica* montre assez les cheminements et les hésitations dans l'établissement de la liste des Écritures néo-testamentaires. Dans cet état, sinon de confusion, du moins de doute sur la canonicité (ou sur l'authenticité) de plusieurs livres … on conçoit que la tâche de l'évêque catholique, sur ce sujet des Écritures, n'allait pas sans difficultés et que le polémiste devait prendre des risques. C'est en vue d'avoir des assises plus sûres, face à des adversaires déterminés à défendre âprement leurs positions très libérales – du moins en apparence – qu'Augustin mettait tout en œuvre pour obtenir de l'Église l'établissement d'un canon définitif. Il n'est pas sans intérêt, à ce sujet, de remarquer que c'est précisément en Afrique – à Hippone – qu'ont été prises les premières décisions en ce sens …[13].

10. ALLGEIER, *Der Einfluß des Manichäismus* (n. 9), p. 9.

11. F. DECRET, *Aspects du manichéisme dans l'Afrique Romaine*, Paris, Études Augustiniennes, 1970, p. 175.

12. See also n. 37.

13. DECRET, *Aspects du manichéisme* (n. 11), p. 175. For other opinions along these lines, see, e.g., J. VAN OORT, *Mani, Manichaeism & Augustine: The Rediscovery of Manichaeism & Its Influence on Western Christianity. Lectures delivered at the State University of Tbilisi & the K. Kekelidze Institute of Manuscripts of the Georgian Academy of Sciences, Tbilisi, Georgia, 26-29 September, 1995*, Tbilisi, Academy of Sciences of Georgia, 1997, p. 46; RIES, *La Bible*, II (n. 5), p. 203 (note also that, here, Ries implies that this statement reflects the views of J. RITCHIE SMITH, *Augustine as an Exegete*, in *Bibliotheca Sacra* 61 [1904] 318-344. However, after consulting that article, it was not clear to me that Ritchie Smith had explicitly made these claims. This is illustrative of a problem with Ries' otherwise very helpful articles: it was not always clear – at least to me – where Ries' own opinions stopped and where those of others began. In what follows, wherever it seems that Ries is reflecting the opinion of another, it will be indicated); *ibid.*, pp. 204 and 210-211 (again it seems that this last quotation by Ries is closely dependent upon that of ALLGEIER, *Der Einfluß* (n. 9); and, W.H.C. FREND, *Manichaeism in the Struggle between Saint Augustine and Petilian of Constantine*, in *Augustinus Magister: Congrès international augustinienne, Paris, 21-24 septembre 1954*, Paris, Études Augustiniennes, 1954-1955, p. 865 (cf. also ID., *The Gnostic-Manichaean Tradition in Roman North Africa*, in *Journal of Ecclesiastical History* 4 [1953] 22 and n.4), Frend makes reference to *epistula*

III. MANICHAEISM'S INFLUENCE ON AUGUSTINE'S
NON-"ANTI-MANICHAEAN" WORKS

Augustine's struggle with the Manichaeans profoundly impacted both him and his ministry. In fact, scholars have observed that in some ways his wrestling with that movement and the problems it raised colored much of the rest of his polemical œuvre[14]. What seems equally clear is that Manichaeism also affected works that were not overtly polemical, much less overtly anti-Manichaean. Specifically, this prolonged strife at least partially explains both the timing and the content of the *Confessiones*, the *De doctrina christiana* and, perhaps, even that all-important *Wendepunkt*, the *Ad Simplicianum*[15].

64, a letter which seems to be securely datable to either late 401 or the first half of 402. See esp. paragraph 3 where Augustine chalks up Quintasius' error in regard to the conciliar decrees to a faulty memory (*tu non memineris*). If the dating of this letter is accurate, its contents offer evidence that in North Africa, like elsewhere, councils often failed to generate immediate and unquestioned conformity to their canons. While both the participants and later generations may have regarded their decisions to be inspired of God, it is far from clear that everyone else was as impressed!

14. See, e.g., BONNER, *St. Augustine of Hippo* (n. 2), p. 194: "... Augustine's disputes with the Manichees ... prepare[d] the way for his treatment of similar issues in later controversies. Thus, writing against the Donatists, the saint found himself discussing the nature of the Church and arguing how certain passages of Scripture are to be interpreted. In the Pelagian controversy, it might be said that all the questions raised: Grace and Free Will; Predestination and Reprobation; Original Sin and the Fall, spring from the problems which he had discussed in his writings against the Manichees". At the same time and while it cannot be doubted that Augustine met with not a little success against the Manichaeans on both an individual and an institutional level, the movement did not immediately die out in either North Africa or other parts of the West. See, e.g., FREND, *Manichaeism in the Struggle* (n. 13), p. 865, where he writes: "As we know from the sermons and letters of Pope Leo, Rome itself contained numerous Manichees who behaved outwardly as Catholic Christians. This was the case in Africa also". For a more general statement, cf. also *ibid.*, p. 859. Apparently, it is the insertion of the adjective "organised" that prevents this former statement from contradicting what Frend had written earlier: "That Manichaeism failed to survive in the West as an organised religion may be due largely to Augustine's writings and controversies in the years 387-399". For this, see FREND, *The Gnostic-Manichaean Tradition* (n. 13), p. 24.

15. The possible links between the *Ad Simplicianum* and Augustine's anti-Manichaean effort seem to be a valid line for further inquiry. First, there is the timing of the work. Its being written within the first year or two of Augustine's ordination as Bishop places it right in the middle of the hottest part of his anti-Manichaean crusade. Second, there is the fact that the Manichaeans compelled Augustine to reassess his doctrine of inspiration as well as his overall attitude (i.e., both form and content) toward the Scriptures. In a word, he was "primed" to be especially moved by whatever conclusions he came to as he studied the Scriptures in the process of answering Simplicianus. Third, it seems also possible that the Manichaeans' emphasis on Paul, insofar as his letters were one of the few bits of the Catholic Scriptures that they also greatly respected, is also likely to have increased Augustine's sensitivity to the deeper points and finer nuances of Paul's arguments. Is it not likely that Augustine, as a talented polemicist, would also be especially attentive in his reading

The links between the *Confessiones* and anti-Manichaean polemics are probably the clearest; they are certainly the ones that have been most often recognized by scholars[16]. Especially helpful is the following statement of J. van Oort: "One who is acquainted with the Manichaean texts and their terminology will read Augustine's *Confessiones* with new eyes. [...] The prevailing tone, the *cantus firmus* of the *Confessiones*, is gnostic-Manichaean"[17]. Especially relevant for anyone who would connect the *Confessiones* to the Bishop of Hippo's anti-Manichaeism is his attempt to interpret Genesis in Books XI-XIII[18]. To give but two examples, note how in the following passages Augustine goes to such great – and dramatic! – lengths to impress upon his readers his conviction regarding the inspiration, rationality, and, hence, the trustworthiness of the Old Testament. At XII,30,41 we read:

> ... may we love you, our God, fount of truth – if truth is what we are thirsting after and not vanity. And may we agree in so honouring your servant [i.e., Moses], the minister of this scripture, full of your Holy Spirit, that we believe him to have written under your revelation and to have intended that meaning which supremely corresponds both to the light of the truth and to the reader's spiritual profit, and with respect to the profit it would yield[19].

of Paul during this precise period? After all, in order to be properly prepared to debate the Paul-loving Manichaeans, both formally and informally, he would have needed to know both Paul's texts and his theology backwards and forwards. For more information on *Ad Simplicianum* as Augustine's great turning point on the issue of grace and its role in election, perseverance, and salvation, see, e.g., D. OGLIARI, *Gratia et Certamen: The Relationship between Grace and Free Will in the Discussion of Augustine with the so-called Semipelagians* (BETL, 169), Leuven, Leuven University Press – Peeters, 2003, *passim*, but esp. pp. 74, 79, 84-85, and 156-159 along with the nn. given there.

16. Two older examples should also suffice to show that this, too, is not a new discovery. See RIES, *La Bible*, III (n. 5), p. 318: "Les *Confessions* ont des relents manichéens à chaque page" (Once again, although it is not entirely clear, this statement is apparently Ries' reflecting the "parfois déconcertante" views of A. Adam which the latter put forth in two different publications in the 1950's. For the full bibliographical information on these, see *ibid.*, p. 317 and n. 26), and ID., *La Bible*, II (n. 5), p. 205: "Deux traités augustiniens sonnent les glas du modernisme de l'époque: *De genesi ad litteram*, réfutation décisive de la cosmogonie de Mani et *De doctrina christiana*, la ruine de l'exégèse des manichéens d'Afrique". This time, Ries is discussing the 1908 article of L. HUGO entitled *Der geistige Sinn der hl. Schrift beim hl. Augustinus*. That Hugo's article was written in the midst of the Modernist Controversy of the early twentieth century does not invalidate either this statement or Hugo's conclusion, made on the basis of many and various considerations, that the *De doctrina christiana* was, at least to some extent, an anti-Manichaean treatise.

17. VAN OORT, *Mani, Manichaeism & Augustine* (n. 13), p. 52. Also interesting in this connection is van Oort's observation/invitation that "the extent to which the *Confessiones* are – thetically and anti-thetically – influenced by Manichaeism has yet to be worked out in detailed studies".

18. On this point, see, e.g., *ibid.*, p. 46.

19. For this English translation, see CHADWICK, *Saint Augustine Confessions* (n. 2), p. 270. Cf. CCSL, 27, p. 240: "... diligamus Te, Deum nostrum, fontem ueritatis, si non

Similarly, at XIII,29,44 and in reference to the repetition of the phrase "And God saw that it was good" in the Genesis 1 creation narrative Augustine records a "conversation" that he had with God about this text:

> I said: Lord (i.e., God the Father), surely your scripture is true, for you, being truthful and Truth itself, have produced it ... [t]o this you replied to me ... with the cry: "O man, what my scripture says, I say"[20].

1. *Engaging the Manichaeans: The Role, Nature, and Content of the Scriptures*

The facts that the North Africans were driven to produce a formal statement on the metes and bounds of the canon by the persistence of the Manichaean threat and that Augustine's anxiety over this same threat can be detected in the background of even his non-"anti-Manichaean" works only begs questions regarding the details of the debate. In order to address some of these, the following sections will briefly discuss the Manichaean *attitude* toward Scripture and the specific *content* of the Manichaean "canon" before discussing the ways in which these ideas were opposed by the Catholic camp.

A necessary preliminary to this, however, is a brief reminder about the essential nature of the "Bible" in the fourth and fifth centuries. Throughout much of what follows, it will be helpful to recall that part of what made it so easy for anyone to focus on this or that portion of the Scriptures is that, during this period, single-volume Bibles were (almost) completely unknown[21]. In other words, while we today automatically think of

uana, sed ipsam sitimus, eundem que famulum Tuum, scripturae huius dispensatorem, Spiritu Tuo plenum, ita honoremus, ut hoc eum te reuelante, cum haec scriberet, attendisse credamus, quod in eis maxime et luce ueritatis et fruge utilitatis excellit". Cf. this sentiment to both XXII, 83 of the *contra Faustum* (cf. CSEL 25, p. 685): "The Prophet (Moses) has compiled a narrative of human actions, under the guidance and inspiration of the Holy Ghost (Ea quippe hominum facta Sancto Spiritu disponente atque inspirante collegit propheta narrator ...)" and V, 8, 23 of the *Gn. litt.*, the first 9 books of which probably date from 401 or soon after (cf. n.15 *supra* and, for these specific lines, CSEL 28,1, p. 152): "... the Holy Ghost ... was present in the one who wrote them". (... spiritus qui inerat scribenti ea ...).

20. For this English translation, see CHADWICK, *Saint Augustine Confessions* (n. 2), p. 300. Cf. CCSL, 27, p. 268: "O Domine, nonne ista scriptura Tua uera est, quoniam Tu uerax et Veritas edidisti eam? ... Tu dicis mihi ... clamans: 'O homo, nempe quod scriptura Mea dicit', Ego dico ...".

21. The "almost" here reflects the still-unresolved debate about the nature, number, and distribution of the codices commissioned in the 4th-century by the recently-Christianized secular leadership. Were these Gospel codices? Complete New Testaments? Could they even have been entire Bibles? Exactly how many were produced? Who, i.e., which individuals or which local churches received them? How quickly (if at all) did any copies make it to the West? For a brief discussion, see J. YATES, *The Reception of James in the*

a single, thin, and very-portable volume when we hear the word "Bible",
all of Augustine's contemporaries – even those who acknowledged that
the canon had been established and permanently closed – necessarily
thought of a collection of several, thick, and usually unwieldy codices[22].
Moreover, given the difficulties and expense involved in their production, we would also do well to recall that it was usually only the wealth-
ier and more-cosmopolitan of local churches that would have possessed
a "complete" collection, much less multiple copies of the various codices.
Of course, even as we note this we are passing over in silence the siz-
able, if unavoidable, problems of quality and accuracy which plagued the
entire literary industry in the ancient world. Professional scribes or copy-
ists were not cheap; non-professionals or "do-it-yourselfers", while
always more economical, were often much less reliable. In short, the
adage "you get what you pay for" was just as true in the 4th-century as
it is in the 21st.

2. *The Manichaean Attitude*

Given the age and geographical distribution of the Manichaean sect, it
should come as no surprise that, just as was the case for the Catholics or
"orthodox" camps, there were significant practical and theological differences among the Manichaeans of different periods and different loca-
tions. This certainly seems to have been true for the fourth-century
Manichaeans in the Latin-speaking portion of the Empire. Most relevant
here is their attitude toward the role of Scripture generally and the way
in which that attitude differed toward the more "uncritical" Catholics in
particular. As Coyle has noted, western Manichaeans were particularly
"biblical" in their thinking and their orientation:

> Because Manichaeism was essentially an Oriental Gnosticism which bor-
> rowed elements from Christianity whenever proselytisation warranted it,
> one must distinguish between the teaching concerning Scripture of Mani
> himself, for whom it played only a minimal role, and of someone like Faus-

West: Could Athanasius have Played a Role?, in J. SCHLOSSER (ed.), *The Catholic Epistles and the Tradition* (BETL, 176), Leuven, Leuven University Press – Peeters, 2004,
271-286, esp. the text and nn. in the subsection entitled "Athanasius and 'Alexandrian'
Bibles in the West".
    22. Cf. J.K. COYLE, *Augustine's* De moribus ecclesiae catholicae, *a Study of the Work,
its Composition and its Sources* (Paradosis, 25), Fribourg, University Press, 1978, p. 156,
where Coyle has observed that in Augustine's time there was no "such thing as a 'Bible',
in the sense of a complete collection of all the canonical books bound together in a single
volume. The most one could expect to find were volumes of 'homogeneous' *libri*: the
four Gospels, for instance, or all the letters attributed to Saint Paul, or the Psalms, or the
prophets".

tus who relied heavily on the Bible and who (along with Adimantus) was most likely the chief formulator of this teaching among the Manichaeans of North Africa[23].

However, this "reliance" did not mean that the western Manichaeans looked at the sacred text the same way as did the Catholics who were their contemporaries. On the contrary, in a way that, *prima facie*, seems more modern and critical, the Manichaeans made no bones about the need to read their sacred texts both selectively and with a willingness to excise from those texts anything and everything that did not support their message and agenda. In fact, to the degree that Faustus can be taken as typical, their only concern …

> was to show that the Catholics were semi-Christians because they were completely uncritical in their use of the Bible and had signally failed to separate the truth of Christ from the superstition of the Jews and the lies which the church had perpetuated about Christ. In short, if the Christian scriptures were properly interpreted and purged of fraudulent interpolations, they would be found to be in harmony with the message of Mani[24].

3. *The Manichaean Canon*

If, then, the western Manichaeans were at once "biblical" and "critically selective", what then can be said regarding the identity and contents of the texts they actually did employ? In other words, to the degree that they cared to define it, what comprised the western Manichaean canon?

In addition to a handful of texts that Mani himself had written, the western Manichaean canon simultaneously excluded much of what the Catholics had long regarded as sacred and included works that the Catholics had/were beginning to downgrade(d) or reject(ed) outright[25].

---

23. *Ibid.*, pp. 145-146 and n. 589. Cf. the similar conclusion of Decret: "Le manichéisme, malgré ses prétentions à la rationalité, n'a pas atteint des positions aussi radicales. Dans l'enseignement de Mani, le primat du *noûs* ne dispense pas de recourir aux Écritures qui demeurent 'fondamentales'. For this see, DECRET, *Aspects du manichéisme* (n. 11), p. 182.

24. LIEU, *Manichaeism in the Later Roman Empire* (n. 5), p. 120. See also DECRET, *Aspects du manichéisme* (n. 11), p. 149: "… à ses yeux [i.e. Faustus'], l'acceptation ou les refus de ces Écritures [i.e., the Old Testament] est le critère décisif qui permet de distinguer le manichéisme du catholicisme, c'est-à-dire, … le chrétien authentique du 'semi-chrétien' …".

25. On this latter point, see J. VAN OORT, *Secundini Manichaei epistula*: *Roman Manichaean 'Biblical' Argument in the Age of Augustine*, in J. VAN OORT – O. WERMELINGER – G. WURST (eds.), *Augustine and Manichaeism in the Latin West* (Nag Hammadi and Manichaean Studies, 49), Leiden, Brill, 2001, p. 164, where, regarding the contents and style of the so-called *Secundini Manichaei epistula*, he observes "[w]hat we actually see here is a Manichaean *auditor* who is trying to recall a former *auditor* [i.e., Augustine] back to the Manichaean fold. And, characteristically, he does so by constantly

Unlike (at least) some of their co-religionists in other parts of the world[26], western Manichaeans passed over the entire collection of Jewish sacred texts precisely because it was too "Jewish" and encouraged worship of Yahweh, who, while recognized as a deity, was to be clearly distinguished from the far-superior God whom Jesus called his Father.

It also quickly becomes apparent that the western Manichaeans' views on the Old Testament also affected their take on what should comprise their New Testament[27]. Again, Coyle is helpful:

> [they] accepted ... the New Testament, which, though it was not given the same importance as Mani's own writings, was nevertheless used extensively. But even in the New Testament they rejected whatever smacked of 'Judaism,' and they claimed to see numerous interpolations, even in the Gospels and the letters of Paul, their preferred New Testament reading[28].

In practice, then, the western Manichaean "canon" – for lack of a better term – consisted of basically four parts, two of which – at least in their "unedited" forms – were acceptable to Augustine and his fellow-Catholics[29]. Indeed, while the role of Mani's own writings in the think-

---

appealing to 'Biblical' texts" which were authoritative for the Manichaeans but, at best, questionable for the catholics". In n. 11 on this same page, van Oort also makes it clear that the texts which were "fair game" – at least in Secundinus' eyes – included "Tatian's Diatessaron, the Gospel of Thomas and the so-called Old and New Testament Apocrypha". Cf. *ibid.*, pp. 168-169 and nn. 32-35 as well as p. 172 and n. 51 for more remarks on the Gospel of Thomas. For more on the Manichaean use of these and other ultimately-non-canonical texts, see n. 34.

26. Here, see, e.g., J.K. COYLE, *What Did Augustine Know about Manichaeism When he Wrote His Two Treatises* De moribus?, in VAN OORT – WERMELINGER – WURST (eds.), *Augustine and Manichaeism* (n. 25), p. 53 and n. 56: "... not all of the Old Testament was repudiated, at least in Egypt ...".

27. Regarding this, F. Decret, has (somewhat enigmatically) observed that: "On sait en effet que les manichéens recevaient tous les livres du Nouveau Testament, celui des Actes des Apôtres excepté". See F. DECRET, *L'utilisation des Épîtres de Paul chez les Manichéens d'Afrique*, in J. RIES – F. DECRET – W.H.C. FREND – M.G. MARA (eds.), *Le Epistole Paoline nei manichei, i donatisti e il primo Agostino* (Sussidi patristici, 5), Roma, Istituto Patristico Augustinianum, 1989, 29-83, pp. 78-79; reprinted as Chapter IV of F. DECRET, *Essais sur l'Église manichéenne en Afrique du Nord et à Rome au temps de saint Augustin: Recueil d'études* (Studia Ephemeridis Augustinianum, 47), Roma, Institutum Patristicum Augustinianum, 1995, pp. 55-106. (Note that all references to this essay use the page numbers of the reprinted edition.) In turn, this should be compared with M. TARDIEU, *Principes de l'exégèse manichéenne du Nouveau Testament*, in M. TARDIEU (ed.), *Les règles de l'interprétation*, Paris, Les Éditions du Cerf, 1987, p. 129, which offers a key caveat regarding the status of the New Testament for the Manichaeans: " ... contrairement à la Bible juive pour les catholiques, le Nouveau Testament n'a pas chez les manichéens statut d'Écriture canonique". These and other passages make it plain that Decret and Tardieu harbor serious doubts about each other's respective methodologies and conclusions.

28. COYLE, *Augustine's* De moribus ecclesiae catholicae (n. 22), pp. 147-149.

29. DECRET, *Aspects du manichéisme* (n. 11), pp. 117-118, is helpful with regard to the Manichaean attitude toward the Catholic New Testament as well as with regard to how

ing of the western Manichaeans would be hard to overemphasize, it was their use of Paul[30] and the Gospels[31] that was at the center of their controversy with the Catholics[32]. The reason for this is not hard to figure out: these books had played an important role in the thinking and theol-

those particular books were viewed in relation to their preeminent authorities, that is Mani's own compositions. Here he notes that: "Les Manichéens, comme ceux que nous voyons défendre leur doctrine face à Augustin, devaient considérer le Nouveau Testament – ou du moins ce qu'ils en retenaient – comme une 'nourriture de nouveau-né [cf. 1 Cor 3,1-2]' dans la démarche vers la possession de la gnose, celle-ci ne trouvant la perfection de son enseignement, la claire vérité – *enodata* – que dans les seules Écritures de Mani".

30. TARDIEU, *Principes de l'exégèse manichéenne* (n. 27), p. 142: "Les manichéens, en revanche, utilisent toutes les lettres pauliniennes et ne privilégient aucune d'entre elles". Note well, however, that in the context from which this quotation was taken, Tardieu makes it plain that "un doute subsiste" regarding both the letters that Paul addressed to the Thessalonians as well as that addressed to Philemon. While, as Decret has pointed out (cf. DECRET, *L'utilisation des Épîtres de Paul* [n. 27], p. 78), both the nature/content and the length of Philemon make its absence less than problematic, it should be noted that, given the Manichaeans rather rabid anti-Judaism, they certainly missed a golden opportunity by not making much of 1 Thess 2,14-16, a passage which many commentators regard as the strongest anti-Jewish statement in all the Pauline corpus. This *lacuna* probably deserves to be investigated more thoroughly in light of the Manichaean predilection for Paul.

31. COYLE, *Augustine's* De moribus ecclesiae catholicae (n. 22), pp. 190-191: "Next in popularity to Paul in the New Testament comes Matthew, who also seems to have enjoyed great use among the Manichaeans of Africa. [...] Noticeably absent (except for a few possible allusions) are the Acts of the Apostles and the Letter to the Hebrews. The Acts do not appear to have been held in high regard by the Manichaeans; and by its very name Hebrews, with its strong basis in the Old Testament, would have ensured itself of Manichaean disdain. I John and II Thessalonians are referred to only once. Philippians, I and II Peter, James, Jude, Revelation and, of the Pastorals, II Timothy and Philemon receive no attention at all; one is led to wonder whether the Manichaeans ever made use of them". For a further nuance to this position, note that on p. 190 and n. 716 Coyle observes that in the works against Faustus, Felix and Fortunatus, "Matthew is quoted even oftener than Paul" and that on p. 191 and n. 720 he observes that "Felix quotes only 1 John out of all the Catholic Epistles". Coyle's caution here about Acts is warranted. In discussing a much older study by N. Lardner, RIES, *La Bible*, I (n. 5), p. 235 notes that it is only Augustine's works that offer us any "preuve formelle" that the Manichaeans rejected the book. DECRET, *Aspects du manichéisme* (n. 11), pp. 162-163 and 173-174 has also commented on the Manichaean attitude toward each book of what would become the Catholic N.T. On p. 163 (about Hebrews) he writes, "… en un mot, c'eût été adjouter de l'ivraie à l'ivraie". On p. 174 (about Acts) he writes, "Toutefois Faustus connaissait bien ces *Actes* puisque, sans les nommer …" *Ibid.*, (about, *inter alia*, the Catholic Epistles) he writes, "En conclusion, si l'on dresse le bilan des *loci* cités se référant aux Épîtres, on peut établir le classement suivant, par ordre décroissant: Rom, Gal et 1 Cor, Eph, 2 Cor, Col, 1 Tim, Tit. On ne rencontre aucune référence à 1 et 2 Thess, 2 Tim, Philm. De même, aucune citation n'est empruntée à l'Apc, 1 et 2 Pet, Iac, et Iud. Quant aux Épîtres de Jean, seule la première est utilisée pour une citation".

32. FREND, *The Gnostic-Manichaean Tradition* (n. 13), p. 21: "African Manichees also used St. Paul extensively. To Felix he was the forerunner of Mani. African Manichaeism is almost a Paulinist heresy. … practically the whole of the debate between Augustine and his former friend, the Manichee Fortunatus, turns on the interpretation to be placed on Pauline texts".

ogizing of North African Christianity for over 200 years[33]. To this tri-
partite list (i.e., Mani's *epistulae*, edited Gospels, and edited Paul), the
Manichaeans added yet another element: various apocryphal Acts and
Gospels[34]. Not surprisingly, these latter books were nowhere near as well
or as readily received by the Catholic leadership. In addition to their containing "deviant" ideas and doctrines, these texts were rejected by fourth-
century Catholics because of their historical links to Gnosticism. Their
reasons for this were not overly complex: such a position supported their
own particular Christology[35].

IV. THE CATHOLIC/AUGUSTINIAN ATTITUDE

1. *Augustine's Position*

Over against both the Manichaean attitude toward and collection of
sacred texts stands the attitude of the North African Catholics generally
and of Augustine particularly. Drawing upon his own experiences and, no
doubt, spurred on by at least some residual fear and guilt, Augustine,

---

33. This chronology assumes the historicity of the story of the so-called Martyrs of
Scilli who were tried and put to death in Carthage in 180 A.D. During the proceedings, one
from among them confessed, apparently in Latin, to possessing at least part of the Pauline
Corpus. They said that in their "capsa" they had "libri et epistulae Pauli, uiri iusti". As
it is assumed that the martyrs were commoners and, hence, would have known little or no
Greek, it is deduced that their books and letters must also have been Latin. This evidence
also allows scholars to conclude much regarding the age and vitality of a Scripture-based
Christianity in Northern Africa in the second century. For the text and context of the quote,
see H. MUSURILLO, *The Acts of the Christian Martyrs*, Oxford, Clarendon, 1972, pp. 86-
88. For a readable article containing various observations about many different aspects of
this text generally and of the line "libri et epistulae Pauli, uiri iusti" specifically, see G.
BONNER, *The Scillitan Saints and the Pauline Epistles*, in *The Journal of Ecclesiastical History* 7 (1956) 141-146.

34. COYLE, *Augustine's* De moribus ecclesiae catholicae (n. 22), p. 149 and n. 612
gives the most complete list of which I am aware: "Of the N.T. apocrypha, we know that
the Manichaeans used the following: Euangelium de natiuitate Mariae; Gospel of Peter;
Acts of Andrew; Acts of John; Acts of Paul and Thecla; Acts of Peter; Acts of Philip;
Acts of Thomas". Of course, many other scholars have weighed in on which apocryphal
works the Manichaeans regarded as important and/or authoritative. See also, e.g., LIEU,
Manichaeism in the Later Roman Empire (n. 5), p. 129 and FREND, *The Gnostic-
Manichaean Tradition* (n. 13), p. 21. A seminal article on both Augustine's and the
Manichaeans' – albeit to a lesser extent for the latter – relationship to all sorts of what
would soon become extra-canonical literature is B. ALTANER, *Augustinus und die neutes-
tamentliche Apokryphen, Sibyllinen und Sextussprüche: Eine Quellenkritische Unter-
suchung*, in *Analecta Bollandiana* 67 (1949) 236-248.

35. COYLE, *Augustine's* De moribus ecclesiae catholicae (n. 22), pp. 148-149: "In order
to bolster their own view of Christ, they accepted some of the biblical apocrypha used by
earlier Gnostics, perhaps even going so far as to compose some of their own".

along with several other ex-Manichaean colleagues[36], spent much energy
during the decade and a half of 390-405[37] defending their faith and coun-
teracting the threats they perceived as existing within Manichaeism. It
seems clear that, although the Manichaeans had preoccupied him from the
first days of his life as a Catholic, his concern to oppose them only inten-
sified as time passed and his responsibilities increased[38].

36. Reconstructing Augustine's personal relationships in the period that he himself was
an evangelist as well as in the period after which he (re-)converted to the Catholic camp
is a challenge which has inspired more than a few scholars. See, e.g., FREND, *The Gnostic-Manichaean Tradition* (n. 13), p. 22; ID., *Manichaeism in the Struggle* (n. 13), pp. 859-
866, esp. 861 and 865; and LIEU, *Manichaeism in the Later Roman Empire* (n. 5), pp.
133-134, 147, 152 with accompanying nn. A search of these and other sources reveals that
at least eight of Augustine's friends and associates had been Manichaean: Romanianus,
Honoratus, Nebridius, Cornelius, Evodius, Profuturus, Fortunatus and, certainly not least,
Alypius. In many cases, because he was "an ardent Manichaean evangelist" (*Ibid.*, p. 133),
it was Augustine himself who was responsible for their association with the *secta*. In no
less than four cases these men, like Augustine, went on to become Catholic bishops in the
North African Church. For the purposes of this study, this last fact is doubly significant.
First, because these men were former Manichaeans, these men were especially well
equipped to help with the struggle against their former group both practically and doctrinally. To various degrees, they knew it "from the inside". Second, and certainly no less
important, is the fact that, as priests and, later, as bishops, they would have been able to
influence official Catholic policy, not least toward Scripture and the canon. Moreover, it
is likely that they would have quickly and zealously sided with any initiative designed to
delimit the canon in order to damage or discredit the Manichaeans. For solid biographical
information on several of these figures, see A. MANDOUZE (ed.), *Prosopographie Chrétienne du bas-empire.* I: *Prosopographie de l'Afrique Chrétienne (303-533)*, Paris, Éditions
du Centre National de la Recherche Scientifique, 1982, s.v. "Alypius", "Honoratus 4",
"Nebridius", "Possidius", and "Romanianus". Alypius is unique in that he was both an
especially dear friend to Augustine and was elevated to the bishopric of his and Augustine's hometown of Thagaste before Augustine was made bishop of Hippo. For his involvement as a bishop in the various North African councils, his willingness to serve as courier
between Jerome and Augustine as well as as a liaison between Paulinus of Nola and Augustine during the struggle against the Manichaeans, and, finally, for his contribution "avec
ardeur" to the various struggles faced by the North African Church (esp. Donatism and
Pelagianism), see *Ibid.*, p. 56. For a more recent discussion of Alypius, now see E. FELD-
MANN – A. SCHLINDER – O. WERMELINGER, *Alypius*, in C. MEIER (ed.), *Augustinus Lexikon.*
Vol. 1 *(Aaron-Conuersio)*, Basel, Schwabe & Co. AG, 1986-1994. This last article is especially valuable for the way in which it highlights the multiple ways the lives of Alypius
and Augustine were deeply intertwined.
37. Interestingly, it is Augustine's correspondence with Jerome that offers us evidence
that the former's concern regarding the Manichaeans generally and the validity of the arguments against them specifically continued on until at least 405, i.e., the very middle of the
period in which he was also deeply entrenched against the Donatists. See R.S. COLE-TURNER,
*Anti-Heretical Issues and the Debate over Galatians 2:11-14 in the Letters of St. Augus-
tine to St. Jerome*, in *Augustinian Studies* 11 (1980) 155-166. More recently, Cole-Turner's
thinking has been followed in large part by E. Plummer. See E. PLUMMER, *Augustine's
Commentary on Galatians*, Oxford – New York, Oxford University Press, 2003, p. 95.
38. RIES, *La Bible*, I (n. 5), p. 233: "En 395, Augustin est sacré évêque à Hippone. La
défense de la Bible sera une de ses préoccupations majeures durant les premières années
de son épiscopat".

More immediately germane for this study is the effort he and his colleagues exerted in establishing and defending the sources of authority upon which that faith was based. An early passage that eloquently expresses the fundamental concerns of Augustine and his fellow Catholics is that of *De utilitate credendi* VI,13. This work dates from 391/392 and is the first work Augustine wrote after his ordination as a priest.

> I am convinced there is nothing more wise, more chaste, more religious than those scriptures which the Catholic Church accepts under the name of the Old Testament. You are amazed, I am sure. For I cannot pretend that I was not formerly of a very different opinion. [...] the Manichees ... with floods of oratory and malevolent criticism tear to pieces books which they do not understand, of which they do not know the purpose or the nature, books which look quite simple but, to those who understand, are subtle and divine; ... All that is in these Scriptures, believe me, is profound and divine. All truth is there, and learning suited to refresh and restore souls, but in such a form that there is no one who may not draw thence all he needs, provided he comes to draw in a spirit of piety and devotion such as true religion demands[39].

2. *Augustine's Accusations: Pre-Judgment and Pride*

As the previous passage makes clear, Augustine was intent on defending his newfound faith on simultaneous fronts: that faith's sacred texts (*in toto*) and that faith's general organizational structure as the unique Church of Christ. In his view, the Manichaeans had failed to properly acknowledge – much less humbly accept – the reality of either of these. Moreover, they wanted to reserve the right to pre-judge every practical and theological issue with which they were confronted. In the worst sense of the term, they were thoroughly *sui generis*[40]. This tendency towards

---

39. For this English translation, see J. Burleigh, *Augustine: Earlier Writings* (The Library of Christian Classics, 6), London, SCM Press, 1953, pp. 301-302. A second "early" work that is also germane here is the *Acta contra Fortunatum*. It reflects a very public debate between Augustine and Fortunatus that took place on 28-29 August, 392. The debate was in no small part focused on the nature and number of the books that the Catholics regarded as inspired. Cf. Ries, *La Bible*, I (n. 5), p. 232. Is it not possible that these works played a part in convincing Augustine and his fellow bishops of the need to address the issue of the canon – just as they did at the synod that took place the next year (i.e., 393) in Hippo? After all, by their very nature, councils and the canons they produce are almost always reactionary, i.e., they are usually only called in reaction to a doctrinal or ecclesiastical threat – whether real or imagined. And passages like these certainly make it clear that Augustine and, undoubtedly, many of his fellow bishops were being threatened by the Manichaeans. A good question – and one almost impossible to answer due to lack of evidence – is how exactly the Manichaeans reacted to the councils of the 390's and their canons. What evidence we do have seems to indicate that they, not unlike some catholics (cf. n. 13) were unimpressed.

40. Decret, *L'utilisation des Épîtres de Paul* (n. 27), p. 105: "Selon l'évêque d'Hip-

pre-judgment, however, was, at least in Augustine's view, only a symptom of a much more malevolent and much more dangerous disease: pride.
Augustine saw the Manichaeans, like all genuine "heretics", as people
whose prideful obstinacy had rendered them stiff-necked with respect to
both the (right) Scriptures and the (true) Church and had led them to follow their own sin-damaged hearts instead of these other, external
sources[41]. It was this twofold failure to submit that aided Augustine in
drawing the lines of battle for his aforementioned two-front defense: by
tying these issues together in an effective – if logically circular[42] – way,
he made it so that every blow he struck registered against both of these
fronts simultaneously.

3. *Augustine's Attack*

Of the many powerful and effective passages that could be marshaled
to illustrate the Bishop's battle plan, it is *Contra Faustum* XI,5 which
seems most apropos[43]. In it, even though Augustine's chief concern is
clearly to delineate the acceptable books[44] from the unacceptable[45], he

pone, ses anciens correligionnaires ... au lieu de soumettre leur foi à l'autorité des Écritures, ils soumettent les Écritures à leur propre jugement, bref, s'en servent pour caution-
ner une foi préétablie".

41. In Augustine, esp. within his polemical literature, this charge is a *topos*. Cf., e.g.,
how he used it at the opposite (chronological) end of his career against Julian of Aeclanum.
In *Contra Iulianum opus imperfectum* VI, 7 we read: "You, or your Pelagian companions
as well, think that you say something when, having abandoned divine authority, you exult
in human vanity and oppose and shout against the truth of the holy Scriptures *by the arguments of your heart*" (italics added). Of course, by the time we get to the Pelagian Controversy, Augustine adds yet another twist by becoming increasingly insistent that even the
correct disposition of the heart is something that is a by-product of the sovereign – and
ultimately irresistible – *gratia Dei*. H.J. LOEWEN, *The Use of Scripture in Augustine's Theology*, in *Scottish Journal of Theology* 34 (1981) 220, captures this aspect well: "For
Augustine ... we do not believe on authority. Rather we have an authority in the Scriptures and in the Church because, through grace, our will has been *made submissive* to
what the Scriptures and the Church proffers. Apart from this authority we cannot believe
rightly" (italics added).

42. For passages which clearly betray the "circularity" within Augustine's system
between the authority of Scripture and the authority of the Church, see, e.g., *Cres.* I, 33,
39; *s.* 23, 3 (where he uses 2 Tim 3,16); and *De Civitate Dei* XX,30,6 (where he [proba-
bly] uses Hebrews 6,18 and Titus 1,2).

43. Also significant is *contra Faustum*'s relatively early date of composition, i.e.,
between 397-399.

44. Of course, by this time and in such contexts, "acceptable" has become a synonym
for "Scripture". Of the literally dozens of passages from the period under consideration
in which Augustine unequivocally assigns to Scripture an exceedingly high – and not infre-
quently the highest – level of authority, see, e.g., *Confessiones* VI, 5, 8; XII, 16, 23; and
epistula 82, 5 and 7.

45. Earlier, in the equally interesting passage of *contra Faustum* XI, 2, Augustine discussed the appropriate criteria for distinguishing between genuine and apocryphal Scrip-

also touches upon the believer's need for submissive attitude[46] as well as upon the role of the Church in process of establishing and preserving authority:

> ... there is a distinct boundary line separating all productions subsequent to apostolic times from the authoritative canonical books of the Old and New Testaments. The authority of these books has come down to us from the apostles through the successions of bishops and the extensions of the Church, and, from a position of lofty supremacy claims the submission of every faithful and pious mind. If we are perplexed by an apparent contradiction in Scripture, it is not allowable to say, The author of this book is mistaken ... In the innumerable books that have been written latterly we may sometimes find the same truth as in Scripture, but there is not the same authority. Scripture has a sacredness particular unto itself. [...] But in consequence of the distinctive particularity of the sacred writings, we are bound to receive as true whatever the canon shows to have been said by even one prophet, or apostle, or evangelist. Otherwise not a single page will be left for the guidance of human fallibility, if contempt for the wholesome authority of the canonical books either puts an end to that authority altogether, or involves it in hopeless confusion[47].

---

ture. Cf. CSEL 25, p. 314: "Aliud est ipsos libros non accipere ... quod denique nos ipsi de uestris ... uel de his, qui appellantur apocryphi – non quod habendi sint in aliqua auctoritate secreta, sed quia nulla testificationis luce declarati de nescio quo secreto nescio quorum praesumptione prolati sunt – ..." For a more general statement see, e.g., ALLGEIER, *Der Einfluß des Manichäismus* (n. 7), pp. 8-9. Since their authors were known, there was, of course, never a thought that the works of later, Christian writers might come to be regarded as apocryphal. Nevertheless, we can frequently find Augustine asserting that these later writers – himself included – should in no way be regarded as substantially authoritative in any way similar to the authority inherent in Scripture. For two of many possible passages, see *contra Faustum* XI, 5 (see the text of this same page *supra*) and *epistula* 148, 15.18. (*Epistula* 148 is variously dated to between 410 and 414.) Augustine's attitude toward his own authority over against both that of Scripture and that of his "orthodox" predecessors and contemporaries is a promising avenue for further research.

46. For examples of passages in which Augustine makes clear the need for submission to the Scripture, see, e.g., *contra Faustum* XI, 2; XVI, 11; XXXII, 19; as well as *epistula* 28, 4 and *epistula* 82, 3, both of which were addressed to Jerome, albeit some ten or eleven years apart. On these last two, cf. n. 37. For the role of the Church, COYLE, *Augustine's De moribus ecclesiae catholicae* (n. 22), pp. 151-153 has done an admirable job in summarizing Augustine's six "proofs" of the Church's credibility as they appear in the *De moribus* and then augmenting these with passages from elsewhere in his corpus. Especially helpful is the following quote taken from p. 152: "... the proof of the Church's credibility lies in such phenomena as her rapid territorial expansion and large numbers of faithful in her martyrs, in the large numbers of her faithful who practice the evangelical counsels to the full, in her continuity through history, but above all in her apostolic tradition ...". Cf. also RIES, *La Bible*, I (n. 5), p. 239: "Augustine restitue aux apôtres, l'arbitrage de l'autorité biblique: ils restent les premiers témoins authentiques de la tradition de l'Église".

47. For this English translation (which falls short of capturing the intensity of the Latin), see NPNF, IV, p. 180. Cf. CSEL 25, pp. 320-321 (noting especially the parts that have been italicized): " ... distincta est a posteriorum libris excellentia canonicae auctoritatis Veteris et Noui Testamenti, quae apostolorum confirmata temporibus per succes-

As one might suspect, to merely accept that a given book was part of the authoritative collection was not enough. One had to also know how to handle and interpret them. While, on the one hand, this was also connected to the need for any reader to belong to the "true" Church[48], on the other, it was also due to the fact that any reader or hearer needed to be careful to submit to *the whole council* of *all* the genuine Scriptures. This was the surest guide for avoiding interpretive problems such as apparent contradictions. Sermon 50, which is certainly directed against the Manichaeans, is thought to date from the period in between the first two councils that pronounced on the canon, i.e., to 394-395. In its concluding Paragraph 13 Augustine, even as he admits the Scriptures' susceptibility to abuse, offers both critique and guidance:

> ... the sect of the Manichees uses fraudulent, not honest, means with the unlearned to get them to set parts of the scriptures above the whole, the new above the old; they pick out sentences which they try to show contradict each other, in order to take in the unlearned. But just in the New Testament itself there is no letter of the apostle or even book of the gospel in which that sort of thing cannot be done, so that any one book may be made to look as if it contradicted itself in various places, *unless the reader pays very careful attention to its whole composition and design*[49].

siones episcoporum et propagationes Ecclesiarum *tamquam in sede quadam sublimiter constituta est*, cui *seruiat* omnis fidelis et pius intellectus. Ibi si quid uelut absurdum mouerit. Non licet dicere: auctor huius libri non tenuit ueritatem ... In opusculis autem posteriorum, quae libris innumerabilibus continentur, *sed nullo modo illi sacratissimae canonicarum scripturarum excellentiae coaequantur*, etiam in quibuscumque eorum inuenitur eadem ueritas, *longe tamen est inpar auctoritas.* [...] In illa uero canonica eminentia sacrarum litterarum, etiamsi unus propheta seu apostolus aut euangelista aliquid in suis litteris posuisse ipsa canonis confirmatione declaratur, non licet dubitare, quod uerum sit; alioquin nulla erit pagina, *qua humanae inperitiae regatur infirmitas*, si librorum saluberrima auctoritas aut contempta penitus aboletur aut interminata confunditur".

48. Here, see T. Toom, *Thought Clothed With Sound: Augustine's Christological Hermeneutics in* De doctrina Christiana (International Theological Studies: Contributions of Baptist Scholars, 4), Bern, Peter Lang, 2002, p. 106: "People tend to find in the scripture what they have been taught to find there, and precisely because of that, Augustine emphasized the Church as the right context for interpreting the scripture". For an older but clearly parallel sentiment, see Loewen, *The Use of Scripture* (n. 41), p. 205: " ... it is clear that Augustine perceived the authoritative function of Scripture to exist in the framework of a rather robust doctrine of the Church, a framework in which the Church provided a visible context of faith and life through which the authority of the biblical teaching found expression and validation".

49. For this English translation, see *WSA* III,2, p.351; for the Latin, cf. CCSL, 41, pp. 632-633: "... Manicheorum sectam non ueritate sed fraude agere cum imperitis, ut scripturas non totas totis, nouas ueteribus praeferant, sed excerpendo sententias, quas uelut aduersas sibi esse conatur ostendere, ut decipiant imperitos. Nulla est autem de ipso Nouo Testamento uel apostoli epistola uel etiam liber euangelii, de quo non possint ista fieri, ut quibusdam sententiis ipse unus liber sibi uideatur esse contrarius, *nisi eius tota contextio diligentissima lectoris intentione tractetur*" (italics added). Here, also note Coyle's com-

4. *Augustine's Impact*

Augustine's defense of both his particular, if universal, Church and his particular canon (read *in toto*) – while it certainly is impressive in its own right – would be little more than a chapter in the history of theology had he not become the West's most influential post-Apostolic theologian[50]. Indeed, were it not for his impact on every generation that succeeded him, few would be likely to be interested in his views on any of the foregoing. Given the restrictions of this forum, a few examples of this impact will have to suffice. For starters, note the way Balbulus, an exegete who died soon after the turn of the tenth-century, could use just Augustine's *name* as a "proof-text". In his *Liber de interpretatione Scripturae*, as a means of resolving an exegetical dilemma, he boldly asserted that: "*si Augustinus adest, sufficit ipse tibi*"[51]. Still more impressive is the way the Bishop of Hippo's texts and legacy were handled throughout the sixteenth-century: at many points during the Reformation both sides made the claim that they, and they alone, were the true descendents of the thought and doctrine of the Bishop of Hippo[52].

ments which he links to his analysis of lines 984-990 of the substantially earlier *De moribus ecclesiae catholicae*: "... in [Augustine's] view ... once any passage in any part of Scripture has been discredited, the whole becomes untrustworthy, and one can end up dismissing the whole Bible as an 'interpolation''. For this, see COYLE, *Augustine's* De moribus ecclesiae catholicae (n. 22), p. 150.

50. Statements to this effect are not at all rare in the literature. For just two examples, note the following two assertions from Drobner and Chadwick, respectively: "... from the Middle Ages to the present, Augustine has remained the most prominent and most widely studied author in western Christianity, second only to biblical writers such as Paul". See H.R. DROBNER, *Studying Augustine: An Overview of Recent Research*, in R. DODARO – G. LAWLESS (eds.), *Augustine and His Critics*, London, Routledge, 2000, p. 18. Chadwick is even more sweeping when he labels Augustine as "the greatest single mind and influence in Christian history". Apparently, Chadwick sees Augustine's influence as even *surpassing* that of Paul! For this, see H. CHADWICK, *Augustine*, in R.J. COGGINS – J.L. HOULDEN (eds.), *A Dictionary of Biblical Interpretation*, London, SCM Press, 1990.

51. Cf. PL 131, col. 998. This is borrowed from RIES, *La Bible*, II (n. 5), p. 207. This statement (which was also new to me), if thoroughly researched, might also yield some interesting results. E.g., how common was it for Balbulus and/or others to use this and other, similar statements? In what context(s)? Is it at all possible that it was regarded as a more-or-less serious didactic tool?

52. A helpful survey of the issues surrounding the reception of the major writers of the Patristic period during the Reformation is available in the two-volume collection I. BACKUS (ed.), *The Reception of the Church Fathers in the West: From the Carolingians to the Maurists*, 2 Vols., Leiden, Brill, 1997. See esp. E.L. SAAK, *The Reception of Augustine in the Later Middle Ages*, in BACKUS (ed.), *The Reception of the Church Fathers in the West*, Vol. I, pp. 367-404, which, although both substantial and expert, still begins (cf. p. 371) by observing that Augustine is so omnipresent in this period that "to chart the reception of Augustine in the Later Middle Ages is to be faced with an ominous task". See also virtually all of volume II, but most esp. Chapters 15 (by M. Schulze), 16 (by I. Backus), and

V. SUMMARY AND SELECTED IMPLICATIONS

In what has proceeded it has been shown that, Augustine, as an influential priest and bishop during the North Africa of the 390's, had a hand in "constructing" his community's Bible, one of the two or three primary sources of truth to which he would appeal throughout the rest of his life[53]. More precisely, this came about because he helped that Church to construct and to enforce a conciliar and, hence, public and binding, pronouncement on the issue of the canon. So, while it is highly improbable that the Bishop of Hippo would have been able to foresee all the implications of this maneuver, it is nevertheless true that both the role and the attitude evidenced by the fourth-and-fifth-century North African Catholics during the process has profoundly affected the ways all western Christians approached the issue of truth in the intervening centuries. Thanks to Augustine and his North African friends – and, at least indirectly, to those resilient Manichaeans – western Christians of all stripes, in spite of great and significant differences – still believe that (at least one of) the avenue(s) for the establishment of truth has been smoothly paved once and for all[54]. If this be doubted, imagine the ruckus that would be generated in many quarters if anyone seriously advocated making significant *addenda et corrigenda* to the Bible. To a lesser extent, this brief sketch has also illustrated how an individual person (e.g., Augustine) or thing (e.g. particular Scriptures) can begin or continue that largely mysterious process of becoming so integrated into the warp and woof of a tradition and, hence, into the fabric that tradition's orthodoxy, as to become a *sine qua non* of the tradition itself.

jonathan.yates@villanova.edu   Jonathan YATES

17 (by J. van Oort), which are dedicated, respectively, to Luther, Zwingli/Bucer, and Calvin. The reception and impact of Augustine on these three is explicitly discussed on pp. 573-579, 631-632, 641-643, 654-656, and 689. On p. 671, for example, J. van Oort, the author of the chapter on Calvin, notes that "[Calvin's] most intimate knowledge concerns the Father who is also cited most frequently: Augustine", before going on to discuss, on p. 679, Calvin's famous, if polemically charged claim from 1552 that "Augustinus totus noster est".

53. Indeed, as any perusal of his works will readily show, in his hands, Scripture could serve alternatively as an encouraging guidepost or as an iron-hard bludgeon.

54. Even during the Reformation, when some of that movement's leaders successfully advocated for further changes in the canon's contents, they always argued that it should be *further restricted* or *delimited*, never – at least as far as I am aware – that it should be *expanded* beyond that used by Augustine. To this day, the Bible of the vast majority of the denominations or confessions who have their roots in the various reform efforts of the sixteenth-century still use a shorter, sixty-six book Bible.

THE LOUVAIN THEOLOGIAN JOHN DRIEDO VERSUS
THE GERMAN REFORMER MARTIN LUTHER

AND WHO COULD IMPOSE THEIR TRUTH...

It has been observed that the fifteenth century was an age of piety, the sixteenth century by contrast an age of theology. One of the reasons for this shift was "Luther's anchoring of ultimate truth in the purity of doctrine, not in the purity of life"[1]. Luther sparked a Reformation centered on doctrinal reform. As a consequence, it was theological truth that was at stake in the debate between the reformers and the Catholic Church. At the same time, it was also the object of general debate among common people, "by means of the avalanche of pamphlets and sermons, Bible translations, songs, and catechisms"[2]. This article will focus on the state of affairs in the 1530s. In 1533 the Louvain theologian John Driedo issued *De ecclesiasticis scripturis et dogmatibus* in reply to Luther's *sola scriptura*-doctrine. During this period, politics was at least as influential on the rapid spread of Luther's positions in Germany and the preserving of Catholicism in the southern part of the Low Countries as was the veracity of the antagonists' theological positions.

I. ON THE SOURCES OF TRUTH

1. *Martin Luther:* sola scriptura[3]

A crucial moment in Luther's personal and intellectual development was the series of lectures he gave in the years 1515-16 on Paul's Epistle

---

1. B. HAMM, *The Urban Reformation in the Holy Roman Empire*, in T.A. BRADY, JR. – H.A. OBERMAN – J.D. TRACY (eds.), *Handbook of European History 1400-1600: Late Middle Ages, Renaissance and Reformation*. Vol. II: *Visions, Programs and Outcomes*, Leiden, Brill, 1995, 193-216, esp. 211.
2. *Ibid.*, p. 211.
3. Among the abundant literature concerning Luther's person and his emphasis on Scripture, see M. BRECHT, *Martin Luther*. Vol. 1: *Sein Weg zur Reformation 1483-1521*, Stuttgart, Calwer, 1981; *Ibid.*, vol. 2: *Ordnung und Abgrenzung der Reformation 1521-1532*, Stuttgart, Calwer, 1986; *Ibid.*, vol. 3: *Die Erhaltung der Kirche 1532-1546*, Stuttgart, Calwer, 1987; H.A. OBERMAN, *Luther: Mensch zwischen Gott und Teufel*, Berlin, Severin und Siedler, 1982; A. BEUTEL, *In dem Anfang war das Wort: Studien zu Luthers Sprachverständnis* (Hermeneutische Untersuchungen zur Theologie, 27), Tübingen, Mohr Siebeck, 1991. Concerning the edition of Luther's works, we refer always to *D. Martin*

to the Romans[4]. In Rom 1,17 he read: "For therein is the righteousness of God revealed from faith to faith: as it is written, The just shall live by faith [Hab 2,4]". According to Luther, this verse proved once and for all that, after the last Bible book was completed, Scripture became the sole trustworthy means for accessing theological truth (*sola scriptura* as the formal principle of Reformation). He considered the Pauline doctrine of justification as the hermeneutic key for understanding Scripture. To elucidate Paul's view, he made an appeal to Augustine's anti-pelagian works and particularly to *De spiritu et littera*[5]. It led him to the conviction that it was impossible for any fundamentally-sinful human being to earn his righteousness by doing good works and fulfilling devotional practices. After Adam's fall, all acts of man – even the so-called 'good works' – were corrupted by a fundamental sinfulness. Hence, it was by faith and faith alone that the baptized could hope for God's graceful initiative. Faith was a response to God's offer of grace as mediated through Jesus' substitutionary death and resurrection (*sola gratia* and *sola fide* as the material principles of Reformation)[6]. From faith flow the fruits of faith, i.e. daily "good works". This Pauline doctrine of justification, which was, in Luther's view, the core of the Gospel, constituted the perspective from which the whole Bible had to be interpreted. Regarding matters that were necessary for human salvation, Scripture was therefore considered as the

Luthers Werke. Kritische Gesamtausgabe, Weimar, Böhlau, 1883-1993; reprints, Graz. Sections: *Werke*, 60 vols., 5 vols. registers, 1883-1993 [=WA]; *Tischreden*, 6 vols., 1912-1921 [=WATr]; *Die Deutsche Bibel*, 12 vols., 1906-1961 [=WADB]; *Briefwechsel*, 18 vols., 1930-1983 [=WABr].

4. See among others: LUTHER, *Vorrede zum 1. Bande der Gesamtausgaben seiner lat. Schriften. 1545* (WA, 54), pp. 179-187, esp. 186, l. 16-20. We do not enter at length into the discussion when Luther's reformational 'breakthrough' effectively took place. We have rather to reckon with a gradual evolution to which several influences contributed.

5. For an introduction in the relationship between Luther and Augustine, see: P.D. KREY, *Luther, Martin*, in A.D. FITZGERALD (ed.), *Augustine through the Ages: An Encyclopedia*, Grand Rapids, MI, Eerdmans, 1999, 516-518. Also: L. GRANE, *Augustins "Expositio quarundam propositionum ex epistola apostoli ad Romanos" in Luthers Römerbriefvorlesung*, in *Zeitschrift für Theologie und Kirche* 69 (1972) 304-330; ID., *Divus Paulus et S. Augustinus, interpres eius fidelissimus: Über Luthers Verhältnis zu Augustin*, in G. EBELING – E. JÜNGEL – G. SCHUNACK (eds.), *Festschrift für Ernst Fuchs*, Tübingen, Mohr Siebeck, 1973, 133-146, esp. 145. Also: M. SCHULZE, *Martin Luther and the Church Fathers*, in I. BACKUS (ed.), *The Reception of the Church Fathers in the West: From the Carolingians to the Maurists*, vol. 2, Leiden, Brill, 1997, 573-626, esp. 576-578; OBERMAN, *Luther: Mensch zwischen Gott und Teufel* (n. 3), pp. 159-162.

6. LUTHER, *Der Brief an die Römer* (WA, 56), pp. 172 l. 3-11, 273 l. 3-9. Also: LUTHER, *Predigten des Jahres 1531* (WA, 34-II), p. 488b l. 25-26: "Ego nullo alio medio habeo articulum iustificationis quam per scripturam, per verbum"; *Predigten der Jahre 1533 und 1534* (WA, 37), p. 325 l. 25-26: "Ego non aliam fidem [habeo], quam quae in scriptura". Vgl. W.-D. HAUSCHILD, *Lehrbuch der Kirchen- und Dogmengeschichte*. Vol. 2: *Reformation und Neuzeit*, Gütersloh, Gütersloher Verlagshaus, 1999, p. 275.

clear and transparent expression of God's Word (*claritas scripturae*)[7]. Scripture was called to be its own interpreter (*sacra scriptura sui ipsius interpres*). As a result, Luther distanced himself from hermeneutical criteria that were alien to Scripture[8]. In his view, it was evident that all binding articles and acts of faith must necessarily be supported by an explicit verse of Scripture. Catholics, however, were unable to overcome the impression that Luther's reasoning was circular: it was by reading Scripture that *sola gratia* and *sola fide* were revealed as core truths, and at the same time, *sola gratia* and *sola fide* were the alleged keys for understanding the contents of Scripture. Yet, Luther appealed to the Holy Spirit who inspired the authors or redactors of Scripture. The same Spirit is at work in the heart of every Christian who reads Scripture and, hence, guaranteed that the faithful theologian, preacher and lay lecturer would understand the Word rightly[9]. Obviously, Luther did not explain why people, both inside and outside his community, all of whom appealed to the same Spirit, arrived at different doctrinal and exegetical conclusions.

For their part, the Catholics, who wanted to guard Scripture from so-called subjective interpretations, were accused by Luther of supplementing and interpreting the Bible with various merely human 'traditions'. Many of these were drawn from the Church Fathers and the scholastic commentators. Equally problematic was the exaltation of popes and Councils as the highest authorities and as those empowered to distinguish valid interpretations from non-valid. Luther, by contrast, was only prepared to assign great authority to the judgments of the four earliest ecumenical Councils (Nicea, Constantinople, Ephesus and Chalcedon), because they were thought to have given authentic explanations of Scripture and to have avoided giving new articles of faith promulgated through

---

7. Luther elaborated his doctrine of *claritas Scripturae* in his work *De servo arbitrio*, which was a polemical reply to Erasmus. See a.o.: LUTHER, *De servo arbitrio. 1525* (WA, 18), pp. 609 l. 4-14, 653 l. 28-33. Other assertions of the *claritas Scripturae*: LUTHER, *Auf das überchristlich usw. Buch Bocks Emsers Antwort. 1521* (WA, 7), p. 647 l. 31 ff.; *Rationis Latomianae confutatio. 1521* (WA, 8), p. 99 l. 4-22; *Der 36. Psalm Davids. 1521* (WA, 8), p. 236 l. 7-17; *Predigten des Jahres 1522* (WA, 10-III), p. 237 l. 24-27.

8. LUTHER, *Assertio omnium articulorum M. Lutheri per bullam Leonis X. 1520* (WA, 7), p. 97 l. 23-24: "per sese certissima, facillima, apertissima, sui ipsius interpres, omnium omnia probans, iudicans et illuminans"; M. Luther to G. Spalatinus, 12 February 1519 (WABr, 1), n° 145, p. 330 l. 115-116: "Vides, quam Euangelii verba seipsa exponant, suasque glosas secum habent, ut nihil necesse sit aliena et humana miscere"; LUTHER, *Operationes in Psalmos. 1519-1521* (WA, 5), pp. 597 l. 37 – 598 l. 2; *Predigten des Jahres 1532* (WA, 36), p. 504b l. 14-18.

9. LUTHER, *Assertio omnium articulorum M. Lutheri per bullam Leonis X. 1520* (WA, 7), p. 97 l. 1-3: "Scripturas non nisi eo spiritu intelligendas esse, quo scriptae sunt, qui spiritus nusquam praesentius et vivacius quam in ipsis sacris suis, quas scripsit, literis inveniri potest"; *De servo arbitrio. 1525* (WA, 18), p. 609 l. 4-12.

an appeal to a formal, external authority[10]. Luther evidently had no objections against 'good' scriptural interpretations made by the Church Fathers, that is, interpretations that were in accordance with the basic evangelical principles of *sola gratia* and *sola fide*. Luther relied most heavily on Augustine and especially on Augustine's writings against the Pelagians. It was in these that he had 'discovered' views that were in accordance with Paul's view on justification by faith alone[11]. At the same time, he was fundamentally convinced that unlike Scripture the Church Fathers (including Augustine) and (later) Councils could err and did in fact[12]. By the same reasoning, Luther rejected the idea that the Pope could assert an exclusive right to interpret Scripture in an authoritative (to say nothing of an infallible) way[13]. He criticized the theologians of Paris, Cologne, Louvain and other universities for depending too much on the major scholastic commentators whose sophisticated constructions and contrived argumentations had wandered too far away from the themes of Scripture. Luther regarded as outrageous their use of dialectics and their appeal to ideas and categories that had been devised by the 'pagan' Aristotle, which they employed in order to elucidate the principal notions in Scripture and the Church's doctrine[14]. As a consequence, he rejected completely or con-

10. LUTHER, *Die drei Symbola oder Bekenntnis des Glaubens Christi. 1538* (WA, 50), p. 262 l. 5-12; *Von den Konziliis und Kirchen. 1539* (WA, 50), pp. 522 l. 6-15; 615 l. 28 – 616 l. 5.

11. LUTHER, *Disputatio Heidelbergae habita. 1518* (WA, 1), p. 353 l. 8-14; *In epistolam Pauli ad Galatas commentarius. 1519* (WA, 2), p. 489 l. 17-19; *Vorwort zu In prophetam Amos Iohannis Brentii expositio. 1530* (WA, 30-II), pp. 650 l. 24-33, 651 l. 1-4.

12. LUTHER, *Auf das überchristlich usw. Buch Bocks Emsers Antwort. 1521* (WA, 7), p. 647 l. 29-30; *Rationis Latomianae confutatio. 1521* (WA, 8), p. 99 l. 4-22; *Der 36. (37.) Psalm Davids. 1521* (WA, 8), p. 237 l. 14-19; *Ein Widerspruch D. Luthers seines Irrthums. 1521* (WA, 8), p. 248 l. 18-20; *Widerruf vom Fegefeuer. 1530* (WA, 30-II), p. 384 l. 9-18.

13. See: LUTHER, *Assertio omnium articulorum M. Lutheri per bullam Leonis X. novissimam damnatorum. 1520* (WA, 7), pp. 96 l. 11-20, 97 l. 21-24.26-29, 100 l. 27-33, 134 l. 28, 135 l. 1; *An den Christlicher Adel deutscher Nation von des Christlichen Standes Besserung. 1520* (WA, 6), pp. 411 l. 33-35, 412 l. 11-14. Also: *Resolutio Lutheriana super propositione XIII. de potestate papae. 1519* (WA, 2), pp. 180-240; *Wider das Papsttum zu Rom vom Teufel gestiftet. 1545* (WA, 54), pp. 195-299.

14. Among the manifold references, see LUTHER, *Disputatio contra scholasticam theologiam. 1517* (WA, 1), p. 226 l. 26; *Disputatio Heidelbergae habita. 1518* (WA, 1), p. 355 l. 2-3; *Praecepta Wittenbergensi praedicta populo. 1518* (WA, 1), p. 509, l. 11-15; *Decem Praelectio in librum Iudicum. 1516 flg.* (WA, 4), pp. 538 l. 2-6, 554 l. 34-38; *Operationes in Psalmos; 1519-1521* (WA, 5), p. 22 l. 6-9; *An den christlichen Adel deutscher Nation von des christlichen Standes Besserung. 1520* (WA, 6), pp. 457 l. 31-35, 458 l. 4-6; *De captivitate Babylonica ecclesiae praeludium. 1520* (WA, 6), p. 510 l. 31; *Rationis Latomianae confutatio. 1521* (WA, 8), pp. 98 l. 30 – 99 l. 7; *Eine Äußerung Luthers über die Heidelberger Disputation* [1518] (WA, 9), p. 170 l. 1-9; *Adventspostille. Luk. 21, 25-36 Euangelium am andern sontag ym Advent. Luce 21* (WA, 10-I, 2), pp. 96 l. 21 – 97 l. 1, 116 l. 10-11; *Vorrede zu Gochii fragmenta. 1522* (WA, 10-II), p. 330 l. 7-

sidered as not binding later traditions, understood as the unwritten beliefs and practices that were chiefly added during the scholastic period (and that were not supported by an explicit word of Scripture). These traditions concerned indulgences, purgatory, clerical celibacy, and many of the outward ceremonies of the Roman Church.

Luther's assertion that Scripture was the uniquely valid way to divine truth was the result of three factors: (1) his nominalist background; (2) his study of the Scriptures as a university professor who used the tools of biblical humanism, and (3) his personal existential search for a merciful God. First is Luther's recognition of the degree to which he had been influenced by late medieval nominalism or the *via moderna* while studying at the University of Erfurt[15]; in its philosophical shape, nominalism is known as 'terminism'[16]. The leading representatives of the philosophical nominalism in Erfurt were Jodokus Trutfetter of Eisenach and Bartholomäus Arnoldi of Usingen[17]. Nominalists clearly distinguished between the domain of material reality and the domain of revelation. Concerning material reality, nominalists believed that, on the basis of particular sensory experiences, the human intellect generated abstract concepts. In opposition to the realists of the *via antiqua*, they denied that these general concepts or *universalia* had a 'real' existence apart from the objects to which they referred[18]. They were convinced that these universal concepts were mere products of abstract thinking and that they were signified by *nomina* or *termini* which were only based on convention[19]. These *nomina* or *termini* could be applied to many particular instances. Hence, the abstract concept 'human' had no proper consistency in reality; it was a mere *terminus* that indicated the particular members of the human species[20]. In short, with the famous 'razor of Ockham' nominalists cut away all superfluous conceptual constructions and made sensory experi-

---

10; *Vorlesung über Jesaia. 1527/29. In Esaiam Scholia ex D. Martini Lutheri praelectionibus collecta. 1532/34* (WA, 25), p. 219 l. 13-14; *Text der Genesisvorlesung. 1535-45* (WA, 43), pp. 93 l. 37 – 94 l. 11; *Text der Genesisvorlesung 1535-45* (WA, 44), p. 776 l. 18-19.

15. On Luther's time as student in Erfurt, see: BRECHT, *Martin Luther*, Vol. 1 (n. 3), pp. 33-58; OBERMAN, *Luther: Mensch zwischen Gott und Teufel* (n. 3), pp. 119-132.

16. M. Luther to J. Trutfetter, 9 May 1518 (WABr, 1), n° 74, p. 171 l. 71-74.

17. C. BURGER, *Nieuw onderzoek naar Luthers wijsgerige en theologische vorming en haar doorwerking*, in *Luther-Bulletin. Tijdschrift voor interconfessioneel Lutheronderzoek* 12 (2003) 61-71, esp. 66-67; BRECHT, *Martin Luther*, Vol. 1 (n. 3), pp. 45, 47; OBERMAN, *Luther: Mensch zwischen Gott und Teufel* (n. 3), pp. 124-130.

18. LUTHER, *Tischrede 2937* (WATr, 3), p. 104 l. 18-22.

19. LUTHER, *Tischrede 193* (WATr, 1), p. 85 l. 27-28. Possibly also: LUTHER, *Tischrede 338* (WATr, 1), p. 137 l. 11-16; *Tischrede 3722* (WATr, 3), p. 564 l. 9-10.

20. See a.o.: LUTHER, *Tischrede 5134* (WATr, 4), p. 679 l. 3-20; *Tischrede 6419* (WATr, 5), p. 653 l. 1-18.

ence and reasoning intellect the most important means of accessing any
and all knowledge of reality.

Distinct from the terrain of the material reality, there was the sphere
of revelation, which concerned the salvation of humanity. Its apprehension was beyond the range of reason and sensory experience. It was
purely the realm of God's Word as contained in Scripture; it could neither be empirically proved nor demonstrated. It was up to human beings
to accept God's Word on faith. In theology, proper, the nominalists were
opposed to idle speculations[21]. In fact, "nominalism was the deconstruc-
tionism of its day"[22]. In sum then, Luther's emphasis on sensory experience and rational argument on the one hand, and his appeal to Scripture
on the other, combined with his aversion to idle speculations, had already
had a significant impact on him during his time in nominalist Erfurt. In
later debates, Luther presented his conscience as bound by these strict
premises, but never was willing to admit that he was even more influenced by his personal struggles[23].

Secondly, in Erfurt Luther also came into contact with humanist circles. They strengthened his appreciation for classical Latin authors and
their approach to rhetoric. Biblical humanists, for their part, helped him
to apply the humanist methodology to Scripture and to base his theological insights on the text of the Bible in its original tongues. According to
the humanists, to 're-fund' theology and ecclesiastical life on the basis of
Scripture signified a choice for the 'spirit', while the Church of their era
was said to be dominated by the 'flesh' (2 Cor 3,6), that is outward ceremonies and sophisticated speculations.

After Luther had obtained his degree of Master of Arts, and, as a consequence of the vow he took on 5 July 1505 to St. Anne during a terri-
fying storm, he had entered the monastery of the Augustinians in Erfurt[24].

---

21. See particularly: M. Luther to J. Trutfetter, 9 May 1518 (WABr, 1), n° 74, p. 171
l. 72-74: "... ex te primo omnium didici, solis canonicis libris deberi fidem, caeteris
omnibus iudicium, ut B. Augustinus, imo Paulus et Iohannes praecipiunt".

22. R. MARIUS, *Martin Luther: The Christian Between God and Death*, Cambridge,
MA, Belknap Press of Harvard University Press, ³2000, p. 35.

23. While at Worms, Luther said: "... Unless I am convicted by scripture and by plain
reason (I do not believe in the authority of either popes or councils by themselves, for it
is plain that they have often erred and contradicted each other) in those scriptures that I
have presented, for my conscience is captive to the Word of God, I cannot and I will not
recant anything, for to go against conscience is neither right nor safe. God help me, Amen"
(quoted in MARIUS, *Martin Luther* [n. 22], p. 294). Also: LUTHER, *Responsio ad condem-
nationem doctrinalem per Lov. et Colon. factam. 1520* (WA, 6), pp. 194 l. 37 – 195 l. 6:
"Nec hoc quaesivi, ut me ad suos autores remitterent quasi mihi incognitos, sed ut scripturae autoritate aut ratio probabili sua vera et mea falsa esse convincerent...".

24. Concerning Luther as a monk and a theology student, see: BRECHT, *Martin Luther*,

This house belonged to the Saxon congregation of the Augustinians, the observant wing of the Order. This congregation, as all observant branches of religious orders, was opposed to laxness in monastic life and aimed to restore the original discipline of its particular rule. In this way, the observant congregations wanted to contribute to the reform of the Church[25]. It is striking however that, in the monastery, Luther's psychological constitution began to play an important role in his view on truth. He tried to observe as perfectly as possible the prescribed practices of fasting and penance and to participate in all the liturgical services. Luther, however, was constantly burdened by a sense of failure respecting his duties towards God. He felt God, the severe Judge, was constantly displeased with him. His anxiety for the Last Judgment and the eternal damnation depressed him, a state of mind which manifested itself in a frequent practice of confession. Besides the observance of the rule, the congregation of the observant Augustinians encouraged its members toward the intensive *lectio* of the Scriptures. The impetus for this idea came from the congregation's vicar-general, Johann von Staupitz[26]. From the earliest stage of his life as a monk Luther took great sustenance of the Scriptures (and particularly the Psalms). His original motivation for studying them grew out of his own existential angst. Though Staupitz devoted himself to the rigorous observance of the rules, he was convinced that a human, and particularly a monk, could not achieve salvation entirely by his own efforts. Hence, it was Staupitz who encouraged the tormented student Martin Luther not to be fixed on his own shortcomings and sins but to trust faithfully in a merciful Lord and in the salvation offered through

Vol. 1 (n. 3), pp. 59-110; OBERMAN, *Luther: Mensch zwischen Gott und Teufel* (n. 3), pp. 132-158.

25. On the Saxon congregation of the Augustinians, see particularly: A. KUNZELMANN, *Geschichte der deutschen Augustiner-Eremiten.* Vol. 5: *Die sächsisch-thüringische Provinz und die sächsische Reformkongregation bis zum Untergang der beiden* (Cassiciacum, 26), Würzburg, Augustinus Verlag, 1974, pp. 383-482; W. ECKERMANN, *Neue Dokumente zur Auseinandersetzung zwischen Johann von Staupitz und der Sächsischen Reformkongregation*, in *Analecta Augustiniana* 40 (1977) 279-296; L. GRAF ZU DOHNA, *Von der Ordensreform zur Reformation: Johann von Staupitz*, in K. ELM (ed.), *Reformbemühungen und Observanzbestrebungen im spätmittelalterlichen Ordenswesen* (Berliner Historische Studien, 14: Ordensstudien, 6), Berlin, Duncker und Humblot, 1989, 571-584; R. WEINBRENNER, *Klosterreform im 15. Jahrhundert zwischen Ideal und Praxis: der Augustinereremit Andreas Proles (1429-1503) und die privilegierte Observanz* (Spätmittelalter und Reformation, N.R. 7), Tübingen, Mohr Siebeck, 1996.

26. For the infuence of J. von Staupitz on Luther and the origins of the Reformation, see: L. GRAF ZU DOHNA, *Staupitz and Luther: Continuity and Breakthrough at the Beginning of the Reformation*, in H.A. OBERMAN – F.A. JAMES – E.L. SAAK (eds.), *Via Augustini: Augustine in the Later Middle Ages, Renaissance and Reformation. Essays in Honor of Damasus Trapp, O.S.A.* (Studies in Medieval and Reformation Thought, 4), Leiden, Brill, 1991, 116-129.

the atoning passion and death of Jesus Christ. Staupitz had developed a theology of grace that was fundamentally founded upon the Bible and particularly upon Paul's Epistles, which, in turn, were interpreted according to Augustine's doctrine of justification[27]. Stimulated by Staupitz, Luther redoubled his study of Augustine's works. In sum, the reformational principles of *sola scriptura*, *sola gratia* and *sola fide* were already found *in nuce* in the preaching and works of Staupitz, and it is clear that Luther was fundamentally influenced by his superior and spiritual father[28]. The reformer readily recognized that he, in developing his "doctrina", was fundamentally indebted to Johann von Staupitz[29].

2. *John Driedo about Scripture and traditions in the Church*

As a reply to Luther's *sola scriptura*-doctrine, in 1533 the Louvain theologian John Driedo (1479/80-1535) published in 1533 *De ecclesiasticis scripturis et dogmatibus*[30]. As a member of the Louvain 'school' of

27. An elaboration of Staupitz' theology: GRAF ZU DOHNA, *Staupitz and Luther* (n. 26), pp. 122-125.

28. See: GRAF ZU DOHNA, *Staupitz and Luther* (n. 26), pp. 119-122; M. WRIEDT, *Luther's Theology*, in D.K. MCKIM (ed.), *The Cambridge Companion to Martin Luther*, Cambridge, Cambridge University Press, 2003, 86-119, esp. 89-90.

29. LUTHER, *Tischrede 173* (WATr, 1), p. 80 l. 6-7; *Tischrede 526* (WATr, 1), p. 245 l. 9-12.

30. DRIEDO, Ioannes, *De ecclesiasticis scripturis et dogmatibus libri quattuor*, in *Operum D. Ioannis Driedonis a Turnhout*, T. 1/[a Ruardo Tapper], Lovanii: ex officina Bartholomaei Gravii, 1556, [8], 269 f.; in f°. For a thorough study of this work's content, see J.L. MURPHY, *The Notion of Tradition in John Driedo*, Milwaukee, WI, Seraphic Press, 1959, pp. 44-235. *Inter alia*, the author was responding to the work of J. LODRIOOR, *De Leer over de Christelijke Traditie in de Theologie van Joannes Driedo van Leuven* (unpublished doctoral dissertation, K.U.Leuven), Leuven, 1948. The core of the latter dissertation was also summarized in an article: J. LODRIOOR, *La notion de tradition dans la théologie de Jean Driedo de Louvain*, in *ETL* 26 (1950) 37-53. Additionally, there was a debate between Murphy and another author: J.R. GEISELMANN, *Das Konzil von Trient über das Verhältnis der Heiligen Schrift und der nicht geschriebenen Traditionen*, in M. SCHMAUS, et al. (eds.), *Die mündliche Überlieferung: Beiträge zum Begriff der Tradition*, München, Hueber, 1957, 123-206; J.R. GEISELMANN, *Das Missverständnis über das Verhältnis von Schrift und Tradition und seine Ueberwindung in der katholischen Theologie*, in *Una Sancta* 11 (1956) 131-150; ID., *Die Heilige Schrift und die Tradition: Zu den neueren Kontroversen über das Verhältnis der Heiligen Schrift zu den nichtgeschriebenen Traditionen* (Quaestiones disputatae, 18), Freiburg, Herder, 1962, pp. 166-183. Also: M. GIELIS, *Een Romeins doctoraat over het Traditiebegrip van Johannes Driedo van Turnhout*, in *Taxandria. Jaarboek van de Koninklijke geschied- en oudheidkundige kring van de Antwerpse Kempen* N.R. 68 (1996) 145-161; F.M.H. HENNISSEN, *Het traditiebegrip in de katholieke controverse-theologie van vóór Trente 1518-1546*, ed. M. GIELIS, in *Taxandria* N.R. 68 (1996) 163-211; M. GIELIS, *Vertaling van de Latijnse citaten uit Driedo's De ecclesiasticis scripturis et dogmatibus en van andere vreemdtalige citaten in Hennissens studie over Driedo's Traditiebegrip*, in *Taxandria* N.R. 68 (1996) 213-241. For a biography of John Driedo, see: H. DE JONGH, *L'ancienne Faculté de Théologie de Louvain au*

theology, he was prepared to defend the faith of the Church (and hence the religious unity of Charles' Empire). He argued that not only Scripture but also the unwritten traditions of the Church allowed one access to the truth.

In his book, Driedo paid much attention to the proper role of Scripture. He did not attack his Protestant adversaries directly. Rather, he took the common heritage of Catholics and reformers as his point of departure[31]. The Louvain theologian argued that Christ had communicated the original revelation to the apostles and the first converts to Christianity. The meaning of the Gospel was initially written in the hearts of the apostles (*evangelium in corde*). In turn, the apostles preached the Gospel to the people. Initially, they did not attempt to write the Gospel down on parchment and scrolls. Rather, they preferred to 'write' it on the hearts of men (*evangelium scribere in cordibus hominum*)[32]. The primitive or 'apostolic' Church believed and accepted the full evangelical truth just as they also observed the rites and the ethical code as commanded by the apostles, before any of the gospels were written[33].

Before long, however, thanks to the inspiration of the Holy Spirit, those of the apostolic era began to record on parchment for the benefit of those who already believed, the sermons, the mysteries, the traditions, the sacraments, the actions and the deeds of Christ, and the practices and doctrines of the apostolic Church[34]. Hence, the Gospel contained the essence of the apostolic faith and preaching[35]. At several places in his book,

premier siècle de son existence (1432-1540): Ses débuts, son organisation, son enseignement, sa lutte contre Érasme et Luther, Leuven, 1911 pp. 156-159; H. DE VOCHT, *Monumenta Humanistica Lovaniensia: Texts and Studies about Louvain Humanists in the First Half of the XVIth Century. Erasmus – Vives – Dorpius – Clenardus – Goes – Moringus* (Humanistica Lovaniensia, 4), Leuven, Librairie universitaire, 1934, pp. 344-345; LODRIOOR, *De Leer over de Christelijke Traditie*, pp. IX-XII; J.L. MURPHY, *The Notion of Tradition in John Driedo*, Milwaukee, WI, Seraphic Press, 1959, pp. 12-43; P. FABISCH, *Johannes Driedo (ca. 1480-1535)*, in E. ISERLOH (ed.), *Katholische Theologen der Reformationszeit*, vol. 3, Münster, Aschendorf, 1986, 33-47; C.F. GUNDERSON – P.G. BIETENHOLZ, *Jan Driedo*, in P.G. BIETENHOLZ – T.B. DEUTSCHER (eds.), *Contemporaries of Erasmus: A Biographical Register of the Renaissance and Reformation*, vol. 1, Toronto, University of Toronto Press, 1985, 405-406; M. GIELIS, *Johannes Driedo: Anwalt der Tradition im Streit mit Humanismus und Reformation*, in M.H. JUNG – P. WALTER (eds.), *Theologen des 16. Jahrhunderts: Humanismus – Reformation – Katholische Erneuerung. Eine Einführung*, Darmstadt, Wissenschaftliche Buchgesellschaft, 2002, 135-153. Nota bene, these publications do not agree perfectly in the biographical details that they provide.

31. LODRIOOR, *De leer over de Christelijke Traditie* (n. 30), p. 2.

32. A possible allusion to Prov 7,3; Jer 31,33; Rom 2,15; 2 Cor 3,2-3.

33. DRIEDO, *De ecclesiasticis scripturis* (n. 30), f. 243r A-B. Also: *Ibid.*, f. 53r A, 238v C, 239v D, 264v D.

34. *Ibid.*, f. 243r B.

35. *Ibid.*, f. 60v A-B, 61r C, 61v B, 237v C- D, 248v C.

Driedo seems to have been prepared to accept that all truths necessary for salvation were in some way contained in Scripture[36].

On the other hand, Driedo warned the Lutherans that the content of the faith could not be discovered by a mere analysis of the inspired text alone, just as there was a part of the truth that could not be deduced from the gospels themselves[37]. Because the Church existed before the New Testament was written, it was through it alone that we are assured of the canonicity and authenticity of Scripture[38]. In other words, the Church accepted those gospels as canonical, precisely because they accurately rendered the essential core of the revelation that had be handed down by the spoken word of both Christ and his apostles.

Moreover, a lot of practices concerning moral and sacramental life, liturgy, Church discipline and even some doctrinal propositions were not explicitly testified by Scripture. They have been passed down by the apostles to the Fathers and their successors, the scholastic theologians. They have reached the present-day Church by way of an uninterrupted chain of succession (a real *successio patrum*)[39]. These doctrines and practices, which are universally observed in Church, are indicated by the term "tradition(s)"[40].

Driedo's third claim was that the universal Church – his theological-technical term to indicate the Church that had passed down faithfully the doctrines and practices from the time of the apostles even as far as the present day – had great authority in doubtful matters of faith and was empowered to give the proper interpretation for obscure and difficult biblical passages[41]. In Catholic circles, it was commonly accepted that Scrip-

36. *Ibid.*, f. 60r C, 243r C, 265r A.
37. *Ibid.*, f. 204r B, 241r B-C, 245v B-C, with a reference to Augustinus, *Ep. LIV. Ad inquisitiones Januarii* V 6, ed. A. GOLDBACHER (CSEL, 34/2), Wien, Tempsky, 1898, p. 165 l. 7-14.
38. To support this statement, Driedo referred explicitly to the words of Augustinus, *Contra epistolam Manichaei quam vocant fundamenti* 5, ed. I. ZYCHA (CSEL, 25/1),Wien, Tempsky, 1891, p. 197 l. 22-23; quoted in DRIEDO, *De ecclesiasticis scripturis* (n. 30), f. 60v D – 61r A and f. 238v C-D. For the Church as a witness to the authenticity and canonicity of Scripture, see also *Ibid.*, f. 1v C-D, 239r C-D, 245v C.
39. The afore-mentioned quotation from Augustinus, *Contra epistolam Manichaei* (n. 38), p. 197 l. 22-23 was also employed as the basis for this part of Driedo's reasoning. See: DRIEDO, *De ecclesiasticis scripturis* (n. 30), f. 238v D – 239r A and f. 266v C.
40. *Ibid.*, f. 227v C, 234v D, 238v D, 239r C, 242v D, 245v B, 248v B-C, 254v C-D, 255r D.
41. See, *inter alia*, DRIEDO, *De ecclesiasticis scripturis* (n. 30), f. 239v B and 61r A-B. To uphold the "authority of the Catholic Church" in rightly interpreting the Scriptures, Driedo quoted there from Augustinus, *Contra Faustum Manichaeum* lib. XI. 2, ed. I. ZYCHA (CSEL, 25/1), Wien, Tempsky, 1891, p. 315 l. 21-25 (Comp.: *Ibid.* lib. XXVIII. 2 (CSEL, 25), pp. 739 l. 7 – 740 l. 14 and lib. XXXII. 21 (CSEL, 25), pp. 782 l. 15 – 783 l. 4). The same idea also in DRIEDO, *De ecclesiasticis scripturis* (n. 30), f. 52v A, 59v B-C, 61v B-C.

ture was less than clear; occasionally it was even obscure[42]. Examples of doctrines and practices that could not be deduced in an obvious way from Scripture were the perpetual virginity of Mary, the significance of indulgences and the prayers for the dead, the rites and the sacrificial character of the mass etc. These were all elements that Luther and his adherents considered as highly problematic. According to the *Lovanienses*, however, they could be traced back to the apostolic era. From our perspective, this lack of historical accuracy is nothing less than amazing.

In sum, Driedo believed that all the dogmatic truths necessary for Salvation could be found in Scripture, either explicitly or implicitly. As for the practice of the sacraments, Driedo seemed to recognize at least a 'starting point' in the Scriptures. There were also regulations concerning Church discipline or liturgical practices that were obviously not contained in Scripture but had been introduced by the apostles or the bishops acting under the inspiration of the Holy Spirit. According to Driedo all these 'traditions' pertained to 'divine law', were immutable and had to be observed strictly by the faithful. Moreover, the apostles and the bishops had also determined some 'ecclesiastical' traditions, which were contextually restricted. They could not be expected to transcend the time, place and the circumstances in which they were originally formulated. Modifications were both possible and in some case necessary for later generations[43]. Divine and ecclesiastical laws, however, both had a binding force; they were distinguished only with regard to their origin.

The Fathers (by which term Driedo meant the patristic writers and the scholastic theologians, but esp. the former) played a great part in the process of preserving, interpreting and unfolding of the original revelation. In Driedo's opinion, there was a direct line between the apostolic era and the time of the Fathers[44]. Augustine particularly had great authority in the Louvain theological milieu. In order to underpin the basic insights of *De ecclesiasticis scripturis et dogmatibus*, Driedo made an abundant appeal to the works the Bishop of Hippo had written against the Manichees and Donatists, in defense of the true Church[45].

---

42. DRIEDO, *De ecclesiasticis scripturis* (n. 30), f. 67r B, with a clear reference to Augustinus, *De doctrina Chrisiana* II, xvi.24, ed. J. MARTIN (CCSL, 32), Turnhout, Brepols, 1962, p. 49 l. 20-23.

43. DRIEDO, *De ecclesiasticis scripturis* (n. 30), f. 250r A, 263v D – 264r A, 266r C, possibly f. 247v B. Also *ibid.*, f. 214v C-D, with a reference to Augustinus, *Ep. CXXXVIII. Ad Marcellinum* I 8, ed. A. GOLDBACHER (CSEL, 44), Wien, Tempsky, 1904, particularly pp. 132 l. 23 – 133 l. 12. Nota bene: This is not a reference to Augustine's *Liber de correctione donatistarum*, as indicated in the margin of the *Opera Omnia*-edition of 1556.

44. DRIEDO, *De ecclesiasticis scripturis* (n. 30), f. 59v A, 265r B-C. Also f. 52v A-B, 208r B-C, 209v D – 210r A, 239v C, 267r C.

45. See: W. FRANÇOIS, *Augustinus als 'onweerlegbare vertolker van de theologie': Johannes Driedo over Schrift, Augustinus en de katholieke traditie (1533)*, in P. VAN

The Fathers were considered to be the primary witnesses to the Tradition; it was the magisterium, however, that had recognized their writings as trustworthy and truthful. The bishops, along with the Supreme Pontiff as their head, could retrace their authority, by way of an uninterrupted chain of succession, to the apostles and Peter. Moreover, by way of references to Irenaeus' *Adversus haereses*[46], to Tertullian, Cyprian, Jerome and Augustine, Driedo stressed that there was a close relationship between apostolic succession and the true faith. Apostolic succession was the guarantee that the 'Church of the present' continued to teach and believe the same doctrines that had been preached by the primitive Church. The visible hierarchy of the bishops with the Supreme Pontiff as its head had to be recognized as the custodian of the Christian revelation; apart from the magisterium, there could only be misunderstanding and error[47]. Driedo explicitly criticized 'heretics' who saw the Church of Christ present where the faith and the words of Christ remained, but who closed their ears to anything said about the legitimate succession and the doctrinal role of the bishops[48].

The role of the hierarchy is made most clear by the authority ceded to General Councils. The Protestants stated that the Church was fallible and that all the doctrines of the faith had to be corroborated by an explicit word of Scripture. Inter alia, they referred to Augustine's *De baptismo contra Donatistas* in which the Church father wrote that later Councils are to be preferred above (or even, have corrected) those of earlier date[49]. Driedo, however, noted that the General Council was truly infallible regarding matters of faith or questions pertaining to salvation (and accepted without question that such a Council was always celebrated in union with the Supreme Pontiff, the bishop of Rome)[50]. For God had promised the Church the support of the Holy Spirit until all would be fulfilled. Driedo's interpretation of the aforementioned statement in

GEEST – J. VAN OORT (eds.), *Augustiniana Neerlandica: Aspecten van Augustinus' spiritualiteit en haar doorwerking*, Leuven, Peeters, 2005, 427-446.

46. Irenaeus Lugdunensis, *Adversus haereses*, lib. IV, 33, 8, ed. A. ROUSSEAU, et al. (SC, 100), Paris, Cerf, 1965, pp. 818 l. 137 – 820 l. 141; lib. IV, 26, 2 (SC, 100), p. 718 l. 43-50. Also an extensive reference to *ibid.*, lib. III, 31 – lib. IV, 2, ed. A. ROUSSEAU – L. DOUTRELEAU (SC, 211), Paris, Cerf, 1974, pp. 30 l. 1 – 46 l. 21.

47. DRIEDO, *De ecclesiasticis scripturis* (n. 30), f. 223r B-C, 224v A-B, 225r B-C, 266r C.

48. *Ibid.*, f. 219r B, 223r C-D, 225v D. Also: *Ibid.*, f. 220r C – 220v B, 223v C-D, 224v D, 226v D.

49. *Ibid.*, f. 204v B-C with a reference to Augustinus, *De baptismo contra Donatistas* lib. II 9,14, ed. M. PETSCHENIG (CSEL, 51), Wien, Tempsky, 1908, p. 190, l. 18-20.

50. It is obvious however that the great majority of the three hundred bishops present at the Council of Nicea came from the eastern part of the Roman Empire. The bishop of Rome was only represented by two priests.

Augustine's *De baptismo contra Donatistas* admits that it is possible for a particular council to err to the degree that its decrees must be corrected by a General Council; he even admitted that this had happened. When Augustine spoke of one General Council correcting the decree of an earlier General Council, however, Driedo insists that Augustine was not referring to matters of faith or to questions pertaining to salvation, but simply to those elements in the Church which are variable according to the circumstances of particular times and places[51].

Although Driedo could not simply pass over the failings of popes and prelates of his own era, he argued that not only the fathers Augustine, Jerome, Cyprian but also Bernard had always taught that the pope is the head of the Catholic, that is the universal Church. He also claimed that, in practice, the Fathers, the martyrs and the councils all appealed to the apostolic See whenever they were in doubt[52]. In addition to this argument for authority, the Louvain theologian offered the doctrinal arguments in favor of the authority of the bishops and even the infallibility of the pope[53]. Interpreting Luke 22,32: "But for you [=Simon] I have prayed that your faith may not fail…"[54], Driedo claimed that Peter had never personally failed due to his special position as an apostle. But this grace of personal infallibility was not passed down to his successors. There remained a possibility that the Supreme Pontiff of the universal Church could become a heretic[55].

Secondly, Driedo affirmed that "it is to be held on faith" (*de fide tenendus*) that the general chair, the See of Peter ("Cathedra Petri"), the universal Church or "flock of Peter" could never fall into doctrinal error. Infallibility was a gift to Peter as pastor of the universal Church (*ut gerenti figuram ecclesiae*). This gift was to be passed on to Peter's successors as pastor and teacher of all Christians[56].

Thirdly, Driedo believed with pious faith (*pia fide*) that the Roman bishop or the people within the Roman diocese could never entirely abandon the faith. Driedo referred to Peter's diocese at Rome as "a norm that does not deviate from the faith". The individual churches throughout the world could be sure that they had not deviated from the original revela-

51. DRIEDO, *De ecclesiasticis scripturis* (n. 30), f. 58r B-C, 59v A-B, 269r D – 269v B.
52. *Ibid.*, f. 229r C.
53. *Ibid.*, f. 253r B.
54. *Ibid.*, f. 233r A-C.
55. *Ibid.*, f. 233r D – 233v A.
56. *Ibid.*, f. 233v A, 235v C-D, 236r A, 236v C-D, 237r C-D. The latter passages both contain a clear reference to Augustinus, *In Iohannis euangelium tractatus* CXXIV, 5, ed. R. WILLEMS (CCSL, 36), Turnhout, Brepols, 1954, p. 684 l. 48-50. Comp.: *Ibid.*, p. 438 l. 9-21.

tion if they could prove that their teaching and faith was in accordance with that of the Church of Rome. The *pia fide* of the third statement, however, suggests a less important theological claim.

In sum, Driedo affirmed that the faith of the universal Church would never be allowed to fail, and that even the diocese of Rome and its leadership would always be preserved from doctrinal corruption[57]. At the same time, Driedo recognized that several popes, at least personally, had been morally corrupt. The fact of the popes' moral failures had profoundly offended Luther and the other reformers[58].

Driedo never clearly formulated the later distinction between statements that were made *ex cathedra* and those that were not. Driedo envisioned the case of an individual pope who was known to be in error, since he publicly taught and defended his error, to which was even added the moral failure of pertinacity. Driedo speculated about how such a pope might be removed from office.

II. THEOLOGICAL AND HISTORICAL CIRCUMSTANCES THAT INFLUENCED THE RELIGIOUS MAP OF EUROPE[59]

1. *Luther's Breakthrough and the German Princes' Struggle for Political and Religious Independence*

Luther's theological and spiritual insights corresponded with the evolving religious susceptibilities of the late Middle Ages. People felt called by God's Word and longed for a more individual piety marked by meditation (e.g. on the Passion of the Christ) and high moral standards. Conversely, people had grown tired of attending the celebration of the sacraments and merely external religious ceremonies such as pilgrimages, masses for the dead, and the selling of indulgences etc. Furthermore, the practice of sermon services in church had arisen separately from the ritual of the mass. Even though the content of these sermons did not always satisfy, the newness of this religious practice exerted a certain attraction on the now-critical audience. In short, these all may fairly be seen as a not insignificant predisposition to the spread of the Reformed ideas.

---

57. DRIEDO, *De ecclesiasticis scripturis* (n. 30), f. 234v C-D, 235v B, 236r B-C. Also *ibid.*, f. 234v A-C, with a reference to Augustinus, *Ep. LIII. Ad Generosum* I 2, ed. A. GOLDBACHER (CSEL, 34/2), Wien, Tempsky, 1898, pp. 153 l. 8 – 154 l. 15.

58. DRIEDO, *De ecclesiasticis scripturis* (n. 30), f. 235r B.

59. Easy-reference introductions to the various particular historical factors that have favored Luther's breakthrough: O. MÖRKE, *Die Reformation: Voraussetzungen und Durchsetzungen* (Enzyklopädie Deutscher Geschichte, 74), München, R. Oldenburg, 2005; also: HAUSCHILD, *Lehrbuch der Kirchen- und Dogmengeschichte* (n. 6), pp. 1-33, 102-106, 184-189.

In Germany the appeal for Church reform was proclaimed loudest. There was dissatisfaction with the 'secularized' mentality of the papal court and the curia. These instances were all too often guided by political and financial interests. The Germans knew that a lot of money was being withdrawn from their country, taken to Rome and never returning. They criticized the outrageous influence (and even arbitrariness) of the papal courts and the Roman influences in episcopal nominations. The Germans insisted upon their right of self-determination in these matters. The parish clergy also seemed constantly in search of prebends and other incomes. By means of both tithing and bequests, abbeys and monasteries were constantly increasing their wealth. People stigmatized monks, nuns, secular priests and prelates as immoral, intemperate, ignorant, or greedy. The concomitant neglect of the essential content of faith and the pastoral work was difficult for many German women and men to boar. These observations all of which reflected the desires and the common practice of the German nation, were first formulated by the *Reichsstände* in 1456 in their so-called *Gravamina (Beschwerungen) nationis germanicae*[60]. They were reissued both in 1497 and 1518. The *Beschwerungen* were used as a guide in determining the *Reichsstände*'s policy toward both the Pope and the Church of Rome. Of course, this is not to say that the German nobility and the cities were only concerned with their subjects' spiritual welfare. On the contrary, they were also driven by political and financial self-interest. Many of these critiques and anticlerical attitudes had already been voiced by the Christian humanists. Some of them were imbued with a German *Nationalbewußtsein*, as e.g. Jakob Wimpfeling and, even in a more radical way, Ulrich von Hutten. The development of a 'national' Christian humanism in Germany made a considerable contribution to the success of the Reformation in that country[61]. It allowed Luther to pass for a German national hero simply by fighting against the papacy and the curia.

---

60. The most thorough study on anticlericalism and Church critics, see: P.A. DYKEMA – H.A. OBERMAN (eds.), *Anticlericalism in Late Medieval and Early Modern Europe* (Studies in Medieval and Reformation Thought, 51), Leiden, Brill, 1993. Also: H.J. GOERTZ, *Pfaffenhaß und groß Geschrei: Die reformatorischen Bewegungen in Deutschland 1517-1529*, München, Beck, 1987, pp. 32-68; ID., *Antiklerikalismus und Reformation: Sozialgeschichtliche Untersuchungen*, Göttingen, Vandenhoeck & Ruprecht, 1995; HAUSCHILD, *Lehrbuch der Kirchen- und Dogmengeschichte* (n. 6), pp. 24-25.

61. On Humanism and Reformation, see: H. JUNGHANS, *Der junge Luther und die Humanisten*, Göttingen, Vandenhoeck & Ruprecht, 1985; M. BEYER – G. WARTENBERG (eds.), *Humanismus und Wittenberger Reformation: Festgabe anlässlich des 500. Geburtstages des Praeceptor Germaniae Philipp Melanchton am 16. Februar 1997*, Leipzig, Evangelische Verlagsanstalt, 1996; E. RUMMEL, *The Confessionalization of Humanism in Reformation Germany* (Oxford Studies in Historical Theology), Oxford, Oxford University Press, 2000.

The changing accents in religious life, anticlericalism and the call for Church reform, all played an important role in the emergence of Reformation among the popular classes. These phenomena however were not new. On the contrary, they were manifested, in different degrees, across Europe. The reason Luther and the Reformation broke through (where John Wyclif, John Hus and others failed), clearly had much to do with politics[62]! In Germany, the various princes (secular as well as ecclesiastical) and free cities insisted on the independence and sovereignty of their respective territories. Seven of them, the so called 'Electors', elected the Emperor of the Holy Roman Empire of the German Nation. The imperial government however had only a limited authority. The Emperor, with the Electors' permission, convoked the *Reichstagen* or 'Diets'. At them, the various princes and the representatives of the imperial cities, together with the Emperor, in spite of their often opposing interests, usually managed to promulgate some unifying measures. With respect to the faith, the German princes consistently urged for Church reform. Reform, however, actually proved to be the most problematic element for German unity.

The Habsburg Charles V, who, since 1519, had been the ruler of the Holy Roman Empire as well as one of the most important players on the European political scene, considered himself to be the primary monarch of Christianity as well as the defender of the Catholic faith. At the Diet of Worms in the spring 1521, Charles commanded Luther to recant. Upon the latter's refusal, he was declared a heretic and an outlaw of the Empire.

---

62. On Lutheranism and political circumstances, see: K. VON GREYERZ (ed.), *Religion, Politics and Social Protest: Three Studies on Early Modern Germany*, London, Allen and Unwin, 1984; E. ISERLOH – G. MÜLLER (eds.), *Luther und die politische Welt: Wissenschaftliches Symposion in Worms vom 27. bis 29. oktober 1983* (Historische Forschungen im Auftrag der historischen Kommission der Akademie der Wissenschaften und der Literatur, 9), Wiesbaden, Steiner, 1984; H.R. SCHMIDT, *Reichsstädte, Reich und Reformation: Korporative Religionspolitik 1521-1529/30* (Veröffentlichungen des Instituts für europäische Geschichte Mainz, 122), Wiesbaden, Steiner, 1986; A. SCHINDLING – W. ZIEGLER (eds.), *Die Territorien des Reichs im Zeitalter der Reformation und Konfessionalisierung: Land und Konfession 1500-1650* (Katholisches Leben und Kirchenreform im Zeitalter der Glaubensspaltung: Vereinsschriften der Gesellschaft zur Herausgabe des Corpus Catholicorum, 49-53.56-57), Münster, Aschendorff, 1989-1997; G. WENZ, *Luther und die politischen Folgen: Eine historische Perspektive aus aktuellem Anlass*, in B. STUBENRAUCH (ed.), *Dem Ursprung Zukunft geben: Glaubenserkenntnis in ökumenischer Verantwortung. Für Wolfgang Beinert*, Freiburg, Herder, 1998, 266-295; G. MÜLLER, *Martin Luther in seinem politischen Verhalten*, in H.-J. NIEDEN – M. NIEDEN (eds.), *Praxis Pietatis: Beiträge zu Theologie und Frömmigkeit in der Frühen Neuzeit. Wolfgang Sommer zum 60. Geburtstag*, Stuttgart, Kohlhammer, 1999, 65-81; J. ESTES, *M. Luther's First Appeal to Secular Authorities for Help with Church Reform, 1520*, in J.R. BAST – A.C. GOW (eds.), *Continuity and Change: The Harvest of Late-Medieval and Reformation History. Essays presented to Heiko A. Oberman on his 70th Birthday*, Leiden, Brill, 2000, 48-76; A. KOHNLE, *Reichstag und Reformation: Kaiserliche und ständische Religionspolitik von den Anfängen der Causa Lutheri bis zum Nürnberger Religionsfrieden* (Quellen

The Edict of Worms (26 May 1521) ordered Luther's arrest and the burning of all his books. The Emperor lacked the means, however, to enforce the edict all over Germany. His first problem was the several opponents that threatened his Empire from the outside. Understandably, this cost him a lot of time, energy and money. The most fearsome adversary of Habsburg hegemony in Europe was the French king, Francis I. Charles was in continuous conflict with him. Their conflict was largely – but not exclusively – over several territories of the southern Low Countries and in northern Italy. Adrian VI (1522-23) did his best to make peace between them. Clement VII (1523-34) however varied his alliances in order to keep either Francis or Charles from dominating Italy. Charles' Empire was also threatened by the Ottoman Turks. To stop them, the Emperor needed the military and financial support of the German princes. These outside threats distracted the Emperor from the interior German scene and prevented him from reacting swiftly against the German 'heretics'.

Also noteworthy is that Charles, who most likely adhered to a humanist form of Catholicism, advocated the convocation of a General Council in order to reform the Church. Pope Adrian VI also favored fundamental Church reform. His successor, Clement VII and his curia however opposed any substantial structural reforms and, consequently, necessary Church renewal was blocked for a long time. Next to Pope Clement's plotting against the Emperor, his refusal to convoke a Council decreased the likelihood that an agreement between Wittenberg and Rome would occur. From our perspective, it seems certain that Clement's policies were an important cause for the schism. Charles, whose chief desire was complete concord throughout all Christendom, rejected a solution at the national-German level and after 15 July 1524 refused a national council. The successive *Reichstagen* failed to assume a univocal stance towards the Reformation that was on the horizon. This failure meant that the decision about its introduction was taken up by the individual princes[63].

This led some princes and cities to strictly enforce the Edict of Worms and to harshly oppress any and every manifestation of the Lutheran faith. Others supported the implementation of Luther's ideas. Luther himself enjoyed the protection of his prince, the Elector Frederick II of Saxony, also known as Frederick the Wise (who reigned from 1486 until 1525) and of his brother and successor Elector John, also known as the Constant (r. 1525-32). Thanks to their protection Luther was allowed to develop his theology, preach his doctrines, and implement his ecclesiastical

und Forschungen zur Reformationsgeschichte, 72), Gütersloh, Gütersloher Verlagshaus, 2001.
    63. Compare MÜLLER, *Martin Luther in seinem politischen Verhalten* (n. 62), pp. 67-69.

reforms. Next to Electoral Saxony, several other princes, mostly in northern and central Germany, as well as magistrates of various free imperial cities, supported Luther's reform and helped to establish his church order. Among them was the Hessian landgrave who took over political leadership of the Reformation-minded party. The princes' efforts of Church reform were connected with their desire for as much independence as possible from the Emperor, their desire to appropriate the wealth and lands of the monasteries, chapters and other ecclesiastical institutions, their wish to influence the nominations for the open bishoprics, and their wish to push back the influence of the independent ecclesiastical juridical system etc. Some German princes discovered in the Reformation the ideological tools they needed to undermine the Roman-Catholic Church's power and to build up ecclesiastical structures that they could control[64].

Central to the success of the Reformation in this early period is the role played by the cities. Educated burghers of these cities had, since about 1500, moved into the princes' corps of officials. From here they had decisively influenced events in favor of Protestantism. The princes who introduced Reformation took as their models the cities "where magistrates now claimed sovereignty not only over the ecclesiastical order and morals, but also over doctrine, which had formerly been strictly reserved to the church"[65].

The free imperial cities were especially situated in the south and the south-west of Germany. During the decisive phase of Reformation, i.e. in the years 1524 to 1530, the cities (e.g. Nuremberg, Strasbourg, and even Ulm) were its primary supporters[66]. It was also in the cities that Luther's insights were quickly spread by way of pamphlets and theological treatises. In short, it was in the cities that his points of faith were initially embraced. In the cities with their various churches and places of pil-

64. G. MÜLLER, *Luther und die evangelischen Fürsten*, in ISERLOH – MÜLLER (eds.), *Luther und die politische Welt* (n. 62), 65-83.

65. HAMM, *The Urban Reformation* (n. 1), p. 205.

66. The standard work remains: B. MOELLER, *Reichsstadt und Reformation*, Berlin, Evangelische Verlagsanstalt, ²1987. Also: B. MOELLER, *Imperial Cities and the Reformation: Three Essays*, Philadelphia, PA, Fortress Press, 1972; S.E. OZMENT, *The Reformation in the Cities: The Appeal of Protestantism to Sixteenth-Century Germany and Switzerland*, New Haven, CT, Yale University, 1975; B. MOELLER (ed.), *Stadt und Kirche im 16. Jahrhundert* (Schriften des Vereins für Reformationsgeschichte, 190), Gütersloh, Mohn, 1978; G. MÜLLER, *Reformation und Stadt: Zur Rezeption der evangelischen Verkündigung* (Akademie der Wissenschaften und der Literatur Mainz. Abhandlungen der Geistes- und Sozialwissenschaftlichen Klasse, 11), Mainz, Akademie der Wissenschaften und der Literatur, 1981; W. REINHARD, *Luther und die Städte*, in ISERLOH – MÜLLER (eds.), *Luther und die politische Welt* (n. 62), 87-112; B. MOELLER, *Korreferat zu Wolfgang Reinhard: Luther und die Städte*, in ISERLOH – MÜLLER (eds.), *Luther und die politische Welt* (n. 62), 113-121; B. HAMM, *The Urban Reformation* (n. 1).

grimage, the late medieval practice of earning one's salvation by way of the accumulation of merits, had come to a head, the faithful continuously gathered indulgences, participated in pilgrimages, processions, masses for the eternal rest of souls. It is no wonder that the city-dwellers were attracted to Luther's claim that one was not saved by performing all these good works and devotional practices but rather by faith in Christ alone. The deconstruction of this 'archaic' religiosity, and a reflective and argumentative employment of the Scriptures, was esp. appealing to the burgher's mentality[67]. The *sola scriptura*-principle "offered the burghers a plausible, simple, comprehensible principle of emancipation and order, which could be extended to all areas of life and be employed to order them and to supply the civic community with a moral holism"[68]. Further, the cities' burghers cherished the corporate ideal that it was important to be a member of the urban community, under the magisterial authority, and they pressed, more than the inhabitants of rural areas, for a larger control over ecclesiastical matters, e.g. in the appointment of parish priests, the administration of schools, poorhouses and buildings etc. The urban inhabitants continuously criticized the clergy's exemption from taxation and the secular legal system. This sense of "fusion of spiritual with civic discipline"[69] repeatedly lead the urban citizens into conflict with the ecclesiastical hierarchy which they regarded as a power foreign to the urban community and beyond the city's control. Essential to the expansion of Reformation theology was its connection with this latent conflict between the urban community and the clerical hierarchy of the 'old Church'. Reformed ecclesiology, which conceived the Church as the community of the faithful who are all equal in God's eyes and who are called to mutual love, and even stressed the general priesthood of the faithful, converged very well with the sense of community among the burghers and their alienation from the Catholic hierarchy. Hence, the cities' magistrates became the Empire's first rulers to evolve a deliberate policy of reform. Yet another factor that assisted the spread of Reformed ideas was the fact that cities were also centers of education and communication. The cities' burghers were, generally speaking, more literate and better educated than the rural population. In the cities the art of printing had particularly developed, thanks, inter alia, to the financial means there available[70]. Humanists used printed books and pamphlets to spread their

---

67. Compare HAMM, *The Urban Reformation* (n. 1), p. 200.
68. *Ibid.*, p. 212.
69. *Ibid.*, p. 214.
70. Compare J.F. GILMONT, *La réforme et le livre: L'Europe de l'imprimé (1517-v.1570)* (Cerf-histoire), Paris, Cerf, 1990.

insights quickly. Reform-minded preachers – a substantial number of whom were former mendicants – proclaimed the new ideas. Humanists, preachers and pamphlet writers found a ready audience among the educated, receptive, but also critical burghers.

Tensions had also risen between the peasants and the land aristocracy. These were often manifested in peasant revolts. The peasants appealed to divine justice, that is, to the principle of equality among all humans. The exploitation by monasteries and religious lords was also a source of anticlericalism. This, too, contributed to the predisposition for reform. Luther acknowledged that the peasants had legitimate grievances against their rulers. The reformer of Wittenberg, however, rejected their use of violence to rectify social injustice or to further the cause of the Reformation. With the consent of Luther, other leading reformers, and some of the urban politicians, the famous Peasants' War was crushed on 15 May 1525. This tragedy signaled a turning point in Luther's development. From then on, he opted for a more moderate line and overtly sided with the German princes[71].

In spring 1526, Luther's princely sympathizers in Germany created the defensive League of Torgau to protect their interests. At the Diet of Speyer (summer 1526) the Emperor proposed to eradicate heresy and rebellion and to enforce the Edict of Worms against Luther. The princes feared for their privileges even as they were intimidated and distracted by the advance of the Turks[72]. This contributed to their decision to postpone the settling of their religious questions. In anticipation of a General Council, each prince and each free city would make its own decisions on religious matters (*Territorialisierung* of the Reformation). This provisional regulation would soon become permanent... It allowed several German princes and cities to boldly implement the Reformation in their territories. In various Protestant territories *Landeskirchen* were founded and the princes assumed the jurisdictional power formerly held by bishops.

In the second half of the decade, however, Charles' military efforts were more successful. In 1525 he crushed Francis I in a battle near Pavia. After this victory over the French, Clement VII feared the Emperor's influence and shifted his allegiance to Francis (1526). This, in turn, led in 1527 to the sack of Rome by Charles V's Spanish and German troops.

---

71. MÜLLER, *Martin Luther in seinem politischen Verhalten* (n. 62), pp. 73-77.

72. Only a few days after the recess, "... on August 29, 1526, a Turkish army inflicted a crushing defeat on the Hungarians at Mohaćs. Vienna stood in their way, and beyond Vienna lay the rest of Christian Europe. The Turks seemed invincible..." (MARIUS, *Martin Luther* [n. 22], pp. 471-472).

Feeding off their anger at being unpaid, their actions quickly spiraled out of control. Not until 1529 was a fragile peace concluded. Charles was now stronger than ever before; only the Turks remained a threat. Consequently, at the second Diet of Speyer, in March-April 1529, the Emperor was able to demand, in the strongest of terms, the revocation of the previous Speyer recess and the enforcement of the Edict of Worms. A majority of princes and cities agreed and banned the introduction of any further religious novelties. A minority of the *Reichsstände* found this unacceptable and produced their own document 'in protest'. As a result this group earned for themselves and for their 'descendents' the title 'Protestants'.

Next to the ongoing implementation of 'evangelical' reforms, in 1529-30, the main princes and cities sent delegates to the Emperor in order to convince him by means of written confessions, that is, summaries of their doctrinal particularities, that their faith was not heretical and that the implemented reforms were not directed against the Habsburg *per se*. The last major chance to resolve the differences between Catholics and Protestants came in 1530 at Augsburg. Here, at the Emperor's behest, a final attempt at reconciliation was put on the table. Philipp Melanchton drafted the Augsburg Confession as a common expression of what the Lutheran party believed in an effort to answer charges of heresy raised by Catholics. The Augsburg Confession was also an effort to compromise with the Catholics; it rejected only the ecclesiastical traditions that the reformers really considered as abuses. Charles V and the Catholic theologians, however, were not impressed. They rejected the Augsburg Confession. The Emperor warned the evangelical-minded princes and cities not to take further initiatives, to preserve the rights of Catholic individuals and monasteries, and to conform, within the next six months, to the doctrine and practices of the Mother Church... In other words, the conditions of the Edict of Worms were re-instigated. As a retort, the Elector of Saxony and the landgrave of Hesse took over the initiative from the cities, and formed, in 1531, a military alliance, the *Schmalkaldic League*, to defend the interests of the evangelical-minded territories. Those who joined the *Schmalkaldic League*, had also to accept the *Confessio Augustana*. It soon became clear, however, that Charles V could not back up his threats. Because he still needed the support of the princes to stop the advance of the Turks, in 1532, the Emperor offered the Peace of Nuremberg to the princes of the *Schmalkaldic League*: no action would be taken against Protestant princes by the Emperor until a General Church Council could be convened. Clement VII, however, refused to respond to the call for a Council. For the Reformation, as a movement, the truce offered a great advantage: It had acknowledged that Lutheranism as a movement would survive[73].

It was only later, when theological arguments and canonical procedures proved unable to contain the situation and after the political troubles with France were resolved again (Peace of Crépy, 1544) that Charles finally decided to take military action in Germany. In the spring of 1547, Charles V won an important victory over the rebellious German princes in the *Schmalkaldic War*. After capturing Elector Johann Friedrich of Saxony and Philipp of Hesse, the key Lutheran leaders, the Emperor attempted to restore important elements of Catholicism in their territories through a temporary settlement known as the *Augsburg Interim*. Matthias Flacius Illyricus and some other Church leaders responded with a campaign of stiff resistance. More conciliatory Lutherans led by Philipp Melanchton drafted the *Leipzig Interim* as a counterproposal: Melanchton was willing to accept the reintroduction of some Catholic ceremonies to keep the Emperor from completely eradicating Lutheranism. The Protestant princes however, who had been striving unceasingly for political and religious independence, proved resilient; in 1552 they forced the Emperor to back down. The *Religious Peace of Augsburg* or *Augsburger Religionsfriede* (1555) recognized the party faithful of the *Confessio Augustana* and hence the religious pluralism of the Empire. It entailed the end of the *Unio imperii et ecclesiae*, the unity of the Western Christian world. The next few decades would clearly and repeatedly show that the various confessions could not co-exist peacefully alongside one another anywhere within the Empire. According to the principle *cuius regio, illius et religio*, the ruler had the right to determine the religion of his subjects and, hence, the various principalities evolved into virtually homogeneous confessional territories. For several decades after the Interim Crisis, however, strife continued within the territorial churches: Supporters of Philipp Melanchton, called Philippists opposed a second group known as Gnesio-Lutherans... Doctrinal disputes proliferated until a center party led by Johannes Brenz, Martin Chemnitz (nicknamed the "second Martin") and Jakob Andreae restored unity in 1577 by convincing two thirds of the Lutheran churches to accept a more detailed confessional statement known as the *Formula of Concord* (1577). It was followed by the *Book of Concord* (1580), which contained the ecumenical creeds, a selection of Luther's texts, and the general Lutheran confessions such as the Augs-

73. G. MÜLLER, *Bündnis und Bekenntnis: Zum Verhältnis von Glaube und Politik im deutschen Luthertum des 16. Jahrhunderts*, in ID., *Causa Reformationis: Beiträge zur Reformationsgeschichte und zur Theologie Martin Luthers. Zum 60. Geburtstag des Autors*, ed. G. MARON – G. SEEBAß, Gütersloh, Mohn, 1989, 25-45, esp. 31-36.

burg Confession of 1530 and the Apology of the Augsburg Confession. Due to the growing influence of Calvinism, however, some German princes had chosen de facto for the Reformed Church. In addition, the Counter-reformation had succeeded in regaining several imperial territories for Catholicism. In short, it was Martin Luther who, on the basis of a widespread call for Church reform, his personal existential and religious struggle, and with the political support of princes and cities, dealt a sharp blow to the medieval ideal of the one European Christian Empire and changed forever the religious map of Germany. The Emperor, for his part, was prevented from settling the religious quarrels in Germany because of his political conflicts with France, the controversy with the pope, the threat of the Turks, as well as because of his transatlantic colonial policy.

2. *The Habsburg Anti-Heresy Edicts and the Preserving of Catholicism in the Southern Part of the Low Countries*

In the Low Countries, the Louvain theologians (as Latomus, Eustachius of Sichem, Driedo), who remained thoroughly loyal towards the Pope[74] and the Emperor, proved to be formidable adversaries of Luther and his adherents. Among the *magistri lovanienses*, John Driedo also regarded the Scriptures, along with ecclesiastical traditions, as an important source of revelation. The Louvain theologians too showed an increasing interest in the authority of Augustine. Despite having many theological resources in common with the Lutherans, they took another position. Louvain was one of the first theological schools to condemn Luther (November 1519). Alongside and within the Catholic majority, some groups of reform-minded people had established themselves in the Low Countries. The early reformers were influenced by the Modern Devotion, just as they also appealed to Erasmus' biblical humanism and to the theological insights of Luther and other reformers. At the same time, however, they claimed that their new religious insights and practices were based on the Bible alone. During the first decades of the sixteenth century, the religious dissent in the Low Countries lacked an outspoken confessional character. As elsewhere in Europe, dissenters were dissatisfied with the abuses and failures of the Roman Church and called for Church reform. The dissatisfaction revealed itself through the ridicule of clerics and the current sacramental practice. The religious dissenters from the early 1520's are

---

74. Certainly, part of Louvain's loyalty to Rome was based upon the fact that the University was a papal foundation (an affection which was reinforced by Louvain's links with Pope Adrian VI of Utrecht).

generally indicated with the term 'Sacramentarians' because of their mere spiritualistic or symbolic conception of the sacraments (e.g. their denial, unlike the Lutherans, of the real presence of Christ in Eucharist). The religious-political map of the Low Countries, however, was not only determined by a discussion at a theological level and by the individual confessional preference of its inhabitants, but also by the social, economical and political context[75]. It was very similar to what happened in northern Germany.

Charles V's efforts to root out heresy might have been frustrated in Germany, but, in the Netherlands, he was determined to safeguard the Catholic faith and to push back the influence of the Reformation. By safeguarding the religious unity of the Low Countries, he also wanted to consolidate and strengthen the State's political unity. Not least among his concerns were also the Low Contries' strategic location and their economic prosperity. The latter was of special importance since it was of significant help in financing his wars in France and Italy. The Emperor, who spent much of his time in Spain, appointed a Governor of the Low Countries (in contrast to Germany) in order to promote and, if possible, to extend the interests of the central government. From 1519 to 1530 Charles V's aunt, Margaret of Austria, was regent in the Low Countries. After her death, in 1531, Charles appointed his sister Mary of Hungary. The Emperor himself authored the broad outlines of his Church and religion policy in the Low Countries, but in reality it was his regents who, in relative independence, implemented the policies within the constitutional and institutional framework of the territories themselves. This however, did not stop the provincial governments and the cities' magistrates from obstructing the central government's policies for the sake of their own customs and privileges (as did the princes in Germany).

In contrast to Germany, Charles succeeded in making the Edict of Worms (in a version that had been customized for the Low Countries) the basis for his anti-reformational policy. Several edicts of increasing com-

---

75. For an analysis of the political situation and the religious climate in the Low Countries, see e.g. A. DUKE, *The Netherlands*, in A. PETTEGREE, *The Early Reformation in Europe*, Cambridge, University Press, 1992, 142-165; A. DUKE, *Reformation and Revolt in the Low Countries*, London, Hambledon, 2003; also: W. BERGSMA, *The Low Countries*, in B. SCRIBNER – R. PORTER – M. TEICH (eds.), *The Reformation in National Context*, Cambridge, University Press, 1994, 67-79; J.J. WOLTJER – M.E.H.N. MOUT, *Settlements: The Netherlands*, in BRADY – OBERMAN – TRACY (eds.), *Handbook of European History 1400-1600*, vol. 2 (n. 1), 385-415; M. GREENGRASS, *The Longman Companion to the European Reformation, c. 1500-1618* (Longman Companions to History), London, Longman, 1998, pp. 129-145; G. MARNEF, *The Netherlands*, in A. PETTEGREE (ed.), *The Reformation World*, London, Routledge, 2000, 344-364.

plexity and severity were issued in line with Worms[76]. The (provisional) climax came with the placard of 1529. The latter was confirmed at the States General of 1531, a meeting attended by the Emperor. The stipulations typical for the anti-heretic placards of the past few years were inserted and included measures designed to counteract secret conventicles in which heretical ideas were passed on (or even devised), to stop the publication and dissemination of dissident literature and vernacular Bibles containing paratextual elements, which were often read and served in the aforementioned conventicles as a basis of heretical conversations ... Further, more measures were promulgated to discourage support of dissenters and to reward those willing to denounce them to the police. It seems that the violation of these imperial placards (particularly those concerning book censorship) was increasingly seen as irrefutable proof of heresy, even though the latter was primarily a canonically defined offence. Hence, the violation of the placards, such as the mere possession of forbidden books came to be regarded as a capital offense punishable by death and confiscation of all property. In 1522, the task of prosecuting heretics had been assigned to a central, State-sponsored Inquisition. Barely a year later, Margaret of Austria, partly under pressure applied by the States of Holland, removed the Inquisitor General Frans van der Hulst from his office. He was succeeded by three inquisitors whose job it was to inquire into the doctrinal orthodoxy of the accused. The question of guilt or innocence, as well as that of punishment, were left to the provincial courts, which had to use the placards as a guide. Because heresy was interpreted as high treason against God (divine lese-majesty), the persecution of the

76. The text of the placards had been edited in P. FREDERICQ (ed.), *Corpus documentorum Inquisitionis haereticae pravitatis Neerlandicae: Verzameling van stukken betreffende de pauselijke en bisschoppelijke Inquisitie in de Nederlanden.* Vol. 4: *Tijdvak der Hervorming in de zestiende eeuw (1514-23 september 1525)*, Gent, Vuylsteke, 1900; vol. 5: *Tijdvak der Hervorming in de zestiende eeuw. Eerste vervolg (24 september 1525 – 31 december 1528)*, Gent, Vuylsteke, 1902. Also: C. LAURENT – J. LAMEERE (eds.), *Recueil des ordonnances des Pays-Bas: Deuxième série:1506-1700.* Vol. 2: *Contenant les ordonnances du 29 janvier 1519 au 31 décembre 1529*, Bruxelles, Goemaere, 1898; J. LAMEERE (ed.), *Recueil des ordonnances des Pays-Bas: Deuxième série:1506-1700.* Vol. 3: *Contenant les ordonnances du 8 janvier 1529 (1530, N. ST.) au 11 décembre 1536*, Bruxelles, Goemaere, 1902; J. LAMEERE – H. SIMONT (eds.), *Recueil des ordonnances des Pays-Bas: Deuxième série:1506-1700.* Vol. 4: *Contenant les ordonnances du 9 janvier 1536 (1537, N. ST.) au 24 décembre 1543*, Bruxelles, Goemaere, 1907; *Ibid.*, Vol. 5: *Contenant les ordonnances du 1er janvier 1543 (1544, N. ST.) au 28 décembre 1549*, Bruxelles, Goemaere, 1910. For a commentary on the edicts and the placards, see e.g.: A. GOOSENS, *Les Inquisitions modernes dans les Pays-Bas méridionaux 1520-1633.* Vol. 1: *La législation* (Spiritualités et pensées libres), Bruxelles, Éditions de l'Université de Bruxelles, 1997, pp. 47-81; J.A. FÜHNER, *Die Niederlande im Herrschaftssystem Karls V. Die Kirchen- und antireformatorische Religionspolitik Kaiser Karls V. in den 17 Provinzen der Niederlande 1515-1555* (Brill's Series in Church History, 23), Leiden, Brill, 2004.

'crime' was reserved to the provincial courts. Ecclesiastical (episcopal
and pontifical) courts and local magistrates were, in principle, suspended
from judging religious dissenters, just as all local privileges were considered null and void. In spite of these regulations, the local tribunals
(particularly in Flanders) continued in claiming their right to take legal
action against people who were suspected of heresy. Local tribunals, however, were reluctant to implement the draconic penalties the edicts
required. This was because the persecution of dissenters was very unpop-
ular and, generally speaking, the cities' magistrates adhered to a relatively liberal version of Catholicism marked by Erasmian humanism. The
magistrates also had a duty to defend their town's privileges (e.g. limit-
ing confiscation, privilege *de non evocando*...) against improper proceedings by both ecclesiastical and external lay officers. They attempted
to preserve the legal usage of *arbitrale correctie*, i.e. the customary right
of using their own discretion to determine the severity of punishment
according to the circumstances of the case. The magistrates in Amsterdam and Antwerp were obvious examples of this position. These com-
mercially-minded cities had also strong trade relations with Lutheran
areas in Germany and the Baltic States. It was imperative that Protestant
traders coming from these regions felt safe and comfortable in Antwerp,
Amsterdam etc. Further, the Antwerp city council was disinclined to
restrict the economically-important printing industry by applying the
severe censorship measures. The provincial councils for their part were
accustomed to mediating between the central government's rigid 'anti-
heresy' policies on the basis of the placards on the one hand, and local
interests and privileges on the other. This tug-of-war between the different spheres of power was most acute in the core provinces, Flemish
speaking Flanders, Brabant, Zeeland and Holland. In the territories of the
French speaking periphery, as well as in the extreme North and East that
did not belong to the original Burgundian hereditary lands and only later
became Habsburg possessions, local and provincial authorities pursued a
more independent line. The central government in Brussels treated regions
such as Gelderland, Groningen etc. with special delicacy and did not subject them to the anti-heresy legislation in force elsewhere in the Netherlands.

    Only when, in the early part of the 1530s, the millenarian Anabaptists
began to make violent attacks and attempted to undermine the established
order, did town magistrates rally to the central government's policy and
begin to persecute the Anabaptists. After this threat to the established
order had disappeared in the South in 1538, and the Münster line in the
North was for the greater part annihilated in 1544-45, the local tribunals

and provincial courts relaxed their efforts and enforced the government's placards only in a limited fashion.

At the end of the 1530s, the government picked up the thread of book censorship. In 1540 another great anti-heresy placard followed. It listed the measures concerning book censorship that had been approved in previous years and, on several points, even made them more restrictive. The placard of 1540 was also geared toward preventive censorship: beginning in 1540, publishing a book that addressed the Scriptures, the faith, or the regulations of the Church without having received an official *imprimatur* from the *ordinarius loci*, the death penalty was uncompromisingly demanded. This measure represented a serious and important hardening when compared to the placards of 1529 and 1531, which local magistrates and provincial councils only selectively enforced. The 1540s nevertheless saw an increase in the degree of repression in the southern provinces of the Low Countries. It all came to a head in 1544-46 and as a result, people with Reformed sympathies fled the southern part of the Low Countries and settled in cities like Wesel, London, Frankfurt and later Emden. These anti-reformation and sometimes repressive policies meant that religious dissenters activities were greatly restricted. They were not, however, exterminated: they merely kept on working within underground networks.

The anti-heresy legislation and the continued persecutions in Flanders and neighboring provinces, the loss of local influence in government and the courts, the exorbitant taxation to finance imperial military campaigns in France and Italy, all led to ever growing tensions between the king and his subjects[77]. In 1555, Charles V was succeeded by his son Philip II. The latter's determination to root out 'heresy' was even greater than his father's. He was, however, confronted with the growing success of Calvinist preachers, especially in the extreme South of Flanders. Calvinism proved to be successful in several towns, as Antwerp and Ghent. Eventually it also influenced the northern part of the Low Countries. The success of Calvinism was increased by its ability to form political alliances with people who were dissatisfied with the regime of Philip II and his 'stadholders'. The dissatisfaction even included several prominent noblemen, who, at the end of 1565, formed an association, the so-called 'Compromise', in order to force a relaxation of the severe anti-heresy legislation. In April 1566, they submitted a petition to the Governess of the Netherlands, Margaret of Parma, entreating her to suspend the heresy laws, to adjourn Inquisition and to establish a new reli-

---

77. WOLTJER – MOUT, *Settlements: The Netherlands* (n. 75), pp. 397-405.

gious policy in consultation and agreement with the States General. One of Margaret's advisers ironically called them *gueux* or beggars. On the basis of Margaret's rather vague reply to the 'Compromise', many thought religious freedom was in sight. Secret conventicles of Protestants turned into public assemblies in the fields outside the city gates and with increasing number of participants (*hedge-preaching*). In addition to the sermons preached throughout the land in 1566, ministers also baptized, married and buried according to the rite of the 'new religion'. Subsequently, the nobles requested freedom of worship, which was already de facto allowed. A radicalization however took place and, beginning in the South of the Low Countries, iconoclasts destroyed the images in the churches. The movement gradually spread to the North[78]. The ferocity of some towns' iconoclasm was clearly exacerbated by political jealousies as well as social and economic tensions. Margaret of Parma wanted to take vigorous action. High nobles in the Council of State, among them the prince of Orange and the counts of Egmont and Hoorn, only took up arms and made efforts to restore order after the Governess agreed to allow public Protestant preaching and had promised to settle the religious problem in consultation with the States General. The iconoclastic movement, however, had at least to some degree undermined the Protestants' cause. In the early spring of 1567, the Governess restored her authority.

After the new Governor, the Duke of Alba, had arrived, in August 1567, a new wave of harsh repression followed under his 'Council of Troubles'. In 1568, William of Orange assumed the leadership of the insurgent noblemen. In 1572 the hostility towards the Spanish regime erupted into a new revolt. On 1 april 1572 the Sea-Beggars captured Den Briel, a small port in the south of Holland. In July William of Orange entered the Netherlands with an army of 20,000. In large parts of Holland and Zeeland the rebels were able to hold their ground against the Spanish armies. William of Orange was declared '*stadholder*' by the rebel States. The States of Holland accepted the *stadholder's* proposal to establish freedom of worship for both Protestants and Catholics. The Protestants, however, soon assumed power and very quickly worked to outlaw public Catholic worship in Holland and Zeeland, even as they accepted freedom of conscience for individuals (including Catholics). On 8 November 1576, the rebel provinces and the States General of the Low Countries concluded the 'Pacification of Ghent', which, along with a few other agreements, dismissed all foreign troops and withdrew all measures against heretics then in place.

78. A. DUKE, *The Time of Troubles in the County of Holland, 1566-67*, in ID., *Reformation and Revolt* (n. 75), 125-151.

The new governor, Don Juan of Austria, arrived in the Low Countries in November 1576. A new revolt, which resulted from Don Juan's decision to resume military activity, commenced at the end of 1577. Before it was over nearly all of the seventeen provinces of the Netherlands had taken up arms against the king. In Flanders and Brabant, the Calvinists obtained leading positions among Protestants. The Dutch Calvinists were perceived as patriots opposing religious repression stemming from a foreign occupying power. Another new Governor, Alessandro Farnese Duke of Parma, re-conquered town after town and restored Catholicism in the southern part of the Low Countries. Thousands of refugees, among whom were many of the economic elite, fled to the northern part of the Netherlands. The rebellious provinces of the North concluded the Union of Utrecht (1579), an 'undying agreement' of military alliance between the northern states, in which freedom of conscience was guaranteed. In 1581 they rejected by the Act of Abjuration (*Plakkaat van Verlatinghe*) Philip II as their sovereign. This rejection laid the foundation for an independent Republic of the United Netherlands. It evolved toward a Protestant State, dominated by the Calvinist element but in which other denominations, e.g. Mennonites and Lutherans, were tolerated. Even Catholics were allowed to practice their faith, but not publicly. By 1587, the Spaniards had almost completely rooted Calvinism out from its original strongholds in the South. Hence, it was mainly the region's political and military vicissitudes (and not the confessional preferences of the faithful) that determined the religious map of the Low Countries for the decades and centuries to come.

CONCLUSION: THE CLAMMY HANDS OF THE CHURCH HISTORIAN

In the sixteenth century reformers and their Catholic opponents were not afraid to claim that they had unique access to divine truth. Luther advanced the thesis that Scripture alone was all that was necessary and sufficient for one to gain access to truth. According to John Driedo, Scripture needed to be interpreted and supplemented by ecclesiastical traditions. Both appealed to Augustine in order to support their respective positions. Luther placed much emphasis on Augustine's anti-pelagian works. Driedo, in defining his doctrine of grace, also appealed to these books. In *De ecclesiasticis scripturis et dogmatibus*, however, the Louvain theologian drew amply upon Augustine's anti-Manichean and anti-donatist works. Here, the Church father presents himself as a 'man of the true Church' and opposed to the *sectae* that undermined the unity of this

Church. It is striking that Catholic theologians would continue to make extensive use of these writings. Both Lutherans and Catholics wanted to demonstrate that their position was in fact the ancient and traditional view. They selectively used patristic (and other) sources with particular goals already in mind.

It is hard to avoid the conclusion that this 16th century discussion about the ways to the truth, was strongly determined by the context in which the protagonists lived, by their educational systems, and existential concerns and fears (*in casu* Luther), by the 'school' to which they belonged (Driedo), by their notions of the Church, by their lack of historical perspective, etc. All parties called upon the Holy Spirit as the ultimate guarantor of their own position, a fact that cannot be overlooked by systematic theologians who are asking 'meta'-questions … Church history clearly shows that both the breakthrough of the Reformation and the maintenance of Catholicism were largely due to political influences. The one who was proclaimed the religious victor, was often the one who was backed by the political, military and even financial powers which dominated that particular region. When systematic theologians ask whether transcendent truth was revealed in a particularly clear and transparent way by way of this often contrived and bloody 16th century debates, the church historian becomes very nervous…

wim.francois@theo.kuleuven.be   Wim FRANÇOIS

THE PROBLEM OF A POSTMODERN (THEOLOGICAL) EPISTEMOLOGY, OR THE TEMPTATION OF A NARRATIVE ONTOTHEOLOGY

I. INTRODUCTION

Augustine seems to be a hot topic again in contemporary thought. Most of the protagonists of hermeneutic and postmodern philosophy explicitly confess the pivotal role of this church father for their thought: Paul Ricœur considers Augustine as one of his main sources of inspiration, Jean-François Lyotard's last book was on Augustine's *Confessiones*, and Jacques Derrida's *Circonfession* can be read as a postmodern version of the *Confessiones*. Yet it is mainly postmodern theology, which likes to present a return to Augustine as inevitable. Here, theology uses the critique on modern reason, exercised by postmodern philosophy, to promote a precedence of faith over reason, or better to understand reason from within the framework of a religious narrative tradition.

Nevertheless, I do not wish to focus on the specific nature of a return to Augustine in this article. The aim mainly consists of interpreting and criticising an epistemology, which starts with particularity and thus with tradition as a particular story. After all, the concept 'postmodern Augustinianism' can be understood in a rather broad sense, to indicate the shift from a modern rationality to an emphasis on faith, particularity, tradition and narrativity. This way it almost characterises the whole of contemporary theology, at least on an epistemological level. 'Progressive' (pluralistic) as well as rather 'conservative' (exclusivist) postmodern theologies often seem to share (to a certain extent) the same epistemology: one that stresses the tradition-dependency of rationality. Contextual-hermeneutical, post-liberal and radical-orthodox theologies agree in denying universal standards and transcendental schemes, and in the endorsing of the constitutive character of tradition and the cultural-linguistic framework of rationality. Of course, this kind of affinity need not be a problem as such. Some questions are inevitable however. What are the criteria for evaluating the different traditions? Is all evaluation only happening from within the own tradition? Is it possible to opt for a different tradition? Is a conversion in fact arbitrary? How and in which direction will our own tradition develop? Does the interruptive power of particularity remain warranted? And does fundamental theology not risk losing its critical character?

In the elaboration of my discussion and critique of this kind of post-modern epistemology, I will limit myself to two thinkers who, in their insistence on the importance of tradition, can be considered as typical for the Augustinian move in epistemology, namely Alasdair MacIntyre and John Milbank. Both authors not only appeal in a broad sense to the importance of particular narratives, but they try to radicalise this postmodern shift in such a way that they oppose the modern-liberal tradition in favour of a reassessment of the Augustinian tradition. Both can therefore explicitly be labelled as postmodern Augustinians. The structure of the article will be as follows: firstly, I will try to demonstrate why I consider Mac-Intyre's model as inconsistent; secondly, I will argue that Milbank consequently elaborates the idea of tradition-dependent rationality, but that his model is undesirable. The text does not aim at a careful exegesis of both thinkers; their role has to be seen as paradigmatical in the clarification of tradition-bound rationality.

II. TRADITION-DEPENDENCY
THE DIALECTICAL-'OBJECTIVE' OPTION (ALASDAIR MACINTYRE)

In contemporary philosophy, the idea of a tradition-dependent rationality has been mainly elaborated by Alasdair MacIntyre. He became known to the philosophical audience by publishing his highly acclaimed *After Virtue*[1]. In this book he opposes the modern, liberal project of a universalising ethical account, in order to return to a kind of virtue ethics that was known in Greek Antiquity. Precisely in its denial of the role of particularity and tradition, modern ethics is considered abstract and empty, and thus unable to provide us with a substantial vision of our goal in life. His epistemology can mainly be found in the sequel to *After Virtue*, namely *Whose Justice? Which Rationality?*[2]. This book can be read as a plea to always understanding philosophy "in terms of the historical context of tradition, social order and conflict out of which it emerged"[3]. Crucial is the idea of an ever-evolving historical story, constituting a tradition, and as such providing the framework for rationality[4].

---

1. A. MACINTYRE, *After Virtue: A Study in Moral Theory*, London, Duckworth, 1981.
2. A. MACINTYRE, *Whose Justice? Which Rationality?*, Notre Dame, IN, University of Notre Dame Press, 1988.
3. *Ibid.*, p. 390.
4. This implies that all rationality has to be understood from within a specific tradition of understanding or research. MacIntyre himself uses the word of 'enquiry-bearing traditions'. Cf. MACINTYRE, *Whose Justice?* (n. 2), p. 354. This idea is closely related to Imre Lakatos' model of 'scientific research programs'. What Lakatos proposes within the con-

In other words: conceptions of rationality always have their own story.

MacIntyre conceives the development of a tradition as an evolution through different stages. He distinguishes three. Every rationality starts in a condition of pure, historical contingency. The beliefs, the practices, the institutions and eventually the founding texts of a particular community constitute a given, which gives rise to a certain rationality, a certain way to understand the world. In this first stage, the authoritative texts and voices have not yet been questioned. However, after a while, incoherencies appear and some lacunae in the particular system of convictions become visible. This marks the transition to a second stage. Normally, this transition takes place when a community is confronted with new situations it cannot adequately deal with by using its original system of beliefs. Therefore inadequacies become identified in this stage, but not yet remedied. This happens in the third stage by developing reformulations and re-evaluations, which should be able to overcome the limitations and inadequacies of the former system. This is the stage of inventivity. Important however is that this inventivity is never to be considered as a free or unbound inventivity: some ruptures may occur, but "some core of shared belief, constitutive of allegiance to the tradition, has to survive every rupture"[5].

So far, it would be possible to reproach MacIntyre as relativism. Because of the radical particularity-dependency we get the impression that he holds on to a pure coherency-theory of truth, and that there are in the end so many truths as there are traditions of rationality. MacIntyre, however, wants to tackle this impression by an account of interaction between different rationalities. According to him, the incommensurability and the untranslatibility of traditions does not exclude that a certain form of dialectics between the traditions can be thought of. MacIntyre points out the fact that a tradition is normally able to respond and to react to new situations by using its own resources and that within the account given above, there is no real interaction with other forms of rationality. It is possible however that a tradition reaches the point that it is no longer able to evolve by using its own standards. A situation may occur where a tradition exposes more inadequacies and previously unknown incoherencies in using its own methods of research. MacIntyre calls this an

text of natural sciences, seems so to get translated by MacIntyre for a context of human sciences. On this affinity, cf. also A.N. MURPHY, *Anglo-American Postmodernity: Philosophical Perspectives on Science, Religion and Ethics*, Boulder, CO, Westview, 1997, pp. 49-62.

5. MACINTYRE, *Whose Justice?* (n. 2), p. 356.

epistemological crisis: the tradition reaches a point where its own survival is at stake. Of course, the occurrence of such a crisis does not have to be fatal. It means that a tradition is falsifiable. It can be put into question as a whole. It is clear that there are two options in case of a crisis: either the tradition actually gets falsified, or it still manages to come up with a solution. A solution demands the invention of new concepts and frameworks, or theories that meet three specific requirements[6]. First, the conceptually enriched schemes must provide a solution to the problems, which gave rise to the crisis. Second, it must provide an explanation of what is was that rendered the tradition sterile or incoherent. Third, these first two tasks must be carried out in such a way that shows some fundamental continuity between the new schemes and the original tradition. If these three things are not compatible a conversion to a rival tradition becomes inevitable. Consequently a conversion is not arbitrary, but motivated by the failure of the own tradition. That specific tradition, which is able to answer the unsolved questions of the original tradition, therefore becomes attractive.

MacIntyre thus believes that the idea of falsification is tenable without returning to the idea of a reality independent of a particular, tradition-bound rationality[7]. The principle of falsification is grafted onto the possibility of uncovering the inadequacies of a tradition, always measured by its own standards. But because of the fact that other traditions sometimes may give better answers to problems of the given tradition, the closeness of a tradition is forced open and gives rise to a kind of dialectics and interaction. MacIntyre himself even speaks of the possibility of "a rational debate between and a rational choice among rival traditions"[8]. The opportunity of a challenge by other traditions rests on the possibility of the apprehension of a 'second first language' and on the skill of 'empathetic imagination'[9]. The language of a tradition may be untranslatable, but this does not preclude the possibility of apprehending another language; apprehension as the condition to judge what exactly remains untranslatable.

---

6. *Ibid.*, p. 362.

7. Cf. *Ibid.*, p. 357: "Facts, like telescopes and wigs for gentlemen, were a seventeenth-century invention".

8. *Ibid.*, p. 352.

9. Jennifer A. Herdt turns attention to the ironical fact that this is precisely a liberal concept, and that by consequence MacIntyre does not manage to stay within his own tradition. Cf. J.A. HERDT, *Alasdair MacIntyre's "Rationality of Traditions" and Tradition-Transcendental Standards of Justification*, in *The Journal of Religion* 78 (1998) 524-546, esp. pp. 531-532.

It is clear that MacIntyre here offers theology a very interesting epistemology. First, he demonstrates the constitutive role of authority and tradition for rationality. Furthermore, it is clear that the element of faith inevitably re-enters: holding on to a specific rationality always implies an element of faith, exactly because all rationality retains an element of contingency. Critical reasoning is, in other words, always already a '*fides quaerens intellectum*'[10]. Second, MacIntyre is convinced that his epistemology does not lead to relativism. The relationship between rationality and a particular tradition does not imply a need to abandon all notions of objectivity. It does not imply that in the end an infinite number of rationality-traditions exist next to one another in total incommensurability. Between the traditions there will always be a kind of dialectics, which makes a certain rapprochement between the 'truths' possible. However, exactly at this point, MacIntyre's project becomes questionable. Crucial is the question of the statute of MacIntyre's interaction-scheme. Is the scheme in itself a merely tradition-bound, particular scheme, or does this scheme, at least concerning the validity of it, transcend the different particular traditions? In his answer to the problem of perspectivism and relativism, he conveys the impression that this is happening. The problem with this however consists of the risk of contradicting the own point of departure. On the other hand, when he presents his scheme as merely particular, it becomes hard to see how he finally does not fall back to relativism.

MacIntyre thus presents us a general model, which explains how a form of dialectics between traditions can be thought of: on the basis of an 'empathetic imagination' a person learns 'a second first language', and so he goes on to investigate the relation between the newly acquainted tradition and the problems that gave rise to the epistemological crisis of the own tradition. MacIntyre presents both the skill of 'empathetic imagination', the possibility of learning 'a second first language', as well as the structure of the development of a tradition, namely the possibility of an epistemological crisis together with the step-by-step plan for the solution, as somewhat tradition-transcendent. That is at least the impression we get. Sometimes, he is even quite explicit.

> The grounds for an answer to relativism and perspectivism are to be found, not in any theory of rationality as yet explicitly articulated and advanced within one or more of the traditions with which we have been concerned,

---

10. Cf. also C. EARLY, *MacIntyre, Narrative Rationality and Faith*, in *New Blackfriars* 82 (2001) 35-43.

but rather with a theory embodied in and presupposed by their practices of inquiry[11].

The principles that should allow interaction and a form of dialectic between the (enquiry-bearing) traditions cannot be reduced to a specific tradition. According to this quote, they enable precisely a 'dialogue' between the traditions, and so seem to be presupposed by the different traditions. This sounds quite logical: to resolve a conflict between rival traditions on a legitimate basis, one cannot use principles that are restricted to just one of the traditions. MacIntyre's problem however consists then of the fact that he falls back on a transcendental logic by speaking of "a theory embodied in and presupposed by". Of course, he could claim that he only proposes a minimal, formal procedure as general, and not articulated substantive standards. But that would not solve the problem. On the contrary, a transcendental logic rests precisely on such a formal procedure. Moreover, it would just be highly ironic to slide back into a formal, procedural logic, exactly because this typifies the modern, liberal tradition he is in fact opposing[12].

Nevertheless, an alternative reading seems possible. The system of interaction could be considered as universal on merely pragmatic grounds, more precisely because it would be for all traditions the most profitable scheme within the light of their own further development. He himself states quite clearly, that each system only has to gain by the idea that another system may be superior on some topic.

> The only rational way for the adherents of any tradition to approach intellectually, culturally, and linguistically alien rivals is one that allows for the possibility that in one or more areas the other may be rationally superior to it. [...] Only those whose tradition allows for the possibility of its hegemony being put in question can have a rational warrant for asserting such a hegemony[13].

Progression then has to be evaluated from the possibilities to explain more in the future; as a possibility that becomes optimised by accepting MacIntyre's interaction-scheme on a pragmatic basis. This would not have to result in relativism, because in the course of time a form of dialectic remains upright: one system will lose out on another, simply because e.g. system A will be able to explain more than system B. Thus to be able to explain more or less then becomes the criterion which allows for a

---

11. MACINTYRE, *Whose Justice?* (n. 2), p. 354.
12. Cf. also J.A. HERDT, *Alasdair MacIntyre's "Rationality of Traditions"* (n. 9), p. 535: "Is MacIntyre's rationality of traditions perhaps just a new Enlightenment method?".
13. MACINTYRE, *Whose Justice?* (n. 2), p. 388.

legitimate comparison between different rationalities. Still, it can be doubted that MacIntyre here succeeds in escaping relativism. The 'more or less', according to MacIntyre's own logic, can no longer be considered as a neutral criterion: there is no 'more or less' as such. Therefore he will have to admit that the 'more or less' is also tradition-bound and so already an internal principle. He will have to admit that with this criterion, it is impossible to install a genuine form of dialectics. The adherents of system A may be convinced that their system is able to explain more than system B, while the adherents of system B may be convinced that it can explain more than system A. When rationality as such is thought of as tradition-bound, one has to admit that all inadequacies as well as all solutions have to be thought of intra-systemically as well. Thus, if an epistemological crisis can only be called so from within the rationality of one's own tradition, nothing states that crises will keep occurring. Finally, it cannot be excluded that some traditions of rationality are able to reach such a high degree of coherence so that a number of traditions will exist next to on another, incommensurable and without interaction[14].

III. TRADITION-DEPENDENCY
THE RHETORICAL-RELATIVIST OPTION (JOHN MILBANK)

In my reading, MacIntyre does not succeed in combining tradition-dependency with a form of dialectics, which allows an overcoming of relativism. As John Milbank rightly notices, there is still too much of an *"air of non-commitment"*[15] hovering above the work of MacIntyre: he talks as a philosopher, too often presenting his own thesis as a new, general and valid model, and thus tradition-independent. Of course, this does not imply that a tradition-dependent epistemology cannot be conceptualised in a consistent manner. On the contrary; the idea of tradition-dependency calls for a radicalisation of MacIntyre's epistemology; it calls for a further purification from hidden, modern presuppositions that will contradict the original point of departure in the end. Such a radicalisation is now precisely the intention of John Milbank himself.

Milbank wants to stress clearer and more radical than MacIntyre the postmodern particularity-dependency of all thought, in order to provide

14. Nowadays, it is still possible to present oneself as a die-hard materialist, or as a die-hard idealist, even as a neo-platonist or as a neo-scholastic.

15. J. MILBANK, *Theology and Social Theory: Beyond Secular Reason*, Oxford, Blackwell, 1990, p. 329.

an alternative for modern, liberal thought, which he labels nihilistic. However, he is fully conscious of the fact that he cannot rationally repudiate
the modern tradition, precisely because all rationality has to be understood in the end as a form of *mythos*. Because all rationalities remain tradition-bound, and all traditions are contingent, historical constructs, we
have to admit that all rationalities are a kind of mythos. Therefore, the
only option consists of the attempt to overrule another tradition rhetorically. In the words of Milbank:

> The encounter of these diverse reasons cannot be contained and mediated
> by dialectical conversation alone: at the limits of disagreement it will take
> the form of a clash of rhetorics[16].

The epistemology of MacIntyre is thus not only made more particu-
larity-bound, but also more narrative and more historicist, exactly by giving up on dialectics. Let us take the example of justification: now this has
to be understood completely intra-textual and on a narrative base, independent of all further interaction:

> The story of the development of a tradition really *is* the argument for the
> tradition[17].

Philosophically seen, Milbank's epistemology can be called relativistic. Only a number of metaphysically unfounded[18], incommensurable
forms of rationality exist. Furthermore, we cannot state that there is a
dialectical relation between these forms that turns a rapprochement with
the 'truth' possible; every rational meta-perspective is impossible.
According to Milbank, this is the reality a post-Nietzschean theology has
to face. The peculiarity of his position is that he manages to make the
solution of what actually is the problem: he will stress that a philosophical relativism does not imply that the end-vocabulary is relativistic too,
precisely on the basis of a radicalisation of the Nietzschean principle.
When there are only rationally unfounded stories, then also the story that
tells us that we should no longer tell meta-stories is unfounded. This
means for Milbank that we do not longer have to agree with thinkers as
Lyotard and Derrida. Firstly, also their story implies some kind of meta-
story, although they do not acknowledge that. Secondly, it is useless to
tell only micro-stories. Milbank stresses that it is crucial to resist the ultra
violent master-story of neo-liberal capitalism; and this does not succeed

---

16. *Ibid.*, p. 347.
17. *Ibid.*, p. 347.
18. This is of course also true for theology. Cf. MILBANK, *Theology* (n. 15), p. 247:
"Theology is just another socio-historical gaze, just another perspective alongside other
gazes".

when we stick to small stories. Small stories are weak stories, and as such powerless.

Thus, the postmodern perspective does not preclude that a meta-perspective or master-story can still be defended. The difference with modernity however consists of the fact that we are aware of the rationally unfounded character: we can no longer defend a master-story on the basis of a rational certainty, but we can still hold on to it on the basis of faith[19]. Applied to the problem of truth: truth remains relative within the light of the general philosophical theory, but this theory allows that a transition to another non-philosophical register is made, which can be understood as a master-story. A philosophical relativism and perspectivism thus can be combined with a theological realism, in such a way that one finally understands truth in the first place as theological. Concerning Milbank's own position and the transition to theology this entails that the claims of the Christian tradition (concerning the reality) come back into play. Maybe we can understand this as a 'U-turn philosophy': philosophically he points out the inadequacy of philosophical reasoning and thus the necessity to speak from within a particular tradition, including the embracing of all the (ontological) claims of that tradition. For the relation between philosophy and theology, this implies that he will finally also have to subordinate philosophy to theology, at least as a Christian. The benefit of this move lies in the fact that he is able to supplement a coherence-theory of truth with a correspondence theory. Philosophically, we have to admit that the Christian story is not better founded or more true than any other story; theologically, and on the basis of faith, nothing prevents us from talking about reality as such, and to develop again an ontology.

Milbank thus succeeds in coherently radicalising the concept of particularity-dependent rationality, and in restoring the claims of theology on the basis of this radicalisation. Moreover, we could think of this as a nonpretentious project. By holding on to the distinction between a philosophical and a theological level, we get the impression it would be possible to stay modest, in spite of all theological claims, which remain rationally seen unfounded. However, staying modest does not seem to be Milbank's choice. By emphasizing the necessity of a strong master-narrative, he risks forgetting that his narrative is rationally unfounded; he risks forgetting about the fictional status of the Christian story as a

19. Cf. MILBANK, *Theology* (n. 15), p. 249: "Theology purports to give an ultimate narrative, to provide some ultimate depth of description, because the situation of oneself within such a continuing narrative is what it means to belong to the church, to be a Christian. However, the claim is made by faith, not a reason which seeks foundations".

mythos[20]. In his *Theology and Social Theory* he still explicitly renders account of the rational unfoundedness of the Christian story, but in his later writings there seems to be little room for a reflection on the mythological nature of Christianity. Here it would be possible to read his theological realism again as a kind of philosophical realism[21]. The problem with this shift consists of the fact that his project is in danger of becoming a quite violent one: the quasi-absoluteness of his claims gives rise to the use of antagonistic-agonistic schemes[22]. Typical for this is the emphasis on the Christian story as a counter-narrative, necessary to fight modern nihilism. In his postmodernism, Milbank directs the distinction between the modern and the Christian story to a climax. In his account, the modern story comes into being as a heresy (starting with Duns Scotus) that in its claim of the existence of a secular sphere gives rise to the nihilism of modern man, to the Godlessness of our times. Postmodern philosophy is according to Milbank only part of the modern story. He considers thinkers as Nietzsche, Heidegger, Deleuze, Lyotard and Derrida as representatives of a single nihilist philosophy. In the end modernity has to be understood as "a refusal of Christianity and the invention of an 'Anti-Christianity'"[23]. Compromises are impossible: the modern story has to be rejected as nihilistic.

In order to understand the true nature of Milbank's claim better, I would like to focus a moment on the paradoxical nature of his claim: Milbank's warrior logic consists of promoting the Christian 'fight' in the name of an ultimate non-violence. He stresses that the peculiarity of Christianity rests on its ontology of non-violence, contrary to the ontology of violence of the modern story. Unfortunately, he seems to be little aware of this paradox and refuses to take in account the violence of his antagonistic-agonistic scheme. Most of the time he clearly denies that his story, or the Christian story[24] as such, entails some element of violence. Typical here is his relation to Augustine and the problem of heresy. Using

20. Cf. also G. WARD, *John Milbank's Divina Commedia*, in *New Blackfriars* (1992) 311-326, esp. 312. Ward stresses here the nearly impossible combination of fictionality and the idea of a masternarrative.

21. Some parts of his *Being Reconciled* give the impression he is again developing a kind of natural theology. Cf. J. MILBANK, *Being Reconciled: Ontology and Pardon*, London, Routledge, 2003.

22. Douglas Hedley therefore stresses the gnostic-dualistic character of Milbank's thought. Cf. D. HEDLEY, *Should Divinity Overcome Metaphysics? Reflections on John Milbank's Theology beyond Secular Reason and Confessions of a Cambridge Platonist*, in *The Journal of Religion* 80 (2000) 271-298.

23. MILBANK, *Theology* (n. 15), p. 280.

24. Milbank makes no distinction between these two: his story of Christianity *is* the Christian story.

De Civitate Dei he wants to demonstrate that Augustine understands the City of God as a 'nomad city', as a city without borders, without a fixed place and open to everyone. He even likes to speak of the open exteriority of the Christian Story; or as he states in his article *'Postmodern Critical Augustinianism'*: "Christianity should not draw boundaries"[25]. A heresy would subsequently not originate when a certain group becomes excluded, but when a group locks itself out because of its emphasis on interiority. The problem with this reading rests on Milbank's ignoring of a certain form of dialectics between exteriority and interiority within the thought of Augustine[26]: also Augustine excludes, also Augustine draws boundaries, sometimes even quite clearly. In that way Milbank creates the impression he wants to cover up the violence of Augustine's story, in order to cover up the violence of his own story. In his *Being Reconciled*, his view on the use of violence has slightly changed. He now opposes pacifism by the use of a distinction between means and goal: the Christian goal of peace may require drawing on violent means in order to reach the goal. Nevertheless, we are not inclined to call his position here more self-conscious, because all violence is presented as an element completely external to his use of the meta-narrative. According to Milbank, it is just a means, necessary in some circumstances. In his words: "In certain circumstances, the young, the deluded, those relatively lacking in vision need to be coerced"[27]. But who are the 'deluded' and who is precisely lacking in vision? His master-story has criteria for this: because of the absolute conception of his story, all those who do not support his version of Christianity are in fact nihilists[28]. They need to be opposed, and if necessary with violence. Therefore, only the Christian war is a justified war, because only for Christians peace is the name of the *eschaton*.

Let us return to the problem of epistemology now. Crucial for us is the relation between the violence of Milbank's story and his radically par-

25. J. MILBANK, *'Postmodern Critical Augustianism': A Short Summa in Forty Two Responses to Unasked Questions*, in *Modern Theology* 7/3 (1991) 229.

26. Cf. also R. DODARO, *Loose Canons: Augustine and Derrida on Their Selves*, in J.D. CAPUTO – M.J. SCANLON (eds.), *God, the Gift and Postmodernism*, Bloomington, IN, Indiana University Press, 1999, 79-111; G. HYMAN, *The Predicament of Postmodern Theology: Radical Orthodoxy or Nihilist Textualism*, Louisville, KY, Westminster John Knox Press, 2001, pp. 75-77; W.J. HANKEY, *Re-christianizing Augustine Postmodern Style: Readings by Jacques Derrida, Robert Dodaro, Jean-Luc Marion, Rowan Williams, Lewis Ayres and John Milbank*, in *Animus* 2 (1997) 1-34.

27. MILBANK, *Being Reconciled* (n. 21), p. 39.

28. Cf. J. MILBANK, *Knowledge: The Theological Critique of Philosophy in Hamann and Jacobi*, in J. MILBANK – C. PICKSTOCK – G. WARD (eds.), *Radical Orthodoxy: A New Theology*, London, Routledge, 2001, p. 32: "it is indeed for radical orthodoxy an either/or: philosophy (Western or Eastern) as a purely autonomous discipline, or theology: Herod or the magi, Pilate or the God-man".

ticularity-bound epistemology. Is this violence in fact a result of too wide-ranging claims and so of an inconsistency concerning his own episte-mology, or does a direct relation between this violence and his episte-mology exist? I at least have the impression that his model is consistent and that the problem precisely resides in his epistemology. Let me make myself clear. The easiest way to explain the violence is by pointing out that Milbank forgets the fictional status (in the sense of rationally ungrounded) of his master-narrative. Nevertheless, this does not answer the question. Of course, the violence is a result of this forgetting. But can this be a reproach within the light of his epistemology? I do not think so. In order to be consistent, he seems to be obliged to this kind of forgetting. A theory, which proclaims the tradition-dependency of all rationality, obliges to start speaking from within the own tradition. By consequence, it is no longer possible to defend the theory of tradition-dependency as a general valid theory[29]. The general theory is self-deny-ing. Therefore, we can compare the theory of tradition-dependency with Wittgenstein's ladder[30]: once up, we have to throw the ladder away. As a result of this however, the theory of tradition-dependency will nearly inevitably lead to making the own story absolute. This would mean that in a fully considered epistemology of tradition-dependency the own story becomes the measure of all reality, that the own story will be presented finally as coinciding with reality.

Let us try to look at the same problem by means of some other con-cepts. A radical tradition-dependent rationality is translatable to the methodological requirement of intra-textuality: in determining truth, one has to stay within the own 'text', within the own story. In general, this requirement is presented as an example of a modest epistemology: we do not pretend to say more than what we understand from within our own story. This modesty however can only be linked to a half-hearted version of this epistemology: one that wishes not to forget about the (ungrounded) fictionality. Therefore, the modesty of this epistemology is essentially a false modesty. The requirement to understand all from within the own text

29. Another example of this logic is the relativism-paradox: when one states that all truth is relative, than one creates the impression that one is making an exception for the idea that all truth is relative. Yet, this does not have to stay an unsurpassable contradic-tion. Relativism is consequent possibility, at least as long as one gives up on stating that all truth is relative. One has to live as a relativist. In other words: the true relativist does not argue with a philosopher; he makes fun of him.

30. Cf. L. Wittgenstein at the end of his Tractatus: "Meine sätzen erläutern dadurch, daß sie der, welcher mir versteht, am Ende als unsinnig erkennt, wenn er durch sie – auf ihnen – über sie hinausgestiegen ist. (Er muß sozusagen die Leiter wegwerfen, nachdem er auf ihr hinaufgestiegen ist)". L. WITTGENSTEIN, *Tractatus Logico-Philosophicus*, Ams-terdam, Athenaeum-Pollak en van Gennep, 1975, 6.54.

is a violent requirement, precisely because this finally implies a refusal of all external positioning. By taking the own text as the final measure, the temptation seems to be irresistible either to execrate all otherness or to encapsulate the Other within the own story: the Other becomes a function of the Self. On a theological-philosophical level, the problem of ontotheology returns: God gets devalued, not because of a metaphysical speculation, but as a making absolute of the category of narrativity. It would be naive to think that theology has overcome ontotheology by switching to the category of narrativity. As God can be reduced to a function of an abstract thought of being, so God can be reduced to an intra-systemic function of a story. And precisely this last possibility becomes actual in an intra-textual approach. When one gives up on each anthropological anchoring of receptivity, interruption becomes a useless concept[31]. It will be nearly impossible then not to withdraw into the artificial security of the own story. God here becomes the final safety pin, and the own ultimate truth will be the only thing that can be heard[32]. Of course, as a counterargument, the theologian could state that the peculiarity of the Christian story consists of being an open story. However, this is not convincing, at least not in relation to an intra-textual epistemology. When the criteria for openness can only be determined intra-textually, every story can claim to be an open story. Just as interruption, openness is a useless concept within an intra-textual approach. Intra-textuality is the impossibility of both.

IV. CONCLUSION

In this article, I have tried to clarify the concept of tradition-dependent rationality, by paying attention to two paradigmatic models of this epistemology. In a first part, I have tried to show that MacIntyre's model is

31. I therefore resist all strong concepts of revelation in the precedence of '*Offenbarung*' over '*Offenbarkeit*' (as e.g. can be found in neo-orthodox and radical-orthodox theologies or in the philosophy of Jean-Luc Marion).

32. In theology, one sometimes tries to defend the absoluteness of one's own truth claims by an appeal to incarnation: we know the truth and we do have knowledge of the divine mystery, because God has given himself to mankind. By this, however, incarnation functions as an excuse for self-glorification. Luckily, not all Radical Orthodoxy-members go along with the refusal of each external positioning. In a critique on John Milbank, Gerald Loughlin stresses that Milbank forgets about the positioning of the Christian story itself by Christ's second coming. Here, eschatology can play the role of a critical corrective which should prevent that we make the christian story as it is known or told today absolute. Cf. G. LOUGHLIN, *Christianity at the End of the Story or the Return of the Master-Narrative*, in *Modern Theology* 8/4 (1992) 369-383.

not consistent. He presents a dialectical model that should allow a genuine interaction between different traditions. But he gets into problems,
when we ask for the statute of his own interaction-model: either he states
that his model is presupposed in all traditions, or he presents his model
as pragmatically seen the most profitable option. In the first case, he falls
back on a transcendental scheme of the formal conditions of possibility.
In the other case he slides back into relativism, because the criterion of
'being able to explain more or less' can no longer be presented as tradition-independent. In a second part, I've tried to show how Milbank consequently radicalises MacIntyre's model, how he accepts a kind of philosophical relativism and how he manages to force a transition to a
theological realism. The problem of his model concerns the desirability
of it. I consider his model as an extremely violent one, whereby this violence is rooted in the radicalised epistemology of tradition-dependency.
The crux of this conclusion consists of the idea of the necessity to forget; the idea that every rationality is tradition-bound, obliges to speak
from within the own tradition and to stop defending the general theory
of tradition-dependency. One must forget tradition-dependency in order
to speak tradition-dependent. This is the only consequent option. The violence of this position then finally translates itself in the impossibility of
interruption. Applied to God: God becomes a function of a story; he
becomes absorbed by and within a story.

Nevertheless, with my critique I do not simply wish to return to a modern, universalistic, transcendental logic. That would be too naïve. The
elaboration of transcendental schemes is unavoidably indebted to a particular context. Therefore, a hermeneutical supplement will always be
needed in order to stay aware of the particularity of the own speech. Modern approaches often do underestimate the constitutive role of the context
and risk to presuppose a kind of direct access to a sphere of noumenality. However, this may not seduce us to carry out a simple reduction to
particularity: such a reduction leads to particularism, to the dangerous
'tribalism' of a 'Gott mit uns'. Both reductions, to universality and to
particularity, are to be resisted. In other words: we can no longer be
plainly modern, but a postmodernism that wishes to be completely 'post'
walks into the same trap.

Personally, I especially fear for an all too hasty denial of a dialectical-
mediating moment of some (abstract) universality[33]. The direct choice

_____

33. The thought of Slavoj Žižek is quite interesting on this point. As a lacanian 'post-
modern' he is completely aware of the impossibility of simply returning to modern
schemes. Nevertheless, he warns for ignoring the necessity of an abstract universality as
a mediating moment, in order not to relapse into pre-modernity. More specific, he speaks

for a particular form of life leads nearly inevitable to a slide back into pre-modernity: in abandoning dialectics between particularity and universality (and between faith and reason) a narrative theology (as a fundamental theology) risks to make a contingent given story absolute and to reduce God to and intra-systemic function. MacIntyre of course is aware of the unavoidability of dialectics, but he is finally inconsistent, for he does not recognise its minimal transcendental condition. Milbank then presents us a false picture of both modernity and postmodernity. Already Immanuel Kant explicitly denied the possibility of a direct access to ourselves as noumenal beings. Such an access would imply the end of the moral struggle; it would reduce us to automatons. But indeed, Kant sometimes does not adequately take enough into account the 'syrupiness' of the pathological (the order of our inclinations). We can never fully escape our being rooted in the particular and pathological. However, here postmodern philosophy offers us a crucial modification of modern insights. With for example Jacques Derrida, we can understand the noumenal as 'parasitic' on the order of phenomenality. Noumenality itself relies on ontic carriers of experience. Applied to the moral law: this is unconceivable without a minimal narrative development. This does not mean that Derrida reduces the order of the noumenal and universal to the order of the phenomenal and particular. He wants to respect the tension that exists between both. He wants to demonstrate that both orders rely on one another, but that they can never be reduced to one another. So the Enlightenment should be understood as elliptically structured[34]. The Enlightenment is divided within itself, constituted by two focal centres which give the overall structure an aporetical outlook. The two focal centres can be associated with a logic of particularity on the one side and a logic of universality on the other side: there is nothing outside of contextuality; nevertheless, we are marked by an unconditional appeal to transcend every context. This tension makes it possible to criticise both all presumed pureness of abstract and formal philosophies and every attempt to reduce claims of truth to its context.

of the impossibility of choosing the "true meaning" directly. Therefore, one has to begin by making the "wrong choice". Translated to our problem: one has to opt for some abstract universality as a "wrong moment", in order to really validate the concreteness of life. Cf. S. ŽIŽEK, *The Puppet and the Dwarf, The Perverse Core of Christianity* (Short Circuits), Massachusetts, MA, MIT Press, 2003, p. 83.

34. J. DERRIDA, *On a Newly Arisen Apocalyptic Tone in Philosophy*, in P. D. FENVES (ed.), *Raising the Tone of Philosophy: Late Essays by Immanuel Kant, Transformative Critique by Jacques Derrida*, Baltimore, MD, The Johns Hopkins University Press, 1993, 117-171.

Let us now return to Milbank for a last time. Milbank resists the deconstructive approach of Derrida as nihilistic. In line with the rest of postmodern philosophy, he would not succeed in overcoming modern formalism. More specifically, he reproaches Derrida for remaining to Hegelian[35]. Derrida postpones every synthesis and prolongs the logic of negativity, but he remains caught within a dialectic logic. But is this necessarily such a problem? Indeed, Derrida gives the impression of being a postmodern Hegelian. And as such, he knows, as a result of his eschatological correction, how to avoid all triumphalism. The latter correction then seems to be largely absent in Milbank's thought. The 'yet-to-come' is here discredited in favour of the 'already'. We can therefore turn the accusation of (modern) Hegelianism against Milbank himself. In Milbank's thought, clear dialectical traces can be found: in his attempt to overcome the duality of reason and faith, and nature and grace he remains heir of Hegel. Moreover, his attempt easily results in an ad hand synthesis, for it is a synthesis identified with his own master-narrative. It is therefore all too easy to reject deconstruction as modern formalism and to leave us with an either/or option: either *Radical Orthodoxy* or postmodern nihilist philosophy. Deconstruction is essentially a sophisticated way to deal with particular truths of faith. Deconstruction refuses all attempts to make them absolute, but understand them as the necessary carriers (and so always deconstructable in their truth claims) of a universal logic of truth and justice. It is to be regretted here that Milbank finally (despite his attempt to overcome the duality of nature and grace) seems unable to escape a strange duality of salvation and damnation. Maybe he is not dialectical enough. A healthy dialectics challenges us to question our own position time and time again and to render account of the complex interplay of the self and the other. It constantly tries to avoid two seductions: on one side it refuses to absorb the other in the story of the self, on the other side it refuses to hypostasize as unbridgeable the distance that separates us from the other. From the perspective of a dialectical postmodern stance, there can be no reduction, nor any unbridgeable asymmetry. The idea then, that one has overcome the totalitarianism of modern metaphysics, by starting from particularity within epistemology, may just be a symptom of a relapse before Hegel, and before Kant, than an actual overcoming.

tom.jacobs@theo.kuleuven.be   Tom JACOBS

---

35. Cf. MILBANK, *Theology* (n. 15), p. 310.

THEOLOGICAL TRUTH IN A CONTEXT OF AESTHETICISATION
RESEARCH MEMORANDA ON HANS URS VON BALTHASAR AND THEODOR W. ADORNO

More than ever, the question of truth has become questionable. The general reticence on this subject can be partly explained as moral prudence: postmodern philosophers remind us that too many victims have been made in the name of truth. In practice, the warning that 'truth' is a dangerous word is outshone by the growing implicit consensus that, in important domains of human life, the question of truth has become simply irrelevant. Especially regarding ultimate Truth, people seem to switch from thinking in terms of orthodoxy towards living according to aesthetic criteria. The question is not if it is *true*, but if it is *authentic*. Regarding religion, the norm is no longer defined by what is true, but by what can serve as an authentic expression of the own subjective creativity. The role model for our quest of meaning is no longer the priest, but the artist. The shift is also tangible within faculties of theology, if professors still dare to speak about dogmas, they hasten to say that the idea of a dogma as a proposition, which formulates the objective truth is superseded: a dogma has to be seen rather as a construction, by means of which historically situated (wo)men try to get a glimpse of the truth.

I. EPISTEMOLOGICAL AESTHETICISATION

The current western context which we just evoked is often characterised by means of the term 'aestheticisation'. This notion often ends up as a phrase. Fortunately, Wolfgang Welsch wrote an elucidating survey of the different aspects involved[1]. Welsch defines aestheticisation as the process in which the non-aesthetic is being made aesthetic or conceived of as aesthetic. Or, to put it another way, aestheticisation is the process in which the aesthetic exceeds its bounds and extends into non-aesthetic spheres. The aesthetic concerns the sensible on different levels: sensorial perception, emotions, and more specific, the beautiful, whether or not

---

1. Cf. W. WELSCH, *Ästhetisierungsprozesse: Phänomene, Unterscheidungen, Perspektiven*, in *Deutsche Zeitschrift für Philosophie* 41 (1993) 7-29.

regarding the arts. In line with this complex notion Welsch distinguishes the processes of aestheticisation into different levels, in which various facets of the aesthetic come into play. First of all, there is a surface aestheticisation: the emergence of a 'spectacle society' or '*Erlebnisgesellschaft*', in which aesthetic practices like entertainment, face-lifting and fashion provide the paradigms for the different spheres in society. More fundamentally, there is an in-depth aestheticisation of the material and social world, and of the human subject. Reality is virtualising – it loses objectivity –, and becomes manipulable by means of mass media, genetic technology, etc. The human subject experiences an increasing possibility of constructing its own identity.

According to Welsch all these processes are manifestations of what he indicates as 'epistemological aestheticisation'[2]. This epistemological aestheticisation refers to a fundamental shift in our perception of what truth, knowledge and reality are: the human being discovers itself as an *animal fingens*, and the world as its design. Welsch sketches this growing awareness as a modern trajectory that began with Kant's transcendental philosophy, over Nietzsche's genealogy of knowledge towards the widespread post-modern view that truth always is the product of a constructive activity. This insight is not only widely accepted in the humanities; positive scientists as well understand their approach in similar ways. According to Welsch this awareness is the inevitable condition of truth in the contemporary context; in this light the emergence of fundamentalisms is to interpret as a self-deceiving strategy to deny the constructed character of truth. All attempts to restore a former truth regime negate the process of epistemological aestheticisation, i.e., the fact that 'in modernity truth has become itself an aesthetic category'[3]. An effective critical answer to this aestheticisation cannot subsist in falling back upon the classical notion of truth, but rather in looking for aesthetic criteria[4].

II. AN AESTHETIC TURN WITHIN THEOLOGY
VON BALTHASAR'S *HERRLICHKEIT*: TRUTH, LIGHT AND RESURRECTION

The strength of Welsch' analysis is that it helps to overthrow the impression that a research program entitled 'Orthodoxy: Process and

---

2. *Ibid.*, pp. 19-27.
3. *Ibid.*, p. 27: "Wahrheit in der Moderne selbst zu einer ästhetischen Kategorie geworden ist".
4. Welsch proposes the possibility of interruption and the explicit awareness of blind spots in every construction as criteria. Cf. *Ibid.*, pp. 27-28.

Product' would be anachronistic because the true would have been simply replaced by the aesthetic. His notion of epistemological aestheticisation points to the fact that in contemporary processes of aestheticisation truth nevertheless continues to be produced. Stressing its pertinence, he challenges us to reformulate the question of truth. Welsch points out that systematic reflections on this new shape of truth will have to start from a radically aesthetic perspective. A most pertinent theological starting-point can be offered by the work of Hans Urs von Balthasar (1905-1988) – it is no coincidence that his formerly largely unnoticed books are receiving greater attention today[5]. In 1961 von Balthasar published the first book of his impressive trilogy, which he conceived according to the three *transcendentalia* 'the Beautiful, the Good, and the True'. After the seven volumes of the theological aesthetics – *Herrlichkeit. Eine theologische Ästhetik* (1961-1969) –, von Balthasar wrote the five volumes of the *Theodramatik* (1973-1983), and finished his *magnum opus* with the three volumes of *Theologik* (1985-1987). In taking theological aesthetics as his point of departure, von Balthasar is purposefully inverting the traditional order of the transcendentals (*verum, bonum, pulchrum*): his whole theological project aims at the rediscovery of (divine) beauty.

According to von Balthasar's diagnostic of the cultural context, beauty is endangered by premodern and modern forms of blindness. This blindness has fatal consequences for the question of truth. Not only is the aesthetic, following the traditional philosophical law of convertibility of the transcendentals, an indispensable path to the truth; moreover, the aesthetic highlights a characteristic of theological truth in particular. For von Balthasar the theological question of truth is rooted at the heart of a theological aesthetics, as becomes manifest in his aesthetic reconceptualisation of faith as a 'theological act of perception' (*theologische Wahrnehmungsakt*)[6]. In this theological act of perception, the '*Wahrnehmung*' (perception), as von Balthasar emphasises by explicitly splitting the term, has to be understood as '*Wahr-nehmen*' (to receive the true)[7]. The first volume of his *Herrlichkeit: Eine theologische Ästhetik* is

5. Especially in the Anglo-Saxon world his work generated a remarkable reception. Cf. the collections: L. GARDNER – D. MOSS – B. QUASH – G. WARD, *Balthasar at the End of Modernity*. Forword by F. KERR and afterword by R. WILLIAMS, Edinburgh, T&T Clark, 1999; E.T. OAKES – D. MOSS (eds.), *The Cambridge Companion to Hans Urs von Balthasar*, Cambridge, Cambridge University Press, 2004.

6. H.U. VON BALTHASAR, *Herrlichkeit: Eine theologische Ästhetik*. I. *Schau der Gestalt*, Einsiedeln, Johannes Verlag, 1961, p. 148; English translation: ID., *The Glory of the Lord: A Theological Aesthetics*. I. *Seeing the Form*. Trans. E. Leiva-Merikakis, Edinburgh, T&T Clark, 1982. All translations are mine, unless explicit reference is made to *The Glory of the Lord*.

7. Cf. VON BALTHASAR, *Herrlichkeit* I (n. 6), pp. 22, 26, 144.

subtitled 'Schau der Gestalt' (Seeing the Form): von Balthasar envisions this perception as the seeing of God's Glory in the concrete figure of Jesus Christ.

Von Balthasar's theological aesthetics is focusing on the possibility of the reception of the *splendor veritatis*, the radiating truth. In line with this theological-aesthetic notion of the splendour of the truth, von Balthasar invokes and reinterprets the traditional notion of the truth as light, and its theological analogy, the *lumen fidei*[8]. Von Balthasar recalls that the metaphysical notion of the light of being (*Seinslicht*) endeavoured to account for the event of truth, an event in which reality discloses itself for human reason, which for its part is also conceived of as a light (*lumen intellectus agentis*). More precisely, this light of reason is understood as the human participation in the light of being. Truth happens when the human reason receives the illumination by the light of being. Von Balthasar explains that theologians transposed this metaphysical illuminism into a Trinitarian mode in order to conceptualise the dynamics of faith and revelation. Through Christ, the divine Light shone into the world, and illuminated the human spirit. In this divine light the believer starts to recognize God's love, which is revealed as the ultimate source of being.

Von Balthasar criticises this theological notion of truth as light because it risks overlooking the specificity of the biblical revelation, which stresses that the Word of God reveals itself in concrete history, up to the incarnation in a concrete historical figure, Jesus of Nazareth. Far too often the metaphor of light had been suggesting that the objective mediation of the 'historical facts'[9] may evaporate into an immediateness between God and soul. In such an illuminist doctrine of theological truth the concrete singularity of historical forms is made transparent to deliver its theological contents. Underlying this concept of truth von Balthasar detects a sign theory that presupposes a dualism between the 'signified light' and the 'referring sign', in which the mediation of the sign is considered as secondary, if not superfluous, with regard to the signified[10]. In theological terms this unwarranted leap from the sign to the signified, or, from the historical to the eternal, comes down to a 'desincarnation'[11] of the truth of faith.

Against such tendencies, which he ascribes to both Neo-Platonist (or Gnostic) framework of premodern theologies and modern Kantian theo-

---

8. We base ourselves on von Balthasar's long chapter on the light of faith (*Das Glaubenslicht*), cf. VON BALTHASAR, *Herrlichkeit* I (n. 6), pp. 123-210.

9. *Ibid.*, p. 141: "historische Fakten".

10. *Ibid.*, p. 145: "bezeichnetem innern Licht [...] hinweisendem Zeichen".

11. *Ibid.*, p. 131: "Desinkarnation".

logical epistemologies, von Balthasar brings to the fore the *fact* of the aesthetic, 'das Faktum ästhetischen "Gestaltsehens"'[12]: in the 'perception of a form' (*Wahr-nehmung einer Gestalt*)[13] the beholder encounters a figure in which the signified cannot be separated from the referring sign: 'the content does not lie behind the form, but in it'[14]. By means of the classical aesthetic terms *species et lumen* (or *forma et splendor*), von Balthasar elaborates a notion of light which is inextricably bound up with the figure in which it appears. His theological-aesthetic reformulation of the *lumen fidei* involves the strong affirmation that this light can never be abstracted from the figure of God's incarnation. Where a Platonising illuminist theory looks for the infinite light of truth behind the finite forms in which it is disclosed, von Balthasar, on the contrary, emphasizes that the light of faith is 'Christomorphous' (*christusförmig*)[15]: in this Christomorphous light, form and light are irreducible. The figure of Jesus Christ can never be left behind. For von Balthasar this is specific for the theological notion of truth:

> The whole mystery of Christianity, that which distinguishes it radically from every other religious project, is that the form does not stand in opposition to infinite light, for the reason that God has himself instituted and confirmed such form. And although, being finite and worldly, this form must die just as every other beautiful thing on earth must die, nevertheless it does not go down into the realm of formlessness, leaving behind an infinite tragic longing, but, rather, it rises up to God *as form*, as the form which now, in God himself, has definitively become one with the divine Word and Light which God has intended for and bestowed upon the world. The form itself must participate in the process of death and resurrection, and thus it becomes coextensive with God's Light-Word. This makes the Christian principle the superabundant and unsurpassable principle of every aesthetics; Christianity becomes *the* aesthetic religion *par excellence*[16].

12. *Ibid.*, p. 144.
13. *Ibid.*, p. 144.
14. *Ibid.*, p. 144: "Der Gehalt liegt nicht hinter der Gestalt, sondern in ihr".
15. *Ibid.*, p. 208.
16. VON BALTHASAR, *The Glory of the Lord* I (n. 6), p. 216; ID., *Herrlichkeit* I (n. 6), p. 208: "Das ganze Geheimnis des Christentums, worin es sich radikal von jedem andern Religionsentwurf unterscheidet, ist, dass die Gestalt, weil sie von Gott her gesetzt und bejaht wird, nicht im Gegensatz steht zum unendlichen Licht, und, obwohl sie als endliche und weltliche Gestalt sterben muss, wie alles Schöne sterben muss auf Erden, dennoch nicht ins Gestaltlose untergeht, eine unendliche tragische Sehnsucht hinterlassend, sondern zu Gott hin *als Gestalt* aufersteht, als die Gestalt, die nun endgültig in Gott selber eins geworden ist mit dem göttlichen Wort und Licht, das Gott der Welt zugedacht und geschenkt hat. Die Gestalt selbst macht den Prozess von Tod und Auferstehung mit, und wird so koextensiv dem Licht-Wort-Gottes. Darin wird das Christliche zum überschwenglichen und durch nichts einzuholenden Prinzip jeder Ästhetik, es wird zur schlechthin ästhetische Religion überhaupt".

Remark that the ultimate theological ground for the indissoluble connection between form and light is not the incarnation, but the resurrection of the flesh.

By stressing the inseparable unity between the light of the Absolute and
contingent forms, von Balthasar's theological aesthetics seeks to counter
a widespread miscomprehension of truth and signification, which he considers at the root of the blindness of premodern theologies, designated by
von Balthasar as 'Platonising' or 'Gnosticising'. *Mutatis mutandis*, von
Balthasar applies the same critique on modern theologies: the role of the
Neo-Platonist illuminist sign theory has been taken over by the Kantian
formalism for which all the sensible is nothing but material for the oper-
ations of the transcendental subject. Against the Kantian worldview von
Balthasar refers to the aesthetic experience, which implies 'the aesthetic
experience is the union of the greatest possible concreteness of the individual form and the greatest possible universality of its meaning or of
the epiphany within it of the mystery of Being'[17]. Here, von Balthasar
explicitly invokes Hegel who stresses the unity between the particular
and the universal in the aesthetic phenomenon, but at the same time he
points at the crucial distinction with the latter's position. Contrary to
Hegel, von Balthasar will never accept that the concrete historical figure
would be idealistically transcended in an absolute knowing beyond the
form[18]. Because the aesthetic implies a radical incarnation, it is the pre-
eminent way to understand the figure of Christ which is the *universale
concretissimum*: epiphany is inextricably bound up with a concrete form,
at a particular place and time.

Long before the rise of post-modern thinking, von Balthasar's theological aesthetics rediscovered an important characteristic of theological
truth: the incarnation and resurrection of Jesus Christ imply the irreducible bond between the light of truth and the concrete historical form,
or, put differently, the universal and the particular. This characteristic
aspect of theological truth at the same time offers a criterion of orthodoxy: von Balthasar sees at the root of all major heresies a tendency of
'desincarnation', as has been exemplified in von Balthasar's critique of
the notion of *lumen fidei*[19]. This misunderstanding ends up in substitut-
ing an illusory eternity for the truth in history. Recognition of the aesthetic

---

17. VON BALTHASAR, *The Glory of the Lord* I (n. 6), p. 234; ID., *Herrlichkeit* I (n. 6),
p. 225: "Die ästhetische Erfahrung ist die Einheit einer grösstmöglichen Konkretheit der
Einzelgestalt mit der grösstmöglichen Allgemeinheit ihrer Bedeutung oder der Epiphanie
des Seinsgeheimnisses in ihr".

18. Cf. VON BALTHASAR, *Herrlichkeit* I (n. 6), p. 222.

19. Cf. *Ibid.*, pp. 305. 314-316.

character of revelation is the condition for orthodoxy. This said, one must remind that von Balthasar's focus on the aesthetic, however, does not lead him to an aestheticisation of theology. In terms of form and light, von Balthasar warns for an aestheticising absolutisation of form as well, because in that case form is eclipsing the light of truth and cutting the beautiful from its transcendental interconnectedness with the true[20].

III. THE PHILOSOPHICAL APORIA OF ADORNO'S *ÄSTHETISCHE THEORIE*

Regarding the question of truth, von Balthasar's project offers inspiring impulses; in the end, however, his focus on the Glory of the Lord (*doxa*) seems to outshine the concrete questions of *orthodoxy*. In principle, von Balthasar should focus on the historical, but in practice serious analyses of historical cases are lacking[21]. Maybe this has to do with the fact that in the systematic outline of his theological aesthetics, the theological overdetermines the aesthetic. To counterbalance this tendency, it might be helpful to confront von Balthasar's intuitions with a thoroughgoing philosophical aesthetics, which precisely starts from a historical-materialist point of view.

Such a philosophical sparring partner of von Balthasar's project can be found in the late work of his contemporary Theodor W. Adorno (1903-1969), i.e., the latter's *Ästhetische Theorie* (1970). As a member of the neo-Marxist Frankfurt School, Adorno formulated a severe critique of Modernity, and proposed an aesthetic turn to break through the modern impasse. Adorno's analysis of the Twentieth-Century context – Nazism, capitalism and Stalinism – comes down to a diagnostic of a modern instrumentalisation of reason[22]. This instrumental reason subsists in the

20. Von Balthasar sees this tendency of aestheticisation at work in many modern attempts to rearticulate theology along the lines of the aesthetic, which boils down to a fusion of the theological and the aesthetic, in which the latter overshadows the former. Cf. VON BALTHASAR, *Herrlichkeit* I (n. 6), pp. 96-97.

21. The nearest von Balthasar comes to an actual historically oriented approach is his biblical theology in the last volumes of his *Herrlichkeit*, where he is integrating insights from the historical-critical exegesis. Cf. H.U. VON BALTHASAR, *Herrlichkeit: Eine theologische Ästhetik*. III,2. *Theologie. Alter Bund/Neuer Bund*, Einsiedeln, Johannes Verlag, 1967/1969, passim. Further research should investigate some minor works which predate his trilogy. Cf. ID., *Theologie der Geschichte*, Einsiedeln, Johannes Verlag, 1959 (= Neue Fassung: 1979); ID., *Das Ganze im Fragment: Aspekte der Geschichtstheologie*, Einsiedeln, Johannes Verlag, 1963. In this article, our observations concern the general tone of his *magnum opus*.

22. A brief summary of this analysis can be found in T.W. ADORNO – M. HORKHEIMER, *Dialektik der Aufklärung*, Amsterdam, Querido, 1947, pp. 9-19.

levelling out of all differences, all singularities in function of a false universality, or, in other words, the imposition of a totalitarian identity upon the non-identical. The universal has become totalitarian; Adorno parodies Hegel by stating: *'Das Ganze ist das Unwahre'*[23]. Against this context philosophy has to become critical theory: it has to face the catastrophe, and to speak up for the repressed, the singular particularity, the non-identical. Modern philosophy itself, however, shares in the instrumental logic of identification and universalisation. It is at this point that Adorno turns towards the aesthetic, in line with his claim that authentic modern works of art have become an asylum for the truth[24]. In a context where truth has become an instrumental notion – true is what is efficient, what serves the whole –, for Adorno, truth should be about the salvation of the non-identical, that which can not be identified as part of the whole. Philosophy, as critical theory, has to become aesthetic theory.

Like von Balthasar's theological aesthetics, Adorno's aesthetic theory is looking for the truth in the aesthetic[25]. And like von Balthasar, Adorno stresses the inextricable bond between form and truth content[26]. For Adorno, the work of art, understood as a concrete, historical construction, is the place where the truth content appears. This appearing of the truth has not to be understood in an idealistic way, as if a philosophy of art should unwrap the idea out of the concrete work. The truth content cannot be extracted from its material form. More than von Balthasar, Adorno points to the paradoxical consequences of this position: how can a work of art, a construction made by concrete, historically situated human subjects, be true, i.e., not subjective[27]? The paradox of the aesthetic is: 'how can making let appear that which is not made [truth][28]? One of Adorno's criteria for truth in art is whether or not the work of art covers up its own character as artefact[29]. Only a work of art, which overtly manifests its

23. T.W. ADORNO, *Minima Moralia: Reflexionen aus dem beschädigten Leben*, Frankfurt am Main, Suhrkamp, 1951, p. 55 ("The whole is the untrue").

24. Cf. ADORNO – HORKHEIMER, *Dialektik der Aufklärung* (n. 22), pp. 24-26, 39.

25. Cf. T.W. ADORNO, *Ästhetische Theorie*, Frankfurt am Main, Suhrkamp, 1970, p. 498. "Alle ästhetischen Fragen terminieren in solchen des Wahrheitsgehalts der Kunstwerke: ist das, was ein Werk in seiner spezifischen Gestalt objektiv an Geist in sich trägt, wahr?". If the English version is used, we refer to: T.W. ADORNO, *Aesthetic Theory*, trans. R. Hullot-Kentor, Minneapolis, MN, University of Minneapolis Press, 1997 (= *AET*).

26. Cf. ADORNO, *Ästhetische Theorie* (n. 25), pp. 124-125, 138.

27. Cf. *Ibid.*, pp. 99, 121, 198-200.

28. *Ibid.*, p. 164: "wie kann Machen ein nicht Gemachtes [das Wahre] erscheinen lassen?".

29. Here one should further investigate Adorno's interpretation of the aesthetic problem of semblance, cf. L. ZUIDERVAART, *Aesthetic Theory: The Redemption of Illusion*, Cambridge, MA, MIT press, 1991, pp. 178-216.

constructed character, its historicity, can be true. As such, Adorno's aesthetic theory does not only elaborate the awareness that 'truth exists only
as that which has become [*Gewordenes*]'[30] – truth as the product of a
process –, but also that truth precisely has to be found in this 'having
become' (*Gewordensein*) – in its being 'processual' (*prozessual*)[31].
Adorno's claim is not only that truth has a history, but that history has a
truth. The truth of an aesthetic product subsists in the historical process
of its production.

A similar radicality can be found in the way in which Adorno's aesthetics links the particular and the universal[32]. For Adorno, art is the
attempt to save the particular, the non-identical, over against the mastery
of the hegemonic universal. This salvation of the particular cannot lie in
a Hegelian reconciliation of the universal and the particular. In the work
of art the relation between the universal and the particular is insolubly
conflictual, because the relation between both terms is inverted. The universal is no longer the primary instance that could be imposed from outside upon the particular; the work of art is thoroughly singular, even idio-
syncratic, and precisely at the heart of this particularity truth has to be
found. This focus does not simply particularise the truth – Adorno's alternative to an oppressive universalism is not a relativistic nominalism[33].
Adorno does not give up the aspect of universality in truth, and especially not in reference to the work of art. As such, the work of art is a
'tour de force'[34], and, given the modern context, more and more appearing as an impossible undertaking.

Adorno is more radical than von Balthasar in pointing to the paradoxical character of the aesthetic. How can one claim that the singular has
any other meaning than its being just one more singular? In order to prevent his theory from ending up in pure paradoxes, Adorno appropriates
a notion of Leibniz' monadology to elucidate the interconnection between
on the one hand, singularity, historicity, and on the other hand, universality. The monad delivers a structure to evoke how in the singular, precisely in its irreducible singularity, a universal meaning can appear. The
monadological way to come to the universal is to follow the '*principium
individuationis*'[35] all the way through: the work of art comes to its truth

---

30. ADORNO, *Aesthetic Theory* (n. 25), p. 3; ID., *Ästhetische Theorie* (n. 25), p. 12:
"Wahrheit ist einzig als Gewordenes".
31. Cf. ADORNO, *Ästhetische Theorie* (n. 25), pp. 262-269.
32. Cf. *Ibid.*, pp. 147, 197-198, 299-301, 521-523.
33. Cf. *Ibid.*, p. 299.
34. *Ibid.*, p. 162.
35. *Ibid.*, pp. 270, 301.

as exactly at the point where it is the most individual, it becomes universal. Adorno himself is aware of the problematic nature of his argument[36]. He uses the structure of the monad as a model to think the truth of art, although he considers Leibniz' rationalistic metaphysics as an outdated solipsism[37]. Notwithstanding the fact that Adorno drops in this recycling operation the idea of a 'pre-established harmony'[38] and that he breaks the solipsistic impasse by pointing to the way in which the materiality of the concrete historical form is always already perforating the self-enclosing tendency of the work of art, his suggestive passages on the aesthetic monad are not convincing[39]. In a way it only strengthens the paradoxicality of the aesthetic when Adorno states for example that art contains truth *'trotz und wegen* ihres monadologischen Wesens'[40] (*'in spite of and thanks to* its monadological nature'). As Adorno himself admits, 'it could be objected that a residual dogmatic trust is operative here [...] To that the reply is that the monads, which artworks are, lead by way of their own principle of particularization to the universal'[41]. Adorno replies in a tautological way: he simply repeats the definition of the monad, and seems to end up in a vicious circle.

Besides the vain invocation of the monad[42], Adorno's philosophical perplexity concerning the question of truth (particularity-universality) in art, also comes to the fore in his attempts to found the constitutive relation between historical form and truth content. It is striking that at these moments he has to introduce theological concepts like 'epiphany', or even 'revelation'. Adorno hastens himself to add that he is using them in a

36. Cf. *Ibid.*, p. 268: "Die These vom monadologischen Charakter der Werke ist so wahr wie problematisch".

37. Cf. *Ibid.*, p. 70: "Kunst ist die geschichtsphilosophische Wahrheit des an sich unwahren Solipsismus".

38. Cf. *Ibid.*, p. 420.

39. Maybe that is one of the reasons why this very complex notion has been overlooked in the reception of Adorno's *Ästhetische Theorie*. Only F. JAMESON delivers a beginning of an analysis of the monad in Adorno's text. Cf. *Late Marxism: Adorno, or, The Persistence of the Dialectic*, London, Verso, 1990, pp. 185-188.

40. ADORNO, *Ästhetische Theorie* (n. 25), p. 289.

41. ADORNO, *Aesthetic Theory* (n. 25), p. 181; ID., *Ästhetische Theorie* (n. 25), p. 270: "Eingewandt könnte werden, dabei sei ein Rest dogmatischen Vertrauens wirksam. [...] Zu erwidern ist, dass die Monaden, welche die Kunstwerke sind, durch ihr eigenes Prinzip der Besonderung aufs Allgemeine führen".

42. The fact that Adorno does not manage to corroborate his intuition on the monadological structure of the work of art, does not mean that this concept is worthless altogether. Further research could be done regarding Walter BENJAMIN's reinvention of the monad (cf. *Ursprung des deutschen Trauerspiels*, in W. BENJAMIN – R. TIEDEMANN – H. SCHWEPPENHÄUSER [eds.], *Gesammelte Schriften*. I.1., Frankfurt am Main, Suhrkamp, 1980, pp. 203-430 [originally from 1928]), which directly influenced Adorno, and also Gilles DELEUZE's Leibniz-interpretation. Cf. *Le pli: Leibniz et le baroque*, Paris, Minuit, 1988.

secularised way. Regarding 'epiphany', for example, this secularisation lies in Adorno's emphasis that the absolute does not come immediately in the present[43]. Highly illustrative is Adorno sketch of the difficult position of the work of art which has to avoid pretending to be a revelation, and at the same time cannot wipe out the last trace of revelation without effacing itself altogether[44]. Adorno's aesthetic theory encounters a further theological limit category when he tries to articulate the truth of the work of art facing the fact that all Beauty must die: he admits that his reliance on its fragile historicity in the end only makes sense in light of the idea of the resurrection of the flesh[45].

IV. THEOLOGY AS AESTHETIC THEORY?

Our brief sketch of the aesthetics of von Balthasar and Adorno regarding the question of truth, brings to the fore a surprising analogy between two influential twentieth century thinkers who in theological circles are generally considered to be each other's opposites[46]. This convergence comes only to the fore after a *close reading*: at first sight von Balthasar's notion of truth as light, for instance, could appear as exactly what Adorno rejects as a 'theological doctrine'. Adorno recurrently associates theology with an idealist understanding of the symbol as the immediately transparent synthesis of the universal and particular[47]. Moreover, contrary to von Balthasar's notion of light, one could pose Adorno's emphasis on the constitutive obscurity of the work of art[48]. A closer look, however, shows that von Balthasar redefines the light of truth as a 'Christomorphous light'. As his theological aesthetics takes its point of departure in the kenotic figure of Jesus Christ, he stresses the historicity of this figure. Moreover, this kenosis links the theological aesthetics, in a striking convergence with Adorno, with a constitutive darkness[49]. To read Adorno

43. Cf. ADORNO, *Ästhetische Theorie* (n. 25), pp. 125, 159.
44. Cf. *Ibid.*, p. 162.
45. Cf. *Ibid.*, pp. 48.410. For a lucid comment on this surprising outcome, cf. G. STEUNEBRINK, *Kunst, utopie en werkelijkheid: Adorno's esthetica en metafysica tegen de achtergrond van Kant en Hegel*, Tilburg, Tilburg University Press, 1991, pp. 477-482.
46. For a clear sketch of the reception of the relation between Adorno and von Balthasar, cf. U. ENGEL, *Umgrenzte Lehre: Zur Praxis einer politisch-theologischen Ästhetik im Anschluss an Peter Weiss' Romantrilogie "Die Ästhetik des Widerstands"* (Religion, Geschichte, Gesellschaft: fundamentaltheologische Studien, 9), Münster, LIT, 1998, pp. 9-123.
47. Cf. ADORNO, *Ästhetische Theorie* (n. 25), pp. 147-148, 159, 204.
48. Cf. *Ibid.*, pp. 65-66, 81, 204.
49. Cf. VON BALTHASAR, *Herrlichkeit* I (n. 6), pp. 619-623.

as a parallel would enable us to elaborate von Balthasar's theological aesthetic understanding of kenosis as historicity, in a more concrete and radical way than von Balthasar did himself[50].

Beyond these inspiring perspectives for the von Balthasar research, the relevance for our research program lies not so much in the fact that von Balthasar and Adorno, decades ago, formulated intuitions that now belong to mainstream thinking – and which form the a priori of our research –, but that they both get into philosophical troubles when they try to found their fundamental option in a systematic way. It is significant that two great thinkers on the aesthetic and truth have to reinvoke ancient categories – the *transcendentalia*[51], respectively, the monad – in order to link the aesthetic and truth. This indicates the highly problematic nature of what today appears as postmodern axioms on the particular and the universal, on truth and historicity. In contemporary philosophy notions as the transcendentals or the monad are mostly regarded as superseded[52]; in fact Adorno himself considered the monad as superseded, but apparently saw no alternative to tackle the question in a philosophical way: how can one claim that the truth appears *trotz und wegen*, in spite of *and* thanks to the historical particularity?

One can reject Adorno's solution, but not the paradox. It seems that the only ground for the current philosophical consensus on truth and particularity is what von Balthasar already indicated as the bare *fact* of the aesthetic. Up to a certain extent the return towards the religious within contemporary philosophy[53], can be understood as a repetition of Adorno's philosophical perplexity, when he had to fall back upon the theological notion of the resurrection in order to elucidate the claim that truth is *de facto* found in historical singularity. Our proposal to use aesthetic theory

---

50. From a different perspective, an impetus for such an interpretation has been undertaken by S. VAN ERP, *The Art of Theology: Hans Urs von Balthasar's Theological Aesthetics and the Foundations of Faith* (Studies in Philosophical Theology, 25), Leuven, Peeters, 2004.

51. On von Balthasar's use of the transcendentals, cf. M. SAINT-PIERRE, *Beauté, bonté, vérité chez Hans Urs von Balthasar*, Paris, Cerf, 1998. Strangely enough, this extensive study does not question the relevance of the transcendentals, it just takes it for granted.

52. In this respect it is significant that in the research program '*Transcendence and Transcendentals*' (1999-2003), at the University of Tilburg, the *transcendentalia* are, from the outset, conceived of as a theological notion, not a philosophical one. Cf. W. LOGISTER – I. LAMERS – F. MAAS – M. DE HAARDT – N. SCHREURS, *Echt waar: Over theologische waarheid*, Budel, Damon, 2003.

53. Cf. D. JANICAUD, *Le tournant théologique de la phénoménologie française*, Combas, Éditions de l'Éclat, 1991; J. DERRIDA – G. VATTIMO, et al., *La religion*, Paris, Seuil, 1996; for a critical approach of such an enterprise, see also F. DEPOORTERE's contribution to this collection, *Gianni Vattimo's Concept of Truth and Its Consequences for Christianity*.

as a model for systematic theology risks being caught in a vicious circle, as we find that, inversely, theology for its part already serves as a model for aesthetic theory. As, in its post-modern search for truth in the aesthetic, theology is lacking a philosophical framework, it is thrown upon itself. The question then is what it means that both Adorno and von Balthasar point towards the resurrection of the flesh – not the incarnation, as one would expect – as the ultimate foundation of a theological (and philosophical?) understanding of truth.

yves.demaeseneer@theo.kuleuven.be   Yves DE MAESENEER

PART TWO

THE SECOND AVENUE OF RESEARCH

THEOLOGY IN CONFRONTATION WITH MODERNITY

A DIMLY LEGIBLE PALIMPSEST

THE VICTORIAN SAGES AND GERUNDIAL HISTORIOGRAPHY

I. INTRODUCTION

Thomas Carlyle, the Victorian historian and moral philosopher, described history as a "dimly legible palimpsest" that was continually scraped and repainted by the artist-historian to display new insights and images all of which built upon what had gone before. The term palimpsest refers to a surface that has been written upon or inscribed several times, the previous text, texts or images having been imperfectly erased and remaining, therefore partly visible. This layering suggests both personal and collective history, our conditioning, hidden secrets, and hidden intentions. This paper is conceived in three parts that form a kind of palimpsest of their own. The first examines the state of history and theology with their distinctive methodologies in light of postmodern embarrassments. The second examines the thought of the Victorian sage, John Henry Newman, in his proposal of a type of "gerundial" historiography that may assist this embarrassment. The third section asks a series of questions that may be instrumental in considering new means of doing theology and history in a postmodern context.

II. THE STATE OF METHOD

One of the most significant embarrassments to contemporary discourse, located within the landscape of postmodernism, is the lingering spectre of method. As William Placher notes in his landmark work, *Unapologetic Theology*, "A good many people – myself included – have encouraged theologians to abandon their preoccupation with methodology and get on with the business of really doing theology"[1]. It would seem that all theology after Plantinga's critique of "Reason and Belief in God" must take into account the paradigmatic nature of postmodernisms and their relative epistemologies[2]. Ronald Theimann, for example, has argued

---

1. W.C. PLACHER, *Unapologetic Theology*, Louisville, KY, John Knox Press, 1989, p. 7.
2. See A. PLATINGA, *Reason and Belief in God*, in ID. – N. WOLTERSTORFF (eds.), *Faith*

that most of modern theology is burdened with establishing foundations, often rather tentative ones, related to Kantian, Hegalian or Heideggerian paradigms that are only accidentally related to Christian revelation[3]. Nancey Murphy proposes that both conservative and liberal thinkers share this failing of theology in its new context[4]. Regardless of how the critique is framed, the practice of theology, history, religious studies, and, indeed, any discipline has in the past two hundred years increasingly become immured by methodologies. The techné of history and theology, to use the two most applicable examples, began as a vehicle for discovering "truth" (von Ranke and Troeltsch). The positivist question itself is predicated on a belief in the final outcome that truths, truth, or even Truth can be discovered. Methodologies provide rules, systems of analysis, skeletons upon which to hang the sinews of a discipline. Methodologies are embarrassed, however, by phenomena that are inconvenient and do not splice easily into the established apparatuses of the methodology. Such phenomena invariably get exiled to the hinterlands of a discipline. Therefore, methodologies may betray the tendency to "whitewash" the complexities of the object of study. In such instances, methodologies are forced into the corner of delimitation, as Richard Bernstein has observed[5]. Ironically it can be the case that methodologies come to limit the very expansiveness they sought initially to explore. History or theology *becomes* that which the methodology can determine. If it is not observable through the lens of a particular techné, it is not history; it is not theology, or whatever. Thus, modern historical and theological discourse has painted itself into a methodological corner. In the attempt to illuminate the landscape of knowledge, increasingly elementary drawings have been sought with the detrimental effect of a loss of confidence in either the truth-value or relevance of academic discourse. The historical-critical methodology, the mainstay of modernist disciplines, has proved either inadequate or archaic in a postmodern reconceptualisation of thought. The use of differing methodologies with differing prejudices may limit the degree to which interdisciplinary engagement is possible. In a post-

and Rationality: Reason and Belief in God, South Bend, IN, University of Notre Dame Press, 1983.

3. R.F. THIEMANN, *Revelation and Theology: The Gospel as Narrated Promise*, South Bend, IN, University of Notre Dame Press, 1985.

4. N. MURPHY, *Beyond Liberalism and Fundamentalism: How Modern and Postmodern Philosophy Set the Theological Agenda*, Valley Forge, PA, Trinity Press International, 1996.

5. See R. BERNSTEIN, *Beyond Objectivism and Relativism: Science, Hermeneutics and Praxis*, Philadelphia, PA, University of Pennsylvania Press, 1985.

modern context, methodology is not as much embarrassed as embarrassing. The eschewal of foundations precludes the preconception or prejudices that methodology entails. Phenomenologists, beginning, it might be postulated with the Victorian sages, have observed that human beings do not think in linear and conceptually circumvented, two-dimensional ways. The Wittgenstinian web has replaced the Comtian line. In the postmodern context, the simplicity of the object has been deemed illusory or eminently deconstructable in light of radical subjectivity. Truth in the postmodern context is constructive and relational. Here may be invoked the work of Gadamer, drawing on the Aristotelian notion of *phronesis*, or the understanding of tacit judgements found in the work of Michael Polanyi, or the, as yet, un-mined insights of Donald Mackinnon[6]. However, the postmodern reconceptualization, with its experimental methodology does not *seem* adequate to establish hierarchical principles that *seem* necessary to undergird religious experience. Such reconceptualization plays havoc with traditional religious notions such as orthodoxy. Thus, postmodern theologies have disseminated into either a sacrifice of rationality in narrative, reconstructed fideisms or a sacrifice of mystery in a god conceived without being. In a postmodern grammatical aesthetic, substantives are as inadequate as verbals; therefore, nothing is finally, or purposefully, or relevantly said. What is needed to relieve these problems seems to be something between substantives and verbals, a kind of "gerundial" methodology that seeks truth in a "saying and unsaying" of questions within the ongoing context of a narrative. A gerundial methodology has the potential to re-establish the complexity of discursive thought through the postulation of a kind of palimpsest, a many-layered and historical narrative that resonates with the epistemological experience of a postmodern sensibility. However, in this gerundial methodology, the relativism of deconstruction is overcome by the foundational principle of the *necessity* of saying and unsaying so that the gerundial imperative becomes the source of "objective" knowledge, understood in the Christian context as the divine reality or the Incarnational principle. Knowledge, in such an environment is three-dimensional, leaping off (and seeping into) the canvas of academia to (re)-animate the lives of humans being in via media. It is Wisdom understood methodologically, and such was the method of wisdom espoused in the work of the Victorian sages.

6. See H.-G. GADAMER, *Truth and Method*, trans. J. Weinsheimer and D.G. Marshall, New York, Crossroad, [2]1991. The insight of Polanyi: M. POLANYI, *Personal Knowledge*, Chicago, IL, University of Chicago Press, 1962. For Mackinnon, see, D. MACKINNON, *Borderlands of Theology and Other Essays*, London, Lutterworth, 1968.

III. Revisiting the Victorian Sages

In light of the present methodological quagmire, the contemporary lover of wisdom might profitably turn to the work of the Victorian sages. The Victorian sages were a group of highly-respected nineteenth-century British thinkers whose work shares a common set of goals and "methods" although ideologically they were often radically opposed to one another. The commonalities of their thought have been elucidated in the now-classic work of John Holloway[7]. Although some of the sages, such as Newman were orthodox Christians, others, like George Eliot were self-professed agnostics, while still others (e.g., Thomas Hardy and Matthew Arnold) were antagonistic to religion. The cohesion in their work was not ideological but methodological. For example, all of the sages were pre-eminently concerned with history, which they envisioned as having four distinct characteristics. First, history is complex. Second, historical development cannot be understood linearly. Third, history inculcates an object (although this object was understood in different ways for the different sages). Fourth, there is a moral imperative in history that prohibits it being understood as an objective science, that is, history and historiography have consequences. Bearing in mind these prolegomenae, the sages eschewed the positivism and the simplistic epistemologies of the day in favour of what might be termed a gerundial methodology that sought Wisdom instead of knowledge. This gerundial methodology was accomplished by a number of techniques including the particular use of language[8]. They also employed a variety of literary genre not confining themselves to academic modes of discourse but also using poetry, drama and the novel to express their ideas. All of the sages proceeded from a proto-phenomenological perspective, that is, they sought to address central questions in the way in which people understood them, in a common-sensical way. Here they stood more in line with philosophers such as Thomas Reid than with the classical empirical line beginning with Locke. Rather than solving problems, their work intended to invite readers into a gerundial process of seeking depth by asking and re-asking central questions. In this way they anticipated the work of Gabriel Marcel

---

7. See J. Holloway, *The Victorian Sage*, London, Macmillan, 1953. Other considerations of the Victorian sages and their various approaches to the questions of their time include: G.P. Landow, *Elegant Jeremiahs: The Sage from Carlyle to Mailer*, Ithaca, NY, Cornell University Press, 1986. See also L.H. Peterson, *Sage Writing*, in H.F. Tucker (ed.), *A Companion to Victorian Literature and Culture* (Blackwell Companions to Literature and Culture), Oxford, Blackwell, 1999.

8. See D. Robinson, *The Mother of Wisdom: Exploring the Parabolic Imperative in the Early Works of John Henry Newman*, in *Louvain Studies* 27 (2002) 153-170.

with his distinction between problem and mystery[9]. Their pre-eminent concern with the nature of narrative connects their work with contemporary thinkers like Paul Ricœur, Frederick Olafson and Arthur Danto[10]. Their emphasis on the centrality of living issues places them in dialogue with thinkers like Dilthey.

1. *Newman as Historian*

The gerundial methodology is pre-eminent in the work of John Henry Newman. One of the principle ways that Newman undertook theological discourse was from the perspective of history. As he clearly demonstrates in *The Arians of the Fourth Century* Newman uses historical discourse as a tool to entertain discussion of matters related not only to the ancient Church, but also to the contemporary Church. Newman employs a historical guise for writing what might be termed the parable of theology. However, Newman's idea of historiography is subtler than that of genre alone. Newman approaches the question of history with the attitude inherent in sage discourse. The sage thought it not only desirable, but appropriate to move easily between history and polemic between theoretical considerations and applications. This multivalency of approach was indicative of the sage outlook. Newman's approach may offer something by way of critique to modern historiographical methodologies and clues to the contemporary crisis not only in history but in other disciplines as well including systematic theology.

2. *Newman and History in* Essays Critical and Historical

Newman's views of church history are presented in the essay/review of the first edition of Henry Hart Milman's *History of Christianity*, now found in Newman's *Essays Critical and Historical*[11]. Milman's work represented the advance of a more scientific spirit in historical inquiries, the balance of which Newman was to take stock over the coming years[12].

---

9. G. MARCEL, *The Mystery of Being: Reflection and Mystery*, South Bend, IN, St. Augustine's Press, 1960.

10. Consider Ricœur's insight about the conflation of fiction and history in P. RICŒUR, *Time and Narrative*, trans. K. Blamey and D. Pellauer, Chicago, IL, University of Chicago Press, 1990. For Olafson see F.A. OLAFSON, *The Dialectic of Action*, in G. ROBERTS (ed.), *The History and Narrative Reader*, London, Routledge, 2001, chapter 5. For Danto see, A.C. DANTO, *Narration and Knowledge*, New York, Columbia University Press, 1985.

11. J.H. NEWMAN, *Essays Critical and Historical*, Vol. II, London, Longmans-Green and Co., 1868, pp. 187-249.

12. See I. KER, *John Henry Newman: A Biography*, Oxford, Oxford University Press, 1988, p. 204.

However, even at this early stage, Newman found it necessary to critique Milman's understanding of the philosophical detachment of the historian.

What is Milman's methodological starting point? "Mr. Milman loves to regard the whole Christian history as much as possible as a thing of earth"[13]. Milman's first mistake, is that he has failed to comprehend or at least chosen to bracket the central insight of Christianity in that "the whole system of Revelation may be viewed in various, nay antagonist aspects"[14]. The essence of Christianity is a gerundial parabolic tension between the divine and the human, the earthly and the heavenly. In another context, Newman described the working method of any discipline, but especially religious study as a "method of antagonism".

By this *method of antagonism* we steady our minds, not so as to reach their object, but to point them in the right direction; as in an algebraical process we might add and subtract in series, approximating little by little, by saying and unsaying, to a positive result[15].

In Newman's opinion, the methodological forthrightness and linearity of a position such as Milman's (contemplating the Church and the event of the Incarnation that the Church replicates is possible from the vantage point of the earthly or the human dimension) is not *necessarily* a hazard. The problem lies in viewing it *solely* from that position, or unduly spiritualizing the heavenly, of saying without unsaying. In other words, Newman is anticipating in Milman's method, with its purposeful bracketing of divinity, the possibility of misunderstanding the reality of the thing precisely *as a whole*. Newman claims: "The Christian history is 'an outward visible sign of an inward spiritual grace:' whether the sign can be satisfactorily treated separate from the thing signified is another matter"[16]. For Newman, the history of the Church and Church history are sacramental in the way the Church itself is sacramental and in the way that it inculcates the source of sacramentality, the Incarnate Christ. The matter and form of the sacrament cannot be segregated without significant damage to the other element. The saying must accompany the unsaying. The gerundial tension between signifier and signified is made real by the institution of both Church and sacrament by Christ their source. "Christianity has an external aspect and an internal; it is human without, divine within"[17]. The truth of sacrament, Church, the Incarnation as doc-

13. NEWMAN, *Essays* (n. 11), pp. 188-189.
14. *Ibid.*, p. 188.
15. H.M. DE ARCHAVAL – J.D. HOLMES (eds.), *The Theological Papers of John Henry Newman on Faith and Certainty*, Oxford, Oxford University Press, 1976, p. 102.
16. NEWMAN, *Essays* (n. 11), p. 188.
17. *Ibid.*, p. 189.

trine, and history come not from the elucidation of any aspect but by the maintenance of the gerundial imperative that gives life to all by virtue of the life bestowed by the Source.

To attempt to touch the human element without handling also the divine, we may fairly deem unreal, extravagant, and sophistical; we may feel the two to be one integral whole, differing merely in aspect, not in fact: we may consider that a writer has not mastered his own idea who resolves to take liberties with the body, and yet not insult the animating soul[18].

The charge of sophistry is precisely the charge Newman continually references in his work against those who claim the finality of any understandings and any "solutions" that resolve or lessen the tension in the midst of the real. Such sophistry may be unintentional. Certainly Newman would never impute an impure or rationalistic motive to any clergyman (Newman was still an Anglican when he wrote the review). However, there is a fundamental problem in Milman's attempt to "write *rather as an historian than as a religious instructor*"[19]. Thus, Newman takes to task the "pure, impartial and dispassionate tone" Milman claims to be adopting. On this claim alone, Newman offers his critique.

Newman's starting point is a restatement of the gerundial imperative as divine warrant. "We maintain then, as we have already said, that Christianity, nor Christianity only, but all God's dealings with His creatures, have two aspects, one external, one internal"[20]. Newman equates the nature of God with the expression of that nature in the Incarnation. The divine nature is replicated in every aspect of creation, that is, "What one of the earliest Fathers says of its highest ordinance, is true of it altogether, and of all other divine dispensations: they are twofold, 'having one part heavenly, and one part earthly'"[21]. For Newman this is the indicator of the "higher system of things". The intricacies of this system are not reducible to simple observations of cause and effect. They are like the actions of the mind and all discourse, as actions of the mind, must remain authentic to their source and inspiration. While our knowledge of things may be narrow, that knowledge cannot be construed as indicative of the whole. The reality cannot be reduced to aspects. "This is the law of Providence here below; it works beneath a veil, and what is visible in its course does but shadow out at most, and sometimes obscures and dis-

18. *Ibid.*, p. 188.
19. Milman's words quoted by Newman.
20. NEWMAN, *Essays* (n. 11), p. 191.
21. *Ibid.*, p. 191.

guises what is invisible"[22]. While the mind always ponders at any given moment the aspect, the reality is nevertheless implicitly present beneath the veil. The scientist may describe but the sage must reveal, building up the reality by layers of image and discourse like the scrapings of a palimpsest, saying and unsaying. The historian as sage cannot be confined to methodologies that present a narrow lie masquerading as the truth. Historians, "cannot set limits either to the extent or to the minuteness of this wonderful web of causes and effects, in which all we see is involved. It reaches to the skies; it penetrates into our very thoughts, habits, and will"[23].

Newman then penetrates into the heart of his argument. The gerundial way is not something extraordinary to the nature of things. If God has created and remains active in creation, then, "He must be acting by means of its ordinary system, or by quickening, or as it were, stimulating its powers, or by superseding or interrupting it; in other words, by means of what is called nature"[24]. Otherwise it must be assumed with the deists that "He has simply retired, and has left the world ordinarily to itself, – content with having originally imposed on it certain general laws, which will for the most part work out the ends which He contemplates"[25]. God is not only origin but sustainer, and the nature of the creation reflections the nature of the divine. The task of those who describe (within the context of the creation) is to describe its nature. God is always present in a pervasive way in the physical world. "He is acting through, with, and beneath those physical, social, and moral laws, of which our experience informs us"[26]. For Newman, this is the essence of Christianity in that it is the teaching of its central principle. Furthermore, as the principle was articulated in the Word as particular and personal, so it remains in its articulation in the observable things around us. For Newman, this complexity is the ordinary course of things, and any scholar or historian who sets out to describe anything must be ready to hint at this gerundial reality. In fact, it is the maintenance of this gerundial nature in the presentation that is the qualifier for the satisfactory nature of the presentation.

It is not too much to say that this is the one great rule on which the Divine Dispensations with mankind have been and are conducted, that the visible world is the instrument, yet the veil, of the world invisible, – the veil, yet still partially the symbol and index: so that all that exists or hap-

22. *Ibid.*
23. *Ibid.*, p. 193.
24. *Ibid.*
25. *Ibid.*
26. *Ibid.*

pens visibly, conceals and yet suggests, and above all subserves, a system of persons, facts, and events beyond itself[27].

For Newman, this is especially true of Christianity. He uses language such as "tends", "springs", "ever-issuing", "round about", "passing on" to bring together *in motion* matters of faith and sight. "What is called and seems to be cause and effect, is rather an order of sequence, and does not preclude, nay, perhaps implies, the presence of unseen spiritual agency as its real author"[28]. This is the basis of Christianity, it is enshrined in its two principle manifestations, the tension inherent ritual and the interpretation of scripture. Newman refers to it as an "animating principle". It gives life by the sacramental principle in the former and the mystical principle in the latter. For the historian, "All that is seen, – the world, the Bible, the Church, the civil polity, and man himself, – are types, and, in their degree and place, representatives and organs of an unseen world, truer and higher than themselves"[29]. There is no disciple, no faculty, no life that can be interpreted, reported or narrated outside of this Incarnational gerundial imperative. History is therefore simultaneously two-fold. The task of the historian is the maintenance of parable.

Newman then turns to the particular methodology of Church history. From appearances, that is, from a superficial aspect, Christianity may appear to be a type of those religions that surround it. It may appear to be describable in the same sort of terms by which other phenomena are described. Newman adds, ironically for 1841: "We may write its history, and make it look as like those which were before or contemporary with it, as a man is like a monkey"[30]. Newman then adds, rather sardonically: "Now we come at length to Mr. Milman: this is what he has been doing"[31]. Milman's mistakes are like the following: (1) Milman has mistaken a contemplation of external appearances from what is end, to the point that it represents, "a denial of what is inside"[32]. (2) Milman ignores or brackets the Almighty in history and thereby commits the ultimate "sin" of the historian; he portrays as real what is in fact, not real. (3) He has assumed an "impartial" position, professing to be only interested in what is demonstrable in an objective way through the evidence, when in fact, his position is just as ideological as that of any believer. (4) In committing these errors he has inscribed a position which is *de facto* hereti-

27. *Ibid.*
28. *Ibid.*, p. 194.
29. *Ibid.*
30. *Ibid.*, p. 197.
31. *Ibid.*
32. *Ibid.*, p. 198.

cal. "Little as Mr. Milman may be aware of it, that this external contemplation of Christianity necessarily leads a man to write as a Socinian
or Unitarian *would* write, whether he will or not"[33].

Accordingly, Mr. Milman, speaking mainly of what is externally seen,
will be led to speak almost in a Sabellian fashion, as if denying, because
not stating, the specific indwelling which Scripture records, and the
Church teaches. Hence the general *effect* of Mr. Milman's work, we cannot deny, though we wish to give as little offence as possible, is heretical[34].

The interesting point here is that orthodoxy is not discerned by virtue
of any of the findings; although, the findings will invariably replicate in
their heterodoxy the method. It is the method that is heretical, the process
that is unorthodox. The Church historian may be heterodox not according
to any positive statements that he makes, but according to his method.
Orthodoxy is carried in the process rather than in the product, although the
product too is orthodox or heterodox insofar as the process is one or the
other. Orthodoxy, as was demonstrated in *The Arians of the Fourth Century*, is contained in the gerundial imperative. Any product that does not
represent a faithful replication of the maintenance of the gerundial imperative is not orthodox. Milman is a heretic because he wishes to objectify
a divine reality. This orthodoxy or heterodoxy again is predicated on its
faithful representation of the source of inquiry, the Incarnation.

We all know it to be an essential and most practical doctrine that the
Person of Christ is Divine, and that *into* His Divine Personality He has
taken human nature; or, in other words, the Agent, Speaker, Sufferer,
Sacrifice, Intercessor, Judge, is God, though God in our flesh; not man
with a presence of Divinity. The latter doctrine is Sabellianism, Nestori-
anism, and Socinianism[35].

If Newman discounts a false "objectivity" in the historical enterprise,
he also rejects any attempts at generalizing the Christian message through
outward comparisons. Such an approach is mistaken, in Newman's opinion, because it views, "the doctrines of Christianity as a sort of conde-
scension, and looks upon its outward and secular aspect as its glory"[36].
In Newman's mind, this approach, far from being "candid and dispassionate", betrays a wrong-headed secularity that refuses to acknowledge
the complexities which reality betrays, either as manifested in history or
in the processes of individual minds. In this, "Mr. Milman's language

33. *Ibid.*, p. 203.
34. *Ibid.*, p. 204.
35. *Ibid.*
36. *Ibid.*, p. 210.

certainly implies that calmness and dispassionateness and an absence of prejudice are shown in being able to hear and to repeat, without wincing, as regards our great Benefactor, the profane things which infidels and scorners say of Him"[37]. False attempts at objective historiography present in fact the reverse of objectivity and dispassion and present calumny against the reality of the thing considered. Such a misguided adherence to a fact-based historiography is impossible in Newman's estimation because the method:

> ... does make a *theory* of the facts which he records, and such a theory as unhappily implies that they belong mainly to that external system of things of which he writes, and must be directly referred to visible causes and measured by intelligible principles. His mode of writing does not merely pass over, but actually denies the existence and presence among us of that higher and invisible system of which we have spoken above[38].

All historical objectifiers, while professing to keep to the facts, are in fact professing a theory and the theory they profess is a lie because it falsely represents the nature of history. In Newman's opinion, there is no separation of history from theology. There can be none. All history is theandric because history is inundated with the gerundial imperative. There is no legitimate separation of the historian from the religious instructor as Milman wishes to maintain. Furthermore, the profession of such a project, detached historiography, is irresponsible because all discourse has consequences and as far as history leads readers to consider as real what is unreal, that is the easy (or possible) delineation between the sacred and the secular, then there is a moral imperative by which it cannot recognize "the rights of philosophy to profess opinions without incurring their responsibilities, to have a sort of *lasciar passare*, which enables it to introduce bag and baggage free of examination; or that it lives on some high cliff, or some remote watch-tower, and is able thence to contemplate with the poet the sea of human opinion, "alterius spectare laborem"; and in a pure ethereal region to discern Christianity abstracted from all religion, and to gauge it without molestation by principles simply incommensurable with its own"[39].

3. *Newman and Sage History*

Like the other Victorian sages, Newman sees history as having four distinct characteristics. First, history, like all truth is complex. It is com-

37. *Ibid.*, p. 213.
38. *Ibid.*, p. 214.
39. *Ibid.*, p. 217.

posed of a matrix of events, feelings, personalities and influences that are untraceable in that they are indiscernible by means of simple analyses of cause and effect. The task of the Church historian or theologian is not to describe aspects of Church life and activity, but rather to present the reality of Christianity from the standpoint of the Incarnation. The historian must employ a method that replicates the reality that she is ultimately historicizing. In other words, the historian must use a gerundial method in that the nature of the thing inculcated, the Incarnation, is gerundial. Second, the reality of history is not linear, just as thought is not linear. The task of the historian is not to simplify the course of history by reducing it to causes and effects and linear understanding. The historian's task is to present the complexity of history in order to make more vivid the essence of reality as it is appropriated by the mind. Linear understandings and logocentric interpretations of history only serve to alienate the mind from their veracity because they do not recapitulate the processes of the human imagination, which Newman understands as the illative sense. The historian's task then is to instil in the person the wonderful complexity and web of history in order to fascinate and attract the interest of the reader. As with Carlyle, all pretences to scientific historiography were wrong-headed and dangerous. History is not a collection of delineated facts. For Newman, the objective of history is the need to invoke the presence of the Word, the Incarnate God, which Newman understands as a unique event that changes all epistemological and moral categories. The object of history is the gerundial God that resists objectification and necessitates a continual engagement. For Newman, theology and church history were inseparable because both illuminated the same object, the parable that is only "known" by a continual "saying and unsaying to a positive result". The positive result is the continuation of the gerundial discourse and thereby the relationship with the object of the discourse. Any historicizing that "reduces" the object to the measurable and identifiable is false and morally suspicious. Third, history, like theology inculcates an object. in Newman's estimation, the historian deceives himself who claims that he has no interests, that he is only reporting the news. Theology (in its basic sense as a Word about God) must always be involved in history because the reality that is considered in history is an Incarnational reality whose human or earthly aspects cannot be teased away from its divine aspects but must remain within the tensile space of a gerundial saying and unsaying between the two natural poles of the Logos. Finally, history always has a moral imperative. History must move the person to action, although it is not necessarily focused as to what action the historian should incite. History cannot be moral in the sense of Foxe (positively) or Gibbon (negatively). Rather it should be inciteful, that is, it should not provide answers but prompt the reader to further consideration of the complexity of the Divine. It brings a person into a relationship. In the case of the Church historian, this is an already named relationship with the person of Christ.

IV. CONCLUSIONS AND QUESTIONS

One of the lasting effects of modernism and its inherent methodologies is academic isolation. Although postmodern thinkers have attempted a deconstruction of the elitist principles of modernism: who reads them? The Victorian sages, like their later postmodern progeny were attempting a re-evaluation of the conceits of modernism. Is it possible that their pioneering efforts may offer twenty-first century theologians and historians not only a method but also a model for thinking and writing that engages the public? Somehow, the sages were able to unite academic respectability with a far-reaching influence that seems to have escaped many of our contemporary thinkers. Who in the parish today is familiar with the work of Lyotard or Marion? Who in the nineteenth century was not familiar with the work of Newman or the novels of George Eliot? For Newman and the other Victorian sages, historians had a particular goal, to illuminate the complexities of history in such a way that life was enhanced by a greater appreciation of the object of human living, Carlyle's Divine Mind, Eliot's Spirit of Sympathy, Newman's Incarnate Word. The sages, therefore, espouse a gerundial methodology, an active historiography that does not seek facticity, or rather the facticity it seeks is gerundial. Truth in history is discerned not by merely "saying" facts. Likewise, it is not found in the "unsaying" of postmodern deconstruction. It is rather in the narrativity of a gerundial saying and unsaying that historical truth is known. Is it possible that the Victorian sages might offer a model of doing theology and history that somehow captures the *via media* between modernism and postmodernism? Sage historiography as a method of wisdom rather than knowledge may be helpful in assisting historical and theological discourse out of its methodological corner. In its "saying" it satisfies some modernist sensibilities, even rehabilitating the historical-critical method as a tool, though not as a goal. In its "unsaying" it satisfies postmodern epistemologies by "deconstructing" to a positive rather than a negative result. In its positive result, it satisfies the need for Christianity to continue to rely on terms like orthodoxy, now reconceptualized as a living product in process, the positive result of which is the continuance of narrative now devoid of undesirable, modernist, linear concepts of development. In Carlyle's estimation history (and Newman might add theology) yields but small profits, and then only to the vigilant and those who approach it with reverent humility. It betrays the qualities not of a *tabula rasa*, but rather:

> ... a Palimpsest [...] still dimly legible there – some letters, some words, may be deciphered; and if no complete Philosophy, here and there an intelligible precept, available in practice, be gathered: well understanding, in the mean while, that it is only a little portion we have deciphered; that much still remains to be interpreted; that History is a real Prophetic Manuscript, and can be fully interpreted by no man[40].

DRobinson@saintmeinrad.edu   Denis ROBINSON O.S.B.

---

40. T. CARLYLE, *Historical Essays* (*The Norman and Charlotte Strouse Edition of the Writings of Thomas Carlyle*), Berkeley, CA, University of California Press, 2002, p. 8.

'TRUTH' ACCORDING TO THE LATER
SCHELLING AND BAADER

AN ATTEMPT AT TRANSCENDING MODERNITY

> Das Wahre ist leicht – nicht das es leicht wäre,
> es zu finden. Aber wenn es gefunden,
> erscheint es leicht und einfach,
> wie ein vollendetes Werk der Kunst[1].

I. INTRODUCTION

In the Bavarian capital of the 1830s two thinkers came to highly relevant conclusions about truth and 'Christian truth' in particular. Permanently balancing on the boundary between philosophy and theology,
Schelling and Baader, both employed as professors at the Ludwig Maximilian Universität of Munich, developed an encompassing vision of reality. It is difficult to call this vision 'metaphysics', because it claimed to
have finally overcome classical – Wolffian – metaphysics. It is also hard
to maintain that their vision boils down to 'theology', since their scope
and their interest are much broader than a reflection upon the Christian
God. Peter Koslowski might have suggested the best characterisation of
their thought, as he described it as a "Theorie der Gesamtwirklichkeit"[2] –
a theory about the totality of reality. It not only included nature, history,
art, (self-)conscience, epistemology and 'Revelation', but also – and that
is what matters here – 'truth' as such.

In the course of their lectures at the university, Schelling and Baader
made painstakingly clear what, in their eyes, was 'truth' and what was not
'truth'. One could generally regard modern philosophy as their main
opponent[3]. Indeed, both Baader and Schelling strongly reacted not only
against their immediate predecessors in philosophy and theology but also

---

1. F.W.J. SCHELLING, *Grundlegung der positiven Philosophie*, ed. H. FUHRMANS (Phili-
sophica varia inedita vel rariora, 3/1), Torino, Bottega d'Erasmo, 1972, p. 119.
2. P. KOSLOWSKI, *Philosophien der Offenbarung: Antiker Gnostizismus, Franz von
Baader, Schelling*, Paderborn, Schöning, 2001. Koslowski almost exclusively reserves the
term for Baader's thought, but I am convinced that it adequately describes the aim of
Schelling's later philosophy too.
3. The word 'modern' does not belong to Schelling's and Baader's vocabulary, in any
case not in the sense we currently are familiar with. Instead, they spoke about "die *neuere*
Philosophie" – the *newer* philosophy, stretching out from Descartes and Spinoza over
Leibniz and Kant to Hegel.

against contemporaries, whom they considered to be indebted to or influenced by these predecessors. Schelling's and Baader's principal argument against the representatives of modern thought was that they reduced truth in several ways. None of them was able to give a reliable account of truth as a whole; they were all one-sided and contented themselves with variegated aspects of truth only. Hence, according to Baader and Schelling, a renewed reflection upon the totality of truth and being was urgently needed.

Baader and Schelling's later thought should be situated against the background of what has become known as 'German idealism'. This philosophical movement is generally regarded as the complex development of philosophical systems from Kant to Hegel in the last decade of the 18ᵗʰ century and the first three decades of the 19ᵗʰ century. The three main representatives of German idealism are Fichte, Hegel and Schelling himself. Strictly speaking, Baader does not belong to this movement, although he exerted a considerable influence on Hegel and Schelling. It is not an exaggeration to state that Baader has been forgotten and even neglected in the historiography of Western thinking. I appeal here to Baader because of his intelligent critique of modern philosophy in favour of a concept of truth that is reconcilable with Christian faith. Also Schelling distanced his later thought from his earlier intellectual evolution, during which, according to his own words, he significantly contributed to 'modern' thinking[4]. Moreover, it seems that Schelling had similar reasons to do so as those upon which Baader based his critique. Both Baader and Schelling pointed to an inherent incapacity of modern philosophy to come up with a notion of truth that is faithful to Christianity as a truly historical reality.

In this essay I will elucidate Schelling's and Baader's daring and unusual position toward truth[5]. One could label their point of view daring and unusual because it undeniably collides with contemporary beliefs. Firstly, I will elaborate upon Schelling's and Baader's method of coming to truth – which immediately involves a discussion of the rela-

---

4. In the course of his lectures in Munich, Schelling more than once came to speak about his attitude towards his early thought. He never denied it completely, but he neither held on to it. He regarded it as a natural stage in the developmental process towards 'positive' philosophy, without, however, reaching it already. See F.W.J. SCHELLING, *Einleitung in die Philosophie*, ed. W.E. EHRHARDT (Schellingiana, 1), Stuttgart, Frommann-Holzboog, 1989, pp. 38-39; SCHELLING, *Grundlegung* (n. 1), pp. 179ff.

5. In this contribution it is impossible to scrutinise the inner differences between Schelling and Baader. If there are any important items of philosophical discordance, they rather concern style and accuracy of argumentation than fundamental issues. The main theological difference between both authors lies in the fact that Baader was a prominent Catholic and Schelling a convinced Protestant. Both, however, were ecumenically engaged and made no point of challenging any other denominations.

tion between truth and the totality of being. Secondly, I will outline how and why they, accordingly, felt obliged to vehemently criticise modern philosophy and, at the same time, how they believed they had transcended it. Not surprisingly, Schelling's and Baader deeply understood that their account of truth was loyal to Christianity, whereas, in the end, modernity's was not. In the conclusion I will argue that Baader and Schelling's thought is not only interesting from a historical point of view, but also highly relevant in light of contemporary debates about truth and theological hermeneutics.

II. TRUTH AND METHOD

Etymologically, 'method' refers to the way (*hodos*) in or by (*meta*) which something is seen or has to be done. A theory and a practice proceed methodically if they follow a certain path consisting of several, clearly discernible stages. Hence a theory and a practice are methodologically sound if they are able to give an account of how they come to results. In modern philosophy, the awareness of different possible methodologies and the search for the one ultimate, all-encompassing and universally valid method became extremely important. Philosophers observed that great progress was made in the sciences if one consistently applied the mathematical model. Descartes and Kant were full of admiration for the '*mathesis universalis*', so that their epistemology can be regarded as a philosophical explanation and justification of how physics and mathematics work. The fact that mathematics works and that its method was successful in other sciences as well, was something they simply took for granted.

Whether truth as such was attained by simply applying mathematical figures and standards on reality, Descartes and Kant did not really ask, at least not in Schelling's and Baader's assessment. Descartes and Kant strongly believed that everything which was scientifically irrefutable was unconditionally true. Schelling and Baader, however, had serious doubts about the desirability of an extension or the universalisation of the mathematical example[6]. So, according to Schelling and Baader, whether this particular kind of truth, in the sense of (scientific) 'correctedness', could be identified with the totality of truth, remained unclear in Kantian and Cartesian philosophy. The deeper grounds of individual human beings

---

6. For an illustration of Schelling's struggle with mathematics, see SCHELLING, *Grundlegung* (n. 1), pp. 97-98; SCHELLING, *Einleitung* (n. 4), pp. 17-18. Schelling argues that mathematics thinks and understands; it does not *know* anything.

who are, astonishingly, able to gain knowledge about the world and themselves, were left unexamined.

According to Schelling and Baader, Descartes and Kant therefore were fundamentally blind for the presuppositions and biases of their own thought. Since they took a radically subjective position from which they, thereupon, approached reality, they overlooked the fact that truth is not something to approximate, but rather a horizon that expresses itself in the human being. Truth is not a strange and passive object that the subject is confronted with and that it tries to incorporate and accommodate, but an active subject-object[7] that comes to full self-conscience in the human mind. It is not the knowing subject that comes first, but truth. Hence, it is not through human beings that there can be decided upon truth; truth is no merit of brave and smart human beings. On the contrary, it manifests itself as something ontologically prior to human existence and human knowledge. And it is a lack of sensibility for this primordiality that, according to Schelling and Baader, lies at the basis of modernity's mistakes and misfortunes.

For Baader and Schelling, an adequate method of finding truth is not the one that tries to 'get to' the truth, as if the truth was not always already there. It is neither a method that speaks of truth as if the subject had to invent what is true and false – which would imply that the subject is able to do that. For, the truth always finds itself within the many relations that root the subject in reality. *Truth is discovered, not invented.* In Schelling's own terminology, truth is 'positive', not 'negative'[8]. Truth is put; it is (like) a brute fact that stands for itself, no matter of how people came across it. Truth happens in a truly historical way, the same way that people live their lives, think and speak, feel and act, eat and drink, in short are being to be. For all these reasons, truth is not found in a priori way, but always *a posteriori*[9]. A method of finding truth comes structurally

7. The term 'Subjekt-Objekt' is a word Schelling used from the early beginnings of his philosophical career onwards. He gave it slightly different meanings, but it remained unchanged in its opposition to modern philosophy and to Kantianism in particular. According to Schelling, modern thought made a forced division between the subject and the object that it did not succeed to overcome. Like Baader, Schelling opined that subjectivity is fundamentally involved in objectivity and vice versa. Cf. SCHELLING, *Einleitung* (n. 4), p. 52: "Against him [i.e. Fichte], it was my purpose to demonstrate the objectivity of spirit ['Geist'] as well as the subjectivity of matter".

8. For Schelling, the meaning of 'positive' is closely connected with its etymological origin, the Latin verb 'ponere' (= to put). Schelling not only often uses different forms of the German verb 'setzen' (= to put), he also intrinsically relates it with truth and the pure facticity of being. Among the most telling passages where Schelling delineates 'positive' and 'negative' (orientations in) philosophy, are the following: SCHELLING, *Einleitung* (n. 4), pp. 8, 13, 18, 21, 26-27; SCHELLING, *Grundlegung* (n. 1), pp. 83, 94, 117.

9. This couple of technical philosophical terms is of crucial importance for an ade-

after truth has happened. It afterwards inclines with the reality of truth and does not impose its own laws.

III. TRUTH AND REALITY

A true concept of truth also has to take into account all different elements of reality. As long as there remain aspects, even the smallest details, unclear or unseen, truth as such is not ascertained. This might sound obvious, as for example someone in court who does not tell everything he/she knows is quickly regarded as a liar. Not to tell the whole truth is to lie. From a philosophical and theological perspective, it is much more difficult to hold on to the totality of truth. How is it possible, at a given moment, to maintain that one is in accordance with all aspects, factors and elements that build up truth and reality? Is it not a mere presumption that absolute truth lies in the range of the (intellectual) faculties of human beings? Is reality not so overwhelmingly complex that our mental and physical forces often have to squeeze the sponge?

In the history of Western thought, the general critique of German idealism has emphasised this kind of putting matters into perspective. Human reason, it is said, is not and will never be able to converge with truth or the totality of being. It was the historical mistake of German idealism to suppose that this is possible and to work out metaphysical and epistemological theories on the basis of this assumption. All contemporary and future thought is warned not to fall again into the errors of Fichte, Schelling, Hegel and their supporters. Moreover, we have learnt, mostly from post-modern thinkers, that striving for totality is oppressive, dangerous and morally reprehensible, because particularity, sheer 'otherness' and the irreducible independence of the other are too easily denied.

Yet, German idealist philosophers were well aware of the limits of human thinking. They would otherwise never have spent so much energy exploring the borderlines between human self-conscience, reason, the world, history, and God. It is certainly wrong to judge German idealism as one clearly definable line of thought that overestimated human reason and naively identified reason with reality. I would rather regard the basic intuition of German idealism as surprisingly helpful with a view to overcoming the problems that modernity, above all in its enlightened form, have bequeathed. German idealism started from a sense of dissatisfaction with the emphasis on mere intelligence as the one and only trust-

quate understanding of Schelling's later ('positive') philosophy. See SCHELLING, *Einleitung* (n. 4), pp. 24, 36; SCHELLING, *Grundlegung* (n. 1), p. 112.

worthy guide in the domains of knowledge, the human soul, nature, politics, art, religion etc. German idealist philosophy wanted to break through the lines of a stubborn but in the end weak and empty rationalism[10]. That is in a few words also Schelling's (and Baader's) deepest motive. Let me further explain this.

Schelling and Baader opposed a philosophical mentality which divided reality into several areas of reflection and research. They claimed that, in such a case, it is impossible to come up with truth in a plausible and convincing way. Instead truth is to be sought and found solely in the intimate interconnection of everything. In this respect Schelling spoke of a (real, general, objective and historical) "Zusammenhang" of all being[11]. Baader on his side consistently drew the attention to a "solidären Verband" of different layers of which reality consists[12]. He correspondingly developed an ingenious theory of the "Penetrabilität", "Durchdringung" and "Inexistenz" of all (levels of) being(s)[13].

Both authors used in this context the strong metaphors of organicity, growing, life, and process and defended a dynamic, developmental and historical worldview. Their appeal to truth and/as reality must therefore be interpreted as a reaction against the philosophical but also deeply human inclination towards dividing, ordering, and pigeonholing reality. At the same time their fascination for the totality of being has appeared in a different light – in any case different from those who all too frivolously dismiss 'totality' as a valuable philosophical and theological category.

IV. TRUTH AND MODERNITY

In this context, which is one of living in and from truth rather than one of approaching to it, Baader and Schelling felt forced to criticise the foundational principles of modern philosophy. In their analysis, modernity fell short in at least two ways. On the one hand, it ignored the positive priority of truth. That means that modern philosophers looked for truth

10. For Schelling's stand towards 'rationalism', see SCHELLING, *Grundlegung* (n. 1), pp. 160-161.
11. SCHELLING, *Einleitung* (n. 4), p. 30; SCHELLING, *Grundlegung* (n. 1), pp. 70, 72, 77, 119, 207.
12. F.X. VON BAADER, *Ueber den solidären Verband des intelligenten und des nicht-intelligenten Seins und Wirkens*, in ID., *Sämtliche Werke*, ed. F. HOFFMANN, Aalen, Scientia, 1963, IV, pp. 295-302.
13. F.X. VON BAADER, *Vorlesungen über speculative Dogmatik* 4, in ID., *Sämtliche Werke* (n. 12), IX, pp. 54-55, 94-100; F.X. VON BAADER, *Vorlesungen über speculative Dogmatik* 5, in ID., *Sämtliche Werke* (n. 12), IX, pp. 273-274.

as something lying before them. They started from an individual subject and asked what had to be done to come to truth. In doing so, they ignored that truth is objective and radically anterior to subjectivity. On the other hand, modern philosophy neglected the totality of truth. Its representatives reduced truth to something to possess or to something that has to be (scientifically) tested. While developing *a priori* methods to achieve truth, modern philosophy forgot that this epistemological strategy might not have the last word about truth.

Against this narrow subjective and reductive orientation Schelling and Baader argued that it is truth itself, conceived as the total reality of nature and history, that enables human beings to come to knowledge and to cope with reality. Truth is not simply the same as 'having right'; it is the horizon and the ontological background thanks to which everything has come into existence and can be understood. In their lectures and their writings, Baader and Schelling further applied and concretised the aforementioned double critique in numerous reflections and considerations. I mention only three of them and I focus on three main representatives of modern thought: Descartes, Kant and Hegel.

Schelling and Baader recognised in Cartesian philosophy the definitive step towards modern subjectivism, as its system took a start with what was held for the most fundamental certainty, the one of 'cogito, ergo sum'. In his critique of Descartes, Baader went so far as to turn around the meaning of the 'cogito'. He replaced the active grammatical verb form by a passive form: "Instead of saying with Descartes: I think, therefore I am, one ought to say: I am thought, therefore I think, or: I am *wanted (loved), therefore I am*"[14]. Indeed Baader loudly protested "against th[e] non audiam, non serviam, non credam, non orem of our philosophy of subjectivity"[15], which he saw as the immediate consequence of a *cogito* instead of a *cogitor*[16].

In his protest, Baader found Schelling on his side, since he also deconstructed Descartes' appeal to the 'cogito' as completely unsatisfactory. He argued that Cartesian philosophy could never transcend a purely subjective kind of certainty[17]. According to Schelling, this was due to the fact

---

14. F.X. VON BAADER, *Vorlesungen über speculative Dogmatik* 3, in ID., *Sämtliche Werke* (n. 12), VIII, p. 339.

15. VON BAADER, *Vorlesungen über speculative Dogmatik* 4 (n. 13), p. 105.

16. For a more elaborate discussion, see my "Cogitor" *ergo sum: On the Meaning and Relevance of Baader's Theological Critique of Descartes*, in *Modern Theology* 21 (2005) 237-251.

17. F.W.J. SCHELLING, *Zur Geschichte der neueren Philosophie. Münchener Vorlesungen*, in ID., *Schriften von 1813-1830* (Ausgewählte Werke), Darmstadt, Wissenschaftliche Buchgesellschaft, 1976, p. 287.

that Descartes never came up with a convincing theory about how things in the external world correspond with mental states of affairs. Descartes' dualism of 'res cogitans' and 'res extensa' laid at the basis of its own incompetence and loss. Moreover, Schelling refuted the so-called speculative significance of Cartesian doubts, because, in the end, they seem to rest on nothing more than mere empirical observations.

In short, a subjective position can never guarantee truth. That is a fundamental idea of Baader's and Schelling's 'theory of total reality' which also contradicted the purpose of Kant's epistemology. In spite of his respect for Kant's historical merits (he brought some order to metaphysics), Schelling accused Kant of a 'regressive' methodology[18]. That means that he ended his reflections with what he should have started with, namely the supersensible. Instead Kant let an adequate philosophy begin with an exploration of the intellectual capacities of human beings. On the basis of that analysis he concluded that nothing certain could be asserted about supernatural reality. However, according to Schelling, Kant's philosophy was in contradiction with its own presuppositions, since its construction of experience in some way presupposes the (existence of the) supernatural[19]. So the truth Kant claims to lay bare cannot be the whole truth, because of a one-sided regressive method.

Baader articulated a similar critique of Kant's epistemology. He considered a theory of knowledge which only put the categories of understanding in the knowing subject inappropriate and unintelligent[20], because it will never be able to make clear how people really experience reality. Hence Kantianism remains merely external to truth, and even Jacobi's philosophy of feeling is, ultimately, nothing better than a Kantian subjectivism[21]. In addition, Baader blamed Kant for the influence he exerted on moral philosophy and the philosophy of religion. Also in these domains, Baader deliberately rejected an emphasis on the subject as the autonomous inventor or creator of (moral) law and (religious) sense. What Descartes brought about in theoretical philosophy, a radical pull towards autonomy and subjectivity, was extended by Kant in practical philosophy. This self-pro-

---

18. It must be stressed that the terms 'regressive' and its opposite 'progressive' are closely connected with the other fundamental word pairs shaping Schelling's later philosophy, such as negative – positive, a priori – a posteriori, subjective – objective, logical – historical, etc. For the identification of Kant and a regressive method in epistemology, see SCHELLING, *Einleitung* (n. 4), pp. 33ff.

19. SCHELLING, *Grundlegung* (n. 1), pp. 169-170.

20. VON BAADER, *Vorlesungen über speculative Dogmatik* 4 (n. 13), pp. 103-104.

21. F.X. VON BAADER, *Vorlesungen über speculative Dogmatik* 1, in ID., *Sämtliche Werke* (n. 12), VIII, p. 24.

claimed autonomy of the subject is, for Baader, as stupid as the act of embracing oneself[22].

As to Baader's and Schelling's critique of Hegel, their most thorough-going objections seem to focus on the *Wissenschaft der Logik*. In this masterly work of metaphysics Hegel tries to describe the fundamental conceptual processes of thought and being. It is here that his 'dialectics' operate in the densest way and that the 'motor' of his mature system has to be situated. If Baader and Schelling do away with the central convictions and implicit assumptions of the *Logik*, it is clear that they wanted philosophy and theology to be freed from any Hegelian temptation[23]. Although their relation to Hegel is very complex and although it changed in the course of their lives, I focus here exclusively on their critical remarks.

Schelling saw in Hegel's system the ultimate continuation of all modern, "negative" philosophy. That means that it did not succeed in giving a true account of ("positive") being and reality. It conceived of reality as one huge chain of necessarily related concepts, thoughts or ideas, which, in the end, were to be identified with actual being. Schelling, however, maintained that anything like that is impossible. At least, he thought that Hegel did not clarify how he founded the transition from the ideal world of thoughts to being. Bridging this gap was the great challenge of Hegel's *Logik*, but apparently he got stuck in – sometimes brilliant, Schelling admits – ideas without realising its goal. According to Schelling, Hegel's merit lies in having developed the notion of process, but how being itself exists in the fashion of a lively and organic process was not made clear in a convincing way. "Life has sunk down to a mere negation. *In essence*, everything has already been posited by the merely logical process; hence nature is only *the empty form of the outwardly being of the concept* and there is no talk anymore of an inner connection, a true process. Nature as such is no real *history*, but mere concept"[24].

Baader for his part ridiculed Hegel's extremely difficult line of reasoning in the *Logik*, in a way that resembles Schopenhauer's assaults[25]. He emphasised that Hegel's philosophy of mere concepts remains much

---

22. VON BAADER, *Vorlesungen über speculative Dogmatik* 5 (n. 13), pp. 263-264.

23. There exist many contributions which evaluate Schelling's critique of Hegel and they mostly conclude that Schelling's argumentation is poor and philosophically inadequate. However, from a theological point of view, his critique points to important shortcomings of Hegel's system. Baader's critique of Hegel has been excellently treated in KOSLOWSKI, *Philosophien der Offenbarung* (n. 2), pp. 543-562.

24. SCHELLING, *Grundlegung* (n. 1), p. 233 (my translation; Schelling's emphasis). Schelling's critique of Hegel has also been elaborated in *Zur Geschichte der neueren Philosophie: Münchener Vorlesungen*, in ID., *Schriften von 1813-1830* (n. 17), pp. 408-446; SCHELLING, *Einleitung* (n. 4), pp. 61-67.

25. F.X. VON BAADER, *Briefwechsel*, in ID., *Sämtliche Werke* (n. 12), XV, pp. 453, 539.

too abstract, negative, and empty, so that he considered it necessary to undertake a constructive revision of Hegelianism[26]. In any case Baader thought that Hegel's philosophy, like most modern attempts, did not show the true way to truth.

V. TRUTH AND CHRISTIANITY

It should now be clear that, in Baader's and Schelling's opinion, modernity's answers to the question of truth were hopelessly insufficient. But even more interesting for our purpose is that they claimed that an authentic interpretation of Christianity and its appeal to Revelation and Creation avoids the problems which modernity established or, at least, did not succeed to overcome. Whereas modern philosophers neglected and rejected the priority and the totality of truth, understood as the development of total reality, Christianity does justice to both these aspects. This claim now needs to be examined in greater detail. For the sake of conciseness, I will only discuss Schelling's and Baader's account of God as an absolutely free creator. This religious conviction and at the same time metaphysical theorem undoubtedly constitutes the very heart of their theologies.

According to Schelling and Baader, Christianity is not (primarily) a matter of doctrinal systems or logical constructions[27]. What prevails when considering Christianity is an objective historical reality that needs to be acknowledged. As a philosopher, Schelling did not doubt that Christianity is true, in the sense that it is *in* truth, that it moves forward from a fundamentally anterior truth, called 'Revelation', and that it consequently bears evidence of this truth. This truth, however, does not depend upon subjective approval from the side of human beings. It is a "positive" truth in the fullest and most literal meaning of the word: it has been posited before any human capacity of understanding came into existence.

Baader harmoniously takes up this fundamental ontological viewpoint. Also for him, God's creation and revelation are 'facts' so (historically) real that a denial of them would boil down to untruth and all sorts of illegitimate distortions of 'the' truth. For instance, Baader frequently emphasised the 'givenness' of being, which, for him, cannot but imply that there is a divine giver[28]. According to Baader, it is God that has enabled peo-

---

26. F.X. VON BAADER, *Revision der Philosopheme der Hegel'schen Schule, bezüglich auf das Christentum*, in ID., *Sämtliche Werke* (n. 12), IX, pp. 299-360.

27. SCHELLING, *Einleitung* (n. 4), pp. 9-10; F.X. VON BAADER, *Ueber Religions- und religiöse Philosophie im Gegensatze sowohl der Religionsunphilosophie als der irreligiöse Philosophie*, in ID., *Sämtliche Werke* (n. 12), I, pp. 325, 333.

28. F.X. VON BAADER, *Vorlesungen über speculative Dogmatik* 3 (n. 14), p. 344; *Vor-*

ple to act in and to come to knowledge about the world in which he pre-viously placed them. And if intelligent beings – such as human beings are (called to be) – look well around in nature and their own soul, then they must, sooner or later, come not only to a reasonable affirmation, but also, perhaps more importantly, to a pious integration of this 'givenness' into their lives. For Baader, this (Christian) creational perspective is so cru-cial that it permeates his whole thinking, especially the fundamental inter-pretational framework of his speculative dogmatics.

It will come as no surprise that this thought paradigm stood and still stands at odds with a modern mind. There is authority instead of auton-omy, there is a claim of objectivity instead of subjectivity, there is ante-riority instead of progression[29] and there is an emphasis on faith and trust instead of a mentality of checking everything on one's own. In short, there is being before reason – and certainly before subjectivism and ratio-nalism – and truth before there is agreement upon it. Schelling explains this in a beautiful way[30]. Reason ("Vernunft"), he says, is always late and negative. It is that human faculty which always has to be persuaded before it inclines, recognises, comes to insight or gives permission. That means that there has to be something to be persuaded of. And that particular 'something' is, upon closer inspection, nothing other than *reality*, always and inevitably preceding the efforts of reason.

VI. CONCLUSION

Through their reflection upon the basis of Christianity as a historical reality, Schelling and Baader have avoided the reduction of truth to a knowable thing or to any other simply cognitive dimension. Moreover, they have done justice to the ontological priority of truth. If truth is to play a role in philosophical, historical, and theological ideas explicitly dedi-cated to that theme, then one must consider the totality of reality and give an account of the radical anteriority of truth. That seems to me Baader's

---

lesungen über speculative Dogmatik 4 (n. 13), p. 103; *Ueber die Nothwendigkeit einer Revision der Wissenschaft natürlicher, menschlicher und göttlicher Dinge*, in ID., *Sämtliche Werke* (n. 12), X, p. 279. In similar contexts Baader plays with the German words "Gabe" (or "Gegebenes") and "Aufgabe" (or "Aufgegebenes"). What is given by God immedi-ately contains an assignment addressed to human beings, whether they want it or not. See F.X. VON BAADER, *Vorlesungen über speculative Dogmatik* 1 (n. 20), p. 37; *Vorlesungen über speculative Dogmatik* 3 (n. 14), p. 355.

29. 'Progression', however, has to be interpreted here not in the peculiar way Schelling understands it. I appeal here to its current significance.

30. See SCHELLING, *Grundlegung* (n. 1), p. 161. In this context, Schelling also remem-bers the etymological roots of "Vernunft", which refer to 'hearing' and 'learning'.

and Schelling's most important lesson. Yet this does not automatically mean that Christianity is pushed forward as the everlasting, one and only true religion – at least, if one is allowed to translate Schelling and Baader's concerns into the discourse of contemporary theological problems. What it does mean, is that one will not truly testify to 'Christian' truth, whenever one does not take into account a harsh reality claim. For, Christianity's message is about reality and it is only true because it is about reality. Schelling's and Baader's thought might then be provocative, "unzeitgemäß" and somehow troublesome, but has the history of ('the') truth not demonstrated that truth itself is always and necessarily recalcitrant and difficult to digest?

joris.geldhof@theo.kuleuven.be   Joris GELDHOF

TRUTH AS ISSUE IN A SECOND MODERNIST CRISIS?

THE CLASH BETWEEN RECONTEXTUALIZATION AND RETROCONTEXTUALIZATION IN THE FRENCH-SPEAKING POLEMIC OF 1946-47

I. INTRODUCTION: TRUTH IN THE DISCUSSION ON THE 'NOUVELLE THÉOLOGIE'

The concept of truth can cover different areas, depending on the point of view from which one approaches the question. Theological truth does not escape this methodological law. In the first half of the previous century, the truth question raised sharp discussions in theological centres where dogmatically and historically-oriented theologians confronted one another from their own point of view. In 1942, Marie-Dominique Chenu (1895-1990) and Louis Charlier (1898-1981), both Dominicans, were jointly condemned by Rome, primarily because they unmistakably brought the catholic *depositum fidei* in discredit with their conceptions on a full integration of history in theology[1]. Several months later, the Louvain theologian René Draguet (1896-1980) underwent the same fate after he indicated that Charlier had not quoted him, although his course at the theological faculty in Louvain had been the main source of Charlier's

---

1. *AAS* 34 (1942) 37. February 4, 1942, both publications of Chenu (M.-D. CHENU, *Une école de théologie: le Saulchoir*, Kain-lez-Tournai, Le Saulchoir, 1937; reprinted in 1985 in G. ALBERIGO, et al., *Une école de théologie: le Saulchoir* [Théologies], Paris, Cerf, 1985, pp. 91-173) and of Charlier (L. CHARLIER, *Essai sur le problème théologique* [Bibliothèque Orientations, Section scientifique, 1], Thuillies, Ramgal, 1938) were placed on the index. So Guelluy erronously mentioned February 6, 1942 (R. GUELLUY, *Les antécédents de l'encyclique 'Humani generis' dans les sanctions romaines de 1942: Chenu, Charlier, Draguet*, in *RHE* 81 [1986] 421-497, esp. 422); on February 6, 1942, the *AAS* only published the fact of the works being placed on the index. On March 26, 1942, the *AAS* published the fact of the submission of both Dominicans: *AAS* 34 (1942) 148. Cf. J.-C. PETIT, *La compréhension de la théologie dans la théologie française au XXe siècle. Vers une nouvelle conscience historique: G. Rabeau, M.-D. Chenu, L. Charlier*, in *Laval théologique et philosophique* 47 (1991) 215-229; É. FOUILLOUX, *Autour d'une mise à l'index*, in J. DORÉ – J. FANTINO (eds.), *Marie-Dominique Chenu, Moyen-Âge et modernité. Colloque organisé par le Département de la recherche de l'Institut Catholique de Paris et le Centre d'études du Saulchoir à Paris, les 28 et 29 octobre 1995 sous la présidence de Joseph Doré et Jacques Fantino* (Les Cahiers du Centre d'études du Saulchoir, 5), Paris, Cerf, 1997, 26-56; J. METTEPENNINGEN, *Beschouwingen bij het 'Essai sur le problème théologique' (1938) van Louis Charlier* (unpublished master's dissertation in theology, K.U.Leuven), Leuven, 2003, esp. pp. 38-41.

Essai sur le problème théologique[2]. The different critiques Charlier received in international periodicals[3] (Chenu's work remarkably only got one recension[4]) carried mainly the stamp of Neo-Scholasticism. Indeed, since the modernist crisis, official catholic theology had been identified with Neo-Scholasticism[5]. After a *retour à la scolastique* (approx. 1850-1920) – Neo-Scholasticism became finally the criterion for orthodoxy, the "party-line" of the church[6] – in the 1920s, 1930s and 1940s, Neo-

2. R. DRAGUET, recension of CHARLIER, *Essai* (n. 1), in *ETL* 16 (1939) 143-145, p. 143: "Pour répondre à une question qui m'a été posée de divers côtés, je me vois obligé de dire que c'est à mon insu que le R.P. Charlier a utilisé mes travaux, qu'il connaissait par des notes d'étudiant. Sa probité scientifique est hors de cause, l'absence de référence à la source principale du livre ayant en fait le caractère d'une simple omission (…)". Cf. J. COPPENS, *In memoriam R. Draguet 1896-1980*, in *ETL* 57 (1981) 194-200, esp. 196-197. Anyway, Draguet had already discussed the theme of the theological methodology in R. DRAGUET, *Méthodes théologiques d'hier et d'aujourd'hui*, in *Revue catholique des idées et des faits* 15/42 (January 10, 1936) 1-7; 15/46 (February 7, 1936) 4-7; 15/47 (February 14, 1936) 13-17. On the relationship between this series of articles and the book of Charlier, see e.g. P. SCHOONENBERG, *Theologie als geloofsvertolking: Een weergave van enige recente uiteenzettingen over de verhouding der speculatieve theologie tot het geloof, gevolgd door een kritische samenvatting* (unpublished doctoral dissertation), Nijmegen, 1948, pp. 168-169: "Draguets invloed blijkt vooral in het eerste deel [of Charlier's publication] waarin we éénzelfde visie op de ontwikkeling van de speculatieve en de positieve theologie vinden als in *Méthodes théologiques d'hier et d'aujourd'hui*".
3. We only mention the sharpest article, nota bene written by a member of the same religious order: M.R. GAGNEBET, *Un essai sur le problème théologique*, in *Revue thomiste* 45 (1939) 108-145. Gagnebet indicated three elements of critique. First of all he asked what kind of scholasticism Charlier was criticising. Then he judged this criticism unfounded, because it was based both on an historical *a priori* and on superficial knowledge of the texts. "Enfin, elle s'appuie sur un certain nombre d'erreurs logiques qui surprennent de la part d'un disciple de saint Thomas – ne s'intéresserait-il, qu'à ce que le docteur commun a dit, et voudrait-il faire abstraction 'de tout ce qu'on veut lui faire dire, fût-ce en se recommandant de ses grands commentateurs'" (*ibid.*, pp. 113-114). Third, Gagnebet asked the question whether Charlier was conscious of the seriousness of what he was criticising, namely scholastic theology. Other articles on the book of Charlier: M.-J. CONGAR, recension of CHARLIER, *Essai* (n. 1), in *Bulletin thomiste* 5 (1938) 490-505; M.D. KOSTER, recension of CHARLIER, *Essai* (n. 1), in *Theologische Revue* 38 (1939) 41-48; F. SCHLAGENHAUFEN, recension of CHARLIER, *Essai* (n. 1), in *Zeitschrift für Katholische Theologie* 63 (1939) 366-371; D.M. CAPPUYNS, recension of CHARLIER, *Essai* (n. 1), in *RTAM* 11 (1939) (13)-(15); W. GOOSSENS, *Notion et méthodes de la théologie. 'L'Essai' du P. L. Charlier*, in *Collationes Gandavenses* 26 (1939) 115-134; J. COTTIAUX, recension of CHARLIER, *Essai* (n. 1), in *RHE* 36 (1940) 459-462; T. ZAPELENA, *Problema theologicum*, in *Gregorianum* 24 (1943) 23-47, 287-326; 25 (1944) 38-73, 247-282.
4. F. STEGMÜLLER, recension of CHENU, *Une école de théologie* (n. 1), in *Theologische Revue* 38 (1939) 48-51.
5. É. FOUILLOUX, *Courants de pensée, piété, apostolat. II: Le catholicisme*, in J.-M. MAYEUR, et al. (eds.), *Guerres mondiales et totalitarismes (1914-1958)* (Histoire du Christianisme des origines à nos jours, 12), Paris, Desclée, 1998, 116-239, esp. p. 167: "Quoi qu'on pense du statut de sa [thomism] restauration trente ans auparavant, le thomisme de 1910 est devenu profondément 'antimoderne'. (…): en 1914, le thomisme est devenu un système clos où philosophie et théologie s'imbriquent de façon indissociable".
6. Cf. F. COPPLESTON, *A History of Philosophy*. Vol. 9: *Modern Philosophy: From the*

Scholasticism experienced a renaissance and an internal pluralisation under the influence of lay intellectuals such as Jacques Maritain (1882-1973) and Étienne Gilson (1884-1978), of Dominicans such as Antonin-Dalmace Sertillanges (1863-1948) and Réginald Garrigou-Lagrange (1877-1964) and of the Jesuit Joseph Maréchal (1878-1944), professor at the Jesuit *Theologicum* near Louvain[7]. The end of the first stage in the development of the *'nouvelle théologie'* was set with the condemnation of Chenu, Charlier and Draguet, but theologically the problem was not yet solved[8]. The Jesuits of Lyon-Fourvière took up the core topic of this

---

French Revolution to Sartre, Camus, and Lévi-Strauss, New York, Image Books, [3]1994, p. 250: "Papal endorsement of Thomism had of course several effects. On the one hand it encouraged the formation, especially in clerical circles and in ecclesiastical seminaries and academic institutions, of one might describe as a party-line, a kind of philosophical orthodoxy".

7. The notion *'retour à la scolastique'* is taken from the book by the same title, written by Gonzague Truc (G. TRUC, *Le retour à la scolastique* [Bibliothèque internationale de critique. Religion et philosophie, 20], Paris, La renaissance du livre, 1919). The periodization 1850-1920 is derived from the *opus magnum* of Joseph Kleutgen (1811-1883); (ID., *Die Theologie der Vorzeit*, Münster, 1853-1863, en ID., *Die Philosophie der Vorzeit*, Münster, 1853-1863), who is generally seen as the 'father of the encyclical *Aeterni Patris*' (1879), as well as – symbolic – from the 'reopening' of the Institut Supérieur de Philosophie in Louvain (1919), which illustrated the beginning of a period of important contributions of lay intellectuals to thomistic thought in the next decades (cf. L. DE RAEYMAEKER, *Le cardinal Mercier et l'Institut Supérieur de Philosophie de Louvain*, Louvain, Publications universitaires de Louvain, 1952, p. 194). Cf. P. CHENAUX, *La seconde vague thomiste*, in P. COLIN (ed.), *Intellectuels chrétiens et esprit des années 1920: Actes du colloque, Institut catholique de Paris. 23-24 septembre 1993* (Sciences humaines et religions), Paris, Cerf, 1997, 139-167; T.F. O'MEARA, *Thomas Aquinas theologian*, Notre Dame, IN, University of Notre Dame Press, 1997, pp. 172-173; G. MCCOOL, *The Neo-Thomists* (Marquette Studies in Philosophy, 3), Milwaukee, WI, 1994; B.J. SHANLEY, *The Thomist Tradition* (Handbook of Contemporary Philosophy of Religion, 2), Dordrecht, Kluwer, 2002, pp. 5-21. See also note 5.

8. The division in two parts goes back to the work of T. TSHIBANGU, *La théologie comme science au XXème siècle*, Kinshasa, Presses universitaires du Zaïre, 1980, pp. 79-110; where he uses the following division: 1938-1946 and 1946-1948. Yves Congar extended the second period: 1946-1950, cf. Y. CONGAR, *Situations et tâches présentes de la théologie* (Cogitatio fidei, 27), Paris, Cerf, 1967, p. 14: "Certains se sont forgé alors l'idée fantastique d'une 'théologie nouvelle' qu'ils étaient d'ailleurs incapables de définir, ainsi que nous en avons fait cent fois personnellement l'expérience entre 1946 et 1950". We do not understand Tshibangu and Rosino Gibellini – the latter compiled the division of Tshibangu and the extension of Congar (cf. R. GIBELLINI, *Panorama de la théologie du XXe siècle*, transl. by J. Mignon, [Théologies], Paris, Cerf, 1994, p. 191) – since they discuss Chenu's *Une école de théologie: le Saulchoir* (n. 1) within the context of the first phase of the 'nouvelle théologie', while this phase for both Tshibangu and Gibellini had begun the year after that publication. Concerning the year that makes the distinction between the two phases, like Tshibangu and Gibellini we opt for 1946 in stead of 1944. In 1944 one heard the last 'sounds' of the effects of the condemnation of the works of Chenu, Charlier, and Draguet (cf. *infra*). Still in 1944 Henri Bouillard published his book on grace (H. BOUILLARD, *Conversion et grâce chez S. Thomas d'Aquin: étude historique* [Théologie, 1], Paris, Aubier, 1944), which formed a 'jesuitic triptych' with the work of

first phase, in particular the place and the value of history within theology, especially in the reflection concerning revelation, truth, dogma, theological conceptuality and methodology (see e.g. the historical-critical method). An article of Jean Daniélou (1905-1975) published in 1946[9] became commonly known as the start of the second phase in the development of the *'nouvelle théologie'*. According to Jean Lacouture, however, this article could also be considered as a response to the criticism from Rome by P. Parente (1891-1986) directed to Chenu and Charlier four years earlier[10]. In his article, *Les orientations présentes de la pensée religieuse*, Daniélou promoted a *ressourcement*, a return to the sources of faith and theology, in particular to the Bible, the liturgy and the Fathers of the Church. In this way, the Jesuit postulated and promoted a way of practising theology that would rely in its source material and its methodology on the whole of history, instead of only on Scholasticism as developed in the sixteenth and seventeenth centuries, e.g. by Cajaetan (1469-1534), Bañez (1528-1604), John of St. Thomas (1589-1644). Neither the Neo-Scholastic way of practising theology, which had been built up and consolidated in the previous century, nor the truth, which had been presented until then as evident, seemed absolute any more. Daniélou's article initiated a chain reaction of polemic writings in French-speaking periodicals concerning theological truth as the most eminent *casus* in the battle over the precise place of history in the practise of theology. For the first time in forty years, the question of truth was not to be taken or left to academics, but had to be considered. Not all scholars did agree as became clear from the sharp response by Réginald Garrigou-Lagrange in *Angelicum*, which appeared in February 1947[11].

Henri de Lubac two years later (H. DE LUBAC, *Surnaturel: Études historiques* [Théologie, 8], Paris, Aubier, 1946) and the article of Jean Daniélou, also in 1946 (J. DANIÉLOU, *Les orientations présentes de la pensée religieuse*, in *Études* 249 [April 1946] 5-21). Nevertheless, the latter is commonly seen as the starting point of the polemic (cf. *infra*). On the 'nouvelle théologie', see a.o. GIBELLINI, *Panorama* (n. 8), pp. 186-240; TSHIBANGU, *La théologie comme science* (n. 8), pp. 79-110; É. FOUILLOUX, *Une Église en quête de liberté: La pensée catholique française entre modernisme et Vatican II (1914-1965)* (Anthropologiques), Paris, Desclée De Brouwer, 1998, pp. 193-300.

9. See note 8.
10. J. LACOUTURE, *Jésuites: une multibiographie*. Vol. 2: *Les revenants*, Paris, Seuil, 1992, p. 494: "*L'Osservatore Romano* ayant en 1941, sous la plume d'un monsignore Parente (this was not published in 1941, but in *L'Osservatore Romano*, 9-10 february 1942, p. 1), attaqué les *'nuove tendenze teologiche'* venues notamment de Paris, le R.P. Daniélou crut bon, au lendemain de la guerre, de lui répliquer en prenant la défense de ce qu'il appelait lui aussi 'théologie nouvelle' pour designer, globalement, les courants très divers d'une recherche soucieuse de ne rien rejeter des efforts de la science moderne".
11. R. GARRIGOU-LAGRANGE, *La nouvelle théologie où va-t-elle?*, in *Angelicum* 23 (1946) 126-145.

R. Garrigou-Lagrange criticised J. Daniélou and his companions in a solemn way – as if he was the personification of Rome[12] – by labelling their vision as modernist thinking: "Où va la nouvelle théologie? Elle revient au modernisme"[13]. The main reason for reaching such a judgement was what he saw as the distortion of truth. Instead of the recognition of objective (catholic) truth, one focussed all one's attention on a subjective truth. The former vision on truth is static, the latter is characterised by a continuing development. Here truth is no longer purely transcendent – a part of revelation that had been concluded with the death of the last apostle and therefore partly still hidden – but a living reality that can be discovered by us through the progress of life if we are receptive to its revelation today. For Garrigou-Lagrange, who quoted Roman documents to provide his vision with the necessary authority, this new vision was a heresy: "Et où va-t-elle aller cette théologie nouvelle avec les maîtres nouveaux dont elle s'inspire? Où va-t-elle si non dans la voie du scepticisme, de la fantaisie et de l'hérésie?"[14].

In this contribution, we will first map the different positions concerning the concept of truth as they announce themselves chronologically. Second, we examine whether or not, at the height of the polemic in February 1947, this can be established as a second modernist crisis. In order to do so, we return to the first decade of the previous century, comparing the judgements of the Magisterium at the end of 1940s with those of that first decade. Two responses to Garrigou-Lagrange and some considerations on the concept of truth in this polemic conclude this concise contribution.

II. THE DIFFERENT POSITIONS IN THE DISCUSSION[15]

Concerning the vision of truth, from the theology-historical point of view, in general the second half of the 1940s can be seen as the time of

---

12. Cf. SHANLEY, *The Thomist Tradition* (n. 7), p. 5: "His (Garrigou-Lagrange) influence was not limited to his own work, since his long-standing prominence at the *Angelicum* (the Dominican pontifical university in Rome) led to such an extraordinary influence in the Vatican that his version of Thomism assumed a quasi-official status. By the time Garrigou-Lagrange attained such power, however, his version of Thomism had been called into question even by his own confreres. His style of Thomism would not stand up well against the new research into the historical Aquinas, and he came to be seen by some as a kind of Thomistic dinosaur".

13. GARRIGOU-LAGRANGE, *La nouvelle théologie* (n. 11), p. 143.

14. *Ibid.*, p. 134.

15. Besides the articles that will be discussed, we will base our contribution on É. FOUILLOUX, *Dialogue théologique? (1946-1948)*, in S.-T. BONINO (ed.), *Saint Thomas au XXe siècle. Colloque du centenaire de la "Revue thomiste" (1893-1992). Toulouse, 25-28 mars 1993*, Paris, Saint-Paul, 1994, 153-195; A. NICHOLS, *Thomism and the Nouvelle Théologie*, in *The Thomist* 64 (2000) 1-19. GIBELLINI, *Panorama* (n. 8), pp. 191-196.

opposing theological parties. We even can state that there was a 'theo-logical battle' on the vision of truth. On the one hand, there was the side of the Jesuits – later followed by the Dominicans of Toulouse – for whom truth is not (entirely) knowable. This truth always wants and needs to be found in and be defined according to every new historical context. The concepts to express this truth as adequate as possible are inspired by the context. Therefore, the notion of truth has been inextricably linked with the particular historical context, and as a result this truth is also particu-lar and temporary in its conceptual expression. In other words, the notion of truth always had to be *recontextualized*.

On the other hand, there was the side of the Thomists, as postulated by Garrigou-Lagrange and shared by other prominent Dominicans. The partisans of this vision can be named the 'Dominican side'. Here, truth was considered as a gift that had been revealed to us. This means truth was to be found during the period of revelation (until the death of the last apostle), and that it has always been defined in concepts which are – like truth itself – immutable and timeless. This notion of truth has been linked inextricably with ecclesiastical authority and is in its conceptual expres-sion uniform and universally appropriate. In other words, the notion always had to be *decontextualized*. This means that there are no other words for truth possible than those given by the Magisterium and ratified by its authority in immutable formulations. Decontextualization is a syn-onym for a concept of truth that has a transcendent and thereby a-histor-ical character.

The first side found its inspiration and point of departure in the already mentioned article of Jean Daniélou of April 1946[16]. Daniélou stated that, until then Neo-Scholasticism presented theological truth as being eternal and invariable in such a manner[17] that one must pay attention not to con-fuse truth with Neo-Scholasticism[18]. According to him, the latter does

16. We follow the chronological order of the articles. By writing that the article of Daniélou was the starting point of the polemic we agree with Gibellini (cf. GIBELLINI, *Panorama* [n. 8], pp. 191-192: "Le renouveau théologique promu par les jésuites français trouva *son expression programmatique* dans un article stimulant, 'Les orientations présentes de la pensée religieuse', paru dans la revue *Études* en avril 1946, et signé de Jean Daniélou"; italics mine) and so we do not agree with É. Fouilloux (FOUILLOUX, *Dialogue théologique?* [n. 15], p. 154: "Ce texte [M.-M. LABOURDETTE, *La théologie et ses sources*, in *Revue thomiste* 46 (1946) 353-371; that is the volume of May-August], *qui lance la con-troverse*, a été plus cité que véritablement lu"; italics mine).

17. DANIÉLOU, *Les orientations* (n. 8), p. 14: "Le monde qui est le sien (scholasticism) est le monde immobile de la pensée grecque où sa mission a été d'incarner le message chré-tien. Cette conception garde une vérité permanente et toujours valuable (...)".

18. *Ibid.*, p. 13: "Et la tentation ici serait cette paresse qui nous ferait prendre le vête-ment de la vérité pour la vérité elle-même, (...)".

not provide an answer to the dangers of modernism, but only guards truth when it was threatened by modernism[19]. A month later, the Dominicans M.-M. Labourdette (1908-1990) and R. Garrigou-Lagrange reacted to this vision. The former mainly in footnotes of an article in the *Revue thomiste*, of which he was editor in chief[20], and the latter briefly but strongly in *Angelicum*. Both May numbers of these periodicals eventually appeared much later than the month of May (cf. *infra*). Labourdette and Garrigou-Lagrange opposed any form of separation between the vision of truth and Neo-Scholasticism. According to Labourdette Thomistic thought is not lacking a dynamic spirit, but the vision of Daniélou is lacking respect for this method and for the truth (Scholasticism is not to be seen as a piece of art in a museum)[21]. Concerning Daniélou's conception of truth Labourdette held that, with the introduction of history (development) in the resulting "pseudo-philosophy" or philosophy of action, relativism was brought in. As a consequence speculative truth had to make a place for a historical truth expressing the mentality and experiences of 'situated' people[22]. Therefore a meta-temporary or timeless truth is no longer conceivable, because truth has been connected to time[23]. In the same sense the Jesuit Henri Bouillard (1908-1981) in 1944 already explicitly stated: "A theology that would not be actual, would be an incorrect theology"[24].

19. *Ibid*, pp. 6-7: "Il s'agissait de parer aux dangers créés par le modernisme. Le néothomisme et la Commission biblique ont été ces garde-fous. Mais il est bien clair que des garde-fous ne sont pas des réponses".

20. See note 16.

21. LABOURDETTE, *La théologie* (n. 16), p. 359, note 1: "(…). Nous croyons au contraire qu'elle (neoscholasticism) est une façon de pensée parfaitement vivante, à la fois ambitieuse et capable d'entrer dans les problèmes nouveaux et de les comprendre, de s'assimiler tout ce que contiennent d'authentique les doctrines les plus modernes, mais trop respectueuse de la vérité, (…)"; *ibid*., p. 359, nt. 1: "L'élargissement que souhaite le P. Daniélou, si on s'en tient à ses expressions, se solderait par une déperdition infiniment déplorable: la perte d'un acquis en lequel réside notre trésor intellectuel le plus précieux et la réduction de la pensée scolastique à l'état de témoin (permanent sans doute, mais comme l'est une statue dans un musée) d'un temps révolu. Le thomisme ne prétend pas moins à la vie que l'existentialisme ou le marxisme, ou l'évolutionnisme du P. Teilhard de Chardin".

22. *Ibid*., p. 362: "La pseudo-philosophie qu'inspirent inconsciemment les méthodes de l'histoire, c'est le 'relativisme', au sens fort d'une théorie, ou plus encore d'une attitude intellectuelle qui remplace la notion métaphysique de vérité spéculative par celle plus modeste de vérité historique, comme expression plus ou moins complète de la mentalité, de l'expérience humaine d'une époque ou d'un groupe d'hommes".

23. *Ibid*., p. 362: "L'idée même que notre esprit puisse arriver à saisir et à cerner, en les mieux assurées de ses notions, une vérité intemporelle, devient proprement impensable".

24. BOUILLARD, *Conversion et grâce* (n. 8), p. 219: "Quand l'esprit évolue, une vérité immuable ne se maintient que grâce à une évolution simultanée et corrélative de toutes les notions, maintenant entre elles un même rapport. Une théologie qui ne serait pas actuelle serait une théologie fausse".

Moreover, Bouillard stated that, throughout time, the (conceptual) notion of truth changes spontaneously within theology on the instigation of truth herself. Truth wants to express herself in each language as 'contemporary' as possible; its permanent content guides the variable notion and this notion makes truth accessible[25]. According to Labourdette, this opinion endangered Christian faith[26]. He therefore opted resolutely for the traditional, speculative vision of truth: the conformity between intellect and reality, instead of a truth being build up and expressed as a bond with time, action or life. According to him this speculative truth is accessible[27]. The response of Garrigou-Lagrange, which was published effectively only in February 1947, fitted in with the vision of Labourdette. So truth is no *adaequatio realis mentis et vitae* but remains the scholastic *adaequatio rei et intellectus* (cf. *supra* and *infra*)[28].

In July 1946 Garrigou-Lagrange wrote in a letter to Labourdette that the article of Daniélou seemed to form some sort of programme for the 'nouvelle théologie' and that one had to be aware of a *retour au modernisme*[29]. On 19 September 1946, the *Osservatore Romano* published a speech Pope Pius XII had held two days earlier for the heads of the

---

25. *Ibid.*, p. 219: "Pour maintenir dans de nouveaux contextes intellectuels la pureté d'une affirmation absolue, les théologiens l'ont spontanément exprimée en des notions nouvelles"; *ibid.*, p. 220: "Jamais la vérité divine n'est accessible en deçà de toute notion contingente. C'est la loi de l'incarnation"; *ibid.*: "Si les notions, les méthodes, les systèmes changent avec le temps, les affirmations qu'ils contiennent demeurent, quoiqu'elles s'expriment dans d'autres catégories. Bien plus, ce sont les affirmations elles-mêmes qui, pour conserver leur sens dans un univers intellectuel nouveau, déterminent des notions, des méthodes et des systèmes nouveaux en correspondance avec cet univers. S'il en était autrement, les formules anciennes, en subsistant, perdraient leur sens premier"; *ibid.*, p. 221: "L'histoire manifeste donc à la fois la relativité des notions, des schèmes où la théologie prend corps, et l'affirmation permanente qui les domine".
26. LABOURDETTE, *La théologie* (n. 16), p. 365: "C'est que dans l'explication du P. Bouillard, l'idée même de vérité prend une signification contradictoire; ce ne serait peut-être pas inquiétant pour une conception hégélienne de l'histoire, c'est dangereux non seulement pour la théologie, mais pour la foi chrétienne".
27. *Ibid.*, p. 368: "Mais ce que nous ne pouvons admettre, c'est l'évacuation complète, en une pareille façon de voir, de l'idée de *vérité spéculative*. Et à qui nous demanderait si nous croyons que la vérité nous soit accessible, nous aurons la naïveté de répondre oui. Nous entendons par vérité la conformité de l'intelligence connaissante avec un réel qui est pour elle un donné, nullement un 'construit'".
28. GARRIGOU-LAGRANGE, *La nouvelle théologie* (n. 11), p. 143: "Où va la nouvelle théologie? Elle revient au modernisme. Parce qu'elle a accepté la proposition qui lui était faite: celle de substituer à la définition traditionnelle de la vérité: *adaequatio rei et intellectus*, comme si elle était chimérique, la définition subjective: *adaequatio realis mentis et vitae*".
29. Étienne Fouilloux quotes a letter out of archives with no further detail: FOUILLOUX, *Dialogue théologique?* (n. 15), p. 170, note 1: "(…) P. Garrigou qui écrivait le 17 juillet à Labourdette: 'L'article du P. Daniélou dans les Études d'Avril dernier paraît être le manifeste de cette théologie nouvelle (…). Mais ici on est bien attentif à tout ce mouvement, qui est un retour au modernisme'".

Jesuit order. Pius stated "that there were said many things concerning the 'new theology' and these words were insufficiently elaborated"[30], and that "the different contemporary visions of truth have to be investigated, certainly when believers have problems with them"[31]. In this task the doctrine of the church is the one and only trustworthy guide[32]. On 22 September 1946, in a speech held for the heads of the Dominican order, the Pope repeated this, now emphasizing the example of Thomas[32b]. The Dominicans and the Jesuits, however, continued the polemic, in particular by the publication at the same time – February 1947 – of the article by Garrigou-Lagrange in *Angelicum* (May 1946) and of one by a group of Jesuit-theologians[33] in *Recherches de science religieuse* (October 1946)[34]. The latter wanted to give an answer to Labourdette and their text was dated November 20, 1946, still before the *Revue thomiste* containing the article of Labourdette had appeared, and, according to the authors two months after they had read his text, being about the time Pius XII for the first time spoke about the '*nouvelle théologie*'[35]. At first the Jesuits agreed with Labourdette in his opposition against a far going historical relativism concerning all human expressions of divine truth, and in his

30. *Il venerato Discorso del Sommo Pontifice alla XXIX Congregazione Generale della Compagnia di Gesù*, in *Osservatore Romano*, 19 September 1946, p. 1: "Plura dicta sunt, at non satis explorata ratione, 'de nova theologia' (...)". In our opinion it is surprising that the Pope makes mention of this fact, since the articles of both Labourdette and Garrigou-Lagrange were not yet published. Is it right to see here the influence of the latter in Vatican circles (cf. note 12)?

31. *Il venerato Discorso del Sommo Pontifice* (n. 30), p. 1: "(...). Dum igitur inocciduam Veritatem vereri sanctum sollemneque habetis, operam date problemata, quae labens fert tempus, studiose investigare et exsolvere, praesertim si ea eruditis christifidelibus obstacula et difficultates progignere possint; (...)".

32. *Il venerato Discorso del Sommo Pontifice* (n. 30), p. 1: "(...). Verumtamen, cum novae vel liberae agitantur quaestiones, catholicae doctrinae principia semper mentibus praefulgeant".

32b. *Fervido Discorso del Sommo Pontifice ai Capitolari dell'Ordine dei Frati Predicatori*, in *Osservatore Romano*, 23-24 September 1946, p. 1.

33. Although the article is not signed by an author, M. Labourdette, M.-J. Nicolas and R.-L. Bruckberger stated that the following persons have contributed to it: H. de Lubac, J. Daniélou, H. Bouillard, G. Fessard and H. U. von Balthasar. Cf. M. LABOURDETTE – M.-J. NICOLAS – R.-L. BRUCKBERGER, *Dialogue théologique: Pièces du débat entre 'La Revue Thomiste' d'une part et les R.R. P.P. de Lubac, Daniélou, Bouillard, Fessard, von Balthasar, S.J., d'autre part*, Saint-Maximin, Les Arcades, 1947, p. 99: "La Réponse des RR. PP. Jésuites n'étant pas signée, nous pensons que chacun de ceux que nous avons critiqués, même en passant, en prend l'entière responsabilité; nous avons donc nommé les RR. PP. de Lubac, Daniélou, Bouillard, Fessard et Von Balthasar".

34. *La théologie et ses sources. Réponse*, in *Recherches de science religieuse* 33 (1946) 385-401.

35. *Ibid.*, p. 385: "Une brochure d''études critiques' nous est arrivé, voilà plus de deux mois, – 'tiré à part' d'un fascicule de la *Revue thomiste* encore à venir, – qui contient un réquisitoire inattendu contre un certain nombre de théologiens jésuites".

coinciding objection against the replacement of speculative truth by a more historical truth[36]. Then the Jesuit side indicated that his method was completely wrong. First, they stated, the method created a "monstrous heresy" and then Labourdette noticed this monster at work everywhere, not having done the effort to examine the different visions[37]. The Jesuits emphasized the diversity of their group, as such they cannot be categorised and over-simplified as one side and judged as such[38]. The fact Labourdette did this, however, gave proof of his subjectivism, exactly the fact he reacted against[39]. By pointing out some distortions Labourdette made of their original texts, the Jesuits in a most subtle way indicated that it would not hurt a partisan of speculative truth to show some respect for historical truth as well[40]. Concerning the core of the debate on truth, according to the Jesuit group, it is obvious that the historical method differs from the dogmatical method, although many misunderstandings concerning relativism arise out of a negation of this difference[41]. Concerning dogmatic relativism the group stated that no theological system can grasp truth entirely in its objectivity, and that each system can only understand 'something' of this objective truth. "Do we have to close our eyes for these *évidences*, thereby escaping relativism or subjectivism", the

36. *Ibid.*, pp. 385-386: "Le R. P. Labourdette ne veut pas qu'on professe 'l'essentiel relativisme historique de toute expression humaine des vérités divines'. (…). Il ne veut pas que la méthode historique s'alourdisse d'une 'pseudo-philosophie' qui 'remplace la notion métaphysique de vérité spéculative par celle plus modeste de vérité historique'. Il ne veut pas que, sous prétexte de critiquer le 'progrès théologique', on opéra 'une perpétuelle refonte de nos conceptions sur Dieu'. (…). Combien le R. P. Labourdette a raison".

37. *Ibid.*, p. 387: "Notre auteur (Labourdette) est sous le coup d'une grave inquiétude. Un monstre d'hérésie a surgi devant son regard, dont il ne pourra s'empêcher ensuite de trouver partout quelque signe. (…). Livres ou articles de revue, ils sont d'auteurs divers, de nature diverse, parus en des circonstances et en des temps divers. Or – tel est le second vice de sa méthode – le R. P. Labourdette, sans prendre la peine d'en analyser aucun, entreprend de les commenter les uns par les autres".

38. *Ibid.*: "Chacun de nous n'en est pas moins indépendant dans son travail. Nous avons conscience entre nous de diversités nombreuses, souvent profondes, dans la méthode et la pensée, (…)".

39. *Ibid.*, p. 388: "(…), rien ne lui apparaît de répréhensible, à supposer des "arrière-pensées". Le voici, désormais, plus que sur la pente, déjà dans l'abîme du subjectivisme le plus prononcé!".

40. *Ibid.*, p. 390: "(…), s'il est assurément blâmable de 'remplacer la notion métaphysique de vérité spéculative par celle plus modeste de vérité historique', un respect plus attentive de l'humble vérité historique, c'est-à-dire un peu plus d'objectivité dans la lecture, pourrait éviter bien des mesures pour rien aux plus jaloux amants de la vérité spéculative".

41. *Ibid.*, pp. 391-392: "Il (Labourdette) semble oublier aussi que les méthodes de l'histoire ne sont pas celles du traité dogmatique, et qu'on ne procède pas non plus dans la recherche comme on fait dans l'enseignement. D'où les malentendus qui le portent à parler de 'relativisme'".

Jesuits asked themselves[42]. In the same sense did they resisted the exclusion of relativism and subjectivism in the area of historical sciences. They therefore held that it is nevertheless not obliged to speak always about a timeless truth, losing sight of concrete, particular elements[43].

Also in February 1947 the superior of the Dominican province of Toulouse, Marie-Joseph Nicolas (1906-1999), and the rector of the Institut Catholique of Toulouse, Bruno de Solages (1895-1983), corresponded on the article of Labourdette[44]. Nicolas stated that he did not understand why concepts, although they cannot adequately reflect the revealed truth, still have to be seen as contingent, and why truth would have to incarnate herself in notions and systems succeeding each other[45]. He continued to hold on to Thomism[46]. In doing so he gave a careful response to the position of de Solages, who in his letter to Nicolas quoted from his own article of August-September 1946 in *Esprit*, where he stated the immutability of revelation. Human reason is not, therefore the synthesis of both revelation and reason is constantly evolving[47].

42. *Ibid.*, p. 397, nt. 1: "Ils (theological systems) ne laissent pas pour autant d'atteindre une même vérité objective, mais chacun n'en exprime à fond qu'un aspect, et tous ensemble ne l'épuisent pas. (…). Faudra-t-il fermer les yeux à ces évidences pour échapper au relativisme ou au subjectivisme?".

43. *Ibid.*, p. 394: "Plus généralement, toute 'expression scientifique rigoureuse de la pensée chrétienne en travail sur les vérités de la foi' laisse forcément en dehors d'elle bien des éléments d'ordre plus concret, que du reste elle ne contredit pas"; *ibid.*, pp. 395-396, nt. 1: "Pourquoi d'ailleurs ne serait-il pas permis de s'intéresser à cette 'vie subjective', nous ne le voyons pas. Rien n'oblige à toujours parler de la vérité intemporelle. On peut croire à bien des choses sans les rappeler à propos de tout et sans en faire l'objet particulier de ses études. Est-il toujours possible, au surplus, si l'on veut vraiment reconstituer une pensée, de ne pas tenir grandement compte de cette 'vie subjective'?".

44. B. DE SOLAGES – M.-J. NICOLAS, *Autour d'une controverse*, in *Bulletin de Littérature Ecclésiastique* 48 (1947) 3-17.

45. *Ibid.*, p. 13: "Les concepts dans lesquels la Foi nous est proposée ne reflètent la Réalité divine que par une analogie lointaine. Ce sont des concepts crées, élaborés souvent, à partir de l'expérience commune, par voie de réflexion philosophique, et auxquels la lumière de la Révélation divine donne le pouvoir de signifier analogiquement, quoique réellement, des réalités divines surnaturelles. On peut convenir que même les concepts contenus dans la Révélation sont à ce point inadéquats que d'autres concepts (non pas certes contraires à ceux qui ont été choisis, mais complémentaires) auraient pu servir à la Révélation de la même vérité éternelle"; *ibid.*, p. 15: "(…), je ne comprends pas cette nécessité, admise comme un postulat, que toutes les notions se mettent à changer sous prétexte que l'esprit humain évolue, qu'elles soient toutes forcément *contingents*, et que la Vérité Divine doive aussi s'incarner successivement dans des systèmes de notions analogues les uns aux autres, qui se remplacent dans l'esprit des hommes".

46. *Ibid.*, p. 17: "Je crois, comme vous, que le Thomisme est le plus vrai des systèmes. Je dirai même qu'il est le seul vrai en tant que système complet".

47. *Ibid.*, p. 9: "(…). Or si la lumière divine est, par nature, immuable, les données de la raison – nous le découvrons chaque jour un peu plus – changent avec le temps. La synthèse ne peut donc que se modifier aussi. Beaucoup même de ceux qui l'ont compris rêvent de posséder en quelque manière ces deux éléments à part l'un de l'autre, sans se rendre

Still in February 1947, namely three days after his response to B. de Solages[48], the Dominicans M.-M. Labourdette, M.-J. Nicolas and R.-L. Bruckberger published a booklet, containing the article of Labourdette (the *Revue thomiste* containing this article was just published)[49], the answer of the Jesuits and the answer of the Dominicans, – which, for reasons of expediencey, was not published in the *Revue thomiste* and of which Labourdette (the main text) and Nicolas (the *postscriptum*) were the official authors. Concerning the answer of the Jesuits, Labourdette wrote: "La Réponse craint pas d'étendre ce débat jusqu'à une rivalité d'Ordres religieux"[50]. Only in his conclusion he wrote something about the concept of truth: he repeated his view truth being the conformity between our intellect and the objects – cf. scholasticism – and not between our intellect and a subjectively lived life – cf. Daniélou, and others[51].

In February 1947, the most important opinion was undoubtedly the one of R. Garrigou-Lagrange. Continuously referring to Vatican documents – having nothing to do with the discussion of 1946-1947 in itself –, he *retrocontextualized* the whole polemic by arguing that the '*nouvelle théologie*' held the concept of truth of Maurice Blondel (1861-1949) and Henri Bouillard (1908-1981), namely truth as *adaequatio realis mentis et vitae*[52]. Garrigou-Lagrange thus positioned the vision of Daniélou and his

compte que, dès qu'on exprime la vérité divine, on introduit dans cette expression même un élément humain". Cf. M.-J. NICOLAS, *Monde, Chrétienté, Christianisme*, in *Esprit* 14/2 (1946) 202-222, esp. 221.

48. É. Fouilloux made an error by writing "the 14th of February" instead of the 15th of February, cf. É. FOUILLOUX, *Le 'dialogue théologique' selon Marie-Joseph Nicolas*, in *Bulletin de Littérature Ecclésiastique* 103 (2002) 19-32, esp. 26.

49. The introduction of the response by a group of Jesuits (see note 35), the lack of only one quotation in the correspondence between de Solages and Nicolas (in particular on the 3d of February 1947), and the first concluding remark in the booklet (LABOURDETTE – NICOLAS – BRUCKBERGER, *Dialogue théologique* [n. 33], p. 65, note (a), dated 1947) lead us to this statement.

50. *Ibid.*, p. 104.

51. *Ibid.*, pp. 135-136: "Que la façon dont le même P. Daniélou, dans un texte que j'ai longuement cité, parle des rapports entre les systèmes théologiques et les diverses spiritualités conduit à chercher la mesure de l'expression théologique non sur l'objet qu'elle veut proposer, mais sur l'expérience religieuse du théologien, ce qui infléchit la notion même de vérité spéculative de la définition classique de conformité à l'objet vers l'idée de conformité avec la vie subjective. (...), mais je maintiens que ses formules ne sont objectivement explicables que dans le sens de cet infléchissement".

52. For instance Garrigou-Lagrange referred to the propositions of the Holy Office (1 December 1924). The fifth proposition concerned the notion of truth, cf. *Il monitore ecclesiastico* 50 (1925) 194-195, esp. 194: "Quapropter veritas non invenitur in ullo actu particulari intellectus, in quo haberetur 'conformitas cum obiecto', ut aiunt Scholastici, sed veritas est semper in fieri, consistitque in adaequatione progressiva intellectus et vitae, scilicet in motu quodam perpetuo, quo intellectus evolvere et explicare nititur id quot parit experientia vel exigit actio: ea tamen lege ut in toto progressu nihil unquam ratum fi-

fellows within the picture ecclesiastical documents in the first decade of the twentieth century had sketched of the so-called modernism. At the time, modernism was countered by the Church by all possible 'weapons' and became condemned on several occasions: publications were placed on the index, propositions were prohibited in the decree *Lamentabili sane exitu* (1907)[53], modernism was condemned in the encyclical *Pascendi dominici gregis* (1907) and there defined as a "collection of all heresies"[54], the oath against modernism was made compulsory to all clerics and seminarians (1910)[55] and the so-called modernists were blamed, removed from their teaching assignments and/or excommunicated. To declare the *'nouvelle théologie'* as the 'new version of modernism', illustrated the anti-modernist climate was still present in Rome as a slumbering fire under the ashes. It is by no means an exaggeration to consider the article of Garrigou-Lagrange as a fire rekindled.

To get a better view on the heated discussions at the time and the connected concepts of truth we focus on the period of the modernist crisis.

III. A SECOND MODERNIST CRISIS?

Before the church turned modernist ideas and ideology into a 'coherent' system and condemned it as such, modernists were an incoherent, unorganized group of scientists who dared to introduce historical science into theology and deprived Neo-Scholasticism of its absolutist methodological position[56]. The encyclical *Pascendi* countered the vision on the condemned modernists, as if they were "martyrs of truth"[57]. Much of their ideas and ideology would determine the vision of the 'Jesuit side'

xumque habeatur". The French text, in *La Documentation Catholique* 7 (1925) 771-773, esp. 771-772.

53. *Lamentabili sane exitu*, decree of Pope Pius X, 7 July 1907: *ASS* 40 (1907) 470-478.

54. *Pascendi dominici gregis*, encyclical of Pope Pius X, 8 September 1907: *ASS* 40 (1907) 593-650, esp. 632: "Iam systema universum uno quasi obtutu respicientes, nemo mirabitur si sic illud definimus, ut omnium haereseon conlectum esse affirmemus".

55. *Sacrorum antistitum*, motu proprio of Pope Pius X, 1 September 1910: *AAS* 2 (1910) 669-672.

56. Cf. *Pascendi dominici gregis* (n. 54), p. 595: "Quia vero modernistarum (sic enim iure in vulgus audiunt) callidissimum artificium est, ut doctrinas suas non ordine digestas proponant atque in unum collectas, sed sparsas veluti atque invicem seiunctas, ut nimirum ancipites et quasi vagi videantur, cum e contra firmi sint et constantes; praestat, Venerabiles Fratres, doctrinas easdem uno heic conspectu exhibere primum, nexumque indicare quo invicem coalescunt, (…)".

57. *Ibid.*, p. 638: "(…); denique, quod quisque bonus horreat, si quem Ecclesia damnatione perculerit, hunc, facto agmine, non solum palam et copiosissime laudant, sed ut veritatis martyrem pene venerantur".

forty years later. It is therefore not incorrect to position modernism as the preamble of the *'nouvelle théologie'* and to see the latter as a 'further-thinking' or progression of modernism[58]. Garrigou-Lagrange, however, considered this 'further-thinking' as a regression, a 'thinking-back'. According to Garrigou-Lagrange, the Jesuits relapsed into the old error of modernism. In his eyes the same weapons should be used to condemn this line of thought as four decennia earlier.

Concerning the notion of truth we try – within the limits of this contribution – to describe the vision on truth of three modernist thinkers, in particular of George Tyrrell (1861-1909), Maurice Blondel, and Édouard Le Roy (1870-1954). Without treating the subject in an exhaustive way, we want to give a concise sketch of both the understanding of the concept of truth to which Garrigou-Lagrange refered and the theological background of the period 1946-1950.

In 1907, George Tyrrell saw truth as related to experience. All theological propositions are 'untrue' if contradicting experience[59]. Moreover, truth can never be completely known and for this reason she will always be the object of constant disagreement on the theological level[60]. The rea-

---

58. The Modernist thought has been summarized briefly and to the point by H. VOR-GRIMLER, *Neues theologisches Wörterbuch*, Freiburg-Basel-Vienna, Herder, 2000, ²2000, p. 423: "Historisch-kritische Erforschung der Bibel und der Dogmen; Bejahung subjektiver Verantwortung unter dem Primat des Gewissens; gegen die rationale Beweisführung der neuscholastischen Theologie die Bemühung um Glaubenserfahrung; Erneuerung der Kirche als Gemeinschaft mit der Betonung der einzelnen Gemeinde und ihres sakramentalen Lebens, die durch das kirchliche Amt mit der Gesamtkirche verbunden bleibt. Drei besonders kritisierte Ausprägungen besagten, Religion entspringe dem unbewußten, somit seien Religion und Theologie dem Verstand als einer religiös belanglosen Funktion eigentlich nicht zugänglich; bei der Offenbarung Gottes handle es sich um das Bewußtwerden eines inneren religiösen Bedürfnisses, das bei den Offenbarungszeugen nur am deutlichsten 'objektiviert' sei, und bei Erstarrung dieser Objektivationen entstehe Tradition; die Dogmen seien nur symbolische Ausdrücke dieser Objektivationen, die sich mit fortschreitender Kultur verändern müßten"; see also, a.o., J. METTEPENNINGEN, *Malheur devenu bénédiction. Un siècle de modernisme*, in *RHE* 101 (2006) 1039-1070; P. COLIN, *L'audace et le soupçon: La crise du modernisme dans le catholicisme français (1893-1914)* (Anthropologiques), Paris, Desclée de Brouwer, 1997; D. JODOCK (ed.), *Catholicism Contending with Modernity: Roman Catholic Modernism and Anti-Modernism in Historical Context*, Cambridge, Cambridge University Press, 2000; É. POULAT, *Histoire, dogme et critique dans la crise moderniste* (Bibliothèque de 'L'Évolution de l'Humanité', 18), Paris, Albin Michel, 1996.

59. G. TYRRELL, *Through Scylla and Charybdis or the Old Theology and the New*, London, Longmans Green, 1907, p. 285: "'Truth' is used differently of experience and of judgment about experience; and therefore the principle in question is that which all admit, namely, that no theory is true which contradicts experience"; *ibid.*, p. 290: "It is that experience, taken as concrete fact and reality, which forms the subject-matter of theological explanation".

60. Cf. *ibid.*, p. 1: "Controversy in some sense is the indispensable condition of our progress in the apprehension of truth. Truth being inexhaustible, controversies must be eternal".

son for this "eternal disagreement" lies in the fact that truth does not coincide with reflection and science, but first of all with experience and life[61]. Thus Tyrrell considered life as *the* criterion for truth claims[62]. Nevertheless, according to him truth does not in the first place belong to particular presuppositions, but is related to 'the entire' (the universal level) where the particular level belongs to[63]. The same truth cannot be put entirely or adequately into words, whatever any dogma may claim[64]. Concerning the latter Tyrrell gave the example of the trinity and incarnation, where it became clear that we are not able to grasp the truth in her core[65]. Nevertheless, he thought it is possible to state that in the first place truth is one, in spite of the fact that she will reveal herself through differing experiences of life, and that she (for this reason) secondly always remain the same, in spite of the fact that revelation always happened and happens in different ways[66]. There are of course serious consequences for the concepts formulating truth throughout history. Tyrrell indicated the distinction between the infinite object (*in casu* truth) and the finite concepts (our human language). One can only hold on to the use of an analogous language, where both scientific and non-scientific language can become complementary[67].

In the year Tyrrell's *Through Scylla and Charybdis* appeared, Édouard Le Roy supported the vision of Tyrrell. According to Le Roy truth can not

---

61. *Ibid.*, p. 77: "(...) for us it (truth) is a product of life and experience, and not of reflection and design".
62. *Ibid.*, p. 196: "Life is the test and criterion of truth, as serviceableness is of any instrument".
63. *Ibid.*: "(...) Nor does truth belong *per prius* to particular propositions, but to the whole mind or world-scheme with which such particulars cohere, and which they involve or imply".
64. *Ibid.*, pp. 156-157: "The mystery, which religious dogma formulates, purports to be a truth belonging to a plane of reality above and beyond that which is subjected to man's scientific and historic inquiry; a truth which *can* be known dimly, but which cannot possibly be known clearly by him under his present limitations; a truth which, being necessarily formulated in the terms of things which belong to the lower plane, defies exact expression and perfect intelligibility".
65. *Ibid.*, p. 97: "(...) we have examples in the Trinity and Incarnation, of the inability of the human mind to strike a truth fair in the centre, (...)".
66. *Ibid.*, p. 301: "Truth is one and one only, whether it come to us through natural or supernatural experience; (...). However various the imagery and language in which revelation utters itself in different ages and cultures, the underlying reality which reveals itself, now more or less purely and unimpededly, is ever necessarily the same, even as human love is ever the same phenomenon, however various the words and deeds in which it spontaneously finds utterance".
67. *Ibid.*, p. 90: "(...) the infinite can to some extent be expressed in term of the finite; but are only insisting on the purely analogous character of such expression. Nor again are we denying the utility, or even the necessity, of such an endeavour; for we should be forced equally to deny the use of all scientific, as opposed to vulgar, modes of conception; whereas these two modes check and supplement one another".

be known her totality and depth, and thus her conceptual expressions are always subject to improvement[68]. Disagreing however with Tyrrell on the theological formulations of truth, Le Roy considered truth in her theological formulations more as 'truth' through the progress of these formulations in the course of time, rather than in a static content[69]. Here Le Roy referred to the definition of the concept of truth in scholasticism. He opposed this concept so severely that he stated that the main difference between his own thinking and the scholastic ideology, was precisely their differing vision on the concept of truth[70]. According to Le Roy scholasticism displayed a static vision on truth, in which truth received epitheta like 'eternal' and 'immutable'. In contrast, Le Roy painted a dynamic picture of truth, in which truth meant 'life', and therefore 'movement' and 'progress', instead of a set of immutable 'results' in the scholastic *Konklusionstheologie*[71]. According to him this scholastic way of thinking lead straight to scepticism[72], exactly the accusation Garrigou-Lagrange, as a thomist, pronounced to the representatives of the 'nouvelle théologie'.

In 1904, Maurice Blondel wrote *Histoire et dogme*, a work in which he – even more than the two above-mentioned authors– linked history with catholic truth and in doing so he further disconnected her from the vision of the scholastici. For Blondel truth is "the incarnation of dogmatic ideas in historical facts"[73]. This eternal truth occurs to us in a contingent form and is to be situated both in space and in time, in short, in a particular form. Blondel named this "the specific character, the ἅπαξ

---

68. É. LE ROY, *Dogme et critique* (Études de philosophie et de critique religieuse), Paris, Bloud, 1907, p. 283: "(...). Cela ne veut pas dire qu'il n'y ait point de vérité dans les théories théologiques, mais seulement que ces théories sont toujours perfectibles parce qu'elles ne contiennent jamais la plénitude de la vérité".

69. *Ibid.*, pp. 283-284: "En somme, elles (theological theories) sont plus vraies par leur succession, par leur convergence, par leur mouvement progressif, que par leur contenu statique. En ce sens, la théologie est bien une philosophie, la philosophie de la foi".

70. *Ibid.*, p. 355: "En résumé, le grand disaccord entre les scolastiques et nous porte sur la notion même de vérité".

71. *Ibid.*: "La leur (the vision on truth of the scholastici) est *statique*: ils se représentent la vérité comme une *chose*, ils lui accolent tout naturellement les épithètes *éternelle* et *immuable*. Nous croyons, au contraire, que la vérité est *vie*, donc *mouvement*; *croissance* plutôt que de certains *resultats*".

72. *Ibid.*, p. 335: "Cette définition (according to the scholastici the definition of truth runs as follows: *adaequatio rei et intellectus*) envisage d'un côté la *chose*, de l'autre l'*idée* que nous en avons; puis elle fait consister la vérité en une conformité de l'idée à la chose. Eh bien! Une telle manière de procéder conduit tout droit au scepticisme, à l'impossibilité de toute vérification effective".

73. M. BLONDEL, *Histoire et dogme: Les lacunes philosophiques de l'exégèse moderne. Extrait de 'La Quinzaine' des 16 Janvier, 1er et 16 Février 1904*, Orne, 1904, p. 57: "Si l'essentielle vérité du catholicisme, c'est l'incarnation des idées dogmatiques dans les faits historiques, (...)".

of Christianity"[74]. This means that the forms, and therefore the concepts as well, in which truth is interpreted and expressed, are constantly in evolution. Undoubtedly aiming at the Neo-Scholastic vision on truth, he stated that not the idea of 'development' is to be considered as heretic, but the idea of 'fixism'[75]. Two years later Blondel formulated his vision on truth even sharper by defining truth as *adaequatio realis mentis et vitae* instead of the scholastic *adaequatio rei et intellectus*, which according to him is a "chimera"[76]. Forty years later Garrigou-Lagrange is still strongly opposed to this vision and he incorporates his criticism in his paradigm of retrocontextualization; the Jesuit side thinks truth the way Blondel did. It is not difficult to understand why Garrigou-Lagrange saw Blondel as the leader of modernism[77].

For modernists theological truth is not a 'static' 'something', that lies in the transcendent atmosphere and is fixed forever in immutable formulas. On the contrary, truth is a 'dynamic' 'reality', that lets herself to be experienced and therefore reveals herself to us within our life. This makes truth, in contrast to the vision of Neo-Scholasticism, 'particular' and has her expression in a never ending process of development, not as a definite definition of something that can be known in its totality, but as a forever provisional description of a reality that never is to be grasped completely. When Pope Pius X in the encyclical *Pascendi dominici gregis* considered modernism as the "collection of all heresies" and had put the publications of the two mentioned authors (Tyrrell and Le Roy; Blondel was only strongly suspected) on the index, it is clear that in 1907 the church also – and probably especially – condemned the non-Neo-Scholastic vision on the concept of truth of the so-called modernist ideology.

---

74. *Ibid.*, p. 58: "En effet, de la seule hypothèse d'une Révélation positive, c'est-à-dire de la présence de l'éternelle vérité en une forme locale, temporelle et contingente, il résulte des conséquences précises; et c'est là vraiment le caractère spécifique, l'ἅπαξ du christianisme".

75. *Ibid.*, p. 59: "Loin donc que l'idée de 'développement' dont tant de croyants s'inquiètent soit hétérodoxe, c'est le fixisme (aussi bien celui de l'historien qui prétend saisir la vérité de la Révélation dans sa première rédaction, que celui du spéculative prêt à éteindre l'infinie réalité dans une synthèse achevée, comme si à un moment donné de l'histoire l'esprit de l'homme avait tari l'esprit de Dieu), oui, c'est le 'fixisme' qui est une hérésie virtuelle".

76. ID., *Le point de départ de la recherche philosophique*, in *Annales de philosophie chrétienne* 77 (1906) 225-249, esp. 235: "(...), afin d'intégrer dans la conscience et la science tout ce qui est spontanément dans la vie, et afin d'intégrer dans la vie tout ce qui se manifeste de vérités dans la conscience et la science. À l'abstraite et chimérique *adaequatio speculativa rei et intellectus* se substitue la recherche méthodique de droit l'*adaequatio realis mentis et vitae*. C'est de cette règle intime que Pascal disait qu'elle commande bien plus impérieusement qu'un maître; (...)".

77. GARRIGOU-LAGRANGE, *La nouvelle théologie* (n. 11), pp. 129-131.

In 1950, Pope Pius XII in the encyclical *Humani generis* disapproved
of the thinking in terms of 'development' and the connected dynamic
conception of truth. According to the Pope, truth is 'untouchable'[78]. The
encyclical is explicitly based on the Neo-Scholastic intellectual framework. This becomes more clear in the passage following immediately on
the subparagraph on truth, particularly where the Pope – baring the foregoing in mind – states "that it is clear why the church still continues
teaching its future priests Neo-Scholastic"[79]. Pius even writes that contempt of scholasticism leads to contempt of the *magisterium docendi*, by
often perceived as blocking the progress of science[80]. In his concluding
remarks the Pope warns that "straying teachers" are not allowed to return
to the church without having admitted unconditionally to teach and adhere
the "complete truth that lives in the church"[81]. Here it is possible to discover a link between *veritas* and *auctoritas*, as they were in the first half
of the twentieth century. The former seems to be appropriated by the latter.

The terminology of *Humani generis* – 'what's in a name?' – does
remind us of those of *Pascendi dominici gregis*. Both are concerned with
misunderstandings, the prohibiting of a methodology in terms of development, and the stress on 'orthodoxy' and Neo-Scholasticism as the one
and only intellectual framework possible. *Humani generis*, however,
never quotes *Pascendi* – contrary to Garrigou-Lagrange – nor can be
found one single reference to the modernist crisis. For this reason it
seems, out of a comparison between encyclicals, rather undesirable to us
to speak of a second modernist crisis within the framework of the polemic
of 1946-1947. Concerning the notion of truth, however, the desirability
can be mentioned because of two reasons. First, both *Pascendi* and
Humani generis try to stop the main cause of many misunderstandings,

78. *Humani generis*, encyclical of Pope Pius XII, 12 Augustus 1950 (the official version of the text mentions 1850), in *AAS* 42 (1950) 561-578, esp. p. 572: "Non enim veritas omnisque eius philosophica declaratio in dies mutari possunt, cum potissimum agatur
de principiis humanae menti per se notis, vel de sententiis illis, quae tum saeculorum sapi-
entia, tum etiam divinae 'revelationis' consensu ac fulcimine innituntur".

79. *Ibid.*, p. 573: "Quae si bene perspecta fuerint, facile patebit cur Ecclesia exigat ut
futuri sacerdotes philosophicis disciplinis instruantur 'ad Angelici Doctoris rationem, doc-
trinam et principia' (C.I.C., can. 1366, 2)".

80. *Ibid.*, p. 567: "Utique, proh dolor, rerum novarum studiosi a scholasticae theolo-
giae contemptu ad neglegendum, ac vel etiam ad despiciendum facile transeunt ipsum
Magisterium Ecclesiae, quod theologiam illam sua auctoritate tantopere comprobat. Hoc
enim Magisterium ab ipsis tamquam progressionis sufflamen ac scientiae obex exhibetur".

81. *Ibid.*, p. 578: "(…); nec denique putent, falso 'irenismo' indulgentes, ad Ecclesiae
sinum dissidentes et errantes feliciter reduci posse, nisi integra veritas in Ecclesia vigens,
absque ulla corruptione detractioneque, sincere omnibus tradatur".

contempt of scholasticism[82]. Second, concerning the notion on truth, the core of the 'heresy' is the same in both encyclicals. *Pascendi* fulminates against truth as *adaequatio realis mentis et vitae* or *conformitas mentis et vitae*; compared to the vision supported by Rome – *adaequatio rei et intellectus* –, *Pascendi* defines this as a "nice word game", but totally meaningless because of a subjective and constantly developing understanding of truth, based on experience and feeling[83]. In *Humani generis* we can read equal notions. So between 1907 and 1950, nothing has changed in the Vatican's opinion on truth.

IV. Responses to the Vision of R. Garrigou-Lagrange

It is obvious the article of Garrigou-Lagrange provoked reactions. The sharpest response came from a member of his own order, more particularly from the afore mentioned Bruno de Solages, rector of the Institut catholique in Toulouse. In 1947, in the second number of the *Bulletin de Littérature Ecclésiastique*, he wrote a destroying critique[84]. He noted that Garrigou-Lagrange did not quote – or at least incorrectly – publications, that he presented many things without or out of their contexts, and that

82. *Pascendi dominici gregis* (n. 54), p. 636: "Quod si a moralibus causis ad eas quae ab intellectu sunt veniamus, prima ac potissima occurret ignorantia. Enimvero modernistae quotquot sunt, qui doctores in ecclesia esse ac videri volunt, modernam philosophiam plenis buccis extollentes aspernatique scholasticam, non aliter illam, eius fuco et fallaciis decepti, sunt amplexi, quam quod alteram ignorantes prorsus, omni argumento caruerunt ad notionum confusionem tollendam et ad sophismata refellenda. Ex connubio autem falsae philosophiae cum fide illorum systema, tot tantisque erroribus abundans, ortum habuit. (…). Tria sunt potissimum quae suis illi conatibus adversari sentiunt: scholastica philosophandi methodus, Patrum auctoritas et traditio, magisterium ecclesiasticum. Contra haec acerrima illorum pugna. Idcirco philosophiam ac theologiam scholasticam derident passim atque contemnunt. Sive id ex ignoratione faciant sive ex metu, sive potius ex utraque causa, certum est studium novarum rerum cum odio scholasticae methodi coniungi semper"; *Humani generis* (n. 78), p. 567.

83. *Pascendi dominici gregis* (n. 54), pp. 632-633: "(…): communi autem sensu docemur, perturbationem aut occupationem animi quampiam, non adiumento sed impedimento esse potius ad investigationem veri, veri inquimus ut in se est; nam verum illud alterum *subiectivum*, fructus interni sensus et actionis, si quidem ludendo est aptum, nihil admodum homini confert, (…)".

84. B. DE SOLAGES, *Pour l'honneur de la théologie: Les contre-sens du R. P. Garrigou-Lagrange*, in *Bulletin de Littérature Ecclésiastique* 48 (1947) 65-84. Reprinted in *Bulletin de Littérature Ecclésiastique* 99 (1998) 257-272. The quotations in the following notes are taken from the original article. Fifty years later, in 1998, both J.-M. Glé and A. Dupleix published an article on de Solages's article: J.-M. GLÉ, *'Pour l'honneur de la théologie'. Bruno de Solages le défenseur de Henri Bouillard*, in *Bulletin de Littérature Ecclésiastique* 99 (1998) 157-165; A. DUPLEIX, *'Pour l'honneur de la théologie'. Bruno de Solages le défenseur de Teilhard*, in *Bulletin de Littérature Ecclésiastique* 99 (1998) 167-179.

he gave a reversed interpretation of what was meant by some of the authors. In short, according to de Solages the article of Garrigou-Lagrange was lacking elementary use of the rules of science. He had better followed the example of Thomas Aquinas, whose teaching he always used "as a club to shatter his enemies"[85]. For instance, Garrigou-Lagrange referred to a description of scholastic truth by Blondel that did not correspond with Blondel's actual writings. Garrigou-Lagrange even stated that this description, the exact counterpart of Blondel's vision on truth, was the basis for the vision on truth of Bouillard[86]. De Solages concluded by writing that Garrigou-Lagrange was a member of the side of those who are trying to condemn Thomas[87]! It is beyond the scope of this contribution to enter further in this highly interesting article of de Solages. We therefore only mention that Garrigou-Lagrange responded de Solages, particularly in the April number of *Angelicum*[88]. He indicated that the essence of his article of February 1947 was a reaction to the new concept

---

85. DE SOLAGES, *Pour l'honneur de la théologie* (n. 84), p. 69: "Il se contente de citer quelques phrases, un morceau de phrase souvent, de chacun des auteurs qu'il attaque. Ceci est déjà de mauvaise méthode quand on veut juger de la pensée d'un auteur. Mais ce n'est rien encore! Ses citations sont inexactes, détachées de tout contexte et interprétées à contre-sens. Là encore le R. P. Garrigou-Lagrange se montre fort mauvais élève de saint Thomas. Celui-ci est préoccupé de l'exactitude des citations"; *ibid.*, p. 66: "(…) des règles de honnêteté. Saint Thomas, qui vivait pourtant à une époque où la critique existait à peine, n'y manquait point. Le R. P. Garrigou-Lagrange, qui manie tout le temps le thomisme comme une massue pour écraser ses adversaires, ferait mieux d'être plus fidèle à l'exemple du Docteur Angélique"; *ibid.*: "La première règle violée est une règle de correction: on n'utilise pas – entre honnêtes gens – dans une controverse publique, des textes dont on ne sait pas qu'ils sont authentiques"; *ibid.*, p. 67: "Mais ce qui est plus grave encore, c'est qu'ayant cité ce texte anonyme sur l'Eucharistie après un autre texte tiré de 'feuilles polycopiées', dont il ne nomme pas expressément l'auteur (…)".

86. *Ibid.*, p. 77: "Mais sans tenir le moindre compte de ses affirmations catégoriques, explicites et soulignées, le P. Garrigou-Lagrange attribue de manière absolument gratuite au P. Bouillard une conception de vérité dont il prétend trouver la source première chez M. Maurice Blondel: 'Et comment enfin maintenir que toutes ces propositions sont immuablement *vraies*, si la notion même de vérité doit changer, et s'il faut substituer à la définition traditionnelle de la vérité (la conformité du jugement au réel extramental et à ses lois immuables) celle proposée ces dernières années par la philosophie de l'action: la conformité du jugement avec les exigences de l'action ou de la vie humaine qui évolue toujours?'"; *ibid.*, p. 82: "Le R. P. Garrigou-Lagrange reproche d'abord à M. Blondel une définition de la vérité. Or cette définition – dont, selon lui, provient tout le mal – il ne la cite même pas correctement et supprime du texte de M. Blondel un mot essentiel à l'antithèse entre les deux conceptions de la vérité, le mot *speculativa*: 'A l'abstraite et chimérique adaequatio speculativa rei et intellectus' avait écrit M. Blondel. On pourrait montrer que, même dans le texte de cet article, vieux de plus de quarante ans, la pensée de M. Blondel n'a pas le sens relativiste que lui attribue le P. Garrigou-Lagrange, (…)".

87. *Ibid.*, p. 84: "Le P. Garrigou-Lagrange, il est – et je le regrette – dans le side de ceux qui firent condamner saint Thomas".

88. R. GARRIGOU-LAGRANGE, *Vérité et immutabilité du dogme*, in *Angelicum* 24 (1947) 124-139.

of truth, such as Blondel presented in 1906[89]. Garrigou-Lagrange now quoted Blondel entirely, but put it clearly, after having made several observations, that he maintained his critique[90]. Blondel's vision on truth and the one of the *'nouvelle théologie'* "would lethally hurt the intellect"[91]. The traditional concept as it was held by all of the councils and the *'nouvelle théologie'* had been put into perspective by the Pope on the 19th of September 1946, according to Garrigou-Lagrange[92]. In the same number of *Angelicum* a letter of Maurice Blondel himself was printed, who reacted against the distortion of his concept of truth in the February-article of Garrigou-Lagrange[93]. The response of the latter to Blondel, which immediately followed, ended with the message that many errors in recent theological literature found their reason both in the new conception of truth and in the abandoning of the traditional concept of truth, an evolution which is based upon the 'philosophy of action'[94]. Thus we gain the impression that Blondel and Garrigou-Lagrange were not on the same wavelength, since Blondel put the accent on his interpretation of *res* and

89. *Ibid.*, p. 125: "Nous avons critiqué surtout la nouvelle définition de la vérité proposée par M. Blondel, (…)".

90. *Ibid.*, p. 134: "Nous maintenons donc notre critique". See also the following note.

91. *Ibid.*, p. 137: "Nous ne pouvons donc que maintenir ce que nous avons dit en particulier en ce qui concerne la définition traditionnelle de la vérité *'adaequatio rei et intellectus'*, la conformité du jugement avec le réel et ses trois lois immuables. Cette définition n'est pas chimérique, il ne faut pas lui en substituer une autre qui glisse vers le pragmatisme. Ce serait blesser mortellement l'intelligence; ce serait oublier que cette définition traditionnelle est supposée par tous les Conciles et requise pour l'immutabilité du dogme. On ne saurait donc être trop attentif aux paroles de Sa Sainteté Pie XII dans le discours publié par l'*Osservatore Romano* du 19 Sept. 1946: (…)".

92. See the previous note.

93. M. BLONDEL, *Correspondance*, in *Angelicum* 24 (1947) 210-214, there p. 210: "D'abord, la citation de mon texte est mutilée; en outre, elle laisse ignorer tout l'ensemble d'une doctrine où j'étudie les multiples aspects de l'enseignement intégral"; *ibid.*, p. 211: "On m'attribue gratuitement des conséquences totalement opposées à mes conclusions les plus formelles. Quand on me reproche de méconnaître la suffisance absolue de la définition de la vérité, adaequatio rei et intellectus, ce serait à moi de protester contre cette réduction aux mots *res* et *intellectus*, à la contenance tout à fait insuffisante: *res* en effet ne suffit pas à désigner les plus hautes réalités, et l'intellect n'épuise pas la science des choses et des êtres, ni la réalité des opérations intimes de notre conscience ou de nos devoirs, ni la vérité profonde de notre destinée surnaturelle. Il y a donc carence dans une doctrine à laquelle on voudrait me réduire".

94. *Ibid.*, p. 214: "Enfin nous avons examiné plusieurs déviations récentes sur la nature de la théologie, sur la grâce, sur le péché originel, sur la transsubstantation et la présence réelle. Nous avons remarqué que ces déviation (sic) provenaient de l'oubli ou de l'abandon plus au moins marqué de *la définition traditionnelle de la vérité* (conformité du jugement au réel et à ses lois immuables) et *de l'acceptation de la définition proposé par la philosophie de l'action* (la conformité du jugement avec la vie humaine selon les exigences de l'action), définition qui glisse, disions-nous, vers le pragmatisme. C'est du reste ce qui motiva le 1er décembre 1924 la condamnation par le Saint Office de 12 propositions extraites de la philosophie de l'action".

intellectus, whereas Garrigou-Lagrange in his response – not as such in his February-article – rather wrote on the words *'chimérique'* and *'substituer'*[95].

V. CONCLUDING CONSIDERATIONS

Within the polemic concerning the 'nouvelle théologie', truth is an issue being the most important *casus* concerning the topic of the integration of historical knowledge in the field of theology. The Jesuit's vision of *recontextualization* is a 'further-thinking' of the modernist's ideology, stating that truth should always be seen within the particular intellectual and historical context, to which the ever developing concepts lend themselves to interpret and express that same truth. The fact that the entire truth cannot be known goes together with the recognition of the particularity of her expression and the subjectivity of the vision on truth. This opposes the opinion of Garrigou-Lagrange, Labourdette and others, who hold a speculative, meta-historical vision on truth. According to them, truth has once been revealed by God and became recognised and ratified by the church in formulas, being – as well as truth herself – untouchable and therefore immutable. Every inclination to particularity is banished. The church followed this line of speculative theology in the first half of the twentieth century, which becomes clear from the reading of *Pascendi dominici gregis* and *Humani generis*. The *decontextualization* which the church and the 'Dominican side' supported in 1946-1947 seems completely different from and opposite to the recontextualization as proposed by the 'Jesuit side'. Garrigou-Lagrange, as the most important representative of the Dominican vision, considered the vision of the Jesuits as modernist and attacked it with the weapons of antimodernism of four decades earlier, as it is proved by his article of February 1947. In the same month a group of Jesuit theologians wrote that the polemic returned *de facto* to the integrism of another time[96]. To conclude we can

95. Cf. the vision of Blondel, see notes 28 and 76.
96. *La théologie et ses sources. Réponse*, pp. 399-400: "La manière insolite dont cette brochure de combat (Labourdette's article in *Revue thomiste*) fut répandue pouvait déjà nous donner à penser. Venant en outre, non du même auteur, – nous tenons à le dire, – mais du même milieu et de quelques petits groupes apparentés, certains échos fort précis de conversations, certaines correspondances, certaines agitations seraient de nature à faire craindre que, si les mauvais jours du modernisme sont, grâce à Dieu, maintenant loin de nous, les mauvais jours de l'intégrisme ne fussent sur le point de revenir... (...). Il y a d'ailleurs par le monde trop d'hérésies, celles-là trop réelles, il y a trop d'erreurs virulentes et meurtrières pour qu'il soit permis de nous attarder entre nous (Jesuits on the one hand and Dominicans on the other hand) à des disputes d'un autre âge".

state that this polemic had its roots in the modernist crisis, but there is probably no reason to see this as a return to this crisis. The '*nouvelle théologie*' did not 'repeat' the modernist crisis, but developed its core ideas. Moreover, in 1946-1947, the impact of the internal pluralisation of neothomism must be taken into account, whereas in the first decade of the twentieth century there was only 'one' form of neothomism. One can state that the thinking in terms of *retrocontextualization* of Garrigou-Lagrange was an extreme and paradoxical attempt to defend and to maintain the decontextualization of truth. This objective, speculative, universal and a-historical vision on truth clashes with the subjective, experience-oriented, particular and historical vision of the '*nouvelle théologie*'. Concerning the comparison with the polemic of modernism, it suffices to conclude by quoting Étienne Fouilloux, who wrote fifty years after that polemic of the '*nouvelle théologie*' that the modernist crisis is "the intellectual matrix of catholic thinking of the twentieth century"[97]. Truth was the issue that played a major role in this 'matrix'.

jurgen.mettepenningen@theo.kuleuven.be   Jürgen METTEPENNINGEN

---

97. Cf. FOUILLOUX, *Une Église en quête de liberté* (n. 8), p. 10: "La crise moderniste constitue la matrice intellectuelle du catholicisme contemporain, dans la mesure précisément où elle se définit par la volonté de relire le message fondateur à la lueur des connaissances scientifiques du siècle dernier"; T. SCHOOF, *Aggiornamento: De doorbraak van een nieuwe katholieke theologie* (Theologische Monografieën), Baarn, Wereldvenster, 1968, p. 54: "Want dit eerste diepgaande conflict tussen een naar vernieuwing zoekende theologie en de traditionele interpretatie van de geloofsleer heeft tot op onze dagen de positie van de katholieke theologie bepaald". Concerning christology as the heart of Christian truth, I mention a part of my own field of research, namely Piet Schoonenberg's christological reflection in the wake of modernism and the 'nouvelle théologie'. Cf. J. METTE-PENNINGEN, *Christus denken naar de mensen toe. De 'nouvelle théologie' christologisch doorgedacht door Piet Schoonenberg*, in *Tijdschrift voor Theologie* 46 (2006) 143-160.

PERCEIVING ORTHODOXY

A COMPARATIVE ANALYSIS OF THE ROMAN CONTROVERSY
IN CATHOLIC EXEGESIS (1960-1961)

I. PRELIMINARY NOTES ... AN ESSAY IN CHURCH HISTORY

The following text is not the average historiographical in-depth study. It is more of an historiographer's essay. We wish to point this out at the outset since it implies setting out from an intuition rather than from an a priori scientifically-developed theory, methodology or hermeneutic. In addition, it implies that the structure of our text is kept to its simplest. Its sole interest is to investigate the meaning of the theological concept 'orthodoxy'. More accurately, it is an investigation from the viewpoint of church history, with an emphasis on church history, not the church historian. This means that we take for granted the possibility of the historian to enter history, or of history to enter the historian, which is all the same. The exact relationship between historian and history is not at stake here. We merely wish to offer history's voice. Seen from that specific angle – i.e., from within the historical debate – we intend to find and possibly grasp some elements that have to be taken into account for any theological understanding of religious orthodoxy – and in particular, of Roman Catholic orthodoxy. In order to do so we will be 'using' an historical event. We will enter into it, describe it, and subsequently analyze it from within with the goal of adding to the theological debate on the nature of orthodoxy.

The event we refer to is a small, a seemingly unimportant event, yet it suits exceedingly well as a reference point that could add to theological discussions on the nature of orthodoxy. The event to be studied is better known as the 'Roman' or the 'neo-modernist controversy'. It occurs in the late 1950s and early 1960s when two Roman pontifical institutes became entangled in a discussion that, at a first and superficial glance, would seem to be an 'inside' quarrel among exegetes. However, the quarrel soon covers a much wider sphere and gains in importance. Our interest for this specific topic was raised by the fact that this controversy – between the Pontifical Biblical Institute (PBI) and the Pontifical Lateran University (PLU)[1] – involved professors of both institutes who, accused

---

1. The former Lateran Atheneum had only recently been elevated to the rank of Uni-

their counterparts of heterodoxy, and was convinced of the orthodoxy of his teaching[2].

Given the fact that church historiographers and exegetes have already commented on this controversy in various publications[3], we do not wish to duplicate their work. Still, some background is necessary. Rather than presenting the reader with a classical historiographic study including a full reconstruction of events, we prefer to select two articles out of the many that swirled in this controversial whirlwind and offer them as *pars pro toto*. One of these articles was written by the PBI professor Luis Alonso-Schökel[4], the other by PLU professor Antonino Romeo[5]. Extensive publications devoted to the neo-modernist controversy reveal that these articles played a central role in the debate, which renders them all the more apt for our purpose[6]. Both texts can also hardly be read separately, given

versity by John XXIII, in the *motu proprio Cum Inde*, of May 17, 1959 (in *AAS* 51 [1959] 401-402). On the history and motives behind the elevation see S. PACIOLLA, *Nec de nomine tantum hic agitur*, in *Nuntium* 8 (1999) 176-179. – M. MANZO, *Papa Roncalli e il Laterano*, in P. CHENAUX (ed.), *L'università del Laterano e la preparazione del Concilio Vaticano II: Atti del Convegno Internazionale di Studi (Città del Vaticano, 27 gennaio 2000)* (Studi e documenti sul Concilio Vaticano II, 1), Rome, Lateran University Press, 2001, 29-39, esp. pp. 34-35.

2. See for instance a note in the preconciliar diary of the American Ecclesiastical Review's editor-in-chief, Joseph Clifford Fenton: J.C. FENTON, *Council Diary*, December 4, 1960: "Bill Cummings has just called. He is coming over and we are going out. He has some real news. It seems that one of the Profs at the Biblical Institute came in the other day and told the class that he had been accused of teaching heresy". A copy of this diary can be consulted at the '*Centre for the Study of the Second Vatican Council*', part of the K.U.Leuven Faculty of Theology.

3. R. BURIGANA, *Tradizioni inconciliabili? La "querelle" tra l'Università Lateranense e l'Istituto Biblico nella preparazione del Vaticano II*, in CHENAUX, *L'università del Laterano* (n.1), pp. 51-66; J.A. KOMONCHAK, *The Struggle for the Council During the Preparation of Vatican II (1960-1962)*, in ID. – G. ALBERIGO (eds.), *History of Vatican II*. Vol. I: *Announcing and Preparing Vatican Council II. Toward a New Era in Catholicism*, Maryknoll, NY, Orbis; Leuven, Peeters, 1995, pp. 167-356, esp. pp. 278-283; J.A. FITZMYER, *A Recent Roman Scriptural Controversy*, in *Theological Studies* 22 (1961) 426-444; B.W. HARRISON, *The Teaching of Paul VI on Sacred Scripture: With Special Reference to the Historicity of the Gospels*, Rome, Pontificium Athenaeum Sanctae Crucis, 1997, esp. pp. 59-72; ID., *On Rewriting the Bible: Catholic Biblical Studies in the 60's*, in *Christian Order* 43 (2002) 155-178; ID., *The Encyclical Spiritus Paraclitus in Its Historical Context*, in *Living Tradition* 60 (1995); M. PESCE, *Il rinnovamento biblico*, in M. GUASCO, et al. (eds.), *Storia della chiesa*. Vol. XXV/2: *La Chiesa del Vaticano II (1958-1978)*, Milan, San Paolo, 1994, 167-216; G.P. FOGARTY, *American Catholic Biblical Scholarship: A History from the Early Republic to Vatican II*, New York, Harper & Row, 1989, pp. 291-296, 323.

4. L. ALONSO-SCHÖKEL, *Dove va l'esegesi cattolica?*, in *La Civiltà Cattolica* 111/3 (1960) 449-460.

5. A. ROMEO, *L'Enciclica "Divino afflante Spiritu" e le "opiniones novae"*, in *Divinitas* 4 (1960) 387-456.

6. See for instance BURIGANA, *Tradizioni inconciliabili?* (n. 3), pp. 57-62. It needs to be stressed here that these two articles did not constitute the beginning or the close of the

the fact that Alonso-Schökel's text triggered Romeo's reaction. It is easy, therefore, to understand how this interaction forced both documents to address the same theological issues – a fact that facilitates illustrative comparison. The main concern of these theologians is biblical historicity and how the concept of historicity fits in the framework of a Catholic theology of revelation. Connected with this concept are issues of biblical hermeneutics, the doctrine of scriptural inspiration and scriptural inerrancy.

In the first section of this paper, we will supply the reader with a review of the contents of both articles, following the authors' lines of argument, and focusing mostly on their use of possible authoritative sources. Second, having separately presented the arguments of Alonso-Schökel and Romeo, we will add a twofold comparative analysis of the articles – *i.e.*, both on a material (theological content) and a structural level – trying to grasp differences and analogies between the authors. We believe that this may offer some insight into the functioning of Roman Catholic orthodoxy within church history. Our main point of interest is a conclusive comparative analysis. Readers interested in the broader significance and place of the Roman controversy within the recent history of Catholic exegesis will find sufficient background reading references in the footnote below[7].

controversy. Rather, discussions had been aroused by an article of Biblicum professor S. Lyonnet, *Le péché originel et l'exégèse de Rom. 5,12*, in *Recherches de science religieuse* 44 (1956) 63-84, and the subsequent reaction of Lateran professor F. Spadafora, *Rom. 5,12. Esegesi e riflessi dogmatici*, in *Divinitas* 4 (1960) 289-298 to it. Also, in 1959, Biblicum exegete Maximilian Zerwick had delivered various lectures, bundled and published as M. Zerwick, *Critica letteraria del N.T. nell'esegesi cattolica dei Vangeli* (Conferenze tenute al Convegno biblico di Padova 15-17 settembre 1959), S. Giorgio Canavese, 1959. Again Spadafora reacted viciously in his commentary on a brief *Monitum* by the Holy Office (See Suprema sacra congregatio Sancti Officii, *De germana veritate historica et obiectiva S.Scripturae, etiam quoad dicta et facta Christi Iesu, debite tutanda*, 10 iunii 1961, in *AAS* 53 (1961) 507; for Spadafora's text, see F. Spadafora, *Un documento notevole per l'esegesi cattolica*, in *Palestra del Clero* 40 (1961) 969-981), stating that Zerwicks points of view regarding the importance of historico-critical exegesis are heterodox. Three decades past the controversy Spadafora still defends his criticism of Lyonnet and Zerwick: "i due padri, ascoltati dal S. Officio, non poterono negare gli addebiti loro attribuiti: insegnamente erroneo (e articoli) sulla ispirazione, sulla inerranza dei Libri Santi, sulla storicità degli Vangeli". See F. Spadafora, *La tradizione contro il Concilio*, Rome, Ed. Volpe, 1989, p. 49. A more detailed discussion of the theological issues debated can be found in Harrison, *The Teaching of Pope Paul VI* (n. 3), pp. 64-66.

7. R. Aubert, *La théologie catholique au milieu du XXe siècle* (Cahiers de l'actualité religieuse), Tournai, Casterman, 1954. – D.P. Bechard (ed.), *The Scripture Documents: An Anthology of Official Catholic Teachings*. Foreword by J.A. Fitzmyer, Collegeville, MN, Liturgical Press, 2002; I. de la Potterie, *L'Istituto Biblico negli ottant'anni della sua storia*, in *La Civiltà Cattolica* 140/4 (1989) 166-172; M. Gilbert, *Cinquant'anni di magistero romano sull'ermeneutica biblica. Leone XIII (1893) – Pio XII (1943)*, in Id. – P. Laghi – A. Vanhoye, *Chiesa e Sacra Scrittura: Un secolo di magistero ecclesiastico*

II. LUIS-ALONSO SCHÖKEL AND DISCONTINUITY IN RECENT
CHURCH HISTORY[8]

September 3, 1960, Rome. While the city is still mingled in the turmoil
surrounding the Seventeenth Olympic Games held at that time, Luis
Alonso-Schökel[9], a Spanish professor at the Pontifical Biblical Institute,
published an article entitled '*Dove va l'esegesi cattolica?*[10]'. As a Jesuit,
he had submitted his text to the redaction of the well-known Jesuit periodical *La Civiltà cattolica*, where it was accepted for print without any
obstacles. As the presence of a question mark in the title of the piece
indicates, the article wished to inquire and understand the direction into
which contemporary biblical exegesis was moving.

This inquiry, Alonso-Schökel states, can only find answers by means
of determining the current trajectory[11] of the exegetical movement – a
trajectory which the author sees fluctuating between two anchor points:
first, Pius XII's promulgation of the encyclical *Divino afflante Spiritu*, in

e studi biblici (Subsidia biblica, 17), Rome, Editrice Pontificio Istituto Biblico, 1994, 11-
33; D. JODOCK, *Catholicism Contending with Modernity: Roman Catholic Modernism and
Antimodernism in Historical Context*, Cambridge, Cambridge University Press, 2000; M.
PESCE, *Dall'enciclica biblica di Leone XIII «Providentissimus Deus» (1893) a quella di
Pio XII «Divino afflante Spiritu» (1943)*, in C.M. MARTINI – G. GHIBERTI – M. PESCE,
Cento anni di cammino biblico, Milan, Vita e pensiero, 1995, 39-100; J.G. PRIOR, *The His-
torical Critical Method in Catholic Exegesis* (Tesi Gregoriana: Serie Teologia, 50), Rome,
Pontificia Università Gregoriana, 1999. R.B. ROBINSON, *Roman Catholic Exegesis Since
Divino afflante Spiritu: Hermeneutical Implications* (Society of Biblical Literature: Dis-
sertation Series, 111), Atlanta, GA, Scholars Press, 1982; C. THEOBALD, *La «Question
Biblique» de Providentissimus Deus à la réception de l'exégèse historico-critique par
Divino afflante Spiritu*, in ID. – B. SESBOÜÉ (eds.), *La parole du Salut: La doctrine de la
parole de Dieu* (Histoire des dogmes, 4), Paris, Desclée de Brouwer, 1996, 345-382.
    8. The specific nature of our essay demands paraphrasing large parts of ALONSO-
SCHÖKEL, *Dove va* (n. 4), in the following few pages. In order to confine the critical apparatus of this essay we will only add footnote references when strictly required.
    9. Luis Alonso-Schökel (°1920-†1998), was born in Madrid, and at the time of our
debate had only been recently appointed professor at the Biblicum. He was appointed professor of Old Testament exegesis in succession of the deceased professor R. Dyson. His
nomination came almost immediately after the defense of his doctorate at the PBI, published five years later as L. ALONSO-SCHÖKEL, *Estudios de poética Hebrea*, Barcelona,
Juan Flors, 1963. To this, he owed A. Romeo's criticism that the author of *Dove va* (n. 4),
is a young inexperienced exegete, with only few (and most recent) publications to his
name ... (See ROMEO, *L'Enciclica* [n. 5], pp. 392-393). Alonso-Schökel remained professor at the Institute, teaching courses such as *Introduction in the Old Testament* and *Biblical Hermeneutics*, until his passing. See for instance E. ZURRO RODRIGUEZ, *Luis Alonso
Schökel (1920-1998): Escritor, escriturario, espejo*, in *Estudios Ecclesiásticos* 73 (1998)
565-573.
    10. ALONSO-SCHÖKEL, *Dove va* (n. 4), pp. 449-460.
    11. We use this term for its etymological and semiotical connection to the Italian '*trai-
ettoria*', cfr. ALONSO-SCHÖKEL, *Dove va* (n. 4), pp. 449-450 ff.

1943[12], and the second, Eugenio Pacelli's ultimate statements on biblical matters, written a few weeks before his death. These are found in a letter to the Belgian Cardinal Jozef-Ernest van Roey, a letter proposed as an address to an international exegetical conference in Brussels in 1958[13]. Having secured these historical reference points, the author asks whether the exegetical movement actually started as late as 1943. Further, what had happened in the 50 years preceding *Divino afflante Spiritu*? And, if in 1943 something new actually occurred, how to interpret this change ...? Therefore, Alonso-Schökel decides to commence his research with a short presentation of some exegetical studies prior to 1950, in order to grasp what is new in contemporary exegesis[14].

Regarding exegetical study of Ancient Near East languages and cultures, Alonso-Schökel singles out some sentences written by the Jesuit Cardinal Louis Billot[15], arguing that, where Billot's phrases displayed a certain reluctance in adopting the contribution of positive sciences in biblical exegesis, *Divino afflante Spiritu* did the exact opposite. By means of citations from that encyclical, Alonso-Schökel concludes that Pius XII petitioned for a positive attitude of exegetes towards scientific methods[16].

12. See PIUS XII, *Litt. Enc. Divino afflante Spiritu de Sacrorum Bibliorum studiis opportune provehendis*, in *AAS* (1943) 297-326. Further referred to as *Divino afflante Spiritu*.

13. See ALONSO-SCHÖKEL, *Dove va* (n. 4), pp. 449-450. The conference took place in Brussels, August 1958, at the occasion of the World Expo, and conference meetings were held in the newly built Vatican pavilion *Civitas Dei*. The Acts were published as J. COPPENS – A. DESCAMPS – É. MASSAUX (eds.), *Sacra Pagina: Miscellanea biblica, congressus internationalis catholici de re biblica*, 2 vols. (BETL, 12-13), Paris, Éditions J. Gabalda; Gembloux, Éditions J. Duculot, 1959. For the Pope's letter to Van Roey, see *Ibid.*, pp. 14-16. The original can be found in the *Archives of the archdiocese of Mechelen-Brussels* (Mechelen) Papers Card. J.E. van Roey, II.A.23.

14. ALONSO-SCHÖKEL, *Dove va* (n. 4), p. 450: "È chiaro allora che non basta prendere il 1943 come punto di partenza della traiettoria: È necessario invece risalire ai principi del secolo, per poter rispondere al significato reale della domanda".

15. The French Jesuit cardinal Louis Billot (°1846-†1931) had been professor at the Gregorian University from 1885 until 1911, and became a key member of the Pontifical Biblical Commission (PBC) in 1923. Billot was appreciated as a specialist in thomistic theology, and as a fierce opponent to theological liberalism. The work referred to is L. BILLOT, *De inspiratione Sacrae Scripturae theologica disquisitio. Editio altera et emendata*, Rome, Pontificia Universitas Gregoriana, ⁴1929. Alonso-Schökel notes in *Dove va* (n. 4), p. 450, n. 1, that the original edition is from 1906. This is not correct, and should have been 1903.

16. Alonso-Schökel refers to *Divino afflante Spiritu* (n. 12), p. 305: "Haec omnia, quae, non sine providentis Dei consilio, aetas haec nostra consecuta est, Sacrarum Litterarum interpretes quoddammodo invitant atque admonent, ut ad Divina Eloquia penitius perscrutanda, illustranda clarius, lucidiusque proponenda, tanta hac luce data alacriter utantur".

As for the use of literary criticism[17] in biblical analysis, again Billot's disapproval is quoted[18], and subsequently confronted with Pius XII's 1943 statement that in examining and exposing the scriptures, and in demonstrating scriptural inerrancy, exegetes are obliged to avail themselves prudently of this method. Next, discussing the doctrine of scriptural inerrancy, Alonso-Schökel admits that Pius XII did indeed maintain this doctrine, imbedded in a doctrine of divine scriptural inspiration[19]. This of course raises problems as to the acknowledgement of the historical character of biblical narratives, for such doctrine tends to deny the importance of the 'human authors' of the scriptures. But, Pius XII is praised for presenting the doctrine in a very subtle way, leaving ample space for interpretation.

Indeed, Alonso-Schökel recognizes the alleged 'historicity' of biblical narratives as a key topic for exegetes in the first half of the twentieth century. For instance, he tries to show how an author such as L. Fonck[20] defended a theory of 'total historicity', holding a complete correspondence between biblical narrative and corresponding historical events. This correspondence is safeguarded through the denial of any 'narrative freedom' on the side of the human authors of scripture[21]. They are in fact reduced to mere instruments of the divine author[22]. For Fonck and those

17. For a definition, description, and additional literature on genre criticism, read PRIOR, *The Historical Critical Method* (n. 7), pp. 33-36.

18. BILLOT, *De inspiratione* (n. 15), p. 154 (Alonso-Schökel only offers his Italian translation of Billot. We prefer to render the original here): "Nam quae illi dicunt genera litteraturae, verius diceres genera vanitatis, in quibus vel nulla excusatio est, vel si est, ignorantia excusat errorem, et temeritas ignorantiam".

19. ALONSO-SCHÖKEL, *Dove va* (n. 4), p. 451.

20. Leopold Fonck (°1865-†1930), was a Jesuit exegete who had been professor of New Testament exegesis at the University of Innsbruck, and later at the Gregoriana. In 1909, Pius X entrusted him with the founding of the Biblicum, and appointed Fonck *consultor* of the Pontifical Biblical Commission. Alonso-Schökel refers to L. FONCK, *Der Kampf um die Wahrheit der H. Schrift seit 25 Jahren*, Innsbruck, Rauch, 1905. For further biographical info and reading on Fonck see F.W. BAUTZ, *Leopold Fonck*, in ID., *Biographisch-bibliographisches Kirchenlexikon*, Bd. II, 1990, Spalten, Traugott Bautz, cc. 68-69.

21. ALONSO-SCHÖKEL, *Dove va* (n. 4), p. 452, paraphrasing Fonck: "C'è infatti una terza maniera di fare la storia – quella in cui una perfetta concordanza con i fatti, sia in generale, sia nei particolari, è presentata con un metodo imperfetto. È questo il caso della storia biblica: in essa c'è perciò storicità totale, estendentesi fino alle più minute particolarità, secondo l'insegnamento dei padri della Chiesa. Del resto, conclude il Fonck; la libertà narrativa dell'agiografo, sarebbe inconciliabile con l'ispirazione".

22. Although not explicitly developped here, Alonso-Schökel holds an incarnational view on the nature of scriptural inspiration and inerrancy. He does develop this view later in his L. ALONSO-SCHÖKEL, *La parole inspirée: L'Écriture sainte à la lumière du langage et de la littérature*. Traduit de l'espagnol par H. de Blignières et P. Hardy (Lectio Divina, 64), Paris, Cerf, 1971, pp. 41-81, esp. pp. 45-46, commenting on *Divino afflante Spiritu* (n. 12): "Avant tout, on voit clairement la double nature de la parole inspirée:

who hold similar positions, narrative freedom cannot coexist with the idea of divine inspiration. Again, Alonso-Schökel offers an opposing quotation from Pacelli, only this time from *Humani generis*[23]. Next, pointing out that Fonck rejected the use of comparative methods in biblical studies; Alonso-Schökel once more confronts this with a paraphrase on *Divino afflante Spiritu*[24].

This methodology – paraphrasing an exegete's ideas, and then confronting them with citations from Pius XII's biblical encyclicals – is again used in a subsequent paragraph discussing the authority of the church fathers in matters of biblical interpretation[25]. Once more, Alonso-Schökel refers to the norms of Catholic hermeneutics promulgated in *Divino afflante Spiritu*. Having discussed these examples, he then comes to a preliminary conclusion, that a '*cambiamento nell'esegesi dopo il 1943*' had taken place. All the while, he stresses that this change did not arrive *à l'improviste*, but rather that it took preparation. Clarifying this, he argues that *Divino afflante Spiritu* had accepted and canonized the private research results of certain exegetes[26]. The argument proceeds, notwith-

divine et humaine. Contre cette doctrine fondamentale peuvent se dresser également des hérésies ou des erreurs analogues aux erreurs christologiques, une espèce de gnosticisme ou de monophysisme qui nie, néglige ou affaiblit la nature humaine de cette parole, et une espèce de nestorianisme qui minimise son caractère divin. En conséquence, il nous faudra toujours revenir à la doctrine de l'incarnation pour y chercher la lumière sur des questions particulières de l'inspiration".

23. Pius XII, *Litt. Enc. Humani generis de nonnulis falsis opinionibus quae catholicae doctrinae fundamenta subruere minantur*, in AAS 42 (1950) 568-570, esp. 575-578. The first part of the encyclical *Humani generis* calls upon the theologians to return to the sources of divine revelation, *i.e.* scripture and tradition. Along with this call, Pius XII condemns the idea that the divine sense of a biblical narrative is concealed by its human sense, and condemns any attempt to a symbolic or spiritualist exegesis. The second part of the encyclical states that theologians should take account of the positive sciences inasmuch as they do not contradict catholic teaching (the so-called *analogia fidei*). This implies among others the acceptance of historiographical research methods in the study of scripture. However, the study of narrative or literary patterns, historico-geographical context, etc., should not tend to diminish the fundamental doctrine saying that every word of scripture is subject to divine inspiration, and hence *absolutely* immune to all error. The primordial role of the divine author of scripture is stressed.
For the citation see *Humani generis*, pp. 576-577: "undecim priora capita Geneseos, quamvis cum historicae compositionis rationibus proprie non conveniant, quibus eximii rerum gestarum scriptores graeci et latini, vel nostrae aetatis periti usi fuerint, nihilominus quodam vero sensu, exegetis amplius investigando ac determinando, ad genus historiae pertinere." In this text, Alonso-Schökel reads recognition of a proper kind of historicity that does not call for a literal historicizing reading of biblical narratives.
24. He paraphrases *Divino afflante Spiritu* (n. 12), pp. 313-314: "Nostra siquidem aetas, ut novas aggerit quaestiones novasque difficultates, ita favente Deo, nova etiam praebet exegeseos subsidia et adiumenta".
25. See Alonso-Schökel, *Dove va* (n. 4), pp. 452-453.
26. Alonso-Schökel, *Dove va* (n. 4), p. 454: "il cambiamento non s'è prodotto come un terremoto imprevedibile: Pio XII raccoglieva nell'enciclica *Divino afflante Spiritu*, ed

standing the fact that the rest of the 1943 document prominently features Pius XII's new approach, its first paragraph clearly reflects and underlines the continuity of its teaching with past magisterial teaching[27]. Thus, *Divino afflante*'s continuity with past teaching is twofold. It lies not solely in its faithfulness to official, *i.e.*, magisterial teaching. There was also continuity with a 'large school' – as opposed to 'strict school' – in the field of contemporary exegesis[28], which had now been accepted[29]. New methods and norms had shifted from the margins of local Catholic exegesis into the core of official teaching[30]. At this point Alonso-Schökel is confident that he has resolved the most preoccupying part of his title question, confirming that in 1943 something new happened, yet that it was in continuity with tendencies already present in the past:

> Coloro che erano stati assenti al movimento dell'esegesi, scoprirono la novità, con stupore o con sospetto; quelli invece che lo avevano seguito con attenzione, si compiacquero del cambiamento e lo fecero proprio[31].

After confirming the presence of new pathways in *Divino afflante Spiritu*, Alonso-Schökel asks: What has happened since? Where has Catholic biblical exegesis been heading since 1943? When Pope Pius XII published his encyclical he was, according to Alonso-Schökel, quite aware of the fact that he had opened a new door, and he had even deliberately inserted a paragraph stressing the importance of exegetical freedom. The question, however, remains: How did exegetes handle their freedom[32]?

---

in certo modo canonizzava, i molti resultati dello studio privato degli esegeti". This is but a thinly veiled reference to the studies of scholars such as M.J. Lagrange.

27. It is of course not to be forgotten that *Divino afflante Spiritu* was actually written on the occasion of the fiftieth anniversary of *Providentissimus Deus*. See *Divino afflante Spiritu* (n. 12), p. 298: "Quandoquidem vero quinquagesimum exeuntem annum addecet, cum Encyclicae hae Litterae, quae princeps studiorum biblicorum habentur lex, editae sunt ...".

28. ALONSO-SCHÖKEL, *Dove va* (n. 4), p. 454: "Bisogna però osservare [...] che, tra l'enciclica Pio XII e gli anni precedenti, c'è continuità proprio nel "nuovo" che enuncia l'enciclica".

29. In this way we understand the opening phrase of Namur bishop A.M. Charue's preface on *Divino afflante Spiritu*: "Un souffle d'air frais après l'orage [...] Comme on dit en style de communiqués de guerre, l'exégèse rationaliste avait un peu partout l'initiative, la nôtre se tenait plutôt sur la défensive". PIE XII, *Encyclique sur les études bibliques. Préface de S.E. Monseigneur A.M. Charue. Introduction et commentaires de L. Cerfaux* (Chrétienté nouvelle), Bruxelles, Éditions universitaires, 1945, p. 7.

30. ALONSO-SCHÖKEL, *Dove va* (n. 4), p. 455: "Nonostante [...], una scelta di passi degli autori della scuola "larga" non solo farebbe da contrapeso a quelli della scuola "stretta", ma mostrerebbe una vera continuità tra quegli esegeti e le norme proposte da Pio XII".

31. ALONSO-SCHÖKEL, *Dove va* (n. 4), p. 455.

32. ALONSO-SCHÖKEL, *Dove va* (n. 4), p. 456: "Ma – ed è qui il nodo del problema – gli esegeti cattolici non hanno demeritato la fiducia in essi posta da Pio XII? Non hanno deviato dal cammino loro segnato?".

Alonso-Schökel clearly struggles with the contents of *Humani generis*[33]. Surely, he recognizes that this 1950 encyclical was written to lament and condemn 'certain' deviations, yet he remains confident that Pius XII by no means intended to regress doctrinally. Rather, when analyzing *Humani generis* Alonso-Schökel feels obliged to mention the condemnation of errors, but perspicaciously remarks that the major part of these errors have to do with 'theological' matters. Therefore they do not really touch the exegetical terrain. To illustrate: the meaning of the formula 'God is author of the scriptures', the doctrines of divine scriptural inspiration and inerrancy, the relationship between the authority of scripture and that of the Magisterium – all of these belong to the field of dogmatics[34]. As to *Humani generis*' paragraph on the crisis of historicity – concerning rather liberal interpretations of the Old Testament historical books which legitimize themselves by referring to the PBC's 1948 letter to Suhard[35] – the author demands attention to *Humani generis*' choice of words[36]. The terminological combination 'limits and cautions' found in that paragraph, according to Alonso-Schökel originates from, once again ... *Divino afflante Spiritu*[37], in which it is clear that 'limits' refer to the necessary respect for the analogy of faith in all exegetical activity, and the aforementioned 'cautions' refer to the obligation of honoring the norms of prudent scientific research[38]. In this line of thinking, the crisis

33. ALONSO-SCHÖKEL, *Dove va* (n. 4), p. 456: "Poiché è un fatto che l'enciclica *Humani generis* del 1950 lamenta esplicitamente alcune deviazioni".

34. ALONSO-SCHÖKEL, *Dove va* (n. 4), pp. 456-457: "Di queste questioni si può dire che il modo concreto dell'ispirazione e dell'inerranza sono problemi di cui deve occuparsi la teologia dommatica".

35. On January 16th, 1948, the PBC wrote a letter to the French cardinal E.C. Suhard (°1874-†1949) which was widely received as a plea for scientific freedom for the exegetes (COMMISSION PONTIFICALE POUR LES ÉTUDES BIBLIQUES, *Lettre au card. Suhard, archevêque de Paris, au sujet des sources du Pentateuque et de l'historicité des onze premiers chapitres de la Genèse*, in *AAS* 40 (1948) 45-48. This was to be the last PBC publication of this kind See BECHARD (ed.), *The Scripture Documents* (n. 7), pp. 318-329, esp. p. 326. – K. STOCK, *I cento anni della Pontificia Commissione Biblica*, in ID., et al., *Atti della giornata celebrativa per il 100° anniversario di Fondazione della Pontificia Commissione Biblica* (Collana documenti Vaticani), Rome, Libreria editrice Vaticana, 2003, 7-21, esp. pp. 14-15.

36. *Humani Generis*, p. 576: "Quemadmodum autem in biologicis et anthropologicis disciplinis, ita etiam in historicis sunt qui *limites* et *cautelas* ab Ecclesia statutas audacter transgrediantur". Italics ours.

37. *Divino afflante Spiritu* (n. 12), pp. 319-320.

38. ALONSO-SCHÖKEL, *Dove va* (n. 4), p. 457: "Limiti sono, a volerli riassumere in una formula, l' 'analogia della fede', poiché non sembra che ci siano stati errori circa le dichiarazioni esplicite del magistero ecclesiastico. Cautele saranno le norme di prudenza che applicate agli investigatori, possono ridursi alla 'solidità ed onestà scientifica'".

This reference to the analogy of faith does not necessarily imply exegesis to be a 'theological' activity. On the contrary, it seeks to underline the conintuity between the results of mere scientific study of the text and the 'religious' or dogmatic reading of it.

of historicity mentioned earlier is limited to the fact that exegetes were treating the matter of scriptural historicity without the needed scientific rigor and respect for the Catholic faith. All this is to say that, in Alonso-Schökel's view, *Humani generis* actually continues a tradition set by Pius XII's first biblical encyclical, which in the end reaches a rather surprising conclusion.

In the final part of the article, Alonso-Schökel cites a paragraph from Pacelli's letter to the Belgian Cardinal van Roey that illustrates this continuity and stresses the importance of exegetical freedom in the Pope's teaching, while at the same time defining the boundaries of this freedom, both with reverence for the use of historical-critical methods and ecclesiastical doctrines[39]. Alonso-Schökel concludes that the exegete's labour should remain faithful both to Catholic teaching and to the principles of serious and solid scientific research. He also points out that this matters, not only in scientific work, but also in the vulgarization of exegetical insight. This, according to the author, is the path stretched out by Pius XII's continual teaching and at the same time the answer to the title question: *Dove va l'esegesi cattolica?*

III. Divino afflante Spiritu and New Opinions

Luis Alonso-Schökel's article evoked an immediate and fierce reaction by Msgr. Antonino Romeo[40] that was published in the December volume of *Divinitas* and at the same time was distributed as a book-

---

39. *Allocution de Son Éminence le Cardinal van Roey et Message de Sa Sainteté le Pape Pie XII*, in Coppens – Descamps – Massaux (eds.), *Sacra Pagina* (n. 13), I, p. 15: "Depuis le début de Notre Pontificat, en effet, Nous avons eu à coeur de favoriser le développement des études scripturaires, et voici bientôt quinze ans, Nous aimions, par Notre Encyclique *'Divino afflante Spiritu'*, 'stimuler de plus en plus dans leurs travaux tous les fils de l'Église qui s'adonnent à ces études' et les encourager à 'poursuivre avec tout leur zèle, tous leurs soins et une énergie toujours nouvelle l'œuvre heureusement entreprise'. Par la suite, vous ne l'ignorez pas, Nous n'avons cessé de prodiguer aux exégètes et aux professeurs d'Écriture sainte les marques de notre sollicitude.
Aussi sommes-Nous heureux d'adresser Nos voeux paternels aux maîtres catholiques qui vont se réunir prochainement à Bruxelles pour mettre en commun les richesses de leur savoir et promouvoir les progrès de toutes les sciences requises à une meilleure intelligence du texte sacré. Dociles à l'Église, gardienne et interprète des Saintes Écritures, et forts de Notre estime pour leur tâche parfois austère mais si importante, qu'ils poursuivent avec confiance leurs recherches: par là "ils contribuent grandement au salut des âmes, au progrès de la cause catholique, à l'honneur et à la gloire de Dieu, et ils accomplissent une œuvre intimement liée aux devoirs de l'apostolat".
40. Antonino Romeo (°1902-†1979), an Italian professor from the region of Calabria, was professor of exegesis at the Pontificia Universitas Lateranense. He was also *aiutante di studio* of the Congregation for Seminaries and Universities.

let[41]. Some 70 pages long, Romeo discusses almost every paragraph of Alonso-Schökel's article, setting himself the task of safeguarding Catholic teaching from all possible attacks[42].

Romeo's critique of the article starts with a title-analysis. Deploring the fact that a fine periodical such as *La Civiltà Cattolica*[43] agreed to publish this kind of text, he starts his analysis with a reference to *Divino afflante Spiritu* highlighting the importance of loyal obedience to and faithful continuation of a history of great interpreters of the Bible. Romeo then sets off claiming that after the publication of *Humani generis*, the modernist biblical crisis has in a way been revived[44]. He lays the blame with conformist and concordist tendencies who wish to adapt their thinking to the world of today. These persons lack all reverence for the past, and share an uncritical enthusiasm for the future, a mentality that, according to Romeo, is philosophically absurd, since humankind has always built on traditions of the past. Contemporary Catholic progressivism however, appears to consider the church's doctrinal tradition as a *nucleus* of truth contained in a large package. Further, the progressivists hold that the package of tradition holds a great deal of ideas, truths and principles belonging to an age long gone. Most of them can easily be left behind since they no longer have any value for modern men and women. With these kinds of arguments, Romeo feels, modern progressivism presents itself as anti-traditionalist[45]. It is dialectically stuck between tradition and

41. ROMEO, *L'enciclica* (n. 5). The booklet was published under the same title by the *Libreria Editrice della Pontificia Università Lateranense*. In referring to Romeo's article, we will use the page numbering of the periodical edition. It is quite significant that the December volume featuring Romeo's text was dedicated to cardinal Ernesto Ruffini (°1888-†1967), former rector of the Lateran University and a well-known defender of neo-thomistic theology.

42. See É. FOUILLOUX, *The Antepreparatory Phase: The Slow Emergence from Inertia (January, 1959 – October, 1962)*, in ALBERIGO – KOMONCHAK (eds.), *History*, I (n. 3), pp. 55-166, esp. 137: "the Lateranum appointed itself the watchdog of Catholicism, as was shown by the attack on the Biblical Institute. Moreover, it provided itself with the weapons for this attack: its journal *Divinitas* was also the vehicle for the Pontifical Academy of Theology, an organization that served as a rallying point for zelanti of every kind".

43. ROMEO, *L'Enciclica* (n. 5), p. 387: "... della istruttiva Rivista La Civiltà Cattolica, tanto caro ai cattolici italiani per i suoi 110 anni di memorande lotte contro le triste realtà e le false dottrine ...".

44. *Ibid.*, p. 388: "La questione biblica è stata riaperta tra i cattolici, in quest'alma Roma (ma non da Romani), in modo deciso e pugnace, proprio poco dopo la promulgazione dell'Enciclica *Humani generis* che mette severamente al bando i fautori di 'novità', e di 'irenismo', quei cattolici cioè che, accesamente 'concordisti' e 'conformisti', vogliono in tutto uniformarsi al mondo di oggi, pomposamente gloriandosi dell''era nuova', l'era cioè caratterizzata dalle distruzioni o minace di distruzioni atomiche".

45. *Ibid.*, p. 389: "Il progressismo moderno si svolge al passato con uno spirito di critica corrodente, considera la tradizione dottrinale come un nucleo di verità e di principi buono per altri tempi ... Il progressismo moderno è antitradizionalista".

transformation, radically prioritizing the latter, using all kinds of criticism to batter the first. Moreover, says Romeo, progressivism – although still in denial – does not confine itself to the boundaries of exegesis, but inserts itself in the field of dogmatics[46]. This is evident because given its material object of study, biblical exegesis can never avoid touching the core of the Christian religion, the revealed truths contained in the scriptures. When inquiring about the person of Alonso-Schökel, Romeo finds out that this – rather young – author's mentality clearly is consistent with the above mentioned progressive anti-traditionalists. So far we have presented the introductory character sketch[47]. Let us now look at Romeo's critiques.

Regarding the idea of a trajectory, in his progressive urge to show how new ways find their place in official Catholic exegesis since 1943, Alonso-Schökel is obliged to show how earlier exegetes had no clue concerning 'scientific methodology' and how suddenly, in 1943, scientific exegesis is given birth, and starts to grow. This is illustrated by means of presenting fragments of the ideas of Billot, Murillo and Fonck[48]. As to Cardinal Billot's disapproval of Orientalists, Romeo argues that Billot was misquoted by Alonso-Schökel. The quotation used is incomplete and thus cannot show how Billot was actually writing about certain apostate or erroneous exegetes[49]. In fact, Billot never really questioned the important contributory factor of positive sciences within biblical research. Further, Romeo mocks the 'persiflage' way in which the Biblicum pro-

46. *Ibid.*, pp. 390-391: "Si inserisce [progressism], in primo luogo, nel campo dommatico, con la rimanipolazione della verità rivelata in termine di pensiero moderno, vuotandola, come fece il modernismo, del suo contenuto trascedente [...] Siamo qui alle fondamenta stesse del Cristianesimo, poichè l'esegesi dei Libri sacri non è un mero esercizio di grammatica o di erudizione".

47. *Ibid.*, pp. 392-394: "Chi è l'autore? Evidentemente, per rispondere al complesso e formidabile quesito, occorea una personalità altamente qualificata, di autorità universalmente ammessa, di esperienza prolungata e vastissima. [...] Da tutto un complesso di indizi, il P. Alonso è da supporsi giovane, sia perchè le sue pubblicazioni sono di data recente, sia perchè sembra non essersi ancora affermato nel campo esegetico. [...] La mentalità del P. Alonso è coerente con l'atteggiamento polemico contro la Tradizione e contro i 'conservatori'".

48. *Ibid.*, p. 396: "Volendo dimostrare che tra il 1943 e il 1958 è avvenuto "uno strano cambiamento di direzione" nell'esegesi cattolica, il P. Alonso se vede costretto ad affermare che prima del 1940 gli esegeti cattolici, a cominciare dai più celebri professori del Pont. Istituto Biblico, non avevano idea del metodo scientifico; che dal 1943 la scienza esegetica cattolica finalmente è nata, è cresciuta, si è sviluppata portentosamente, tutto nel breve giro di 15 anni".

49. *Ibid.*, p. 397: "Il P. Alonso sembra non aver compreso il testo del grande teologo che cita. L. Billot pensava ad Orientalisti che avevano apostatato o ammesso qualche errore".

fessor presents an author, opposing his paraphrases of the author's ideas to an arbitrary citation from *Divino afflante Spiritu* and then concluding that there is a substantial difference between their respective points of view[50]. This is, in itself, Romeo concludes, bad exegesis.

A less formal critique concerns Alonso-Schökel's treatment of Fonck. Romeo explicitly criticizes Alonso-Schökel of citing *Humani generis* incompletely in order to refute Foncks' teaching[51]. As to the impossibility of reconciling scriptural inspiration and narrative freedom, Romeo points out that Fonck in no way wished to dismiss the 'freedom' of the author[52]. Concerning the concept of narrative freedom, Romeo feels that 'narrative' freedom is equal to the freedom of falsifying history, and is thus not applicable as a concept. If Pius XII's teaching tries to safeguard human freedom, Romeo asserts that the same can be said about Fonck years before. The discontinuity between both is solely the result of Alonso-Schökel's unfair presentation of paragraphs. So, according to Romeo, not only does Alonso-Schökel quote incompletely, he also misrepresents and even disfigures the encyclicals of Pius XII.

For instance, discussing Fonck's so-called disparagement of comparative exegetical study the PBI professor seduces readers into thinking that *Divino afflante Spiritu* had introduced an entirely new concept in the Catholic doctrine on bible studies, mentioning a comparative method. This is a pertinent falsehood, and in fact, the encyclical never really mentioned this method[53]! Just as he quietly introduced the concept of 'narrative' freedom, Alonso-Schökel pretends his proper 'new' teaching to be that of Pius XII, a process of attribution that Romeo considers unforgivable[54]. Fonck however, in no way disapproved of the contributory use of

---

50. *Ibid.*: "Rincresce il dovere constatare che il P. Alonso manca a tal punto di buon gusto da non comprendere che dinanzi a uomini della statura di L. Billot, L. Fonck, L. Murillo, egli dovrebbe senz'altro inchinarsi riverente. Ma, forse egli non ha tempo di pensarci, tutto preso com'è dai tempi nuovi. Con testi maneggiati come egli fa, il P. Alonso potrà dimonstrare qualunque cosa. Questo suo metodo esegetico, che ha come unica direttiva una tesi da dimostrare per 'fas' o per 'nefas', dimostra che siamo molto lontani dalla scienza genuina, la quale è privilegio di ben pochi, anche dopo il 1940".

51. *Ibid.*, p. 401: "Per opporlo [Fonck] all'Enc. Humani generis, [...] il recente articolo cita un solo passo della *Humani generis* (sempre e solo lo stesso passo!), e lo cita incompleto, attribuendo invece al P. Fonck affermazioni false o inesatte".

52. *Ibid.*, p. 401: "Il P. Fonck non ha mai menomamente posto in questione la libertà dell'agiografo, sia esso narratore, sia esso profeta o poeta".

53. *Ibid.*, p. 403: "Ma che cosa intende l'Alonso con la formola 'metodo comparativo'? Parebbe, a chi legge, che sia imposta dalla *Divino afflante Spiritu*. Questo alto Documento, invece, non nomina neppure il 'metodo comparativo' [...] Attenti alle insidie! Poche righe prima, il P. Alonso aveva lanciato la formola 'libertà narrativa', come espressione del tutto anodina, quasi che fosse usata e insegnata dalle Encicliche di Pio XII".

54. *Ibid.*, p. 425: "O egli [Alonso Schökel] ignora i fatti, ed allora è un incompetente che non dovrebbe arrischiarsi a scrivere per il pubblico su questioni toccate da un alto

positive sciences in the exegetical field, but only of scientism, according to Romeo. Reading Alonso-Schökel's preliminary conclusion, the Lateran professor concludes that as far as he is concerned, no doctrinal transformation occurred in 1943. On the contrary, *Divino afflante Spiritu* and *Humani generis* never did canonize a 'large' school in contemporary exegesis[55], but perpetually remained faithful to traditional teaching. The new methods, the acceptance of positive sciences, are not new but were used by Catholic exegetes such as Billot, Fonck and Murillo already in the nineteenth and the beginning of the twentieth century. Repeatedly Romeo stresses that there was neither change, nor inconsistency nor discontinuity. In his view no new doors had been opened, and there was no necessity to ever do so[56].

Following the line of Alonso-Schökel's text, Romeo highlights his struggle with *Humani generis*. In some ironic phrases, Romeo shows himself utterly surprised that an encyclical of such importance for the orientation of Catholic exegesis is discussed in only twenty-three lines. He then refers to the PBI professor's insight that matters such as scriptural inspiration and inerrancy, hermeneutics, etc. are more theological than exegetical. Romeo reacts to that arguing that all pontifical documents, and not in the least *Divino afflante Spiritu*, regard the Catholic exegete as a theologian! Biblical exegesis is *'fides quaerens intellectum'*, science that presupposes an act of faith[57]. Next, Romeo spends most of his energy

Documento Pontificio, giudicando e smentendo affermazioni del Papa, del grande Pio XII che esalta sperticamente quanto gli attribuisce la ... liberazione dell'esegesi cattolica. O egli conosce i fatti, ed allora bisogna che ci si preoccupi di impedire la denigrazione o l''escamotage' sistematico delle due grande Encicliche del grande Pio XII''.

55. *Ibid.*, pp. 406-407, firmly declines Alonso-Schökel's dichotomizing of a strict and a large school, arguing that: "I falsi dilemmi 'stretto' o 'largo', 'esagerato' o 'moderato', non sono di ordine intellettuale, bensì di ordine volitivo e morale".

56. A few among many possible illustrations: *Ibid.*, p. 405: "Egli vuole, come afferma esplicitamente, mostrare concretamente il cambiamento intervenuto nell'esegesi dopo il 1943. Ma quanto vien detto dopo non mostra affatto, nè 'concretamente', nè 'astrattamente', il cambiamento"; *Ibid.*, p. 409: "Oggi, alla distanza di 17 anni, dopo che il grande Pio XII è morto, il P. Alonso ci dà la notizia di un cambiamento, di un mutamento, di un novità, introdotto dalla *Divino afflante Spiritu*, tale da aprire una nuova ed ampia via [...] Quali novità?".

See also HARRISON, *The Teaching of Pope Paul VI* (n. 3), p. 52. He notes: "less than a decade earlier, an editorial in *La Civiltà Cattolica* by a professor of the Biblical Institute, Luis Alonso-Schökel, had sparked a vehement protest from another scripture scholar, Antonino Romeo, in *Divinitas*, the review of the Pontifical Lateran University, mainly because Alonso Schökel had claimed that Pius XII was very conscious of opening a new and wide door through which many novelties would be entering the precincts of Catholic exegesis – novelties that would have surprised excessively conservative minds".

57. ROMEO, *L'Enciclica* (n. 5), p. 424: "Tutti i Documenti Pontifici, e in prima linea la Divino afflante Spiritu, insegnano che l'esegeta cattolico, sopratutto se è sacerdote, non

refuting Alonso-Schökel's opinion that *Humani generis* merely offers some directives to resolve the aforementioned crisis of historicity. Moreover, these are directives that in short can be described as: 'perform cautious, solid and honest scientific work and remain loyal to the Catholic doctrinal tradition'. Romeo rejects this, pointing out that Alonso-Schökel simply bypasses the dogmatic complexity, and even more, that he ignores the very presence of condemnations of deviations and errors in the 1950 encyclical[58]. Finally, Romeo quickly passes along to Alonso-Schökel's final anchor point: Pius XII's 1958 letter to the conference of Catholic exegetes in Brussels. It is no wonder that one finds continuity between the teaching in this letter and the former teaching of Pius XII[59].

The crucial issue here appears to be of the dis/continuity of Catholic doctrine, yet both authors find continuity. This contestation leads us to see that the problem lies at a more fundamental level. In order to grasp the differences between both authors we will move from a mere description of their standpoints and begin our comparative analysis.

IV. CONCLUSIVE COMPARISONS

1. *Material Comparison*

When examining the topics discussed in the neo-modernist controversy the dissenting voices of Luis Alonso-Schökel and Antonino Romeo are striking. Yet, what is perhaps most striking is that, when we look closely,

---

è un mero filologo, ma è anche un teologo". At this stage Romeo backs his own critique with citations out of cardinal Augustin Bea's commentary on the 1943 encyclical in *La Civiltà Cattolica* 94/4 (1943) 220-224. Romeo firmly stresses the authority of Bea (°1881-†1968) by dropping that the latter had been rector of the PBI (from 1930 until 1949) and one of the major redactors of *Divino afflante Spiritu*. On Bea, see S. SCHMIDT, *Augustin Bea, der Kardinal der Einheit*, trans. S. Spath, Graz, Styria, 1989, esp. pp. 99-145.

58. ROMEO, *L'Enciclica* (n. 5), pp. 432-433: "È assai significativo il fatto che il P. Alonso non è riuscito a trovare nella *Humani generis* alcune direttiva dottrinale. [...] Vi trova soltanto ciò che non vi è. Secondo lui, le uniche direttive della *Humani generis* sono 'solidità e onestà scientifica'. [...] Preme molto al P. Alonso di ridurre tutte le gravissime deviazioni ed errori dottrinali condannati dalla *Humani generis* a semplici imprudenze di malaccorti volgarizzatori".

59. *Ibid.*, p. 411: "Questo documento, presentato con molta enfasi dal P. Alonso nella prima e nell'ultima pagina del suo articolo, come termine della 'traiettoria' di cui ci intrattiene, non contiene assolutamente nulla che possa menomamente confermare o puntellare la sua tesi. [...] Non vi è nulla, in questo breve messaggio, che non sia stato detto da Leone XIII, da S. Pio X, da Benedetto XV, da Pio XI. La santa anima di Pio XII non avrebbe mai potuto immaginare che queste sue alte parole pastorali sarebbero state utilizzate per farlo figurare tra quei 'novatori' e 'irenisti' che aveva con inflessibile rigore condannati nell'Enciclica *Humani generis*".

their disagreement predominantly appears to occur on the material level, i.e., on the level of theological content[60]. In other words, as theologians they disagree on almost all theological issues, which is all the more interesting because each of those issues touches the core of a Catholic theology of revelation.

In summation, there is a seemingly unsurpassable dichotomy in the discussion on the inerrancy of the scripture. Connected to it, one senses strong disagreement on the doctrine of scriptural inspiration. Alonso-Schökel clearly stresses the importance of 'narrative freedom' of the human authors of scripture, and considers that position supported by *Divino afflante Spiritu*. The inspired nature of the human authors however is not fully denied. Rather, it is mirrored in a cooperative perspective. The core of the matter is that Alonso-Schökel defends a theory of mutual collaboration of the human and the divine authors of scripture. This in turn provides space for a complex interplay between divine inspiration on the one hand, and historico-geographical contingency on the other[61]. It also rules out any claim for an 'absolute' scriptural inerrancy, so heavily stressed by Romeo. Romeo's defense of Fonck on the subject of human freedom did not imply him to somewhat lessen his claim of absoluteness regarding the inerrant nature of scriptures[62]. As a logical

60. In the following we will suffice with briefly touching the theological divergences between the authors. We will thereby show some attention to their own backgrounds. This study does however not provide enough space to elaborate in detail their positions with regard to revelation, inspiration, inerrancy and so on. Furthermore, the nature of this article does not ask for such elaboration, as our main interest will lie in the structural comparison.

61. It is highly relevant for the understanding of these discussions to see that the background of the controversy is constituted by the preparations of the Second Vatican Council. For instance, BURIGANA, *Tradizioni inconciliabili* (n. 3), p. 52, notes that "le diverse interpretazioni della *Divino Afflante Spiritu* […] rappresentano una delle chiavi di lettura dei vota per comprendere le posizioni della Lateranense e dell'Istituto Biblico". Especially the discussions in the subcommission *de fontibus revelationis*, part of the Preparatory Theological Commission at Vatican II illustrate this. See for instance J. RATZINGER, *Dogmatic Constitution on Divine Revelation: Origin and Background*, in H. VORGRIMLER (ed.), *Commentary on the Documents of Vatican II*. Vol. III, New York, Herder, 1969, 155-166, esp. 157-158.

As a further illustration we may offer the following citation originating from the antepreparatory votum designed by the professors of the PBI, *Acta et Documenta Concilio Oecumenico Vaticano II Apparando*. Series I (*Antepraeparatoria*), Vol. 4; Pars I/1, pp. 121-136, see p. 130: "in evangeliis explicandis duo principia applicanda et inter se concilianda sunt, historicitas et inerrantia. Quisquis in nomine fidelitatis historicae prorsus restringit libertatem evangelistarum, nullam viam apertam relinquit ad diversitates narrationum re et non solum verbum explicandas. Ideo rigidam statuens historicitatem non salvaret inerrantiam vel saltem eam in periculum adduceret. Illa conciliatio positive perfici potest, habita ratione intentionis hagiographi".

62. ROMEO, *L'Enciclica* (n. 5), p. 401: "Il Magistero Ecclesiastico insegna inequivocabilmente, oggi come ieri, che tutto ciò che è 'Parola di Dio', anche gli obiter dicta, è

result, Romeo cannot attribute freedom to the human authors of scripture, unless formally[63].

Given all of the above, one comprehends the Biblicum's strong accent on the necessity of applying scientific, *i.e.*, historiographic methods in biblical exegesis. This is all the more understandable when taking in account that Alonso-Schökel – completely in the tradition of his PBI colleagues[64] – holds a revelation theology that perceives revelation primarily as an historical *event*, and as an *historical* event. Crucial are the deeds and words of Jesus Christ, handed down to us through the mediation of narratives told by human authors, and thus – again – marked with contingency. The viewpoint is that of the historiographer.

Antonino Romeo and the professors of the PLU do not fully dismiss the historical sciences, but their point of departure clearly lies elsewhere. They start from a dogmatic perspective that draws upon insights of speculative neo-scholasticism[65]. For them, a revelation theology features a propositional view of revelation[66]. Revelation consists of a well-defined set of propositions, which are contained in the scriptures and in tradition[67]. Tradition in turn is represented by – and at various occasions it

totalmente immune da errori, per il fatto che Dio non può nè errare nè indurre in errore. Su questo punto, come su tutti gli altri, la preziosissima Enciclica *Divino afflante Spiritu* (1943) non solo ha confermato, ma ha fortemente ribadito e precisato l'Enciclica *Providentissimus* del 1893".

63. *Ibid.*, p. 401: "naturalmente non può ammettere una 'libertà narrativa', che viene definita [...] la libertà che la tradizione e gli Evangelisti si prendono con la realtà storica dei fatti e dei detti di Gesù, ciò che, più semplicemente e apertamente, senza eufemismo, significa falsificare la storia".

64. See A. INDELICATO, *Difendere la dottrina a annunciare l'Evangelo. Il dibattito nella Commissione centrale preparatoria del Vaticano II* (Testi e ricerche di scienze religiose: Nuova serie, 8), Genua, Marietti, 1992, p. 83.

65. See M. PANGALLO, *L'istituzione della cattedra di S. Tommaso e la filosofia tomista al Laterano negli anni del Concilio*, in P. CHENAUX (ed.), *L'università del Laterano* (n. 1), 41-48, and also note that in the same volume of *Divinitas* that featured Romeo's article, articles can be found such as C. FABRO, *Attualità del Tomismo nell'80° dell'Enciclica "Aeterni Patris"*, in *Divinitas* 4 (1960) 28-60, and A. PIOLANTI, *Azione e supposito nella dottrina di S. Tommaso*, in *Divinitas* 4 (1960) 102-122.

66. The following may illustrate how the discussion on the French 'nouvelle théologie' is involved here. G. ALBERIGO, *Christianisme en tant qu'histoire et "théologie confessante"*, in ID. – M.D. CHENU – E. FOUILLOUX – J.P. JOSSUA – J. LADRIERE, *Une école de théologie: Le Saulchoir* (Théologies), Paris, Cerf, 1985, 9-35, see p. 13 paraphrasing Chenu's critique: "Seule une théologie qui a perdu le sens de la transcendance de la Parole de Dieu traduit l'absolu en formules autoritaires en les soustrayant à l'histoire. Dans la mesure où l'historicité est la condition de la foi et de l'Église, le théologien n'a d'espoir de trouver ses sources que dans l'histoire, et celles-ci ne sont pas constituées par la nature des choses ou des formes intemporelles, ou des essences métaphysiques, mais par les événements".

67. In the redaction of the preparatory schema *De fontibus Revelationis* (which was largely performed by Lateran professors, see A. INDELICATO, *Formazione e composizione*

seems is simply equal to – the Magisterium of the church, and therefore Romeo deems it necessary to defend the traditional teaching of the church as much as possible. Hence, he also stresses the continuity in church history. Alonso-Schökel, for instance, adopting the mentality of the historiographer has fewer problems stating that Pius X's attitude toward biblical criticism caused a climate of anxiety, and noticing changes to all that under Pacelli's reign.

The result of this neo-scholastic theological mentality – and certainly one that does not significantly attempt to develop a doctrine of general revelation and its pendant, natural theology – is that an author such as Romeo finds it necessary to affirm that *Humani generis* defends an '*immunitas absoluta ab errore*' of the scriptures[68]. As we have seen, this is legitimized by accentuating the importance of divine inspiration, highlighting the crucial role of the divine author. This again shows how the human authors end up deprived of their freedom in order to safeguard the veracity of each single biblical pericope. Historicity in this account becomes full equivocity between narrative and history.

These opposing theologies obviously have led to two contradictory reconstructions of half a century's developments in Catholic teaching on biblical studies, defending either discontinuity or continuity in official Catholic teaching since the end of the nineteenth century. The conclusion of mutual theological exclusiveness in the controversy now puts us in the centre of our second comparison.

---

delle commissioni preparatorie, in G. ALBERIGO – A. MELLONI [eds.], *Verso il Concilio Vaticano II (1960-1962): Passagi e problemi della preparazione conciliare* [Testi e ricerche di scienze religiose: Nuova serie, 11], Genua, Marietti, 1993, 43-65, and esp. 54-56; R. BURIGANA, *Progetto dogmatico del Vaticano II: La commissione teologica preparatoria (1960-1962)*, in ALBERIGO – MELLONI [eds.], *Verso il Concilio Vaticano II (1960-1962)*, 141-206, see esp. p. 145), all of this led to discussions on the exact relationship between scripture and tradition. The neo-scholastic attitude toward the problem leads to questions such as 'does scripture contain all revealed truths, or is tradition larger than scripture'. Such discussions seem to imply a quantitative view of revelation, lacking genuine historical concern. Cfr. R. BURIGANA, *La Bibbia nel Concilio: La redazione della costituzione "Dei Verbum del Vaticano II* (Testi e ricerche di scienze religiose: Nuova serie, 21), Bologna, Il Mulino, 1998, pp. 87ff.: "Nel *De fontibus* forte era la dipendenza dalla scolastica e dalla apologetica cattolica".

68. This viewpoint is not only expressed in Romeo's article, but can also be read in Spadafora's part of the antepreparatory votum of the Lateran theological faculty, which sees the adherence to an absolute inerrancy of scripture as a token of orthodoxy. See *Acta et Documenta Concilio Oecumenico Vaticano II Apparando*. Series I (*Antepraeparatoria*), Vol. 4; Pars I/1, pp. 169-275, see p. 264: "Uti patet, agitur hic de inerrantia iuris: impossibile est quod Sacra Scriptura, divinitus inspirata, errorem contineat; ex facto quod tota S. Scriptura Deum habet auctorem, necessario sequitur eam in omnibus et singulis partibus esse Verbum Dei ac per consequens ab omni errore immunem".

2. *Structural Comparison*

The above mentioned dissent lies on the level of different theological perceptions. The next question then is: How is all of the above related to contemporary theological debates on the nature of orthodoxy? In order to contribute to the understanding of this issue, we feel a complementary comparison is helpful. In addition to comparing the authors on the material level, we need now ask different questions. The matter is no longer, what are these authors saying? What does their theology of revelation enhance? Rather, the question is, how are they saying it? On what basis are they saying it? In the above paragraph we noted the presence of contradicting reconstructions. Among others, it is this element of 'construction' and 'reconstruction' that interests us in the final part of our text. Why and how do these authors reconstruct Catholic history in the way they do? Even this last question already takes too much for granted. It is necessary for us to start from a very general basic level of comparison, and then see what comes out of it. Presenting the structure of the arguments in a general way may also be the best way to offer some meaningful thoughts for those investigating the nature of Catholic orthodoxy.

In what follows we will, therefore, present some basic analogies uniting both authors. We feel that exactly these structural analogies might clarify their theological disagreements and their impossibility to overcome them. Still, these analogies will only offer elements that should be taken in account. They have no other intention than to bring forth humble suggestions. They even may not seem more than a collection of self-evident statements, but we are convinced that also the self-evident is worth considering.

Looking for analogies, most basic thing one notices is that both Luis Alonso-Schökel and Antonino Romeo regard themselves as fully Catholic. More generally stated, both authors are convinced of the orthodoxy of their own theological positions. If on nothing else, they agree on this. Yet, as we have pointed out, they defend mutually exclusive theological standpoints. In the case of Antonino Romeo – and the same could be said regarding Spadafora, Ruffini[69], and others[70] entangled in the

---

69. For Spadafora's attitude see F. SPADAFORA, *La critica e gli evangeli*, in *Settimana del Clero* 22 (1959) 7; 29 (1959) 6-7. For Ruffini, E. RUFFINI, *Literary Genres and Working Hypotheses in Recent Biblical Studies*, in *American Ecclesiastical Review* 145 (1961) 362-365 and ID., *The Bible and Its Genuine Historical and Objective Truth*, in *American Ecclesiastical Review* 146 (1962) 361-368.

70. Interestingly, one could make the exact same study on the American pendant of the Roman controversy, that took place at the same moment, featuring hostile discussions between authors in the *American Ecclesiastical Review*, and members of the Catholic Bib-

Roman controversy – this eventually culminates in accusations of heterodoxy toward the opponent. On this basic level, orthodox appears to be
a matter of orthodox self-perception or orthodoxy self-consciousness.

Let us widen the analogy. However much they perceive themselves to
be orthodox theologians, Luis Alonso-Schökel and Antonino Romeo face
the same problem. Neither of them is capable of founding his respective
theological standpoints from within their own theological discourse. It
looks as though an orthodox self-perception cannot serve as an adequate
basis to convince the opponent of their own orthodoxy. In other words,
they share the need for an external ground that legitimates their theological standpoints – which, as we have seen, include doctrines on inspiration, revelation, inerrancy, and so on. One could even say that they need
to legitimate their self-perception.

Automatically the question rises as to where this legitimizing ground
lies? The answer shows us yet another analogy. Notwithstanding the fact
that the Lateran professor repeatedly and explicitly charges the Biblicum
professor with being an anti-traditionalist progressivist, lacking respect for
the importance of historical perspectives, it is undeniable that within the
scope of the controversy both Romeo *and* Alonso-Schökel turn their interest toward the past[71]. They look backward, into history, in view of cop-
ing with their lack of an external basis. They share a need and recognition of church history as a basis. Orthodoxy turns out to require the
function of memory, but which memory? Whose memory?

Their diachronic gaze is not a blind man's leap into the past. In fact,
it can be qualified as a diachronic-*hermeneutical* gaze. In other words,
Alonso-Schökel and Romeo do not simply turn to history;, they turn to
church history. More importantly, they turn to a particular perception of
church history. Naturally, the particularity of their perception is shaped
by their personal theological preferences, preferences shared with their
theological peer group or broader social background. (It is clear that
within the context of the neo-modernist controversy we are referring to
the professors of the Pontifical Biblical Institute and those of the Pontifical Lateran University).

In summation, within the context of the controversy, both Luis Alonso-
Schökel and Antonino Romeo share a legitimizing perception of church
history. This is not an arbitrary insight. The analogy is deeper in that both
authors share an obvious preference for 'authoritative texts', and at var-

lical Association. See FOGARTY, *American Catholic Biblical Scholarship* (n. 3), pp. 276-
310.
    71. The question as to their precise view on history and historicity, belongs to the
domain of theological discourse, and is therefore not addressed here.

ious occasions decide to accentuate the authority of the document at hand. Set in general terms, one might argue that an orthodox self-perception involves a diachronic-hermeneutical turn toward historical ecclesiastical documents that are – once again – *perceived* as authoritative.

Finally, although this may occur as an element shaped by pure contingency, in the process of the neo-modernist controversy, our two authors not only share a legitimizing diachronic-hermeneutical movement toward ecclesiastical documents perceived of as authoritative. What strikes us is that both perform their movement referring to the exact same historical documents. In this case the documents are the encyclicals *Divino afflante Spiritu* and *Humani generis* of Pius XII. When contemplating the wide-ranging structural analogy between both authors it is easy to see how it reinforces, rather than resolves their disagreement on the material level. The shared element of perception turns out to be the actual basis for their dissent.

"Perception" is the one element that continually returns, in a threefold manner. There is both the element of perception of the self, perception of the other, and the perception of the past. Both appear in a complex interplay that cannot be evaded when discussing orthodoxy from the standpoint of church history. In our view the issue of perception constitutes a serious challenge to any debate on the nature of orthodoxy. The concept of perception needs further study and refinement. Perhaps it would be interesting to investigate not only historical, theological and philosophical ideas on the notion of perception, but also to study esthetic theories on the concept on both the individual and the social level[72]. This is exactly the reason why we have opted for a terminology of the senses, writing 'perception' rather than the inadequate term 'interpretation', which bears mostly intellectual connotations.

Still, this is not the end of the matter. We wish to close our essay by concluding that history itself puts Catholic theology before serious questions. When the theologian takes for granted the fact that one cannot escape history, the following questions become crucial to the investigation of orthodoxy: Is it in any way possible to find or develop criteria that can – from inside history's course – decide which person or group's self-perception, perception of the other, and/or perception of its past is gen-

---

72. As an example, we would suggest to study both the plastic and theoretical work of a contemporary artist such as Joseph Beuys (°1921-†1986), whose anthropological widening of artistic creation and perception could offer fruitful insights. An interesting study on this has been published as H.M. HORST, *Kreuz und Christus: Die religiöse Botschaft im Werk von Joseph Beuys*, Stuttgart, Katholisches Bibelwerk, 1998. Yet, we believe that Horst's presupposition of theology as a criticism of art withholds the author of actually grasping Beuys' work.

uine, or orthodox? Is one of the adversaries necessarily wrong, presupposing that orthodoxy is to be seen as an non-divisive and universally legitimate concept? Should it not rather be perceived as a vessel of fruitful contradictions, a combining of opposites in the line of the metaphoric language of biblical parables?

karim.schelkens@theo.kuleuven.be   Karim SCHELKENS

ORTHOPRAXIS AS A CRITERION FOR ORTHODOXY?

EDWARD SCHILLEBEECKX' VIEW ON THE DEVELOPMENT AND THE CHARACTERISTIC OF RELIGIOUS TRUTH

There are many ways to consider the development of tradition as well as the nature of truth in Christian belief. Some would look upon truth as an autonomous and transcendent reality, independent of particular history. According to these views, historical events are the mere mediators of the independent truth. For others the historical and contextual dependence is the main characteristic of religious truth. They emphasise that truth is always constituted in and through history. Edward Schillebeeckx can be regarded as one of the theologians for whom a historical and hermeneutical approach to the development of Christian doctrine is beyond dispute. Schillebeeckx argues that development of Christian truth should not be understood as the preservation of earlier doctrinal articulations but rather as a development of critical translations of Christian experience from one historical era to the next.

In this paper I will examine Schillebeeckx' approach to the development of religious truth, with special attention to his notion of orthopraxis as a criterion of orthodoxy. An analysis of "The Understanding of Faith", in which Schillebeeckx expounds his theological method, will show that the category of experience is a very central one in his thought. In his method of correlation, (human) experience figures as the bridge between tradition and culture. According to Schillebeeckx, experience functions as the ground for theological truth. Despite his attention to the historical and contextual, Schillebeeckx' emphasis on experience risks being regarded as a way of claiming a universal truth. Therefore, from a post-modern point of view, the question must be raised as to what Schillebeeckx means by 'human experience'. Whose experience is at stake here? Can we hold to the idea of a universal human experience in a post-modern and pluralistic world? And if not, does that inevitably mean that Schillebeeckx' notion of orthopraxis cannot inspire present-day Christians? Should we give up on the relation between theory and practice? Taking these questions as a guideline we will examine the possibility of (still) considering orthopraxis as a criterion of orthodoxy in contemporary theology.

I. DEVELOPMENT OF DOCTRINE

In an article he wrote on the occasion of Ted Schoof's departure of the Theological Faculty in Nijmegen in 1994[1], Schillebeeckx expounds his view on dogma and the development of doctrine. There he states that the infallibility of a dogma can never be situated in concrete human articulation. A dogma is a complicated whole of the heart of infallible truth on the one hand and the human shell in which this truth is situated on the other hand. The heart of truth is not reachable by human beings, not even by a bishop or a pope. The translation of the heart of truth can always be improved. This implies that divine revelation never comes straight from heaven, but that it takes place in a process of human experience in history. For Schillebeeckx, revelation is God's work only if it is the work of searching and interpreting human beings. Making a distinction between revelation and experience is for Schillebeeckx a "false dilemma"[2].

This short description already reveals Schillebeeckx' emphasis on history and experience when thinking about the development of Christian tradition and Christian doctrine. This fits within the broader framework of his theological work. It is Schillebeeckx' aim to present Christian belief as an understandable and acceptable option for rational human beings. Therefore, he states, theology must consider itself as apologetic theology and must show that "the Christian faith gives a humanly meaningful, intelligible and responsible interpretation of man and his world"[3]. A modern articulation of the faith is a crucial point of attention. Schillebeeckx rejects the opinion that the language of faith can only be meaningful to the insider. If this were the case, the Church would "become a completely irrelevant, closed group, a sect that has nothing to offer to others and to which others are therefore indifferent"[4]. Therefore Schillebeeckx concludes, following Paul van Buren, that all theological language and interpretation should have a 'secular' meaning, a meaning that can be understood in and by the world. The relationship between the theological language and the lived human experience replaces for Schillebeeckx the criterion of objective verification or falsification as it is formulated in linguistic analyses[5].

1. E. SCHILLEBEECKX, *Breuklijnen in christelijke dogma's*, in E. SCHILLEBEECKX – M. VAN KEULEN, et al. (eds.), *Breuklijnen: grenservaringen en zoektochten. 14 Essay's voor Ted Schoof bij zijn afscheid van de theologische faculteit Nijmegen,* Baarn, Nelissen, 1994, 15-49.
2. SCHILLEBEECKX, *Breuklijnen* (n. 1), pp. 18-19. Quotation on p. 19.
3. E. SCHILLEBEECKX, *The Understanding of Faith: Interpretation and Criticism*, trans. N.D. SMITH, New York, Seabury Press, 1974, p. 13.
4. *Ibid.*, p. 17.
5. *Ibid.*, p. 17.

Still this does not mean that Schillebeeckx is not aware of the fact that the mystery of Christianity is never totally expressible and explainable. In the original (Dutch) version of "The Understanding of Faith" he nuances his apologetical chief principle by stating that we always have to be conscious of the fact that our contemporary interpretations of faith are inadequate attempts at putting forward the mystery in a meaningful and objective manner so that it becomes real for human beings[6].

The fact that even Christians today do not understand the language of the Church any more, is for Schillebeeckx a significant sign that the ecclesiastical articulations have ceased to refer to real experiences in daily life in a recognizable way. If the users of Church language, more specifically the community of faith, no longer understand it, how difficult is it then for people outside the church! Schillebeeckx situates this problem in the theological speaker and not in the experiencing listener. He who articulates theological language should make sure that this language expresses human experiences[7]. It is Schillebeeckx' conviction that from the beginning of Christianity doctrinal articulations have always been expressions of human experiences and that the theologians should continue to assure the affiliation between dogmas and daily life. As he demonstrates in "Jesus"[8] Christianity started with an experience (the *abba*-experience of Jesus and the Easter experience of the disciples). It is, as he further elaborates in "Christ"[9], the same experience that is told in the scriptures and in the later Christian tradition. If this tradition today wants to be meaningful, it has to articulate this same experience in such a language that it can be shown to be related to contemporary experiences.

Due to the fact that theology fails to succeed in this assignment, one should systematically subject the doctrinal and theological language to a process of what Schillebeeckx calls 'hermeneutics of experience'[10]. This process reveals that only an articulation that is related to the real experience of people turns out to be a meaningful articulation. To do this properly, a theologian should critically investigate his own sphere of understanding, which can only be done when an investigation of the history of constantly changing spheres of understanding is analysed[11]. These analyses make it possible for the theologian to take into account his own pre-

6. E. SCHILLEBEECKX, *Geloofsverstaan: Interpretatie en kritiek* (Theologische Peilingen, 5), Bloemendaal, Nelissen, 1972, p. 19.

7. SCHILLEBEECKX, *The Understanding of Faith* (n. 3), pp. 14-16.

8. E. SCHILLEBEECKX, *Jesus: An Experiment in Christology*, London, Collins, 1979.

9. E. SCHILLEBEECKX, *Christ: The Christian Experience in the Modern World*, London, SCM, 1980.

10. SCHILLEBEECKX, *The Understanding of Faith* (n. 3), p. 16.

11. *Ibid.*, p. 30.

suppositions, which are related to the sphere of understanding of his time. Schillebeeckx gives as an example that a theological interpretation in his time always has to be an existential interpretation, because this is the way in which people express and understand themselves in Schillebeeckx' time. He uses the word existential here in the sense of "man living in the world with his fellow-men in a social system"[12]. A doctrinal or theological articulation therefore must be accepted by the community of faith as being in connection with their contemporary experiences. For Schillebeeckx this is one of the criteria that guarantees a true theological interpretation of the experience in Jesus Christ[13].

II. THEOLOGICAL CRITERIA FOR ORTHODOXY[14]

Schillebeeckx feels the need to reflect upon the criteria of what people call orthodoxy or 'right faith'. This reflection is essential because of the intern pluralisation among Christian believers and theologians, which is for Schillebeeckx a "factual problem" that "can no longer be ignored" (46)[15]. Not only in his own country, but in places all over the world Schillebeeckx has met pluralistic tendencies in Christianity. In the 1960s he had a lot of international contacts, especially in the context of the Second Vatican Council. He realises that the pluralism among Christians has the tendency to lead to closed and fundamentalist positions in the theological debate (both on the progressive as on the conservative side) and Schillebeeckx does not intend to remain silent about this matter. Instead he wants to understand the complexity of the situation (a situation he approaches without specific negative or positive feelings because, for him, it is a situation that cannot be altered) and tries to formulate an answer to this plurality by formulating criteria for orthodoxy that can function as universal criteria for Christians, despite the different opinions they have. In Schillebeeckx' opinion pluralism in theology can be overcome by communication, which is made possible by the fact that "there are logical structures which are universally valid and therefore make communication between different interpretations of reality possible" (54).

12. *Ibid.*, p. 32.
13. *Ibid.*, p. 32.
14. For this section we will follow Schillebeeckx' explanation in SCHILLEBEECKX, *The Understanding of Faith* (n. 3), pp. 45-77. The page numbers will be indicated between brackets.
15. Here he speaks only about Christian pluralism, and not about the pluralism among world religions. He acknowledges that this is a major problem for the future but limits his scope here to the problem in christian theology.

Therefore, pluralism cannot be the last word. In Schillebeeckx' view, being conscious of pluralism means implicitly transcending it, for at the moment of consciousness of pluralism one does not take one's own frame of thought as exclusive (55). Still this does not mean that the process of communication is not difficult.

Although for many Catholics the teaching office of the Church guarantees the truth in situations of pluralism, Schillebeeckx doubts whether the word of authority of the office can really bypass the dialectics that exist in the community of faith. For Schillebeeckx the teaching of the Church implies a theology which is only one of many theologies which all claim to express the same faith. Some people would suggest that the teaching authority can be guaranteed by the official charisma, but this argument does not convince Schillebeeckx. Although he is not denying that the Holy Spirit can help the Church and its leaders, he does not think it possible to explain all the decisions and pronouncements of the institutional Church directly by the charismatic help of the Holy Spirit. Inspired by the linguistic philosophies he studied in the 1960s, Schillebeeckx wants to come to a principle of verification on the basis of which a correct reinterpretation of faith can be distinguished from an 'heretical' interpretation (55-56). In "The Understanding of Faith" he formulates three criteria for verification, underlining that he does not attempt to be exhaustive. We will mainly focus on the second criterion, namely that of orthopraxis.

1) The first criterion Schillebeeckx proposes, is that of the proportional norm. Schillebeeckx states that, overlooking the different structures that have arisen in the course of history as a result of the expressions of Christian experiences, one can distinguish 'structural rules' that still preserve their intelligibility as models for every new structuring, even if the structure has lost its efficacy in a different social framework. Out of the relation between the articulations of faith and the referential context in which that articulation occurs, one can in Schillebeeckx view deduce constant but purely proportional principles which will be a safe guide for our interpretation of faith (61). In his later work, Schillebeeckx maintains this proportional understanding[16]. In his view theology always contains an iden-

---

16. For example in *Church: The Human Story of God*, trans. J. Bowden, Londen, SCM, 1990, pp. 40-45 and in his 1983 retirement lecture *Theologisch geloofsverstaan anno 1983: Afscheidscollege gegeven op vrijdag 11 februari 1983 door Mag. Dr. Edward Schillebeeckx o. p. hoogleraar Systematische Theologie en Geschiedenis van de Theologie aan de Katholieke Universiteit Nijmegen*, Baarn, Nelissen, 1983, pp. 14-15. See also D.P. THOMPSON, *Schillebeeckx on the Development of Doctrine*, in *Theological Studies* 62 (2001) 303-321, esp. 309-311.

tity of meaning through the times. In "Church"[17] he clarifies this in the following diagram:

the given articulation of the proportion

$$\frac{\text{Jesus' message}}{\text{social-hist. context of Jesus}} = \frac{\text{new testament message}}{\text{social-hist. context of NT}}$$

is reproduced in the proportion of, for instance,

$$\frac{\text{patristic understandig of the faith}}{\text{social-historical context then}} = \frac{\text{medieval understanding of the faith}}{\text{social-historical context then}}$$

and finally this given and reproduced proportion needs to be reproduced again in the proportion:

$$\frac{\text{contemporary understanding of the faith anno 1989}}{\text{our social-historical and existential context anno 1989}}$$

The diagram demonstrates that it is only in the relationship between message and situation that one can find Christian identity, which cannot be grasped as such. "Christian identity, the one and the same, is thus never the equal, but the proportionally equal"[18]. By proposing the criterion of the proportional norm Schillebeeckx introduces a theoretical element in the interpretation of faith. However, he immediately adds that this theoretical element is not sufficient for the verification of the orthodoxy of faith. "This aspect of knowledge only functions within the totality of the Christian existence and praxis" (63). At the beginning of his explanation about the criterion of the proportional norm he emphasises that one can never practice theology on a merely theoretical level. Therefore action or orthopraxis must be an inner element of the principle of verification (59).

2) Schillebeeckx states that the structure of revelation itself (Jesus' decent into humanity as the manifestation of God) reveals that "only a real and authentic concern for our fellow-men and therefore for the meaning of human existence can really give meaning to the objective truths of the Christian creed" (48). This means that speaking about God is in the meantime a particular way of speaking about human beings. With Hans Fortmann he agrees that one's pronouncements about redemption, for

17. SCHILLEBEECKX, *Church* (n. 16), p. 42.
18. SCHILLEBEECKX, *Theologisch Geloofsverstaan anno 1983* (n. 16), p. 15. Translation by D.P Thomspon, in THOMPSON, *Schillebeeckx on the Development of Doctrine* (n. 16), p. 311.

example, will only make sense if the reality of redemption is made concrete in the historical dimension of our human and social life (48). Schillebeeckx associates himself here with the liberation theology that arose in the 1960s. In the spirit of liberation theology Christian faith should not promise comfort and redemption in the hereafter but should make visible the possibility of liberation in the life of human people, here and now. As Schillebeeckx puts it: "the future cannot be interpreted theoretically, it has to be brought about" (59). Therefore orthodoxy and orthopraxis are unbreakably linked together.

Schillebeeckx is convinced of the fact that the criterion of orthopraxis can function as a universal criterion, because it is based on universal negative experiences of contrast. Although one can distinguish a variety of positive views of man in christianity, one should realize that they are all based on a common negative dialectic. Schillebeeckx expresses this by means of the words of E. Bloch who states that in all positive views of man, man can be seen as seeking the threatened *humanum* (64-65). Where the definition of this *humanum* is positively only expressed in plural forms, it can be negatively regarded as the universal pre-understanding of all these different views of man. Schillebeeckx considers this pre-understanding to be the same universal pre-understanding of the Gospel. The universal salvation that is proclaimed in the Gospel and is expressed in the symbol of 'the kingdom of God' is in his view closely connected with this human pre-understanding (65). Schillebeeckx says that on this universal basis the hermeneutical circle and the question-answer correlation of Barth, Bultmann, Tillich, Ebeling, Moltmann, Pannenberg, etc. should be renewed and extended with the idea of orthopraxis. The past should not only be re-interpreted in the light of the present, but then we remain theologising on the theoretical level. Schillebeeckx repeats here his main conviction: "future cannot be theoretically interpreted, it must be done" (66). This means that the theory, theology is presenting, will have to appear in the praxis of the Church itself. The Church should, in Schillebeeckx' view, realize "a renewal of existence, in which 'existence' concerns man as an individual person and in his social being" (66). Schillebeeckx does not consider this stress on orthopraxis as a new or trendy demand inspired by existentialism. To relate orthodoxy with orthopraxis can be justified as a continuation of the original functioning of the Christian doctrine. After all the creed was not used as a purely doctrinal or theoretical formulation of orthodoxy, but rather as an integral part of the church's liturgy of baptism, "in other words, the theoretical element of (and in) an action of the church" (68). Therefore, Schillebeeckx holds that we must consider the theological movements that reduce orthodoxy to a theoretical doctrine as heretical.

They constitute the great heresy which threatens all forms of Christianity, while proclaiming themselves as 'orthodox' movements (68). For Schillebeeckx it is clear that if they are not concerned about the renewal of the world or of man's existence they can not be considered orthodox.

3) By adding a third criterion for orthodoxy Schillebeeckx wants to draw the attention to the role played by the community of faith in the process of doctrinal development. According to this third criterion the acceptance of a theological interpretation by the community of faith, forms an essential element in the whole of the criterion of verification. The individual theologian is not the only subject sustaining the hermeneutics, but the community of the Church as a whole is responsible (70). Still Schillebeeckx is very realistic about the difficulties of putting this criterion into practice when a theologian formulates a new interpretation of faith. "It is only after a great deal of friction that a new interpretation can be either accepted or rejected. Naturally, in the course of this debate all kinds of new problems will have arisen" (71). But this fact should in no case be used as an excuse for not taking the role of local churches seriously. Schillebeeckx relies here on the teaching of Vatican II where it was affirmed that the universal Church was made present here and now in the local church (71)[19]. When Schillebeeckx stresses the importance of acceptance by the people of God, he understands this in a very concrete way, namely, that it is about the acceptance in the local Church. Still this does not mean that local churches can claim to realise in an authentic and exhaustive way the Christian faith. They are always subject to the criticism of the other local churches. But taking this into account, the way in which a theological interpretation is (or is not) accepted in a local community can be, in Schillebeeckx' view, a source for theology within the universal church, as an indication of the Holy Spirit on the basis of which the given interpretation can be regarded as 'orthodox' (71).

III. DEVELOPING A METHOD THAT CAN MEET THE CRITERIA

Schillebeeckx develops a theological method that can meet the demands of providing a satisfying and orthodox theological interpretation today. He calls it a method of correlation, following P. Tillich who in the 1950s, drew up a theological method which correlates human questions and theological answers[20]. Schillebeeckx refines Tillich's system by

19. Schillebeeckx refers to *Lumen Gentium* 28 and *Ad Gentes* 20.
20. P. TILLICH, *The Method of Correlation*, in ID., *Systematic Theology*, Volume I, Chicago, IL, Chicago University Press, 1951, 59-66.

stressing the universality of the Christian message and by indicating the importance of the human experience, which functions as a bridge between human questions and theological answers.

Inspired by the philosophy of linguistic analysis, Schillebeeckx formulates some objections towards Tillich's point of departure, which states that theology should formulate theological answers in such a way that they appear as meaningful answers to existential human questions. In Schillebeeckx' view, Tillich makes a 'category-mistake', because, seen from a linguistic point of view, a religious answer cannot be given to a non-religious question. In doing so, one ends up giving a meaningless answer. Schillebeeckx supposes that Tillich was aware of this problem and that he therefore formulates the human questions in light of the Christian answer. Although it resolves the linguistic problem (there is a correlation between a religious question and a religious answer) it creates, nevertheless, another problem that is very important for Schillebeeckx. It undermines the intention of the correlative method to present the Christian message as a universal message "because the answer to such a re-formulated question is only valid for the Christian and is not universally valid: it is not a truth that binds all men"[21].

Therefore, a new method of correlation is needed and should (in Schillebeeckx' view) contain two fundamental elements, namely negative dialectics on the one hand and a positive sphere of meaning on the other. A method of correlation based on these two elements provides in the first place a human answer to a human question and only in a second move a religious answer.

1. *Negative Dialectics*

As demonstrated above, Schillebeeckx maintains that one can distinguish something universal in all the human answers to man's deepest questions about meaning. Although it is sustained by an unexpressed positive sphere of meaning, this underlying universal pre-understanding is negative. Schillebeeckx calls this common resistance to the threat to humanity "a praxis which is motivated by hope"[22]. According to him, there is a critical solidarity in resistance to the inhumanity among men. As soon as this universal pre-understanding is positively articulated (theoretically as well as practically), a plurality of projects arieses. Because this universal pre-understanding is also the basis of the Gospel, Christianity does not have to bind itself to one specific philosophical way of thinking in order to be understandable. Because the Christian message is

---

21. SCHILLEBEECKX, *The Understanding of Faith* (n. 3), p. 85.
22. *Ibid.*, p. 92.

grounded on a universal experience, it can be understood by everyone. This proves that Christian identity has to do with human integrity. As Schillebeeckx says it: "The Christian answer is at one with man's universal protest against the inhumane"[23]. This does not mean that Christians should not be critical towards the human answers that are given to the human question of the threatened *humanum*. Schillebeeckx stresses that the Christian should always resist believing that the human being can realise the *humanum* in history. After all, the power to realise an individual and collective peace is reserved for God. This is what Schillebeeckx calls the "eschatological reservation"[24]. Taking this into account a satisfactory method of correlation is possible. It points out that on the human question of the threatened *humanum*, a human answer can be given (resistance against this threatening) and that in this human context of experience the Christian message appears as a meaningful possibility that is understandable for all. This implies that a correlation is possible between "what is affirmed in the gospel message as a promise, a demand and a criticism and what man experiences as emancipation in his resistance to the threat to the *humanum* that he is seeking"[25].

2. *Positive Horizon of Meaningfulness*

Schillebeeckx states that the negative dialectics are in need of an intrinsic supplement, namely the justified trust that the experience of meaningfulness is not entirely beyond our reach. People already act on the conviction that life itself is or is not worth living. They may try to avoid this question on a theoretical level, but in their praxis they have already given an answer[26]. Schillebeeckx states that it is undeniable that human life includes particular experiences which are signs or glimpses of an ultimate total meaning of human life. According to him it is the trust in this meaning of life that is the basis presupposition of man's action in history[27]. Therefore it is possible to regard human life as more than simply meaninglessness, but as a manifestation of essential goodness, even apart from revelation. For Schillebeeckx it is clear that man's questions about himself and about the meaning of life are sustained by the reality of creation and are thus, implicitly rooted in the soil of all religious experience, namely God's act of creation. This implies that the question is implicitly religious and can be answered with a religious answer. In

23. *Ibid.*, p. 93.
24. *Ibid.*, p. 94.
25. *Ibid.*, p. 94.
26. *Ibid.*, pp. 95-96.
27. *Ibid.*, pp. 96-97.

Schillebeeckx' view it is therefore possible to speak in this case correlatively about God in a non-religious context[28]. The human belief that life is meaningful and that good will prevail can be identified as a result of the fact that people are created by God. For Schillebeeckx it is obvious that the positive glimpses of meaningfulness people experience are resulting from God. This makes the correlation between human questions and theological answers possible.

With this new method of correlation (with the two-fold structure), Schillebeeckx proposes a Christianity that functions as a particular expression of a general human striving for humanity. His method guarantees the relation between the Christian message and the experiences of human beings as well as the link between theory and praxis. Schillebeeckx is convinced of the fact that his method of correlation proves that the Christian way of thinking is not strange for modern human beings and that theological and doctrinal articulations are always situated in the human striving for more humanity. This means that the Christian message incites Christians to *practically* create a better world, together with all people of good will. Therefore, the method of correlation is capable of meeting the requirements to produce theological interpretations that are orthodox in the sense as it is understood by Schillebeeckx.

IV. CONTEMPORARY QUESTIONS REGARDING SCHILLEBEECKX' METHOD

Schillebeeckx presents the relation to human experiences as the outstanding criterion to test theological or doctrinal articulations on their meaningfulness. This gives him the reputation of a theologian of experience, sometimes with the connotation of esteeming experience more than revelation. It cannot be denied that experience plays a crucial role in his theology. Still Schillebeeckx cannot be regarded as a liberal theologian who sells off the Christian tradition to experience or who only takes experience as a source for theology. Although he demands theology to be understandable, he also pays attention to the unfathomable character of revelation. The problem is not the fact that experience plays an important role for Schillebeeckx, but that it is not always clear what the expression 'experience' actually involves. Which experiences are at stake here and maybe more important whose experiences? Should the Christian mes-

---

28. *Ibid.*, p. 98.

sage relate to the experience of the theologian or the bishops, or to the experience of the Christian community or simply to the experience of all people? Schillebeeckx' major conviction seems to be that the listeners (and not only the speakers) of the message should be able to understand it as related to their experiences. Sometimes he specifies this group as 'the living community of church' or 'the community of faith'; at other times he thinks this group a greater one, namely 'the people' of his time who are living in the secular society he also lives in. At a certain moment Schillebeeckx states that theological language should take the "human language of experience" as a model[29]. The question rises whether such a general human language exists in reality. Schillebeeckx seems to use the word to refer to the experiences of Western, secularised and modern people who live in a society that only believes in what is rational and scientifically understandable. In this society there is a belief in the technical and scientific process of society and in the reign of liberal values. Schillebeeckx himself is convinced of the fact that society is heading for more humanity and therefore, in his view, to a realisation of the Kingdom of God[30]. His belief in the positive progress of history makes him consider all human striving for humanity as a striving for the Christian vision of the Reign of God. Consequently he looks at all human experiences as if they were Christian experiences.

This makes it difficult to discover whose experience is functioning as a guiding norm in Schillebeeckx' 'hermeneutics of experience'. Is the Christian theologian to test his articulations by the experiences of all people in society or is it his or her task to test them by the experiences of contemporary Christians? For Schillebeeckx the distinction between both is not very clear nor is it a crucial one for him. Schillebeeckx is convinced of the fact that most people of his time (whether they would agree or not) are Christians. In a context where secularisation only began to show its real proportions, this was a natural view.

However, society has been changing a lot since that time. Where Schillebeeckx could still discern two groups in society, namely people who were still Christians and people who were no longer Christians, this seems absolutely impossible today because of the variety of religious attitudes in society. People do not situate themselves only on the line more Christian – less Christian, but constitute their own religious identity in

---

29. *Ibid.*, p. 36.
30. In later publications (SCHILLEBEECKX, *Church* [n. 16]; ID., *Theologisch Testament: Notarieel nog niet verleden*, Baarn, Nelissen, 1994) Schillebeeckx seems less convinced of the values of modern society and the possibility of man to create a better world.

relation to different religious and philosophical traditions. The society in which Christian theologians today work and live is a pluralist society. People of several religious traditions are taking part in society, next to people who are indifferent towards religion or those who are in search of a meaningful view of life inspired by different religious traditions at the same time. Thus, a Christian theologian today is confronted with a diversity of dialogue partners. Schillebeeckx directed his theology to Christians and to people who turned their backs to Christianity because of the fact that they were losing touch with the doctrinal language. It is clear that the situation today is much more complex than that. Next to a far-reaching secularisation pluralisation is a reality. This implies that the theologian today should reconsider his theological task in view of these changes.

In the current situation, it seems impossible to apply Schillebeeckx' 'hermeneutics of experience' in the broadest sense of the word. Christian doctrine cannot adjust itself to the experiences of all people living in our society. Studying the later work of Schillebeeckx it becomes clear that he modifies his method of correlation towards an internal Christian correlation whereby the Christian tradition and the experiences of Christian believers (and not universal 'human' experiences) are thought in a mutual relationship. Modern Christians look at the original Christian experiences from within their experiences in modern society and *vice versa*. The changes in the social-economic contexts in which experiences of faith take place trigger evolutions in the experiences of faith themselves. If Christian faith ought to be understandable for contemporary Christians, this mutual influence should be taken serious[31]. Thus the conclusion that correlation between Christian message and universal human experience is not possible today does not involve a complete denial of the necessity of relation the Christian message to present-day experiences of believers! When Christians cannot see the connection between their tradition and everyday life, they will cease considering their faith as meaningful and inspiring. This was the case in Schillebeeckx' time and is certainly the case today. Theological and doctrinal articulations should also today be in relation to the living faith of the Christian community. We should take Schillebeeckx' concerns very seriously in this matter!

---

31. SCHILLEBEECKX, *Church* (n. 16), p. 35. Still, in this work Schillebeeckx maintains the idea of a universal "protesting experience of contrast" (p. 29) as a basis for his method of correlation. This gives his thought on this method at least an ambiguous character. The distinction between the experiences of Christians and 'universal' human experiences never becomes clear.

V. ORTHOPRAXIS AS A CRITERION FOR ORTHODOXY TODAY?

Taking the former into account, it would be very unwise to evaluate Schillebeeckx' criteria for orthodoxy as inapplicable to our present situation. The problems he points to regarding the difficulties Christians have understanding their own faith if it is not articulated in contemporary language are also urgent today. Schillebeeckx' emphasis on the role of experience in the process of the renewal of faith shows that theologians need to realise more than only a translation of the language of faith. They really have to take into account the experiences of the community of faith and they have to guarantee the alliance between faith and life, between doctrine and praxis. We cannot go back to the time in which the hierarchy of the Church was the articulator of orthodox faith and in which the believers only had to endorse the doctrinal articulations without making any reflection or without confronting them with their own way of believing. Christians today are people who make critical reflections about the content of the Christian faith and who are participating in an active way in the process of seeking religious truth.

We can illustrate this with the reaction of some Christians to 'the case Schillebeeckx' in Rome where accusations were made by the Congregation for the Doctrine of Faith regarding his theological thoughts[32]. Schillebeeckx' orthodoxy was questioned and several Christians protested the charges made by the leaders of the Church. In doing so, they actually brought one of Schillebeeckx' own criteria for orthodoxy in praxis, namely that the pronouncements of the hierarchy should be accepted by the community of faith as corresponding to their perception.

Ted Schoof collected the various reactions people gave in personal letters or in public opinions concerning the 'Case of Schillebeeckx'. In his view the letters demonstrate that Christians take responsibility for the Christian tradition, and that they even claim the right to have a say in the teachings of the Church[33]. Nobody denies that the Congregation for the Doctrine of Faith has a right to exist and that the Catholic Church needs an authorized medium to test the insights of faith, but many Christians

---

32. For more information about the Schillebeeckx case, see L. SWIDLER – P. FRANSEN, *Authority in the Church and the Schillebeeckx Case*, New York, Crossroad, 1982; T. SCHOOF – M. O'CONNELL, *The Schillebeeckx Case: Official Exchange of Letters and Documents in the Investigation of Fr. Edward Schillebeeckx, O.P. by the Sacred Congregation for the Doctrine of the Faith, 1976-1980*, New York, Paulist, 1984; P. HEBBLETHWAITE, *The New Inquisition? Schillebeeckx and Küng* (Fount paperbacks, 106), Glasgow, Collins, 1980.

33. T. SCHOOF, *Getuigen in de 'zaak Schillebeeckx': Theologische lijnen in de publieke en persoonlijke reacties*, in *Tijdschrift voor Theologie* 20 (1980) 402-421, esp. 405.

are convinced of the fact that this testing should take place in an open dialogue and that room should always be left for diversity in the understanding of faith. In their letters the writers assert this because of their
belief that the Holy Spirit is active whenever Christians are seeking faith
in an honest and sincere way. They also refer to the Gospel that rejects
oppression and servile obedience and wants people to be free[34]. Furthermore, in several reactions people made clear that they expect the Church
to act following her own teachings. In the case of the charge against
Schillebeeckx, they point out that the manifold references to human rights
made by John Paul II should not contradict the way in which the Church
is dealing with people. Thus, the Church cannot make use of intimidation
or intellectual repression and at the same time defend human rights. Christians count on the authenticity of the Church[35]. This demand corresponds
to what Schillebeeckx describes as the need for orthopraxis as a criterion
for orthodoxy.

Recent studies about Christian belief in the contemporary Western context[36] indicate that people today, under the influence of individualisation
and de-traditionalisation, are very sensitive to the authenticity of religious
institutions as well as of individual believers[37]. This general observation
is also true for contemporary Christians because they are children of their
time. It seems a tendency that Christians expect to be stimulated by the
leaders of the Church to reflect upon their faith, to discuss it with other
believers and to search for the bond between their faith and their individual lives. As the reactions above show, they want to do this without
being condemned for it. Therefore they see the Church's Magisterium as
a partner for dialogue and not as the institution that can dictate how one
ought to believe. Moreover, they hold that the way in which one gives
shape to his or her belief is more important than the list of things in which
one believes[38]. Therefore people will only engage in a religious tradition
on the basis of personal experiences and not on the authority of an insti

34. SCHOOF, *Getuigen in de 'zaak Schillebeeckx'* (n. 33), p. 408.
35. *Ibid.*, p. 411.
36. K. DOBBELAERE – L. VOYÉ, *Religie en kerkbetrokkenheid: Ambivalentie en vervreemding*, in ID. – M. ELCHARDUS – J. KERKHOFS – L. VOYÉ – B. BAWIN-LEGROS, *Verloren zekerheid: De Belgen en hun waarden, overtuigingen en houdingen*, Tielt, Lannoo, 2000, 117-152; A. VAN HARSKAMP, *Het nieuw-religieuze verlangen*, Kampen, Kok, 2000; R.J. SCHREITER, *Nieuwe contouren van geloof: Verkenning van de stand van zaken in de huidige westerse wereld*, in *Tijdschrift voor Theologie* 39 (1999) 34-47; F. JESPERS, *Gelegenheidsgelovigen: Bewust genieten van genereuze tradities*, in *Tijdschrift voor Theologie* 40 (2000) 111-121.
37. VAN HARSKAMP, *Het nieuw-religieuze verlangen* (n. 36), pp. 58-66; 74; JESPERS, *Gelegenheidsgelovigen* (n. 36), pp. 113-116.
38. SCHREITER, *Nieuwe contouren van geloof* (n. 36), p. 42.

tution. This engagement is mostly situated on a local level, where people feel the freedom to reflect upon their faith and where they encounter fellow believers to share this reflection[39]. It looks like present-day Christians want to give shape to their personal way of believing in a process of reflection together with other believers and in dialogue with the institutional Church. Their personal experiences play a great role and they pay attention to the bond between the theoretical and the practical.

In light of these conclusions one cannot think about orthodoxy today without taking into account the specific situations of Christian believers in our context. Schillebeeckx' criteria for orthodoxy surely show us a way for taking seriously the experiences of Christians today. But his theory (which dates already from the 1960s) should be reconsidered and extended starting from contemporary research on Christian belief today. For, as we made clear, the context of Schillebeeckx and our context differ in many ways.

The most important question regarding orthodoxy today is the question of definition. Is the concept of orthodoxy about articulations of a hierarchical institution that believers only have to accept as articulations of the truth? Or is it about a process in which Christians, looking for the heart of their belief, enter a dialogue with each other in an authentic way in order to give shape to a faith that is related to their daily live? Following Schillebeeckx, I suggest that the latter should not be ignored in the contemporary discussion on orthodoxy and seeking truth. The question of taking believers' experiences serious next to maintaining a balance between orthodoxy and orthopraxis seems for me a crucial one today. This requires a continuous dialogue in our community of faith, in such a way that the community will always be restless in their searching for faith, as Schillebeeckx predicted.

annekatrien.depoorter@theo.kuleuven.be   Annekatrien DEPOORTER

---

39. *Ibid.*, pp. 38-40; JESPERS, *Gelegenheidsgelovigen* (n. 36), p. 117.

THE ROLE OF PARTICULARITY
IN THEOLOGICAL EPISTEMOLOGY

RELIGIOUS EXPERIENCE:
FROM PROCESS TO PRODUCT

During the past few years, I examined the notion and the phenomenon of religious experience in the dogmatic history of the Christian West[1]. There is an important evolution that might throw a light on the hypothesis of this project: in Antiquity and the Middle Ages, religious experience has to be interpreted in terms of a process, whereas in Modernity, it becomes more and more a product. By process, I mean something existential, something ongoing, a never ending and dynamic progression. A product on the other hand has a twofold meaning. First, it is something that can be made or produced by a subject. Second, a product is something finished or completed. It results from a production process.

I. AUGUSTINE

We begin our genealogy of religious experience with Augustine. The most important reason for this is his treatment of the subject matter. Augustine is an excellent representative of an extensive Christian tradition in Latin Antiquity that interprets religious experience rather intellectually, though it does not lack a certain existential component[2]. Though it is difficult to identify religious experience exactly in Augustine's work, it is wrong to decide that there is no such phenomenon in his work at all. Even though religious experience is not an explicit theme in his oeuvre, it is always there beneath the surface. We refer to his mystagogic catechesis and to the involved style of the *Confessiones*[3]. We cannot help but

---

1. General studies on the history of religious experience: W. HAUG – D. MIETH (eds.), *Religiöse Erfahrung: Historische Modelle in christlicher Tradition*, München, Fink, 1992; L. BOEVE – L.P. HEMMING, *Divinising Experience: Essays in the History of Religious Experience from Origen to Ricœur*, Leuven, Peeters, 2004.
2. H. GEYBELS, *Experience Searching for Theology & Theology Interpreting Experience: Augustine's Hermeneutics of Religious Experience*, in BOEVE –HEMMING, *Divinising Experience* (n. 1), 33-57; C. HARRISON, *Augustine and Religious Experience*, in *Louvain Studies* 27 (2002) 99-118.
3. O. PERLER, *Arkandisziplin*, in *Reallexikon für Antike und Christentum* 1 (1950) 243-273; C. JACOB, *Arkandisziplin, Allegorese, Mystagogie: Ein neuer Zugang zur Theologie des Ambrosius von Mailand* (Athenäus Monographien Theologie. Theophaneia: Beiträge zur Religions- und Kirchengeschichte des Altertums, 32), Hain-Frankfurt a.M., 1990, quoted in E. PAUL (ed.), *Geschichte der christlichen Erziehung. Band 1: Antike und Mittelalter*, Freiburg, Herder, 1993, 77, n. 11.

feel that his confessions are written in a spirit of strong existential involvement: "Our heart is restless, until it repose in Thee", the Church Father exclaims at the very beginning of his *Confessiones*[4].

Apart from this existential embeddedness, the concept of religious experience in Augustine's works should primarily be interpreted intellectually[5]. For him religious experience is connected to the search for the good and the beautiful, and especially the search for the true, as it is revealed in Christ. As soon as he starts writing, he is driven by a restless search for truth relying on his own reason and on divine mercy. This restlessness is explicitly manifest in his countless conversions: to Manicheism, to scepticism, to Neoplatonism, and finally to orthodox Christianity.

In this early period his ultimate motivation is the truth, within the context of an intuitive feeling of total existential dependence on the creator. It is this interweaving of existential and intellectual searching that forms the essence of religious experience for Augustine, and it is exactly because of this interweaving that it all seems strange to a post-modern audience for whom experience is often synonymous with emotion. Nevertheless, it is dangerous to completely ignore the cognitive aspect of religious experience.

It is by no means exceptional for religious experience to be a rather intellectualistic concept within the late Antique context of Augustine. The search for truth is much more than an academic pursuit; it is above all a way of life. In order to clarify his way of thinking, we have analogously examined aesthetic experience in Augustine's work. What we now describe as "aesthetic experience" was also more intellectualistic than emotional in the thought of Augustine and his contemporaries. In Augustine's thought, and in that of Antiquity and the Middle Ages in general, there is continuity between religious experience and Christian culture – the latter qualifying or "in-forming" the first[6].

What is Augustine's hermeneutic of religious experience like? In his early period he does not use Scripture for his hermeneutical framework as much as in his later works, but very soon his experiences as a human

---

4. T.J. VAN BAVEL, *De la raison à la foi: La conversion d'Augustin*, in *Augustiniana* 36 (1986) 5-27; N. FISCHER, *"Erfahrung" in Augustins "Confessiones"*, in *Internationale Katholische Zeitschrift Communio* 25 (1996) 206-220.

5. B. ALAND, *Cogitare Deum in den Confessiones Augustins*, in E. DASSMANN – K. SUSO FRANK (eds.), *Pietas: Festschrift für Bernhard Kötting* (Jahrbuch für Antike und Christentum, Ergänzungsbände, 8), Münster, Aschendorff, 93-104, p. 93.

6. On the concept of beauty: P.K. ELLSMERE, *Augustine on Beauty, Art, and God*, in R.R. LA CROIX (ed.), *Augustine on Music: An Interdisciplinary Collection of Essays* (Studies in the History and Interpretation of Music, 6), Lewiston, NY, Mellen, 1988, 97-113.

being turn into religious experiences within the framework offered by orthodox Christianity. He asks his audience to imagine being completely dependent, mortal, and sinful; all of these being experiences he is familiar with and whose meaning is clarified in Scripture and by the authorities. Beginning with his ordination as a priest, his existence is so permeated by Scripture that he speaks biblically. This biblical speaking, which we also encounter in many other antique and medieval authors, can be considered as the external evidence of religious experience – a union of Christian tradition and Christian existential experience. Another characteristic that will influence religious experience in the coming centuries can be extrapolated from Augustine's hermeneutics: religious experience is not a source for knowledge of God but an existentialization of faith. It is an epistemological method, but it does not contain knowledge in itself.

II. THE MIDDLE AGES

1. The Age of Transition

Even though Augustine is possibly the most influential Christian thinker ever, his intellectualistic version of religious experience did not prevail during much of the Middle Ages. The first reason for this is a cultural one. In the deserts of Egypt in the fourth century, new forms of religious living – anchoretism, cenobitism, and ascetic movements – based on ideas of Origen emerge; and, from the middle of the fourth century, the experiences of the desert fathers and mothers are not just being described but are being held up as the norm. We find many traces of this practice – which we describe as the theologising of religious experience – in the works of Cassian and Benedict[7]. The fact that both of these authors wrote for religious communities and not for individual Christians, was probably a large factor.

Aside from this cultural aspect, there is a second, historical reason why Augustine's view on religious experience loses its relevance. The intellectualistic antique paradigm of which he is such an important representative, declines after the fall of the Roman Empire. Part of the reason for

---

7. D. BURTON-CHRISTIE, *Scripture, Self-Knowledge and Contemplation in Cassian's Conferences*, in E.A. LIVINGSTONE (ed.), *Papers Presented at the Eleventh International Conference on Patristic Studies Held in Oxford 1991* (Studia Patristica, 25), Leuven, Peeters, 1993, 339-345; A. VOGÜÉ, *Cassien, le Maître et Benoît*, in J. GRIBOMONT (ed.), *Commandements du Seigneur et libération évangélique: Études monastiques proposées et discutées à Saint-Anselme (15-17 février 1976)* (Studia Anselmiana, 70), Rome, Anselmiana, 1977, 223-235.

this is that the rechristening of the West from the sixth century onwards is led by missionaries from monastic circles, and in the monasteries existential education is more important than the intellectual education of the student of faith. The spiritual father of this way of life was Origen, whose views were spread in the West by the aforementioned Cassian and especially Benedict[8].

Unlike Augustine, Origen and Cassian feel that religious experience is not primarily a cognitive concept but a concrete practice. For Augustine the secret of religious experience lies in the analogy between the Trinity and the human mind conceived to be in accordance with the Trinity; for Cassian it lies in the triad Bible, prayer, and existential experiences of faith. Experience even becomes the explicit theme of monastic practice. It is generated by the monk who takes example from Christ in prayer and lecture of the Bible and thereby anticipates eternal beatitude[9]. The distinction between heaven and earth fades in this participative paradigm. There is, however, not yet a rift between them.

Since Cassian, prayer became the methodical motor of religious experience as existential experience. In prayer a monk reaches a deeper consciousness of God's presence in daily life, and the boundary between immanence and transcendence becomes blurred. For monastic theologians of that time, prayer has become such an important source for reflection that countless tracts on all the different kinds of prayer are written throughout the Middle Ages[10].

Benedict has spread Origen's and Cassian's views on monasticism in the Latin West. His practical guidelines for monastic life have laid the foundations for what religious experience will mean for theology up until the twelfth century: religious experience is the same as experience of God and it is generated by prayer. It is verified by living according to Christian virtues and professing the Christian faith. The theological works of this period, from the fourth to the eleventh century – on any type of theology: exegetic, moral, dogmatic – serve only one purpose to generate religious experience as an encounter with God[11].

8. J. Leclercq, *Aux sources de la spiritualité occidentale: Étapes et constantes* (Tradition et spiritualité, 4), Paris, Cerf, 1964.

9. A. Guillaumont, *Le problème de la prière continuelle dans le monachisme ancien*, in H. Limet – J. Ries (eds.), *L'expérience de la prière dans les grandes religions: Actes du colloque de Louvain-la-Neuve et Liège (22-23 novembre 1978)* (Homo religiosus, 5), Louvain-la-Neuve, Centre d'Histoire des Religions, 1980, 285-294.

10. M. Sheridan, *Models and Images of Spiritual Progress in the Works of John Cassian*, in *Studia Anselmiana* 115 (1994) 101-125.

11. G. Holzherr, *Die Benediktsregel: Eine Anleitung zu christlichem Leben*, Zürich/Einsiedeln/Keulen, Benziger, ²1982, p. 42.

2. *The Early Middle Ages*

From the ninth century onwards, the unified model of Western theology starts to break up. Contrary to Modernity (see infra), when there will be a real rupture, religious experience will not be attacked for its content but for its methodology. The conflicts between Paschasius Radbertus and Ratramnus on the one hand and between Berengar and Lanfranc on the other, indicate the first fissures in monastic theology[12]. In the conflict between the first two, Paschasius Radbertus and Ratramnus, the issue is methodological. In the second conflict, a small fissure becomes a real rift, and it becomes ever more clear that a new method of theologising is emerging in which religious experience's share in theological epistemology gradually diminishes. Instead, discursive reason, based on the dialectical rereading of Augustine and not on the rediscovery of Aristotle, takes its place in the academic theology training from the twelfth century onwards.

Even before this rift becomes final, Anselm tries at the end of the eleventh century to compromise between 'the old and the new' way of theologising. He tends to cling to the old method but allows for the existence of the new method. Anselm radically casts off the monastic way of thinking by completely eliminating the existential factor in comprehending the mysteries of faith: *sola ratione*! On the other hand, he himself remains a monk. His intuitions are formed in the context of the practice of prayer, and he continues to defend the priority of faith over reason even when reason reaches different conclusions[13]. A generation later Abaelard will reverse that order bringing him into conflict with Church authorities[14].

---

12. A. CANTIN, *Foi et dialectique au XIᵉ siècle* (Initiations au Moyen-Âge, 1), Paris, Cerf, 1997; ID., *La position prise par Lanfranc sur le traitement des mystères de la foi par les raisons dialectiques*, in G. D'ONOFRIO (ed.), *Lanfranco di Pavia e l'Europa del secolo XI nel IX centenario della morte (1089-1989)* (Italia sacra. Studi e documenti di storia ecclesiastica, 51), Rome, Herder, 1993, 361-380; and ID., *Ratio et auctoritas dans la première phase de la controverse eucharistique entre Bérenger et Lanfranc*, in *Revue des Études Augustiniennes* 20 (1974) 155-186; and J. DE MONTCLOS, *Lanfranc et Bérenger: Les origines de la doctrine de la Transsubstantiation*, in D'ONOFRIO (ed.), *Lanfranco di Pavia*, 297-326. See also G. MACY, *The Theologies of the Eucharist in the Early Scholastic Period*, Oxford, Clarendon, 1984.

13. G.R. EVANS, *Anselm* (Outstanding Christian Thinkers), London – New York, Continuum, ²2001, p. 5; C.E. VIOLA, *Authorithy and Reason in Saint Anselm's Life and Thought*, in D.E. LUSCOMBE – G.R. EVANS, *Anselm: Aosta, Bec and Canterbury: Papers in Commemoration of the Nine-Hundredth Anniversary of Anselm's Enthronement as Archbishop, 25 September 1093*, Sheffield, Continuum, 1996, 172-208.

14. C.J. MEWS, *Abelard and His Legacy* (Variorum Collected Studies Series, 704), Aldershot, Ashgate, 2001.

3. *Monasticism versus Scholastic Theology: Religious Experience in the High Middle Ages*

After Anselm, theology goes two separate ways: the monastic experientially oriented way, and the scholastic rationalistic theology way. Spiritual masters predominate in the first current of thought and scholarly masters in the second. The first belong to monasteries, the second to the rising cathedral schools, from which gradually emerge the first universities. At first the demarcation between both paradigms of theology is difficult to determine, but from the late twelfth century onwards the separation is a fact. The universities educate professional theologians. The theology of the monasteries reverts to spirituality, however, at least according to modern perception. This explains why many monastic thinkers from Antiquity and the Middle Ages have not been regarded since Modernity as true theologians.

The Monastic Current: Bernard of Clairvaux, the *doctor experientiae*

The conflict is personified *in nucleo* by Bernard of Clairvaux and Peter Abaelard. We will focus *in extenso* on Bernard, whom we give the title *doctor experientiae*, because in his work the monastic reflection on religious experience reaches its apotheosis. He surpasses all his predecessors and his contemporaries in the field of systematic theological reflection on religious experience. Bernard proves himself to be a worthy successor to Augustine. He emphasizes self-knowledge as the basis for knowledge of God; he describes the path towards God as leading from the sensible to the intelligible, as the inner road leading to the ascending road, and so on. He is even more a successor of the monastic theologians because his religious experience is more a matter of existentially experiencing the doctrines of faith than of intellectually understanding them. Though both are different, they are not separate[15].

According to the *doctor experientiae*, a Christian has need of an affective access to Christian tradition. If that is lacking, he or she cannot get in touch with this tradition which is based on experience in the first place. This religious experience is not a matter of intuitive emotions or vague forms of spiritualism but of a lifelong existential growth process in which life is given meaning through Christianity. Bernard uses all possible dra-

---

15. D. HELLER, *Schriftauslegung und geistliche Erfahrung bei Bernhard von Clairvaux* (Studien zur systematischen und spirituellen Theologie, 2), Würzburg, Echter, 1988; U. KÖPF, *Religiöse Erfahrung in der Theologie Bernhards von Clairvaux* (Beiträge zur historischen Theologie, 61), Tübingen, Mohr Siebeck, 1980.

matic and rhetorical techniques to actively involve his audience in his argumentation and to stimulate their desire for religious experience. To ensure that existential experience would be interpreted as Christian experience, he appeals to the experiences of his audience, to his own (in-) experience, to experiences the regular faithful cannot have because they are unique, and more of the same.

Bernard displays a surprising dynamism in his thoughts on religious experience. The possibilities are nearly unlimited on the side of the subject, as well as on the side of the object. On the side of the subject, Bernard places an inexhaustible capacity for gaining new experiences even though some experiences are unique; for instance, no one but Mary has had the experience of giving birth to God's Son. But the subject continually evolves and so it constantly has new experiences. The side of the object, Christian tradition, is nearly as limitless. Specifically, Scripture contains an inexhaustibly rich report of Christian experiences.

We encounter the same dynamism in Bernard's description of the "experiential process." A believer who has experienced God will do anything to revive that experience since (at least) the lustful religious experience will give rise to the desire for a repeat of that experience. This repetition cannot be commanded but it can be stimulated by practicing neighbourly love and by communicating the experience by committing to a Christian life. In other words an authentic religious experience can be verified by (Christian) ethics.

For Bernard the core of Christian religious experience is the experience a believer has of the Christian God. God reveals himself as the content of an experience that He himself causes within the individual through the Word. The believer experiences God's interventions as feelings of pleasure or discomfort. The believer is affected (*affici*) in such a way that his passions can experience it. Religious experiences can therefore be internally perceived as (dis)pleasurable. The believer can then later extract knowledge about God from the contents of his experience. Knowledge gained through sensory perception relates to clearly defined external objects, but experiential knowledge relates to experiences of good and evil, happiness and misery, pleasure and displeasure, all referring to God as their source.

Religious experience happens inside the subject, distinguishing this type of knowledge from external sensory perception and from discursive reason. It is affective knowledge not perceived by the intellect but by the internal senses, especially by taste, with which human beings taste the sweetness of God. Bernard inspires this description of religious experience on the workings of the external senses but stresses that religious experience is perceived through the inner senses[16].

A striking characteristic of religious experience according to Bernard is that religious experience is an immediate experience. It is not mediated by anything outside itself, not even by discursive reason, which only tries to interpret the experience after the fact. The immediate relationship with God will become a crucial characteristic of the medieval Christian religious experience in all those circles described as "mystical" that honour Bernard's legacy. The mystics of the thirteenth century tend to radicalize that characteristic in their opposition to the scholastics[17].

To understand why spiritual theology becomes so radical in the thirteenth century, it is important to find out the exact reason for the conflict between Bernard and Abaelard. It is hardly surprising that Bernard, after being urged to do so by William of Saint-Thierry, considers Abaelard's work to be dangerous. Abaelard's œuvre focuses on the relationship between faith and reason, on the rights of the one and the autonomy of the other[18]. Especially that last part is cause for worry for monastic theologians. According to Bernard, and to William of Saint-Thierry, Abaelard has too high a regard for human reason. Anselm's *sola ratione* is transformed from an intuition to a standardized method of practicing theology. Abaelard's thought did indeed have drastic consequences, as it started theology off in a whole new direction. He defends the use of a dialectic method for understanding faith. For Bernard a virtuous life is the best testament a believer can give of his Christianity, but Abaelard lacks this existential reflex. For the "new Aristotle," understanding is a precondition for faith so faith can become subject to the rules of the intellect. Bernard thinks this is one bridge too far, since it does not accord a different status to religious truths than to any other kind of truth that could be subject to a dialectical analysis. Bernard and William manage to convince the pope to condemn Abaelard, but in the course of history it is Abaelard's method that prevails[19].

16. W. ZWINGMANN, *Affectus illuminati amoris: Über das Offenbarwerden der Gnade und die Erfahrung von Gottes beseligender Gegenwart*, in *Cîteaux* 18 (1967) 193-226.

17. See A. DEBLAERE, *Mystique: 2. Aux origines d'un essor exceptionnel de vie contemplative*, in *Dictionnaire de spiritualité* 10 (1980) 1904-1919.

18. T.M. TOMASIC, *William of Saint-Thierry against Peter Abelard: A Dispute on the Meaning of Being and Person*, in *Analecta cisterciensia* 28 (1972) 3-73; P. VERDEYEN, *La théologie mystique de Guillaume de Saint-Thierry*, Paris, FAC-éditions, 1990.

19. J. JOLIVET, *Arts du langage et théologie chez Abélard* (Études de philosophie médiévale, 57), Paris, Vrin, ²1982, p. 341; A. LECRIVAIN, *Dialectique*, in S. AUROUX (ed.), *Les notions philosophiques: Dictionnaire* (Encyclopédie Philosophique Universelle, 1), Paris, PUF, 1990, 633-639.

Scholastic Theology and Religious Experience:
The Autonomy of Reason

When the existential experiencing of Christian faith was eliminated as a method by academic theology, the face of theology changed forever. It is no longer informed methodically by experience but by dialectics. This evolution is manifest in scholasticism, even more so in nominalism, which is entirely based on abstract syllogistic categories[20]. Precisely this change of theologising starts the evolution from process to product in our understanding of religious experience.

The experientially oriented theology fits within the metaphysical framework of (Neo)platonism which can more easily than Aristotelian metaphysics imagine the relationship between God and man due to its participative structure. Medieval mystics actually had more difficulty envisaging God's transcendence than they did his immanence[21]. Therefore, they have no problems with the immediacy of the relationship with God, unlike the scholastic doctores. The conflicts between both systems reveal their incommensurability, as the controversy between Ruusbroec and Gerson clearly shows. Gerson makes an attempt to envisage religious experience within a scholastic framework, but the rift between mercy and nature has become definitive. Thus, mankind becomes incapable of having a direct and intimate relationship with God, and the scholastics begin to theologize extensively about the sacraments as the pre-eminent means for divine mercy and for encounters with God[22].

Just like during the transition from Antiquity to the Middle Ages, when the intellectualistic paradigm of religious experience lost ground to the affective paradigm, this period is witness to an equally radical evolution, namely, the splitting up of theology into an affective/mystical branch and a dialectical/scholastic one. As soon as these two options diverge from each other, each side becomes ever more radical. On one side of the scale, religious experience is emancipated from traditional monastic culture and individualized as well as democratised within a whole new set of spiritual movements[23]. In monastic circles, an experientially oriented mysti-

---

20. M. GRABMANN, *Geschichte der scholastischen Methode*, 2 vol., Darmstadt, Wissenschaftliche Buchgesellschaft, 1988; = ID., *Geschichte der scholastischen Methode*, 2 vol., Freiburg-im-Breisgau, Herder, 1910-1911; P. VIGNAUX, *Nominalisme*, in *Dictionnaire de théologie catholique*, 11/1 (1931) cc. 717-784.

21. R. FAESEN, *What is a Mystical Experience? History and Interpretation*, in *Louvain Studies* 23 (1998) 221-245.

22. On the conflict: A. COMBES, *Essai sur la critique de Ruysbroeck par Gerson* (Études de théologie et d'histoire de la spiritualité, 4, 5(1-2), 6), Paris, Vrin, 1945-1972.

23. C. MORRIS, *The Discovery of the Individual (1050-1200)* (Church History Outlines, 5), Londen, SPCK, 1972.

cal theology emerges manifested in the spirituality of the mendicant orders and among beguines, bogardes, and female Cistercians. The radicalization becomes apparent in a set of new or renewed spiritual practices such as strict asceticism, fasting, flagellation, etc.

On the other side of the scale, the universities become ever more rationalistic. This period of the rediscovery of Augustine's dialectics and later of Aristotle's metaphysics is interpreted as an intellectual pursuit. That is, it is accepted as a logical understanding of the mysteries of faith to uplift the soul, stimulate contemplation, and increase the love for God. The theme of religious experience disappears from academic theological reflection until the eve of Modernity.

III. MODERNITY

1. *Religious Experience in Protestantism*

In Protestantism, religious experience is again elevated to the position of an object of reflection. There is a continuous thread running from Cassian to Bernard to Luther. They all try to safeguard the experiential aspect of a faithful Christian life and consider the existentializing of Christianity as a crucial subject for their theology, but there is still a difference. Luther is very sensitive to the rift that had grown down the center of the medieval synthesis. The concept of religious experience affords him the possibility to make the gap bridgeable.

Luther

Luther is strongly dependent on Bernard for the development of his views on religious experience. For Bernard and Luther, religious experience plays an important part in the interpretation of Scripture because the deeper meaning of Scripture is only accessible to experienced believers. Through the experiences of sin, suffering, and death that are part of human existence, a believer can acquire knowledge of God and Christ. Hence his often quoted motto, "Sola autem experientia facit theologum"[24].

To Luther, just as for Bernard, religious experience is not a source of knowledge about God (it will become just that in some later Protestant movements). On the contrary, existential experience that is not informed (given *forma*) by the sources of Christian faith is given a very negative qualification. Compared to Bernard, Luther has a pessimistic outlook on

---

24. W. VON LOEWENICH, *Luthers Theologia Crucis*, München, Kaiser, [6]1982.

human existence and much more trust in the certainty offered by the Holy Ghost. In addition, his view on religious experience was formed, in contrast with Bernard's, mainly on the basis of negative experiences like the fear for his own salvation. At the same time that fear, as well as the consciousness of sin, provides the opportunity to find the way to God again which is a positive thing[25]. This shows the split in Luther's personality. On one hand, he is very modern and is frightened because of the gap between grace and nature. On the other hand, he tries to close the gap with medieval means (religious experience in the best tradition of monastic theology).

Because Luther's writing can be interpreted in so many ways, numerous splinter groups that emphasize only the Scriptures appear after his death. Paradoxically enough, this emphasizing of Scripture led to two opposite reactions: one which focuses on rationalizing theology even further, and one which focuses on the experiential aspect. Contrary to Catholicism, where experience disappears from theological reflection and is reduced to something practiced by the rank and file of the faithful, there is much theological reflection on religious experience in Protestant splinter groups[26].

Reaction to Luther: the Counter Reformation

Catholic religious experience develops outside theology in the grass roots of the Church. All forms of art blend into a rhetorical and pathos-filled *Gesammtkunstwerk*. After the Concilium of Trente, Thomism dominates Catholic theology leaving no room for reflection on religious experience (excepting the nineteenth-century Tübinger Schule). Meanwhile, in the sciences a new empirical experiential concept had emerged (experience being used in rationally structured experiments), and Catholic theology follows the example of scientific method by approaching the articles of faith in a rational manner.

2. *Protestant Developments in the Seventeenth and Eighteenth Centuries*

In the eighteenth century, the concept of religious experience comes to the forefront once more in Protestant theology under the influence of philosophers who reflect on the subject of religion. More than the theologians do, the philosophers realise that the existing apologetics, based

---

25. G. EBELING, *Luther: Einführung in sein Denken*, Tübingen, Mohr Siebeck, [3]1978, pp. 239-258.
26. See the catalogue of G.C.B. PÜNJER, *Geschichte der Christlichen Religionsphilosophie seit der Reformation*, 2 vol., Braunschweig, 1880.

on rationalistic natural theology, no longer suffice in an ever more mechanistic world-view. They correctly feel that the entire apologetics should go in a new direction, more specifically in the direction of experience. Experience does however get a changed status as a result of the altered position of the subject. Basic existential experiences become the points of departure for religion instead of the other way around. In other words, in the expression "religious experience", "religious" turns into an adjective instead of a substantive. At the same time, religious experience changes from a method into a precondition for religious knowledge, religious experience evolves from something gained through divine mercy to something produced by the subject[27].

Well-meaning attempts to make revelation acceptable to reason by giving arguments for it that anyone can understand, lead to, as we already mentioned, the failure of a rational defence for religion in philosophical circles. In England, which is traditionally known mainly for empiricism, we encounter numerous rationalistic thinkers (like Toland, Clarke, and Tindal) and also a form of religious enthusiasm that is very experientially oriented (Shaftesbury being a moderate representative). The rationalism that eliminates existential experience from the epistemological process will, just a century later, make the reintroduction of existential experience in theology possible. In this period the first alternative forms of apologetics appear. John Locke states that faith does not provide any scientific knowledge but a kind of belief because it is based on revelation. Belief entails that things are true because they were revealed to be so by God, and not because it has been empirically demonstrated.

David Hume deviates from the traditional rationalistic apologetics even more than Locke does. Even though he was probably an atheist, and it is unclear whether he was being ironic or not, Hume thinks that the origin of religion can be found in a basic existential experience such as fear. Contrary to the Middle Ages, when existential experience was formed by Christian tradition, the subjective existential experience of fear lies at the basis of the emerging and forming of religion. Experience again becomes a subject for discussion on the anthropological plane but with repercussions for religion[28].

27. F.E. MANUEL, *The Eighteenth Century Confronts the Gods*, Cambridge, MA, Harvard University Press, 1967, pp. 57-64.

28. J.C.A. GASKIN, *Hume on Religion*, in D.F. NORTON (ed.), *The Cambridge Companion to Hume*, Cambridge, Cambridge University Press, 1993, 313-344; D.J. HANSON, *Fideism and Hume's Philosophy: Knowledge, Religion and Metaphysics*, New York, Lang, 1993.

3. *Schleiermacher and James*

After the slow reintroduction of religious experience in seventeenth- and eighteenth-century thought, it is brought to the forefront of theological discussion once more in the eighteenth and nineteenth centuries (Schleiermacher, James). The contrast with medieval views becomes extremely great. In the Middle Ages an existential religious experience is the summit of religious life but at the same time it is secondary. Even explicitly mystical writers, always contend that mystics only experience of God what others know about Him. For Schleiermacher and James, it is the experience itself that is the most important. Both feel religious experience is the main point of departure and the defining component of religion.

There is yet another major difference from the Middle Ages. In that period religious experience is an existential experience that must be made to relate to Christian tradition. In many modern versions of religious experience, that relationship is turned around and the individual existential experience becomes constituent for religion. Schleiermacher, for instance, breaks with the medieval and Lutheran belief that religion and experience are not identical. He reinstates the immediate relationship with God of the medieval mystical authors but in a context in which the subject has become autonomous.

Concerning the experiential aspect itself, it is no longer a matter of medieval affectivity (being passively affected) but of subjective emotional forms of expression in opposition to the rigid rationalistic theology. Schleiermacher shows that religion also affects the inner self of mankind: religion must touch man existentially. Schleiermacher locates that feeling in the innermost reaches of the soul, since not much can be said about the essence of religion that does not manifest itself within the soul. It can hardly be expressed linguistically. The emotion escapes any control by the consciousness or by the will. An additional difference from the medieval view is that this emotional event is formally unconnected to the contents of the religious experience and that religious experience is no longer an incentive for moral action[29].

Schleiermacher is a typical modern author, as is made manifest by five characteristics he attributes to religious experience: differentiation (religion is disconnected from ethics and politics), undogmatic (more attention for emotions), individualization (minimalization of the ecclesiastical

---

29. C. ALBRECHT, *Schleiermachers Theorie der Frömmigkeit: Ihr wissenschaftlicher Ort und ihr systematischer Gehalt in den Reden, in der Glaubenslehre und in der Dialektik* (Schleiermacher-Archiv, 15), Berlin, de Gruyter, 1994, pp. 105-125.

aspect of religiosity), pluralisation (equality of the different claims for truth by different religions, i.e. philosophies of life), and de-institutionalisation (which eliminates the rigidity of the traditional organisational forms of religion). Surprisingly each of these five characteristics recurs in numerous present-day religious movements. In other words Schleiermacher has given religious experience a definition that is still relevant today. It still pays to be careful though, since some things are incorrectly attributed to Schleiermacher. He is for instance not the founder of non-cognitive theology, nor does he reduce religion to emotion, nor is he hostile to every form of institutionalisation.

William James professes to give a purely phenomenological account of the concept of religious experience. James' pragmatic approach has made a significant contribution to the sentimentalistic and subjectivistic conception of religious experience. He severs every tie with institutionalised religion. His subject in the *Varieties of Religious Experience* is the individual who claims to have religious experiences. The references to God are only secondary. In fact James proves himself to be a radical follower of David Hume, since James only takes religious experiences seriously in so far as they change the world, thereby making an empirical difference (making the study of the phenomenon possible)[30].

James is on the other side of the spectrum than Augustine: on the one hand an intellectualistic account of religious experience, on the other hand an emotional one. On the emotional side every theological factor is relinquished in favour of a personal interpretation by the subject. Even the source of the emotion can be almost anything: it is vaguely called divine but not given any further qualification. The divine is that which is revealed in the experience that was instigated by the divine. The source of emotion is not experienced as something real but that is irrelevant for James. What makes an experience religious is that it is a special type of experience that James describes as a mystical state of consciousness. Given the subjectification of religious experience, objective criteria that guarantee the authenticity of the religious experience are no longer conceivable. The traditional "distinction of the minds" is a thing of the past for him. In Catholicism it had been tradition and the magisterium that provided these criteria of old, safeguarding Catholic theology from subjectivism for a time longer.

James' Wirkungsgeschichte is radical. There are many characteristics of religious experience named in this study that are still relevant today in

---

30. R.B. PERRY, *The Thought and Character of William James (Briefer Version)*, Cambridge, MA, Harvard University Press, ²1967, p. 259.

numerous religious movements in the fringes and outside of the Christian Churches. Some of these experience-sensitive movements include the charismatic, feminist, and pluralistic movements. But there are also many movements outside the traditional churches that have composed their own religious consciousness from elements of Christianity and other religions (the so-called new-age spirituality). Having religious experiences becomes more important than traversing the road towards a religious experience (following a method). A thinker like William James is assimilated quite well in these circles, which explains why terms like subjectivism, de-institutionalisation, non-cognitivism, emotionality, and so on are so popular in present-day religious feeling (even in traditional Church circles).

IV. CONCLUSION

This historical overview has clearly shown that Christian religious experience was defined differently in each stage of the history of Christianity, and the current debates still bear the marks of those different accounts. Religious experience is not a ready-to-use concept that Christians can just adopt from the past (Augustine, Cassian, Bernard, Luther), but a concept that is continually contextualized throughout twenty centuries of Christianity. The general evolution of the content of religious experience can easily be summarised as the evolution from process to product (in the meaning of something that can be produced). In Antiquity and in the Middle Ages, religious experience is a life-long process of cooperation between God and man. Since Modernity, religious experience is more and more understood as an autonomous product of the subject.

hans.geybels@theo.kuleuven.be   Hans GEYBELS

TRUTH, ROCK MUSIC AND CHRISTIANITY

CAN TRUTH BE MAINTAINED IN THE DIALOGUE
BETWEEN THEOLOGY AND ROCK MUSIC[1]?

In his book *Hungry for Heaven*, rock journalist Steve Turner defines the specific experience at stake in rock 'n' roll music as a continuous 'search for redemption'[2]. If Turner is right in his analysis, he irrevocably places rock music on the agenda of actual theology[3]. More specifically, Turner's conclusion evokes the question of the soteriological truth of Christianity and its relation to the existential experience of rock music.

This last question makes up the thread of this contribution. In the first part, we present the (religious) experience of rock 'n' roll as presented by Turner in his book and as a challenge to theology today. Secondly, we compare two theologians who, in the name of the Christian truth, each developed a dialogue with rock music. The fact that both theologians immediately contradict each other is a challenging observation which directs their claims to Christian truth in the forefront. A final section examines the observed contradiction by trying to overcome it.

I. THE (RELIGIOUS) EXPERIENCE OF ROCK MUSIC:
TRUTH WITHOUT REDEMPTION

The connection between rock music and religious experience was already there from the outset. Apart from the contribution of rhythm and

1. I would like to thank Yves De Maeseneer and Paul Daponte for their comments and suggestions.

2. S. TURNER, *Hungry for Heaven: Rock and Roll and the Search for Redemption*, London – Sydney – Auckland, Hodder & Stoughton, 1988, p. 6.
3. This had been noticed by many practical theologians: I. KÖGLER, *Die Sehnsucht nach mehr: Rockmusik, Jugend und Religion*, Graz – Wien – Köln, Verlag Styria, 1994; M. SCHÄFERS, *Jugend, Religion, Musik: Zur religiösen Dimension der Popularmusik und ihrer Bedeutung für die Jugendlichen heute* (Theologie und Praxis, 1), Münster, Lit, 1999; U. BÖHM – G. BUSCHMANN, *Popmusik – Religion – Unterricht: Modelle und Materialien zur Didaktik von Popularkultur* (Symbol – Mythos – Medien, 5), Münster, Lit, 2000; G. FERMOR, *Ekstasis: Das Religiöse Erbe in der Popmusik als Herausforderung an die Kirche* (Praktische Theologie Heute, 46), Stuttgart – Berlin – Köln, Kohlhammer, 1999; B. SCHWARZE, *Die Religion der Rock- und Popmusik: Analysen und Interpretationen* (Praktische Theologie Heute, 28), Stuttgart – Berlin – Köln, Kohlhammer, 1997; H. TREML, *Spiritualität und Rockmusik: Spurensuche nach einer Spiritualität der Subjekte*, Ostfildern, Schwabenverlag AG, 1997.

blues as well as country music, the history of rock 'n' roll also points to the important influence of gospel music with regard to its origin and development[4]. Turner too examines this influence exploring the life of both Elvis Presley and Jerry Lee Lewis, two artists generally considered to be the founding fathers of commercial rock 'n' roll. Their biographies show how they became acquainted with the energy of gospel music, the way in which music could function as a way of exceeding the everyday life and the exuberance by which the gospel choirs succeeded in exciting the local community. Finally, both artists remembered the themes that were sung about in gospel: the music was about love, hope, desperation and redemption[5].

However, Presley and Lewis never became church ministers: their music inaugurated a definitive rupture with gospel. Whereas gospel viewed everything in the light of the worship of the Christian God, rock 'n' roll embodied the 'secularization' of this devotion. It abandoned the Christian message of redemption and replaced it by the celebration of the everyday life. This evolution had far-reaching consequences, and according to Turner, the history of rock 'n' roll is the story of the existential experience provoked by this 'decision'. Unlike gospel, rock music wanted to live out the human condition without any definitive surrender to the redemptive message of Christianity. For rock 'n' roll, there is only the music of the 'forever now' and no perspective exceeding this immanent experience[6].

Already Presley and Lewis experienced the consequences of this evolution: they both struggled with the fact that their music generated experiences contradicting the ones of Christian faith; Lewis, for instance, called himself 'too weak for the gospel'[7]. Like Presley, he experienced the discrepancy between his own music and the message of Christianity. For Turner, this irreconcilable tension summarizes the essence of rock 'n' roll:

> Ultimately, it was the redemption feel rather than the redemptive message that Southern rock 'n' roll took to the world. Confused, tortured and unsure

4. For the history of rock 'n' roll, see among others: D. HATCH – S. MILWARD, *From Blues to Rock: An Analytical History of Pop Music*, Manchester, Manchester University Press, 1977; N. COHN, *Awopbopaloobop alopbamboom: Pop from the Beginning*, Frogmore, Paladin, 1969, 1970 (new edition).

5. For the history of gospel music, see: D. CUSIN, *The Sound of Light: A History of Gospel Music*, Ohio, Popular press Bowling Green, 1990.

6. This element has been convincingly examined by R. PATTISON, *The Triumph of Vulgarity: Rock Music in the Mirror of Romanticism*, Oxford, Oxford University Press, 1987.

7. Turner cites Lewis from an interview with Rolling Stone: "I was raised a good Christian. But I couldn't make it. Too weak I guess", in TURNER, *Hungry for Heaven* (n. 2), p. 18.

of their own salvation, their personal lives vacillated between the repentant and God-fearing to outright debauchery, drugs and violence. Their music, too, alternated between secular and sacred. Both Presley and Lewis recorded albums of gospel songs, but they could never envisage a marriage of rock 'n' roll with religion. To them, that would have been like fornicating on an altar[8].

According to Turner, this tension is not only an interesting historical fact; it qualifies the essence at stake in rock music as such. Rock music is the autonomous attempt to reach out to the ultimate meaning of life outside the framework of any institutionalised religion. The ultimate motivation of rock is the idea that "we are in the wrong place"[9] and that we all long for a liberation from out of this deserted situation. On the basis of this presupposition, Turner reinterprets well-known moments within the history of rock music as examples of this existential longing – *The Beatles'* decision to move towards India to experiment with other religions, *The Doors'* flirtation with shamanism, and *The Rolling Stones'* with black magic. For Turner, this spiritual journey likewise explains the popularity as well as the omnipresence of drugs within the rock scene.

Although rock stands for the attempt to satisfy autonomously the hunger of human existence, its history is the proof of the impossibility of this project. Each attempt thoroughly analysed by Turner, ends up with the conclusion that rock music indeed presents experiences of exuberance but nevertheless fails to deliver that which it fundamentally cares for. The only result remains the rough observation that we still "need to break free from this fallen world"[10]. After fifty years of rock 'n' roll, Turner concludes that rock music did not survive its rupture with gospel: it did not succeed in its attempt to provide a message as redemptive as the one of gospel. The experience of rock music might be a religious one but remains from the very outset structurally irreconcilable with the message of Christianity. In his final chapter, Turner concludes:

> These experiences, because they are not subject to any tried and tested revelation from God, don't adequately answer the basic questions that religion has always asked: Where do I come from? Why am I here? How should I live? Where am I going[11]?

In short: in rock music truth rises to the surface as truth without redemption: it represents the experience of being human, of having a body, of being mortal and of not being able to realize autonomously any

---

8. TURNER, *Hungry for Heaven* (n. 2), p. 27.
9. *Ibid.*, p. 6.
10. *Ibid.*, p. vii.
11. *Ibid.*, p. 231.

redemption out of this world. It is because of this conclusion, that rock music challenges the agenda of actual theology.

II. THE TRUTH OF CHRISTIANITY AND THE EXPERIENCE OF ROCK

If rock music stands for an existential 'hunger for heaven' as well as for the attempt to fulfil this hunger autonomously, it seems to challenge the redemptive message of Christianity in its very core: how the Christian truth, claiming to stand for 'good news for everyone', relates itself to the experience of rock music?

1. *Joseph Ratzinger: Theological Truth without Dialogue*

Analysis of Rock Music

In his writings about Christian liturgy and church music, Joseph Cardinal Ratzinger, the present pope Benedict XVI, frequently refers to the phenomenon of popular music[12]. The argument on the basis of which he condemns pop as well as rock music is the one of truth: church music counts as the *true* expression of the unique redemption whereas popular music *a priori* counts as an untrue one.

In order to understand this clear and provocative conclusion, it is important to clarify some of Ratzinger's presuppositions. First and foremost, he understands today's western culture as a culture in crisis. The origin of this crisis is to be found in the emancipation thought of the Enlightenment, which, from the seventeenth century onwards, started to claim a 'free thinking' and deliberated itself from the hegemony of Christian faith. With this emancipation movement, western culture cut loose its own religious roots and moved towards an autonomous and secularized worldview. For Ratzinger however, the one who cuts his/her own roots, in the end alienates him- or herself and enters the realm of 'untruthfulness'.

Pop and rock music are the most obvious examples of this untruthfulness[13]. Both phenomena embody the cultural schizophrenia into which

---

12. J. RATZINGER, *Das Fest des Glaubens: Versuche zur Theologie des Gottesdienstes*, Einsiedeln, Johannes Verlag, 1981, pp. 86-111; ID., *A New Song for the Lord: Faith in Christ and Liturgy Today*, trans. M.M. Matesich, New York, Crossroad, 1996, pp. 94-127; J. RATZINGER, *The Spirit of the Liturgy*, trans. J. SAWARD, San Francisco, CA, Ignatius Press, 2000, pp. 136-156. In what follows, we only focus on his writings as a theologian. We will not examine the standpoints from which he wrote as Prefect of the Congregation for the Doctrine of the Faith, nor the documents written by Pope Benedict XVI.

13. Although Ratzinger in his final judgement condemns pop as well as rock music,

the Western culture has ended up because they both show the impotence, cynicism and illusion to which human pride – *hubris* – gives rise. On the one hand, Ratzinger considers rock music an autonomous attempt to realize a pseudo-redemption out of this earthly life. It is the human search for a beatific collective feeling by means of loud music, compelling rhythms and stupefying narcotics: an ecstatic experience in order to exceed the pain of being: "People are, so to speak, released from themselves by the experience of being part of a crowd and by the emotional shock of rhythm, noise, and special lighting effects. However, in the ecstasy of having all their defenses torn down, the participants sink, as it were, beneath the elemental force of the universe"[14]. Pop music on the other hand is the choice of man for the most evident as well as most banal option: the option to willingly behave oneself according to the code imposed by the culture industry. Consequently, pop and rock music confirm the thesis that today's Western culture is just rambling around. The whole of popular music counts as the delivery to a false ecstasy which either reduces the existential experience of human life to an irrelevant problem (pop) or solves it by an illusory spurious solution (rock).

The Answer of Theology

Since for Ratzinger the origin of this cultural crisis has to be found in the autonomous thinking of the Enlightenment, its overcoming consists in the abandoning of this emancipation thought. Ratzinger's answer to the thought of modernity limits itself to the postulation of its invalidity. His argument is the one of truth. This can be derived from the way in which Ratzinger copes with popular music. Since the experience of rock as well as pop music is built upon the basic presuppositions of autonomous thinking, it participates in a creativity which is doomed to fail:

> In this way, however, it becomes apparent that human creativity that does not want to be receptivity and participation is by its very nature absurd and untrue since humans can only be themselves through receptivity and participation. Such creativity is a flight from the *conditio humana* and therefore untrue. This is the reason why cultural disintegration begins wherever

in his analysis he presupposes a difference between the two. He thereby follows the distinction often made among scholars in popular music: pop music then is understood as the industrial product with which the culture industry provides the anonymous masses. Next to it, rock music is presupposed as the music made out of the attempt to come loose of this industrial framework. See G. BUSCHMANN, *Rock, Pop and All That DJ-Culture – Thesen zu Popularmusik, Religion und Kirche aus religionspädagogischer Perspektive*, in *Praktische Theologie* 33 (1998) 41-54.

14. RATZINGER, *The Spirit of the Liturgy* (n. 12), p. 148.

faith in God disappears and a professed *ratio* of being [*Vernunft des Seins*] is automatically called into question[15].

From this quotation, it becomes clear how Ratzinger conceives of the structure of truth. The abandonment of the belief in God equals the denial of a given *"ratio* of being". The result is a flight out of the human condition and the entrance into the realm of untruthfulness. Conversely, truth equals the right acceptance of the *conditio humana*, the belief in God, and, finally, devotion to the given ratio of being.

Ratzinger defines truth as the true humanity which became absolutely visible in the concrete and historical life of Jesus of Nazareth. The incarnation counts as God's liberating answer to the human need of redemption and therefore as the one and only truth. Access to this truth is the humble acceptance of the human condition which in Ratzinger's thought automatically seems to lead to the acceptance of God as Savior and the truth of redemption.

Popular music should be condemned because it counts as the autonomous attempt to care for one's own salvation. Since it denies the truth of the incarnation, it can only produce falsehood. In his dialogue with rock and pop music Ratzinger very well preserves the truth of the unique redemptive message of Christianity. However, in making an absolute connection between truth and Christianity, he threatens to lose the dialogue with culture, *in casu* rock music. The only dialogical attitude the theologian can assume, is firstly to condemn this kind of music, and secondly, to wait until its artists accept the true insight.

2. *Hubert Treml: Dialogue without Truth*

The Analysis of Rock Music

In his book *Spiritualität und Rockmusik*[16], the pastoral theologian Hubert Treml interprets rock music as one of the channels along which people today search for the ultimate meaning of life. Rock music is not a flight out of everyday reality but the process by which this reality is taken seriously: "Die Sogenannte Flucht ist dann in Wirklichkeit eine Konfrontation, eine Auseinandersetzung mit den Anfragen des Lebens"[17]. This confrontation is realized on three specific domains. Rock music is *corporal* music, focussing on the experience of the *everyday life* and thus

---

15. RATZINGER, *A New Song for the Lord* (n. 12), p. 119.
16. H. TREML, *Spiritualität und Rockmusik: Spurensuche nach einer Spiritualität der Subjekte. Anregungen für die Religionspädagogik aus dem Bereich der Rockmusik* (Glaubenskommunikation Reihe Zeitzeichen, 3), Stuttgart, Schwabenverlag, 1997.
17. *Ibid.*, p. 192.

creating a personal (religious) *identity*. In applying each of these domains as the source of an exuberant experience, rock music frees those regions repressed and negotiated by modern rationality[18].

Treml interprets rock music as a religious search: its music stands for the existential experience in which artists express their human longing for what supersedes the concrete here and now. By doing so, the music of rock mediates an experience of transcendence. For this argument, Treml refers to the prominent appearance of religious questions in, for instance, lyrics and interviews as well as the factual function rock music has for many youngsters today. This function is the one of 'Ersatzreligion' ('surrogate religion')[19] since it offers youth a place where they can find a certain identity, where they can drop in with their religious questions, where certain rites give them the feeling of being accepted in a community and where their religious search is cared for by rock artists or groups.

Treml concludes by stating that rock music announces itself as a 'powerful contemporary religious experience' making possible the experience of transcendence within the one of everyday life[20]. Just like Ratzinger, Treml recognizes a religious dynamic within the experience of rock. Whereas for Ratzinger this dynamic is equal to a false flight out of everyday life, Treml interprets this experience as an authentic search for meaning in need of theological valorisation.

The Answer of Theology

Treml theologically embraces the experience of rock music by stating that its authentic search for meaning touches on the same transcendent reality as the one Christians denominate as 'God'. Rock embodies an experience with "dem Lebensgeheimnis, das wir ChristInnen Gott nennen"[21]. In order to think this relation, Treml reduces the Christian experience to the experience of transcendence and removes the moment of truth out of the Christian denomination:

> Christentum ist eine Gemeinschaft, die aus ganz eigenen Erfahrungen göttlicher Offenbarung ihre spezifische *Interpretation* transzendenter Wirklichkeit entfalten konnte. Die Wahrheit liegt nicht in der Interpretation, die

---

18. Treml follows the analysis of R. SIEDLER, *Feel It in Your Body: Sinnlichkeit, Lebensgefühl und Moral in der Rockmusik*, Mainz, Grünewald Verlag, 1995.

19. TREML, *Spiritualität und Rockmusik* (n. 16), pp. 220-225.

20. *Ibid.*, p. 235: "Im Umgang mit Rockmusik wird *Transzendenzerfahrung im Alltag* möglich. Deshalb ist auch hier *religiöse Identitätsbildung* zu verorten, freilich – wie für eine zeitgenössische Spiritualität eher wahrscheinlich – *unbewußt* und *nicht begrifflich*".

21. *Ibid.*, p. 220.

sich als relativierbar erweist, weil sie auf geschichtlich veränderbaren Begriffen beruht, sondern in der *Wirklichkeit*, die sie zu benennen sucht[22].

Treml situates the moment of truth in the experience of transcendence and not so much in its interpretation. For, every interpretation is historical and contingent and therefore *relative* to the reality it interprets. In other words: truth is to be found in the *that* and not in the *what* of transcendent reality. This approach enables Treml to interpret other religious experiences, for instance those of rock music as *expressions of truth*: these too count as another interpretation of the transcendent and mysterious reality[23].

The argument of Treml consists of two different elements. First of all, there is the level of *truth* which concerns the mystery of the transcendent reality. Within this domain the criterion is whether or not the mystery of transcendent reality is acknowledged. The way in which this reality is recognized, interpreted or denominated is, as far as this level is concerned, of minor importance, since the relation between interpretation and reality is a *relative* one. As long as the transcendent reality is recognized, truth is at stake. Secondly and strictly separated from the level of truth, Treml thinks the level of *interpretation*. Since no universal unanimity can be reached here, the dialogue between the Christian tradition and other religious traditions cannot be based upon the universal level of truth but needs to be grounded on a particular Christian argument. Here, Treml applies Christianity's universal message of salvation as the perspective by which Christian theologians have to interpret these non-Christian experiences. In his dialogue with rock Treml abandons the discourse of truth since his main concern is to create an open climate which will not be blocked by too particular notions of truth[24].

In his theological dialogue with culture, Treml opts for a radical openness. In the way he concretizes this dialogue, however, he is in danger of losing the element of truth within Christianity. For, in his model, the

22. *Ibid.*, p. 96.
23. *Ibid.*, p. 220: "Aber nicht erst wenn man über das Geheimnis des Lebens singt, ist man im Kontakt mit ihm, nimmt Beziehung auf. Diese die erste Wirklichkeit transzendierende Begegnung mit dem Lebensgeheimnis, das wir ChristInnen Gott nennen, ereignet sich möglicherweise auch auf non-verbaler Ebene. In der Rockkultur, die vorwiegend auf körperlicher und damit nicht-begrifflicher Kommunikation beruht, könnten sich Phänomene finden, die auf einen solchen Sachverhalt verweisen".
24. *Ibid.*, p. 96: "Gehen wir vom allgemeinen Heilswillen Gottes aus, dann müssen wir damit rechnen, daß sich Gott nicht nur über christliches Begriffsgut dem Menschen mitteilt. Vielmehr ist anzunehmen, daß er schon immer in den einzelnen Menschen wirkt". In a footnote, Treml refers explicitly to certain documents of the Second Vatican Council: *Lumen Gentium*, 13.16; *Nostra aetate*, 1.4; *Dei Verbum*, 3; *Ad Gentes*, 7.

moment of truth is reduced to the acceptance of transcendent reality. Consequently, Treml keeps silent about the message of redemption, not to mention its value of truth.

III. To Conclude: Rock, Truth and Christianity

The approaches of both Ratzinger and Treml not only differ fundamentally, they are also irreconcilable. The theological debate on the religiosity of rock music as well as the search for an adequate theological reaction seems thereby to have arrived at an impasse. The fact that both tendencies hope to prove their own right only by portraying the other position as either 'prejudiced conservative' or as 'ordinary progressive', bears witness to this impasse. Treml, for instance, presents Ratzinger's statement as a simple "misunderstanding"[25] of what rock music is all about[26]; Ratzinger, on the other hand, only asks whether the pastoral embracement of popular music really imparts a valuable element to Christian faith[27].

In what follows, we further examine this impasse. It is our conviction that the 'conservative versus progressive' polarisation misleads the debate. We do not want to follow Treml where he suggests that the origin of this impasse has to be attributed to Ratzinger's unwillingness to take serious the experience of rock music. In the following paragraphs we suggest that the impasse has to do with the way in which both authors conceive the truth of Christianity. First we focus on the concern shared by the two authors and secondly on the way in which the two approaches become

---

25. *Ibid.*, p. 212: "Im Anschluß an die bisherigen Ausführungen zur Rockmusik kann deutlich werden, wie sehr die Interpretation Ratzingers – und vieler ähnlicher Stimmen – auf einem Mißverständnis beruht: Zwar versuchen Jugendliche mit Hilfe der Rockmusik ihrem Alltag immer wieder zu entfliehen, sie wollen sich dadurch aber nicht einer Verantwortung entledigen, sondern wieder neue Kraft schöpfen für die Dinge, die ihre konkrete Lebenssituation ihnen abverlangt. Rockmusik ist weniger Flucht als Hilfe bzw. Begleitung zur Ausbildung einer Identität, in der ja das Ich, die eigene Person, gerade nicht verloren gehen, sondern aufgehoben sein soll". The same reproach can be found by P. WIRTZ, *Nicht nur mit Engelschören: Zum Verhältnis von Christentum und Rock-Musik*, in *Entschluß* 44 (1989) 6, 10-15, esp. 10; KÖGLER, *Die Sehnsucht nach mehr* (n. 3), p. 249 and SCHÄFERS, *Jugend, Religion, Musik* (n. 3), pp. 10-11.

26. For a further elaboration of this reproach, see my *Cardinal Ratzinger and Rock Music: Is Conversation Impossible?*, in J. HAERS – P. DE MEY, *Theology and Conversation: Developing a Relational Theology* (BETL, 172), Leuven, Leuven University Press – Peeters, 2003, 849-906.

27. RATZINGER, *A New Song for the Lord* (n. 12), pp. 108-109: "Is it a pastoral success when we are capable of following the trend of mass culture and thus share the blame for its making people immature or irresponsible"?

problematic. The actual challenge for the theological dialogue with rock music – the third part – consists in a conversation avoiding these problematic aspects.

1. *One Concern, Two Accents*

Notwithstanding the alleged irreconcilability of both standpoints, elements of a concern, shared by both authors, do become visible. Both authors are, for instance, convinced that rock music is an important 'sign of the times' and therefore should be taken seriously as a dialogue partner for theology today[28]. In addition, both assume that Christianity stands for a message of universal significance and therefore needs a dialogue with contemporary culture. The two authors however have their own accents. In his dialogue with rock music, Ratzinger wants to safeguard the singularity and the uniqueness of Christian truth. He stresses the irrevocable difference with rock music and elucidates that Christian faith does not only stand for a subjective experience, but after all for a message of redemption 'given' to humanity. Treml, on the other hand, accentuates the dialogue with culture: the message of Christianity only makes sense when it is able, in one way or another, to join in with culture. While focussing on this dialogue, Treml minimizes the differences between rock and Christianity. The religious experience at stake in rock music should be interpreted by theologians as an 'anonymous Christian' experience.

We want to safeguard both accents without ending up in a mutual exclusion. From Ratzinger's thought we retain the focus on the unique message of theological truth. From Treml, we keep the radical openness for dialogue as well as his concern for affirmative links between culture and theology. In what follows, we want to hold together these two aspects of truth. Therefore we first examine how these two elements seem to exclude each other in the thought of the two authors.

2. *The Mutual Exclusion of Truth and Dialogue*

According to Treml, the moment of truth is the moment in which the human being recognizes the *that* of transcendent reality. As long as this reality is accepted, truth is at stake. For Treml, this truth is recognized whenever the human being faces the relativity of everyday-life or whenever he/she becomes conscious of his/her own mortality. First of all, what strikes one most is that the very content of truth for Treml seems to be

---

28. Ratzinger however explicitly distances himself from a too social interpretation of these "signs of the times" as well as of the whole project of Vatican II: *Ibid.*, pp. 112-115.

empty since it only consists in the vague recognition of a transcendent reality. Furthermore, Treml seems to presuppose the relation between the existential experience and the recognition of this transcendent reality as an immediate and self-evident one.

However, two problems arise. Due to his vague conception of truth, Treml is forced to reduce the specific Christian notion of revelation to only *one of the many* relative interpretations of the universal transcendent reality. First of all, one might ask to what extent Treml's proposal really enables the Christian theologian to dialogue with rock music, since his scheme seems to saw off the branch on which the theologian is sitting. Secondly, if we take for granted the findings of Turner in his book *Hungry for Heaven,* the immediateness presupposed by Treml seems to be absent. Turner's conclusion indeed states that rock searches for the limits of this earthly existence, but that this experience does not testify the religious experience of transcendence. He clearly shows how this experience may give rise to religious connotations but, finally, does not seem to accept an affirmed certainty about the presence of transcendence. By presupposing an evident bridge between the existential experience and the religious experience of transcendence, Treml loses rock music as his dialogue partner. As a rock journalist, Turner observes exactly the opposite: rock music testifies to the absence of such an evident bridge and expresses the wide range of experiences to which this absence gives rise to.

In searching for the relation between theological truth and existential experience, Treml loses his two dialogue partners: the truth of Christianity, since this has to be reduced to a vague notion of transcendence, and the experience of rock, since this has to be forced into an experience of transcendence which is actually absent in rock music.

The two elements forcing Treml to these problematic conclusions, are absent in the dialogue of Ratzinger. On the one hand his concept of truth is not empty at all: the universal truth corresponds absolutely to the Christian message of redemption, promised by God and guaranteed by the life, death and resurrection of Jesus Christ. This truth correlates with the deepest desire of man and answers his most profound existential needs. For Ratzinger, truth has nothing to do with the vague and anonymous acceptance of transcendence, but with the one and unique credo of Christian faith. On the other hand, Ratzinger does not bridge the existential experience of rock with the experience of transcendence, since for him rock music lacks any transcendent reality. A remarkable consequence is that Ratzinger more than Treml seems to be in agreement with the conclusions of Turner's *Hungry for Heaven.* Ratzinger's definition of rock music as an attempt to install a self-made redemption corresponds roughly with the conclusion of Turner who interprets rock music as the autonomous search for redemption as well.

Nevertheless, the dialogue of Ratzinger with popular music remains problematic. In fact, there is another problem of immediacy at work in Ratzinger's scheme. For Ratzinger, pop and rock music are expressions of the cultural crisis into which Western society moved since it structured itself on the foundations of autonomous thinking. The 'solution' to this crisis is the humble attitude of receptivity. Ratzinger seems to take for granted that this attitude will bring back the modern mind to the Christian faith and to the acceptance of its credo. Ratzinger presupposes an immediate link between an attitude of receptivity and the leap of faith[29]. One might ask whether this immediacy is not called into question by rock music itself. For Turner not only defines rock as the autonomous attempt to install a ready-made redemption, he also recognizes within this experience the awareness of the ultimate impossibility of this project. The despair and the desolation to which this awareness gives rise are experiences which, at least potentially, testify to the humble recognition of man's need of redemption and therefore to an attitude of receptivity. Although Ratzinger is right by stating that this possibility would not bring us to an experience of transcendence (as Treml supposes), it would however interrupt the immediacy by which he presupposes the relation between humility and Christian faith.

Ratzinger's dialogue with popular music does preserve the absolute and unique truth of Christianity but threatens to lose its connection with the wide range of feelings as experienced by people today. Since, for Ratzinger, truth is uniquely testified by the Catholic faith, the only dialogue possible is the proclamation of the one and only truth of Christianity and the hope rock music finally assumes this truth as well.

3. Rock Music, Truth and Redemption

In its dialogue with popular music, theology should not avoid the issue of truth and redemption. For these two questions are, insofar as Turner is right in his observations, the most central ones of the experience at stake in rock music. In addition to this, theologians should take seriously the whole range of experience to which the music of rock bears witness. Rock is not only the autonomous and self-sufficient attempt to redeem

---

29. *Ibid.*, p. 124: "Whoever is really touched by it knows somehow deep down inside that the faith is true even if this person still has far to go before comprehending this insight with the mind and will".

oneself in a common, mysterious and ecstatic experience but might also include the humble experience of not being able to fulfil this project[30]. Theologians should reckon with this wide range in a nuanced way and therefore not generalize this kind of music to only one part of it.

Maybe the conception of truth as worked out in the pastoral constitution of the Second Vatican Council can suggest a fruitful way out of the impasse in which the theological dialogue with popular music seems to find itself. In *Gaudium et Spes*, the council fathers proposed a new *topology* of the one and unique truth of Christianity[31]. This truth is on the one hand unique and *absolute*. On the other hand, it is constantly *relative* to the joy, the hope, the sadness and the anxiety of people today[32]. Truth can not be found *as such* but is always *in relation to* concrete and plural experiences. One of the most remarkable consequences of this new topology is the criterion of the no-exclusion. In searching the truth, *Gaudium et Spes* states that no single experience is a priori excluded from the process of making this truth visible, not even the experiences which ignore, neglect or turn away from the redemptive message of truth[33].

On the basis of this challenging combination of both uniqueness and relativity, *Gaudium et Spes* offers a possible framework to dialogue with the experience at stake in rock music. It enables theology to maintain the truth of Christianity in the dialogue with culture. It shows how this dialogue does not need the reduction of the Christian truth to a vague and anonymous religiosity, as Treml seems to suppose. On the other hand, it forces theology to look time and again for new places where truth is to be found. Since truth is not an abstract and isolated credo, it deserves an

---

30. For an interesting discussion of this tension, see: J.-M. BÜTTNER, *Sänger, Songs und triebhafte Rede: Rock als Erzählweise* (Nexus, 36), Basel – Frankfurt, Stroemfeld, 1997, pp. 405-570.

31. H.-J. SANDER, *Theologischer Kommentar zur Pastoralkonstitution über die Kirche in der Welt von heute "Gaudium et Spes"*, in P. HÜNERMANN – B.J. HILBERATH (eds.), *Herders Theologischer Kommentar zum Zweiten Vatikanischen Konzil*, Band 4, Freiburg – Basel – Wien, Herder, 2005, 581-886, esp. p. 585: "Das Zweite Vatikanische Konzil hat einen Ortswechsel des christlichen Glaubens vorgenommen, mit dem die katholische Kirche zur Weltkirche geworden ist. Diese Ortsbestimmung hat einen zweifachen Gehalt; er ergibt sich aus der Problemstellung einer Weltkirche. Sie erfährt sich als überall präsent, aber sie muss diese Präsenz auch überall einlösen können. Das, was sie vor allen Menschen ist, muss sie bei ihnen jeweils auch werden".

32. *Gaudium et Spes*, 1.

33. SANDER, *Theologischer Kommentar zur Pastoralkonstitution* (n. 31), p. 836: "Daraus ergibt sich eine so weitgehende Achtung vor der Pluralität der pastoralen Orte, an denen die Wahrheiten des Glaubens gefordert sind, dass die *Nicht-Ausschließung* zum Kriterium für die Darstellung der Wahrheit wird. Dieses Kriterium geht so weit, dass es selbst die einschließt, die gegen die Kirche wegen dieser Wahrheit vorgehen" (italics mine). See also: *Gaudium et Spes*, 92.

open and widespread perspective within which no single experience can be excluded a priori.

As far as the method of this theological dialogue is concerned, theologians should avoid looking for new existential bridges which would be able to bridge truth, redemption and the experience of rock music. Treml's view shows us that the price to be paid for such a bridge is high, and, theologically speaking, too high. The plea of Ratzinger has another price to pay since his method excludes *a priori* any authentic attitude of receptivity within the experience of rock music. If theologians really want to command the importance of Christian truth within a fruitful dialogue with culture, they should be able to clear out its exact relationship with authentic non-Christian humility. Ultimately, this is the question by which the experience of rock music challenges theology today.

johan.ardui@theo.kuleuven.be   Johan ARDUI

HICK'S PLURALISTIC HYPOTHESIS

AN INTRASYSTEMIC READING OF THE EVIDENCE?

The writings of John Hick have always been permeated with the question of theological truth and the truth of theological language[1]. In his extensive theological and philosophical *œuvre* we can, in my opinion, discern two main phases, distinguished from each other by what is commonly called his *Copernican Revolution* or as Hick describes it himself: the crossing of the theological Rubicon[2]. Following a similar classification in the works of Wittgenstein and Heidegger, I would even dare to speak about a Hick I and a Hick II. Even though there is a certain continuity of thought between the two positions that he takes up, there is nevertheless a discrepancy noticeable regarding his outlook on truth and on the way in which it is determined.

In this article I would first like to shed some light on the critical realism of John Hick and the epistemological presuppositions that enable it (Hick I). In the second part of this paper I will concentrate on Hick's so called Copernican revolution and the consequences it has for his critical realism and for the way in which he perceives theological truth-claims (Hick II). The third part will be devoted to the problems of Hick's pluralistic hypothesis and how his hypothesis contains a paradox in the sense that it is an intra-systemic approach that purports to adopt a universalistic standpoint.

I. Hick I: An Epistemological Apology

As a skilled apologist Hick has tried to defend the cognitive claims of theology against all sorts of criticisms that relegate religion and its truth-claims to the realm of the non-cognitive and non-realist use of language. In the wake of such figures as Feuerbach, Marx, Nietzsche and Freud,

---

1. J. Hick, *The Nature of Religious Faith*, in *Proceedings of the XIth International Congress of Philosophy. Bruxelles, 20-26 August, 1953*, Volume IX, Amsterdam, North-Holland, 1953, 57-62. Id., *Faith and Knowledge: A Modern Introduction to the Problem of Religious Knowledge*, Ithaca, NY, Cornell University Press, 1953. Id., *Theology and Verification*, in *Theology Today* 22/2 (1960) 12-31; Id., *Meaning and Truth in Theology*, in S. Hook (ed.), *Religious Experience and Truth*, New York, University Press, 1961, 203-210.

those critics see religious language rather as an expression of our human emotions, or moral and spiritual ideals than as a sort of knowledge that references to a Transcendent Being[3]. Basically Hick is concerned about the question whether or not theology in the literal sense of the word God-talk (*theos-logos*) can be seen as cognitive. Against the questioning of the frame of reference of religion, Hick holds to the belief that religion is able to make truth-claims: hypothetical articulations of 'what there is' and 'how things are'[4]. He presents himself as a critical realist in the sense that he is convinced that the modern subject makes a vital contribution to the perception of the world[5]. The subject is constitutive for our experiences of the world to the extent that the impact of the world on our senses is being shaped and coloured by human concepts and images.

To gain an insight into the critical realism of Hick, I it is necessary to pay attention to his epistemological presuppositions. More specific I want to concentrate on Hick's conception of knowledge of God and how this knowledge is related with other forms of knowledge.

1. *A Modern Thinker*

Hick lays down the principles of his epistemology by rejecting what he describes as the Catholic-Thomistic tradition. Here faith is put on a par with the acceptance of and the assent to intellectual propositions, which can hardly be taken as true on the basis of our own experiences and insights: they require a 'leap of faith', as it were[6]. Hick omits this tradition, characterized by fideism and intellectualism, in favour of a more modern view, in which divine revelation does not consist of the communication of some immutable religious truths but should rather be seen as the self-revealing acts of God in and through human history and human

2. J. HICK, *The Non-Absoluteness of Christianity*, in J. HICK (ed.), *The Myth of Christian Uniqueness*, New York, Orbis Books, 1987, 16-36, esp. p. 16.

3. With Hick, I am especially referring to those who hold on to the logical positivist argument that religious utterances are neither verifiable nor falsifiable and are as such non-cognitive in nature. Cf. J. HICK, *An Interpretation of Religion: Human Responses to the Transcendent*, New Haven, CT, Yale University Press, 1989, pp. 190-209.

4. HICK, *An Interpretation of Religion* (n. 3), pp. 172-189.

5. Hick makes a distinction between two realist views. On the one hand we can identify a naïve realism, holding that the world is just as we perceive it to be, and on the other hand we have a critical realism, holding that the world as we experience it is a distinctively human construction arising from the impact of a real environment upon our sense organs, but conceptualized in consciousness and language in culturally developed forms. These two forms of realism stand in opposition to non-realist or idealistic views which see the perceived world as a series of modifications of our own consciousness. Cf. J. HICK, *Disputed Questions in Theology and the Philosophy of Religion*, New Haven, CT, Yale University Press, 1993, p. 4.

6. HICK, *Faith and Knowledge* (n. 1), pp. 11-13.

experience[7]. With this, Hick places himself in line with modern thinkers, especially William James, who hold that the certainty of faith can be based on personal religious experience and that faith is no longer the taking as true of a set of propositions. In Hick's view our awareness of God is thus mediated through our subjective experiences of the world: we experience the supernatural through the natural.

To corroborate this assertion, Hick tries to show how every form of knowledge is in fact mediated as a result of which he is able to stake the claim that our knowledge of God is in line with our everyday experience. Although the object of religious knowledge is unique this does not hold true for the epistemological process of religious knowledge. It would be a sign of a misplaced naiveté to assume that Hick claims that religious belief would be the same as sensory perception. He does however claim that faith is a form of knowledge that is closer to sensory perception than to a blind acceptance of intellectual propositions. With this move he wants to give religious knowledge a stable foundation in a general modern epistemology.

But how does he substantiate this? He takes the Wittgensteinian concept of 'seeing-as', in which an object is ambiguous to the extent that one can assign multiple contents and meanings to it, as the centre of his epistemology[8]. On the basis of that theorem it is possible to claim that one person identifies a flying object in the sky as a plane, while another person sees the same object as a bird and a third person can even identify it as a U.F.O. Hick, however, expands this basic notion of 'seeing-as' into that of 'experiencing-as' in which we also have the equivalents for the other senses. We do not only see the object in the sky as a plane, we can also hear it as a plane and, as need be, feel it as a plane or even smell it as a plane. Hick then applies this concept of 'experiencing-as' on the human experience of the universe. According to Hick the Enlightenment has shown us that the universe is in its essence ambiguous, to the extent that it stimulates religious as well as naturalistic responses. The Enlightenment has questioned our taking for granted of the immanence of the divine in our daily lives. Every aspect of human life now seems to be open to a religious as well as a naturalistic interpretation without being able to pronounce upon the truth of one or both[9]. As such, the events of our lives can, on the one hand, be seen as contingent occurrences or, on the other hand, as moments that mediate to us the activity and the pres-

7. *Ibid.*, pp. 27-29.

8. J. HICK, *God and the Universe of Faiths: Essays in the Philosophy of Religion*, London, Macmillan, 1973, p. 39.

9. HICK, *An Interpretation of Religion* (n. 3), pp. 73-125.

ence of God. In other words, an awareness of God manifests itself not in isolation from the other objects of experience, but thanks to a shared epistemological structure Man meets God in and through his social and material milieu.

The believer and the atheist are thus not living in two different worlds, but in an ambiguous universe that they both experience in their own way. Although this is grist to the mill of the atheists in that religion can, in the final analysis, be seen as a purely subjective undertaking while ordinary sense perception has a compelling objectivity, Hick parries this critique by saying that all experiencing is 'experiencing-as'[10]. Hence there is no unmediated experience in that the modern subject always plays a constitutive role within the interpretation of that experience. As such every experience is indebted to the tandem of recognising and identifying[11]. This involves that our experiences of the world are vague and ambiguous until they are interpreted by a subject as significant in a particular way. Significant in the sense that we recognise and identify those experiences as a part of the familiar world we live in. To recognise and to identify is to be 'experiencing-as' in terms of concepts which are social products, having their life within a particular linguistic environment[12]. Hick is at pains to show how each experiencing has to do with a form of recognition that goes beyond the purely sensory and is thus a form of 'experiencing-as'. By doing so he tries to score the point that the day-to-day experiences share a characteristic feature with religious experience[13].

2. *Three Levels of Meaning*

In that intertwining process of experience and interpretation, Hick distinguishes three levels of significance, which correspond to the standard philosophical triad of world, man and God.

Initially Man becomes aware of his environment through his senses. This is the material world which we experience and know daily. At this level we are actively interpreting and experiencing subjects for the very reason that we apply concepts to our sensory perceptions and hence experience ourselves as living in a familiar material world of mutual interacting objects. Although there is according to Hick in each form of knowledge a subjective element, the ambiguity and thus the personal freedom at this level is still minimal. Although quotidian experiences already

10. *Ibid.*, p. 140.
11. *Ibid.*, p. 41.
12. *Ibid.*, pp. 41-42.
13. *Ibid.*, p. 42.

involve a selection of that with which our senses provide us, everyday experience still presupposes a realistic interpretation. The material world is an objective environment whose laws we must obey and towards which we must behave correctly if we want to survive. At this stage, interpretation is a more or less unconscious activity, a sort of habit in the course of which our sensory perceptions are couched in cultural forms[14].

This basic level of awareness and experience is, however, not typical of the human race. A characteristic of Man, contrary to animals, is that he is not only aware of the fact that he is living in a material world that imposes itself on him, but especially that he is a part of a network of interpersonal relations. Man is aware that he lives in relation to others *vis-à-vis* whom he has a certain responsibility. This second scope of significance is grafted on the first because the ethical significance of a situation can only become clear in and through the material world. Whereas our interpretation of the material world still runs into a stubbornness (significance was still to a certain extent enforced upon us), our own freedom is much greater in the ethical sphere: we can back out of part of the moral claims that are imposed upon us. Being ethic is in theory not that different of everyday life. Hick prefers to see it as a particular way of living in the material world[15].

Besides the material and the ethical significance, Hick defines a third sphere as well. This third one, the religious, relies on the first two but our personal contribution here is maximized. Religious experience is thus the interpretation of the world as 'something more', something bigger and other than one would determine on first sight. It is to experience an 'Absoluteness' or an 'Eternal One' in and through daily life: "We experience life as divinely created and ourselves as living in the unseen presence of God"[16]. Just as is the case in the ethical sphere one can ignore the religious inclination and interpret one's experience purely naturalistically. According to Hick we are rationally justified in both cases. The primary religious awareness has thus, according to Hick, little or nothing to do with a rational conclusion or an intuitive feeling that there is a God. It's the consciousness of a divine presence within human experience. It is not an argumentation for a universal truth, but a personal encounter between God and man. A mediated experience with a living God[17]. Entering in a conscious relation with God consists in adapting a particular attitude to the ethical and the social world. Religion is thus not only a way

---

14. HICK, *God and the Universe of Faiths* (n. 8), pp. 45-46.
15. *Ibid.*, pp. 46-47.
16. J. HICK, *Christianity at the Centre*, London, SCM Press, 1968, p. 55.
17. HICK, *Faith and Knowledge* (n. 1), p. 115.

of knowing but especially a way of living[18]. The faithful can by no means explain how he knows that the divine presence is mediated through human experience; he just interprets his experiences that way.

In the wake of Wittgenstein, we can say that we live in a realistic environment that we experience as meaningful in one way or another. The meaningfulness is practical or pragmatic in nature in that it enables us to adopt a certain attitude to the experienced environment. We can then conclude this epistemological exploration by saying that for Hick faith is the interpretative element within the religious person's awareness of an ambiguous universe. To believe is to make a cognitive choice between a naturalistic and a religious interpretation of the universe.

3. *The Right to Believe*

But are we then entitled to define this religious awareness of God as knowledge of God? Does faith entail any claims about 'what is' and 'how things are'? Can we not gather from the analysis of Hick's epistemological system that (Christian) faith is rather a way of perceiving the world that is neither verifiable nor falsifiable and as such not fact-asserting? Hick answers this in the negative. He denies the objections raised by the logical positivist that religious language is not verifiable and as such factual empty. For Hick religion cannot be considered to be the "odd man out". It is not an optional language game that only gives psychological comfort to its adherents. Hick decides to fight the logical positivists on their own territory by asserting that religious language can be verified and is meaningful[19]. The verification of the Christian belief in God is, however, only to be verified in a future time and existence. It would be verified if God's purpose for us would be fulfilled according to the Christian tradition and in communion with God and Christ. Hence for Hick it is not because the Christian experience of the universe is not verifiable here and know that it is not meaningful. The main question is then not whether someone's experience of existing in the presence of God is genuine, but rather whether it is rational for someone to trust his or her experience as veridical and to behave on the basis of it. Hick holds on to the general principle that in the absence of adequate grounds for doubt it is rational to trust our putative experience and that we are then in cognitive touch with our environment. For unless we trust our own experiences, we can have no reason to believe anything about the nature or the existence

18. *Ibid.*, p. 115.
19. *Ibid.*, pp. 169-200; ID., *Faith and Verification*, in *Theology Today* 17/1 (1960) 12-31.

of the universe in which we live[20]. Accordingly, the religious person experiencing life in terms of the divine presence is rationally entitled to believe what he or she experiences to be the case[21].

Hick is convinced that the experience of living in the presence of God is *prima facie* a good and sufficient argument for religious belief. It is thus entirely rational to trust our own religious experience and the wider tradition to which it belongs[22].

4. *A Kantian Interludium*

I think it is obvious how the Kantian insight into the constitutional role of the subject in the interpretation of sensory perceptions is at the centre of Hick's epistemology and critical realism. In his *Kritik der Reinen Vernunft* Kant developed the thesis that there has to be made a distinction between *noumenon* and *phaenomena*; between how things are in themselves and how they appear to rationally endowed subjects. Hick borrows this central Kantian insight and applies it to the more problematic area of religious epistemology[23]. There are however some differences to be noted. Whereas Kant reached his distinction between the *Ding-an-sich* and the phenomenon through an analysis of the structures of 'Space and Time' as structuralizing components of human reason and not of the objective reality, Hick employs another approach. He is convinced that we can deduce the distinction by an elementary reflection on our daily experience. Hick argues that the same object can be perceived by different people in different ways, depending on their own cultural backgrounds. The great difference between the position of Kant and that of Hick is couched in the fact that the categories of reason are for Kant a-priori and universal whereas for Hick they are variable and culture dependent[24]. In other words for Hick it is possible to live without religious categories and they are variable through time.

II. HICK II: TOWARD A PLURALISTIC THEOLOGY

Although the notion of critical realism is still able to be heard in the work of John Hick to this very day, the nature and contents of his religious truth-claims have been changed. In the past it was the concept of

20. HICK, *An Interpretation of Religion* (n. 3), pp. 214-215.
21. *Ibid.*, p. 216.
22. *Ibid.*, p. 228.
23. *Ibid.*, pp. 240-246.
24. *Ibid.*, p. 242.

the Christian tradition that enabled Hick to interpret his religious experience cognitively as the experience of a personal and gracious God, mediated through Christ. In spite of the interpretative process, Christian faith
rendered knowledge of the *noumenal* reality; about 'what there is' and
'how things are'[25]. After his Copernican revolution all truths are to be
found on the phenomenal or particular level; they no longer apply to the
divine reality in itself – they lose their universal scope. Hick II has
become a post-modern in that he dismisses all theories of religion that
claim universal applicability and demand the allegiance of the whole
human family. They fall into the discredited class of meta-narratives.
Instead Hick recommends a pragmatic test for the evaluation of the
world's religions and dismisses all meta-narratives in the face of an
inscrutable universe and an ineffable divinity. Since objective truth is
beyond our grasp we must follow whatever ideas we find useful; the different religions must jettison their grandiose meta-physical claims and
become more modest as they are just another set of narratives.

1. *The History of a Change*

The Copernican revolution in the thought of John Hick began to take
shape at a congress in Birmingham in 1970. The symposium was aimed
at the inquiry into the relations between the different religions with an eye
toward the understanding of different, conflicting truth-claims. Different
religions hold different and even sometimes contrasting opinions about
the nature of the ultimate reality; about the way in which God acts; about
the nature and the destiny of human kind[26]. It is at this congress that Hick
entertains for the first time the idea that the different religions are not
mutually excluding entities: "It seemed to me that our conference discussions offered hints of another approach, and one which may prove a
path along which progress can be made"[27]. He makes a distinction
between the various human encounters with God through the different
religious experiences on the one hand and the different theological doctrines that were developed to express those experiences on the other
hand[28]. Here the Kantian distinction between *noumenon* and *phenomenon*
is used to graft his – still to be developed – theory of religious pluralism

25. HICK, *Faith and Knowledge* (n. 1), pp. 215-217; ID., *Christianity at the Centre*
(n. 16), pp. 57-69.
    26. J. HICK, *The Outcome: Dialogue into Truth*, in ID. (ed.), *Truth and Dialogue in
World Religions: Conflicting Truth Claims*, Philadelphia, PA, Westminster Press, 1970,
140-155.
    27. HICK, *The Outcome: Dialogue into Truth* (n. 26), p. 149.
    28. *Ibid.*, p. 149.

onto his critical realism. He develops the hypothesis that all religions are, in their experiential roots, in contact with one and the same divine reality but that the different experiences, in interaction with different ways of thinking in different cultures, have led to different and contrasting elaborations of that experience[29]. At this point Hick draws some parallels between a religion and a culture: just as it is impossible to judge a culture in terms of true or false, it's also impossible when a religion is involved. Religions are therefore for Hick expressions of the variety of human types, temperaments and ways of thinking[30]. Whereas he used to try to justify the universal out of the particular, he now tries to demonstrate how the universal is being reflected in the particular.

In the same article Hick responds to the thesis of Wilfred Cantwell Smith who understands religious truth neither as propositional nor as cognitive or fact-asserting, but rather as subjective. Religious truth becomes true if it is personalised in a dynamic, actual existence: "a religion becomes true in the life of a man of faith who is related to God within the historical context of that religion"[31]. On the one hand Hick endorses the practical bias in the proposition of Cantwell Smith but on the other hand he has difficulties in agreeing with the separation between subjective and propositional (objective) truth[32]. For Hick, existential truth is only possible to the extent that a religion takes part in a more universal, more objective truth. A religion can only become subjectively true because its truth already existed as a more universal truth "about what there is and how things are"[33]. If this would not be the case, the truth of a religion should merely be judged from the fact that it is authentically lived, apart from the fact that it refers to an objective truth. In other words Christianity cannot be true according to Hick if there is no God. But if he makes this claim, he still has to cope with the problem of the conflicting truth claims: how can different references to the same objective truth collide with each other?

2. *Conflicting Truth-Claims and Mythological Language*

Again, Hick tries to solve this problem with the help of the Kantian paradigm. He makes a distinction between different truth-claims on different levels[34]. On a first level there are differences in the way one con-

29. *Ibid.*, p. 151.
30. *Ibid.*, p. 142.
31. *Ibid.*, p. 143.
32. *Ibid.*, p. 147.
33. *Ibid.*, pp. 146-147.
34. J. HICK, *Problems of Religious Pluralism*, London, Macmillan, 1985, pp. 89-90.

ceives of experiences and hence responses to the divine reality. These
so-called 'fact of faiths' or 'primary affirmations' are unchangeable and
refer to the basic experience out of which faith originates. Even though
this experience can take a variety of forms (personal/impersonal, a severe
judge/a close friend), Hick sees them as supplementary rather than as
competing truth-claims. On a second level we can describe some differences in theological and philosophical doctrines and theories between the
various religions. These 'theological doctrines' interpret and systematize
the basic convictions of a particular religion into a coherent whole. Hick
does not deny that there are various conflicts on this level, but he deems
them as part of a developing human history and of the cultural aspect of
a religion, as a result of which they will sooner or later be superseded[35].
The greatest problem with religious truth-claims can however be found
on a third level: every religion has its own founder and its own sacred
scriptures, in which the divine reality has made itself known. Each of
them requires an absolute response and seems thus *prima facie* incompatible with others. Although Hick is still optimistic about the possibility of a meeting between the religions and the possible discovery of a
common ground on this level, he introduces already his concept of *myth*,
which will be elaborated in his future writings[36].

In *God and the Universe of Faiths* Hick gives for the first time an elaborate account of the Incarnation as an instance of mythical language[37].
Hick disclaims the classical notion of *myth*, as it was used by Bultmann[38],
and defines it more as "a story which is told but is not literally true [...]
but which invites a particular attitude in its hearers"[39]. The truth of a
myth thus no longer concerns cognitive truth, but is reduced by Hick to
a practical matter. It is more about the aptness of the reaction evoked by
the myth. Myths are as such no literal stories but they are more some
kind of rhetorical trick, vehicles for communication. People are much
more moved by a story than by abstract images[40].

The different religious traditions are rich in myths, but there is nothing that compels us to see them as exclusive. According to Hick they can
more rightly be seen as different forms of art with their roots in different

---

35. HICK, *The Outcome: Dialogue into Truth* (n. 26), p. 153.
36. *Ibid.*, pp. 154-155.
37. HICK, *God and the Universe of Faiths* (n. 8), pp. 148-179.
38. "The use of imagery to express the other world in terms of this world and the
divine in terms of human life, the other side in terms of this side", R. BULTMANN, *New
Testament and Mythology*, in ID. – H.W. BARTSCH (eds.), *Kerygma and Myth, a Theological Debate*, New York, Harper and Row, 1961, 1-45, esp. p. 10.
39. HICK, *God and the Universe of Faiths* (n. 8), pp. 166-167.
40. *Ibid.*, p. 168.

traditions[41]. But if we perceive, for example, the doctrine of the Incarnation as mythological language with its only function being to evoke a proper attitude towards Jesus of Nazareth, can the salvation through Christ be considered as a reality? In Hick's opinion it can[42]. Although we can blast Hick and his mythological use of language because of a subjective and an expressivistic approach, the mythical talk about Jesus still contains underlying truth-claims about God in that "it still expresses attitude of reverence and commitment to one who has enabled and whose memory still sustains the Christian form of salvatific encounter with God"[43].

3. *The Outcome: A Soteriocentric Pluralism*

Since his article *The Theology of Religious Pluralism* in 1984 and his masterly synthesis *The Interpretation of Religion* in 1989, it has become clear that the god-talk in the different religions is only a phenomenal instance of a more profound reality: *The Real*[44]. It is also in this phase that he makes the transition from a cognitive complementarity between the different religions to an equality in salvific efficacy "The great world Traditions have in fact all proved to be realms within which or routes along which people are enable to advance in the transition from self-centredness to Reality-centredness. And, since they reveal the Real in such different lights, we must conclude that they are independently valid"[45]. The ultimate referent for every religious speech for every theological truth-claim becomes more and more vague and unknowable. We have no cognitive access to it anymore. Only a practical faith – *the transition from self-centredness to Reality-centredness* – can testify to *the Real*.

III. PROBLEMS WITH THE PLURALISTICH HYPOTHESIS

As we have seen, Hick's postulation of a *noumenal* reality, *The Real*, as the sole referent for all religious language is an instance of the distinction between object and subject that has coloured modern Western rationality for centuries. Hick adheres to the conviction that every form

41. *Ibid.*, p. 176.
42. *Ibid.*, pp. 176-179.
43. B. HEBBLETHWAITE, *John Hick and the Question of Truth in Religion*, in S. ARVIND (ed.), *God, Truth and Reality: Essays in the honour of John Hick*, London, Macmillan, 1993, 124-134, esp. p. 129.
44. Hick uses this term because it is, according to him, familiar to all traditions, without being exclusive property of one of them. Cf. HICK, *An Interpretation of Religion* (n. 3), pp. 10-11.
45. HICK, *Problems of Religious Pluralism* (n. 34), p. 44.

of religious speech has a cognitive content in the sense that this speech has ultimately an existent referent: *The Real*. On the basis of his critical realism, Hick has found a middle way between an absolute and a relativistic standpoint. Every religion passes judgement upon a *noumenal* reality and upon a soteriological process that sets us in proper attitude over against that reality. According to Hick, the core of each religion is salvation, understood as a transformation from self-centredness to Reality-centredness. To what extent that transformation has taken place within a person can only be measured by the life of that person. Those who show compassion and respect certain moral standards are, according to Hick, in a proper relation to *the Real*[46]. Hick holds that it is important for salvation *that* you have chosen a tradition, *which one* you have chosen does not matter. The differences between the different religions are then reduced to historical elements that are especially cultural but also psychological in nature.

1. A Covert Inclusivist

Hick can thus rightly be seen as an inclusivist in the sense that the adherents of other religions are saved through something he has seen through and they do not have. All religions, even secular movements, are unwittingly responses to *the Real*. Hick repudiates the accusation of inclusivism by pointing to the fact that he does not reject the goals of the different religions in favour of one amongst them, but in favour of something that is beyond them. Of course all inclusivists do the same and with the same argument: their goal is always something above and beyond the particularities of the other religions[47]. According to S. M. Heim, Hick clearly employs a meta-theory by postulating that there is a true meaning hidden behind the mythological uses of language by every tradition (a soft reductionism). The real truth of a religion can only be apprehended within the pluralistic meta-theory. It is Hick's vision on salvation that structures his pluralistic hypothesis. In the end there can be only one religious goal and it is only moral behaviour which indicates to what extent that goal has been realised[48].

By importing Kant's epistemological scheme, *the Real* has been pushed deep into the *noumenal* so that it is protected from every particularity which could endanger its neutrality. All tradition-specific elements are

---

46. Hick, *An Interpretation of Religion* (n. 3), pp. 300-303.
47. S.M. Heim, *Salvations: Truth and Difference in Religion*, Maryknoll, NY, Orbis Books, 1995, p. 30.
48. *Ibid.*, p. 32.

drawn into the cultural forms of the 'experiencing-as' and it is only salvation which bridges the gap between both[49]. The different religious traditions are functional routes to the ultimate reality but every possible truth concerning the content is excised as irrelevant or even dangerous to the extent that it would promote narrow views. I am in agreement with Heim that the notion of pluralism is inclusivistic and particular in character[50]. This would not be a problem were it not that such a characterisation acts contrary to the profile the pluralists assign their own undertaking. All religions bring salvation, be it according to a plan only a pluralist can understand. As long as religions fight amongst themselves about truth-claims that do not matter in the end, they are wrong: "Unenlightened, sincere devotees of various faiths may be saved both historically and cosmically, but not on the basis they imagine. It is the Real, or faith, or justice as pluralist know them that redeem. [...] pluralistic theology regards itself as the 'crown and fulfilment' of every religious tradition"[51].

2. An Intra-Systemic Approach

As we have seen Hick makes in his pluralistic hypothesis a distinction between the primary affirmations and the theological doctrines. Whereas the first are the so-called basic assertions or basic beliefs of faith, the second are the consequence of theological reasoning. They interpret and systematize the basic convictions into a coherent whole. It is a philosophical speculation within the borders of a particular tradition[52]. Whereas the denial of the primary affirmations amounts to heresy, the denial of doctrines only leads to heterodoxy[53]. So for Hick doctrines are functional to the extent that they provide a coherent frame of reference within which one can speak about truth. Theology for Hick is only a creation of the human mind that interprets religious experience in a systematic fashion and relates it to our other knowledge. A religion is, in other words, only intra-systematically true. Truth and doctrines are coherent and consistent within a given frame of reference, more precisely within one of the various phenomenological manifestations of *The Real*.

Although Hick has reacted against Cantwell Smith's conception of theological truth as subjective, I am convinced that Hick in his pluralistic hypothesis does nothing other than that for which he reproaches Cantwell Smith: "I hope that Cantwell Smith is not saying that the truth of a reli-

49. *Ibid.*, p. 34.
50. *Ibid.*, p. 101.
51. *Ibid.*, p. 102.
52. HICK, *An Interpretation of Religion* (n. 3), pp. 372-373.
53. HICK, *Faith and Knowledge* (n. 1), p. 220.

gion or a faith consists simply in the fact that it works, producing good fruits in human life, even if its basic associated beliefs should be false"[54]. In Hick's pluralistic hypothesis however, it are only those 'good fruits' that matter for it is impossible to check up whether or not our basic beliefs are true, given the fact that the *noumenal* reality can never be known, except through its phenomenological manifestations. There is nothing that guarantees us that those phenomenal manifestations do justice to the *noumenal* reality which lies behind it.

3. *A Functionalistic Approach to Doctrines*

Because doctrines are judged especially to the extent that they promote the individual or communal transformation that the pluralists deem necessary, I think we are entitled to say that pluralists are inclined to adapt a functionalistic definition of religious doctrines. For Hick, in the end it does not matter anymore whether something is true or not or what is epistemologically preferable, but it matters how one can reach certain theological and practical goals. Goals Hick has set out under influence of his pluralistic doctrine.

A purely functional reading of doctrines, however, is contrary to the intentions of those who have designed those doctrines: they purport to say something about 'what there is' and 'how things are', apart from the transformative aspect Hick attributes to them. Because of this Hick has little attention for the substantial contents of religious doctrines. He is of the opinion that doctrines are historically variable in the sense that they can be changed whenever they do not function properly anymore. This change is legitimate under the condition that the transformation process from self-centredness to Reality-centredness is not endangered.

In the various articles in which Hick examines the conflicting truth-claims he never pays sufficient attention to the fact that there are authentic, cognitive incongruities between the different truth-claims that are important for the communities which confess them. He does not see, for example, the bodily resurrection of Jesus as a part of the essence of Christianity and so it is unnecessary for salvation and liberation. It is a historical fact on which one can choose to disagree[55].

The strength and at the same time the weakness of Hick's pluralistic hypothesis is that he does what even the most fundamental exclusivist would not dare to do: he argues without problems that several of the most important doctrines of different faith-communities are fake, without hav-

---

54. HICK, *The Outcome: Dialogue into Truth* (n. 26), p. 147.
55. HICK, *An Interpretation of Religion* (n. 1), pp. 364-365.

ing an eye for their cognitive content or epistemological plausibility. He writes them off on the simple fact that the attitudes they evoke do not fit the list that he assumes to be important for salvation. The only goal of a doctrine in Hick's theory is the bringing about of a transformation to a *limitless better possibility*[56]. If doctrines are important, cognitively relevant and even constitutive for the salvation of the community which confesses them, one cannot abandon them as easily as Hick proposes. And especially not in favour of the weak pragmatic criteria he proposes.

IV. CONCLUSION

Whereas Hick I could still be viewed as a fervent supporter of the right to and the rationality of faith and its truth-claims, Hick II can be seen as someone who, such as he has defined his own critics in 1967, "calls into question the nature and status of theology as a whole"[57]. While Hick aims at impartiality by seeking to adopt an all-embracing point of view, above all particular traditions, he is unwittingly making truth-claims by describing that universality and is in the process refuting those of others. While he is attempting to absorb all religions in his pluralistic frame of reference, he does them wrong by suggesting that the conflicting truth-claims are of no importance at all for the salvation that he advocates from within his pluralistic framework. Hick fails to see that truth-claims are exclusive in character: not everybody can be right. For Christians this implies specifically that the pluralistic hypothesis can only be true if the doctrine of the Incarnation is false. Putting Jesus into perspective amounts to denying him: "Suppose that Jesus Christ is not God but just a man. Then the cross shows the love of one human being for others. It is human, not divine love. The cross shows the love of God for us, because it is the son that went to the cross for us"[58].

frederik.glorieux@theo.kuleuven.be   Frederik GLORIEUX

---

56. HICK, *Problems of Religious Pluralism* (n. 34), p. 86.
57. HICK, *God and the Universe of Faiths* (n. 8), p. 1.
58. A. MCGRATH, *Making Sense of the Cross*, Downer's Grove, IL, InterVarsity Press, 1992, p. 40.

IS AN ACTUAL GOD INTELLIGIBLE?

INCARNATION-THEOLOGICAL GLOSSES TO VATTIMO AND MCKINNON

The term incarnation had a rather dull and boring ring to it, until recently. As a doctrine, its history is almost as ancient as the Church itself – an antiquity. In the following fundamental theological suggestions, I endeavour to make the reader more receptive to a subtler approach by presenting some of my own humble perspectives. My interest in this subject developed from a grander project, in which I wish to show how philosophy and systematic theology can come together (again) regarding this particular doctrine. More specifically, I will investigate what recent philosophical mediations the doctrine has given rise to. Moreover, I will try to discover in what measure (critical) evaluation of the doctrine can contribute to a better understanding of the scope and the nature of a particular concept of tradition. Recontextualizing Christian articles of faith has become a salient enterprise. Therefore, it almost goes without saying that the current critical consciousness can be used as a starting-point. Even though the theme of incarnation is only hesitantly raised in current debates, it is not wholly absent.

In this article, I shall attempt to map the specific contributions of Donald Mackinnon's incarnation-theology, and formulate some provisional suggestions on that basis. Instead of giving a bookish outline of his theological exploits, I will immediately confront his views with what is relevant today. Therefore I will plunge straight into the matter by raising a known problem, secularization. Secularization is generally understood to be a *non*-presence of God. In this regard and by way of introduction, I refer to Gianni Vattimo (°1936). This Italian philosopher greets the phenomenon of secularization with joy; in addition, the incarnation is a key component of his appreciation. 'Incarnation' is traditionally described as the '*becoming*' human of the Word (John 1,14). The doctrine is about a dynamic event that challenges an exclusively logical approach in its paradoxical formulation at Chalcedon (451)[1]. Any event is dynamic *a forte-*

---

1. This does not necessarily mean that incarnation is an absurdity against reason, see for example: G. O'COLLINS, *The Incarnation: The Critical Issues*, in S.T. DAVIS – D. KENDALL – G. O'COLLINS (eds.), *The Incarnation*, Oxford, Oxford University Press, 2002, 7-9.

riori, meaning it is irrevocably bound up in the incontrovertible order of the concrete world. In this regard, it is a credit to our times to have discovered that every reflection must remain devoid of meaning unless it is intentionally oriented by a subject that knows it is inescapably situated. Philosophers like Martin Heidegger (1889-1976) and Emmanuel Levinas (1906-1995) initiated a sensitivity for a more subtle concept of truth that resists an approach *sub specie aeternitatis*. Philosophy itself, as a search for truth, has lost its capacity to be exhaustively defined; it exists where it is practiced.

Nevertheless, there is a certain, and I feel justified, concern apparent in current thinking, which can be simplified thus: the claims of totality made by Modern thought have been exposed, creating a new openness for thinking about transcendence. But the post-modern subject must also beware a *regressus* into pre-critical immediacy[2]. Therefore it should hardly be surprising that when incarnation is written about at all, it is preferably in a context of *kenosis* or a limitation of God (cf. Phil 2,7).

I. Incarnation as *Kenosis* in Vattimo

In the creed of Nicea (325) we read: "He [i.e. Jesus Christ] has descended from Heaven for the salvation of us, humans". If incarnation were still to be approached in a Neo-Platonic manner, as is suggested at first glance by the Johannine prologue, it would not gain much support. Johann Sebastian Bach's choir sings 'Nun komm, der Heiden Heiland', in which the incarnation is symbolized by a descending series of notes, only moves the contemporary listener aesthetically. Similarly, contemporary religious philosophers feel a certain discomfort when confronted with the theme of incarnation. The suspicion that no theological scheme can satisfactorily connect with the post-modern subject, justifies hiding behind the comfortable safety of a vague and detached term like 'transcendence'.

Several present-day philosophers have nevertheless begun to wonder at the return of philosophy to religion. Gianni Vattimo is one of them. While there is generally an insistence upon a Heideggerian waiting for a coming divinity – a wait that is sometimes implicitly exalted to become the divinity itself – Vattimo attempts to come to terms with his specific Christian heritage in his somewhat autobiographical essay *I believe that*

---

2. Cf. for example G. VATTIMO, *The Trace of the Trace*, in J. DERRIDA – G. VATTIMO – H.-G. GADAMER (eds.), *Religion*, Cambridge, Polity Press, 1998, 79-93, esp. pp. 90-93.

I believe. In his clear and concise hermeneutical reflections, he gives the process of secularization a positive evaluation and rethinks the notion of incarnation.

The search by post-modern thought resembles the activity of psycho-analysis. The modern metaphysical framework demands a diagnosis of its subconscious causes, preferably being power structures. This implies a loss of faith in the independence of pure reason. Underlying motivations that hide outside or beyond conscious thinking use the mind as an instrument to realise a utopian dream: 'Die totale Organisation der Gesellschaft'[3].

Post-metaphysical philosophy must develop a framework that is favourable to the freedom and historicity of existence[4]. Truth can no longer be considered a supersensory compendium of objectivity, but is ultimately reducible to a will to power. Indeed, Friedrich Nietzsche's nihilism, but especially Heidegger's resignation, are an example to the Italian philosopher for his own 'weak thinking', which can be described as a hermeneutical-nihilistic philosophy. Not because the aforementioned philosophers can be said to have contributed to the secularization of thought, but rather because Vattimo feels they are in touch with their specific Judeo-Christian foundations. The autobiographical Italian puts it this way: "[...] At a certain moment I found myself thinking that the weak reading of Heidegger and the idea that the history of Being has as a guiding thread the weakening of strong structures, of claimed peremptoriness of the real that is given 'there, outside', like a wall against which one beats one's head, and that in this way makes itself known as effectively real [...] was nothing but the *transcription* of the Christian doctrine of the incarnation of the Son of God"[5].

Given the fact that the incarnation is interpreted as secularization, it is hardly surprising that Vattimo characterizes incarnation unilaterally in terms of *kenosis*. An ontology of decline, of which secularization is considered an excellent example, is contained in the revelation of the Christian doctrine of incarnation: "[...] The only great paradox and scandal of Christian revelation is the incarnation of God, the *kenosis* – that is the removal of all the transcendent, incomprehensible, mysterious and even

3. This phrase was coined by T.W. ADORNO, *Reflexionen zur Klassentheorie*, in ID. – R. TIEDEMANN (ed.), *Soziologische Schriften I*, Frankfurt am Main, Suhrkamp, 1972, p. 385.

4. G. VATTIMO, *Credere di credere: È possibile essere cristiani nonostante la Chiesa?*, Milan, Garzanti Editore, 1996. ID., *Belief*, trans. L. D'Isanto and D. Webb, Cambridge, Polity Press, 1999, pp. 28-29.

5. VATTIMO, *Belief* (n. 4), p. 36 (italics added).

bizarre features [...]"[6]. Following in the footsteps of René Girard (1923), he realizes that secularization is the positive result of Jesus' proclamation, rather than a way of emancipating oneself from it. Secularization is the way in which the *kenosis* "[...] continues to realize itself more and more clearly by furthering the education of mankind concerning the overcoming of originary violence essential to the sacred and to social life itself"[7]. Vattimo is innovative because he presents secularization as a constitutive element of authentic Christianity[8]. He wonders, rhetorically, whether the deterioration of subjectivity in our current consumer-society may not actually be the bringer of evangelical salvation[9].

But – and here comes the theologian's question – what is it that Vattimo suggests? The assumption that we are witness to a description of the process of secularization that borders on a remarkable idealization, may be too impulsive. But is Christ's descent ultimately not exchangeable with Nietzsche's Zarathustra? On the one hand, for Vattimo, God is *not* present, since he survives through his non-terminal death. On the other hand, the process of secularization can be adequately described, according to him, as a process of *kenosis*. This ambiguity seems more like an incongruity to me, unless the incarnation is really a *metaphor*, serving an ultimately philosophical purpose, being the discovery of the history of being[10]. As Vattimo himself writes: "The discovery of the substantial link between the history of Christian revelation and the history of nihilism means nothing more and nothing less than a confirmation of the validity of Heidegger's discourse on the end of metaphysics"[11]. The philosopher is continually stressing the necessity of demythologising *transcriptions* of the Christian message, given the ontotheological persistence with which it is guarded within the Church's dogmatic framework.

There is a typically modern train of thought here, which is, ironically, very similar to that of David Friedrich Strauss (1808-1874) in *Das Leben Jesu*. According to Vattimo, the removal of history from its 'sacred' or 'religious' origins, has made room for a mature faith that is free of childish superstition. The break with tradition heralded by the philosophical avant-garde of postmodernism can therefore be situated within a larger framework with Hegelian features. Philosophy's return to religion can in

---

6. *Ibid.*, p. 55.
7. *Ibid.*, p. 48.
8. *Ibid.*, p. 50.
9. *Ibid.*, p. 51.
10. This is even more apparent in *After Christianity*. See G. VATTIMO, *Dopo la cristianità: Per un cristianesimo non religioso*, Milan, Garzanti Editore, 2002. ID., *After Christianity* (Italian Academy Lectures), New York, Columbia University Press, 2002.
11. VATTIMO, *After Christianity* (n. 10), p. 40.

fact be understood as a continuation of the disintegration of religion itself. Post-modern nihilism becomes a new dialectical moment in the advancement of the *Götterdämmerung*. In this regard, incarnation can no longer be understood as a literal interpretation[12] or a rediscovery[13]. *Kenosis* must not shy away from a radical demythologization. If it does, the danger is real that the return of philosophy ends in reactive fundamentalism.

II. INCARNATION AS *KENOSIS* IN MACKINNON

Donald MacKinnon is not a systematic thinker. His reflections on incarnation give a rather fragmented impression. This aspect also has to do with his special fascination for living discourse[14]. His own pedagogic mastery enables him to connect theological and philosophical texts with the vivacity of the human condition, in which things hardly ever appear to us clearly. It is significant that MacKinnon continuously enlivens his rather laborious account with narrative examples. By doing this, he implies that the appeal of real life is most excellently evoked by narrative discourse.

Initially MacKinnon would certainly agree with Vattimo's conviction that neither a philosopher nor a theologian can assume apologetic authority: "The apologetic concern [...]", MacKinnon writes, "is the death of serious theologizing [...] equally of serious work in the philosophy of religion [...]." He expects "[...] protesting raids upon the theologian's cherished homeland" from (contemporary) philosophers[15]. However, he repeatedly emphasizes that theological truths reside at the edge of (natural) thought. Therefore a (hermeneutical) philosophy must maintain "a certain openness of texture or porosity" without using fixed horizons[16].

MacKinnon believes that Christianity confronts us with the paradox that some events have an *ultimate, transcendent* meaning, even though their *contingent* nature cannot be denied[17]. That is why incarnation can be a paradigm for all of Christianity: "For here we are involved with

12. *Ibid.*, pp. 44-45.
13. *Ibid.*, pp. 48-50.
14. "The living discourse not only point to unnoticed possibilities of well-doing, but [...] hint, or more than hint, at ways in which things fundamentally are". D.M. MACKINNON, *The Problem of Metaphysics*, London, Cambridge University Press, 1974, p. 79.
15. D.M. MACKINNON – G.W. ROBERTS – D.E. SMUCKER (eds.), *Borderlands of Theology*, London, Lutterworth, 1968, p. 54.
16. MACKINNON, *Borderlands* (n. 15), p. 153.
17. *Ibid.*, p. 87.

what is totally concrete, its details historically disputable, and at the same time with that for which ultimacy is claimed"[18]. When briefly examining his epistemology, it becomes clear that it too is characterized by a paradoxical nature. MacKinnon is looking for the metaphysical moment in a development that takes place in life itself. Still, he remains very much aware of the fact that a metaphysical problem is always most poignant within a concrete environment[19]. As with Immanuel Kant (1724-1804) it is above all the practical sphere in which the metaphysical influences human existence[20].

On the one hand, MacKinnon wishes, unlike Vattimo, to preserve a metaphysical moment based on the presumption that the human mind discovers rather than invents or constructs[21]. In every religious experience we are confronted with an eccentric orientation: religious meaning and religious insight are accumulated in a higher and ultimate sense that is *given* to us. In this regard, MacKinnon welcomes the *via negativa* as an excellent cure for the deception of projection[22].

On the other hand, MacKinnon problematizes every escape from the vulnerable historicity that belongs by nature to all human knowledge. His relative appreciation of utilitarianism stems from its aptitude for correcting any deontology that tends towards fixation[23]. This is apparent from the fact that his ideas about incarnation are strongly, though not consistently, affected by the *implications* contained within the doctrine[24]. The British theologian knows very well that the reality of suffering aggressively withstands the idealistic artifice of any speculative theology. Think-

18. D.M. MACKINNON, *Themes in Theology, the Three-fold Cord*, Edinburgh, T and T Clark, 1987, p. 234.

19. "It is indeed out of the crisis of the traditional moral order as we discern it that our metaphysical question is born". D.M. MACKINNON, *Explorations in Theology*, London, SCM, 1979, p. 112.

20. MACKINNON, *The Problem* (n. 14), p. 69.

21. This epistemological attitude – in which not only the mind, but also faith is presented as receptive or responsive – is similar to Antoon Vergote's insights. This religious psychologist discerns a derision of human need in religious experience. A. VERGOTE, *Over de grens, da capo*, in D. HUTSEBAUT – J. CORVELEYN (eds.), *Over de grens, de religieuze 'behoefte' kritisch onderzocht* (Studia Psychologica), Leuven, Universitaire Pers Leuven, 1987, p. 211. Note that Vattimo seems to have no trouble with the notion of 'religious need'. Cf. DERRIDA – VATTIMO – GADAMER (eds.), *God* (n. 2), pp. 110-111.

22. In his own words: "If men would give sense to what they say, they must be agnostic before they dare invoke the resources of anthropomorphic imagery [...]". MACKINNON, *Borderlands* (n. 15), p. 95. We cannot dwell here on the similarities between MacKinnon and Derrida in interpreting Kearny. These were also noted by P.D. MURRAY, *Theology in the Borderlands: Donald MacKinnon and Contemporary Theology*, in *Modern Theology* 14 (1998) 362.

23. See for example MACKINNON, *Borderlands* (n. 15), p. 156.

24. See for example MACKINNON, *Themes* (n. 18), p. 235.

ing becomes therapy (as well), since reflection explores its own boundaries and puts every *quidditas* to the test of real life.

An Anglican, MacKinnon is firmly anchored in this tradition and takes it seriously. Though he continues to attribute a relative autonomy to the Christian belief that recognizes Jesus as divine-human redeemer, he does not make this tradition turn hermetically in upon itself like George Lindbeck (1930) did: "The admission of the sovereignty of the Christology is not, for the philosopher [...] a device whereby he is able to say that theology has its own place, its statements their own special logic, and that is enough for him to point out this uniqueness and to defend it against those who would impugn or criticise it"[25]. Nevertheless, he is also aware that Jesus' being the revelation of a personal God will always be couched in a Christian system of beliefs.

The divine gift of self always remains a mystery, but despite the incompleteness of the doctrine of incarnation, "[it] still represents a tremendous effort to do justice to the belief that in Jesus Christ we have to reckon before all else with a quite unique movement from God to man [...] the reality of the divine [...] self-limitation, even [...] a wholly unique act of such divine self-limitation that discloses in a way altogether without parallel God's relation to the world he has created. It discloses that relation in a way without a parallel because this act of self-limitation is itself the ground of that relationship"[26]. This passage displays sympathy for the kenotic interpretation, but it is important to note that this limitation is understood as a precondition for God's personal *presence* with humans.

Still this presence has an existential shadow: "If Christian faith is true [...] its truth is constituted by the correspondence of its credenda with harsh, human reality, and with the divine reality that met human reality and was broken by it, only in that breaking to achieve its healing"[27]. In Christ, God becomes present as someone who *really*, existentially, assumes all the ambiguities and tragic depths of finitude in an infinite and creative giving of the self and thereby offers new perspectives where there did not seem to be any before. Hope cannot be considered a cosmic optimism that hides the painful reality of human existence from view. In this kenotic interpretation of the doctrine the pain regains its physical form. The threatening complexity of suffering, as it can be elucidated in literary drama, serves to disrupt the comfortable and often sterile, narcotic discourse of theologians and philosophers[28]. Otherwise there is the risk

25. MACKINNON, *Borderlands* (n. 15), p. 60.
26. MACKINNON, *Themes* (n. 18), p. 140.
27. MACKINNON, *Explorations* (n. 19), pp. 21-22.
28. MACKINNON, *Borderlands* (n. 15), p. 101.

of forgetting: "The mystery of God's presence in human existence is diminished through induced forgetfulness of the depth to which he descended"[29].

III. SEVERAL EXPLORATORY NOTES ON RELIGIOUS COMPREHENSIBILITY

MacKinnon's intellectual modesty is apparent from his interest in refining questions and presenting intuitions, rather than in offering answers. There is a recurring appeal in his books to keep searching for a meaningful *idiom* for coming to grips with incarnation conceptually[30]. In what follows, I will attempt to clarify that the *existential* and *personal* character of any religious (or theological) discourse cannot be discarded as *passé*. I am convinced that a meaningful hermeneutic is characterized first and foremost by an existential sensitivity. What is existential about religious language? Søren Kierkegaard (1813-1855) would say it is its style, and that is not far off the mark[31].

In the *Concluding Unscientific Postscript*, written under Kierkegaard's pseudonym Johannes Climacus, we read that style does not function as an aesthetic or literary category, but as the way in which the existence of the communicator becomes concrete in the communication. In addition the phenomenon of style confronts us with a moment of finitude in subjective speaking, i.e. the impossibility of communicating directly in the domain of existence. Let us examine the subject of style as an existential phenomenon.

Style unmistakably belongs to that order of facticity to which we cannot relate directly. A writer can never completely objectify his own style for himself during his literary or academic activity. His own style is not wholly perceptible to him. It has to do with his own unique personhood, his singularity. He cannot read his own texts as he would read others' texts. There is always something that escapes phenomenality, and this elusiveness has to do with his singularity. The selfness of the subject is manifest as something that is at the same time outside the self. The notion of style makes the elusive facticity of self apparent. Nevertheless, the theologian consolidates this uncomfortable feeling by continuing to speak.

---

29. *Ibid.*, p. 104.
30. MACKINNON, *Explorations* (n. 19), p. 98.
31. For this paragraph, I am grateful to Professor R. Visker for touching upon the phenomenon of style in his course on the history of contemporary philosophy. Note that there is a certain similar perceptiveness in MacKinnon's texts, be it rather implicit.

Why this digression? We can accord the notion of style an open texture by applying it to incarnation. Is it meaningless to propose that the Christian God acquired his own style in the personal exploits of Jesus? Analogically, we could suppose that we have no direct access to this style, because we share the same facticity, i.e. the specific human condition and its inherent aspects of particularity and historicity. This thought also indicates that the doctrine of incarnation, because of its inevitable paradoxical language, is not meant to make God accessible to representative thinking. Also, the specific style of religious language in general – and *this* type of speech in particular – confronts us above all with our own concrete singularity. This singularity is impossible to define satisfactorily using only an objective set of concepts that dissolve human existence. Maybe that is what poet T.S. Eliot (1888-1965) meant when he wrote: "The hint *half* guessed, the gift *half* understood, is Incarnation"[32]. Finally, style on the one hand and religious language on the other hand are related to *deiktic* or demonstrative language. The indicatory gesture receives its particularity and its specific meaning by referring to (pointing at) something. Plato and Aristotle as they are shown on the fresco *The Athenian School* by Raphael are the perfect metaphor for the paradoxical and dialectical character of the hermeneutic *deiksis* that functions in theological discourse: to point outside the framework (Plato), is at the same time to point at the framework itself (Aristotle).

Finally, I wish to contemplate the conditions for religious speech. I will restrict myself to the demand for minimal comprehensibility. What makes religious speech comprehensible? Revelatory speech should not be 'inhuman'; it must reach out to human beings in their particularity instead of crushing them[33]. Assuming that there is a God who addresses himself to us (using language), he must want us humans to understand him. Supernatural meanings must therefore be related to natural ones[34]. Therefore,

32. T.S. ELIOT, *Four Quartets*, trans. H. Servotte, Kapellen, Pelckmans, 1996, p. 90 (italics added).

33. We refer to W. Benjamin's 'mythical violence' of divine words. This concept is in fact used in a political context. See W. BENJAMIN – R. TIEDEMANN (eds.), *Sprache und Geschichte: Philosophische Essays*, Stuttgart, Reclam, 1992, pp. 104-131. In his posthumously published *Philosophie der Mythologie und Offenbarung*, F. Schelling argues that religion has a meaning, which it edifyingly manifests on its own. The truth of myth, and *mutatis mutandis* of religion as well, is tautegoric. The tautegoric interpretation of myth, according to Schelling, is not really an interpretation as one does not look for a second, ideal content that could also be expressed in philosophical or scientific language. If we can truly relate to God, this contact will inevitably be concrete and personal. See also J.E. WILSON, *Schellings 'Mythologie: zur Auslegung der Philosophie der Mythologie und Offenbarung'* (Spekulation und Erfahrung, 31), Stuttgart, Frommann-Holzboog, 1993.

34. See F. KAULBACH, *Der philosophische Begriff der Bewegung: Studien zu Aristoteles, Leibniz und Kant* (Münstersche Forschungen, 16), Köln, Böhlau, 1965, pp. 13-

it could be called a semantic *symphysis*: supernatural meanings can connect to natural and autonomous meanings, and both meanings cannot fundamentally contradict one another. By nature, revelatory language remains external to any immediate recuperation, but it must be receptive to the meaning-structure of terms we are familiar with. If this were impossible, all speaking about God would be senseless, or in fact: there would indeed be no other way to describe him than in terms of emptiness and of the symbol of the break. This indicates that a God who remains distant from the *personal* figure who emerges so perceptibly in the formula of incarnation cannot be encountered in any way, much less understood.

On the other hand, a 'realistic' but relative distinction between immanent and supernatural meaning can hardly be contested fundamentally. This implies, in the first place, that God's transcendent freedom is respected – a post-modern concern. He cannot be exhaustively subordinated to the idealistic artifices of the human mind[35]. The division between God and the particular history can never be absolute. Even though one should make distinctions between the different orders of speech, the statement "God reveals himself in Jesus" does not simply mean that the heart has its own logic, like Blaise Pascal (1623-1662) believed, nor can the acceptance of this statement be based purely on obedience. I believe the most important task of the fundamental theologian should be to develop a kind of congruence so that both approaches, belief and knowledge, can meet after all[36]. I use the verb 'to meet' purposefully. Since, according to the doctrine, God is not a deistic principle, not a total Other, but has subjected himself to the specific conditions of human existence, including suffering, through his Son, we can meet him in a concrete way. A successful fundamental theology always presents an epistemological and

---

23. Also see: M. Moors, *Het noemen van Gods naam: "Hij die Is" : Over filosofie en openbaring*, in M. Moors – J. Van Der Veken (eds.), *Naar Leeuweriken grijpen: Leuvense opstellen over metafysica* (Wijsgerige Verkenningen, 13), Leuven, Universitaire Pers Leuven, 1994, p. 231.

35. Note that it would be impossible to even conceive of incarnation in this way, since it inevitably contains a dimension of existence and facticity. And this can never be satisfactorily converted into a concept, since the medium of thought is ideality.

36. Max Scheler cannot one-sidedly condemn philosophy adversely or declare it incompetent. That would make human beings, who are without question *homo religiosus*, quite schizophrenic. Personal unity would split up into separate aspects: persons would divide into a thinking, an acting, and a religious being, without the possibility for these elements to be oriented towards the same thing. Nevertheless, this is attempted in most post-modern 'anthropologies', by emphasizing the many breaks and discontinuities between different language games. Scheler, however, develops a *conformity* between reason and faith, without ignoring the independence of both modes of knowing. Cf. M. Scheler, *Vom Ewigen im Menschen: Religiöse Erneuerung*, Leipzig, Der Neue Geist, 1921, p. 348. MacKinnon also seems to endorse something similar, though less well developed: MacKinnon, *Borderlands* (n. 15), p. 221.

existential boundary, but never remains silent beyond them. On the contrary, that is where the theologian becomes a person; that is where a reality with its own 'effective' and even systematic logic deploys, though it will probably be unable to envelop subjective idealities.

CONCLUSION

I return to the rather speculative question posed in the title: is a God who is present in human history, comprehensible? Vattimo would probably say not. The progressing development of secularization is one of God's *absence*. The philosopher describes the dynamics of *kenosis* one-sidedly as a receding and impersonal event. Christian revelation dissolves over time, leaving behind a dull and meagre fraternity. God becomes a unilaterally 'rejecting' divinity, about whom we should wonder whether he has not become a philosopher's God again[37]. A big problem in Vattimo's hermeneutics is that particularity, in its emancipation from all 'otherworlds', increasingly turns in upon itself, bringing with it the danger that the particular story of secularization will submerge itself[38]. This is a point of similarity of his demythologizing philosophy with the mythologizing concept of incarnation of John Hick (°1922). Both share an inability to account for the personalistic aspect of a factual presence[39].

MacKinnon would probably answer the question above, positively. In factual existence and nowhere else, systematic theology and philosophy can approach one another on the questions posed by fundamental theology. The inevitable down side of this contingence is in fact the incompleteness and vulnerability of the human search for understanding. Still this down side does not imply a passive mode of thinking. On the contrary: the particular, always practical order is where the incarnation first gains its meaning of vulnerable presence. At the same time, MacKinnon does the eccentric orientation of the Christian subject justice, so that a comfortable retreat into particular tradition and the security of institution

37. MacKinnon is wary of such 'arrogance': "The temptation that must beset the theologian whose temper is that of the explorer of the unknown, even the forbidden territories of the world of ideas, is not to be identified quickly with a superior disdain for the proved simplicities of traditional wisdom". MACKINNON, *Explorations* (n. 19), p. 135.

38. See for example the particular and nihilistic community itself as the only correction or criterion of interpretation, resulting in a very one-sided imagery. VATTIMO, *After Christianity* (n. 10), pp. 67-68.

39. To Vattimo, incarnation contains a sea of possibilities, rather than facticity: "Since the Christian God was incarnate in Jesus, we *may* also *understand* God through the other forms of natural being appearing in many non-Christian religious mythologies". VATTIMO, *After Christianity* (n. 10), p. 27 (italics added).

is no longer an option. It is clear that incarnation has become a dynamic and appealing event in which the problem of suffering is even more poignant. In this critical existential unrest, particular tradition can become an authentic framework for an encounter with God in Jesus.

I have tried to explain that incarnation will never be simply and exhaustively definable in my reflective excursion in which the notion of style was elastically extended. On the other hand, it is this style that enables us to continue to practice theology, which is more than some religious-philosophical preliminaria. A factual God, I believe, is comprehensible, because he appears within facticity – the human sphere. Because God has acquired a style through Jesus, or, from a hermeneutical point of view, has received a style in contextual testimonials, religious language itself can continually refer to a positive singularity that may not be fully expressible, but must still be expressed. And all this is on the basis of the condition of minimal critical understanding. In our continual communication, which is inevitably a communal event, this eccentric singularity is realized further. What is never expressed, remains without style, and is therefore unreal; it evaporates in an impersonal cloud of unknowing. The main challenge put to us by postmodernism, which is also inevitable existentially, is to find a way in which a universal moment can be preserved in religious speech and understanding.

christoph.moonen@theo.kuleuven.be   Christoph MOONEN

GIANNI VATTIMO'S CONCEPT OF TRUTH AND
ITS CONSEQUENCES FOR CHRISTIANITY

In 1996, the Italian philosopher Gianni Vattimo (°1936) published a booklet entitled *Credere di credere* (believing that one believes); translated into English as *Belief*[1]. Ever since, Vattimo has defended in his work the idea that there are no longer any decisive, philosophical arguments for an atheistic position. As a consequence, he states, it is possible again to take seriously the God of the Bible. This seems to show great promise in an era in which Christianity is challenged to search for a future beyond the fruitless alternatives of post-modern disintegration and fundamentalist rigidity.

Vattimo's philosophy is inspired by two sources, namely Nietzsche and Heidegger. He is also a follower of Hans-Georg Gadamer and chooses, like this predecessor, for a radical hermeneutical position. Major works of Vattimo's include *The Adventure of Difference* (1980)[2], *Weak Thought* (1983)[3], *The End of Modernity* (1985)[4] and *The Transparent Society* (1989)[5]. In 1986, he edited a compilation that appeared in 1988 in French translation with the explicit title *La sécularisation de la pensée* (the secularization of thought)[6]. The concept of secularization has become of overriding importance in the work of Vattimo and is one of the core-ideas of his thinking. In 1994, Vattimo participated in a congress dealing with philosophy of religion that took place on the island of Capri. Jacques Derrida and Gadamer also spoke at that congress, at which

---

1. G. VATTIMO, *Credere di credere: È possibile essere cristiani nonostante la Chiesa?*, Milan, Garzanti Editore, 1996. ID., *Belief*, trans. L. D'Isanto and D. Webb, Cambridge, Polity Press, 1999.

2. ID., *La avventure della differenza: Che chosa significa pensare dopo Nietzsche e Heidegger*, Milan, Garzanti Editore, 1980. ID., *The Adventure of Difference: Philosophy After Nietzsche and Heidegger*, trans. C. Blamires, Cambridge, Polity Press, 1993.

3. ID. – P. ALDO ROVATTI (eds.), *Il pensiero debole*, Milan, Feltrinelli, 1983. Vattimo's contribution to this compilation has been translated into English as: ID., *Dialectic, Difference, Weak Thought*, in *Graduate Faculty Philosophy Journal* 10 (1984) 151-164.

4. ID., *La fine della modernità: Nichilismo ed ermeneutica nella cultura post-moderna*, Milan, Garzanti Editore, 1985. ID., *The End of Modernity: Nihilism and Hermeneutics in Post-modern Culture*, trans. J.R. Snyder, Cambridge, Polity Press, 1988.

5. ID., *La società trasparente*, Milan, Garzanti Editore, 1989. ID., *The Transparent Society*, trans. D. Webb, Cambridge, Polity Press, 1992.

6. ID. (ed.), *Filosofia '86*, Rome, Gius, Laterza & Figli, 1986. ID., *La sécularisation de la pensée*, Paris, Éditions du Seuil, 1988. ID., *Metaphysics, Violence, Secularization*, in G. BORRADORI (ed.), *Recoding Metaphysics: The New Italian Philosophy*, Evanston, IL, Northwestern University Press, 1988, 45-61.

Vattimo announced his return to religion[7]. This religious turn can also be concluded from the chapter on religion in his 1994 book *Beyond Interpretation*[8] and more explicitly from the already mentioned *Belief*. Vattimo has recently elaborated his view on Christianity in *After Christianity*, which appeared in 2002[9].

In what follows, we shall proceed in three steps: first, we shall discuss Vattimo's understanding of truth and how it makes it possible to take religion seriously again; second, we shall see how Vattimo argues that this concept of truth is not relativist; and third, we shall examine what Christians can learn from Vattimo about Christian faith in a so-called post-modern context.

I. How a Return of Religion Became Possible

The starting point of Vattimo's philosophical undertaking is the idea that Nietzsche's proclamation of the death of God and Heidegger's announcement of the end of metaphysics are ultimately dealing with one and the same event that presents itself to thought. The death of God in Nietzsche, Vattimo states, is only the death of the metaphysical God, the *moral* God of the philosophers, who have always thought God as the final guarantee of truth and morality. So, when *Nietzsche* proclaims the death of this God, he *teaches us that reality has no ultimate foundation*. Vattimo links this instruction of Nietzsche explicitly with Heidegger's teaching on the end of metaphysics. He describes metaphysics, following Heidegger, as "the thought [...] that identifies Being with the objectively given" and as "the belief in an objective order, which must be recognized so that thought might conform with it"[10]. So, when Heidegger speaks about the end of metaphysics, he announces the end of any thought that determines reality as an objective, unchanging and eternal "structure solidly tied to a sole foundation that philosophy would have the task of knowing, or perhaps that religion would have the task of adoring"[11].

---

7. See for this: G. VATTIMO, *The Trace of the Trace*, in J. DERRIDA – G. VATTIMO – H.-G. GADAMER (eds.), *Religion*, Cambridge, Polity Press, 1998, 79-94.

8. G. VATTIMO, *Oltre l'interpretazione: Il significato dell'ermeneutica per la filosofia* (Lezioni Italiane), Rome – Bari, Laterza and Figli, 1994. ID., *Beyond Interpretation: The Meaning of Hermeneutics for Philosophy*, trans. D. Webb, Cambridge, Polity Press, 1997.

9. G. VATTIMO, *Dopo la cristianità: Per un christianesimo non religioso*, Milan, Garzanti Editore, 2002. ID., *After Christianity* (Italian Academy Lectures), New York, Columbia University Press, 2002.

10. VATTIMO, *Belief* (n. 1), p. 17 and ID., *After Christianity* (n. 9), p. 13 respectively.

11. VATTIMO, *After Christianity* (n. 9), p. 5.

This end of metaphysics can also be defined as the realization of nihilism, described by Vattimo as "the final consummation of the belief that Being and reality are 'objective' data which thinking ought to contemplate in order to bring itself into conformity with their laws"[12]. Nihilism further implies that reality is always a construction of the subject. Vattimo formulates this as follows:

> Finally thinking becomes aware that what is actually real is, as the positivists assert, a 'positive' fact, a given established by science. *Establishing, however, is precisely the act of the human subject* (though not of the individual subject), and the reality of the world of which we speak is identified as the 'product' of scientific experiments and technological apparatus. *There is no longer a 'true world' or, better, truth is reduced entirely to what is 'posited' by the human being, namely the 'Will to Power'*[13].

So, even natural science is not able to describe reality in its pure objectiveness, its pure 'being there'. The results of natural science are provoked by actively interrogating reality with the help of experiments and apparatus, which are set up in order to test hypotheses based on frames of interpretation, paradigms and theoretical schemes, with which a natural scientist approaches reality and which colour his/her perception of that reality. In this regard, Vattimo refers to the highly influential book *The Structure of Scientific Revolutions* of Thomas Kuhn. Natural scientists verify or falsify hypotheses with the help of certain paradigms, axioms and theorems that in turn cannot be verified or falsified. The history of the natural sciences can then be understood as the constant alternation of continuous development within a particular paradigm and revolutions in which an old paradigm is replaced by a new one. However, these revolutions, as Vattimo stresses, "are complex historical events which cannot be explained according to the logic of proof and confutation"[14]. Phrased differently, the paradigms that make verification and falsification possible are not themselves subject to verification or falsification.

Nihilism also necessarily implies another understanding of truth. Since there is no objective reality anymore, it is no longer possible to think truth merely in the traditional way "as the reflection of reality's eternal structure", as the correspondence between our thought and the things as they really are (*aedequatio intellectus et rei*). Truth is not timeless anymore, but thoroughly historical and can only be reached through dialogue and consensus[15]. This also implies a particular view of tradition. In an

---

12. VATTIMO, *Belief* (n. 1), p. 29. See also *After Christianity*(n. 9), p. 105.
13. VATTIMO, *Belief* (n. 1), p. 30 (my italics).
14. VATTIMO, *After Christianity* (n. 9), pp. 6-7.
15. *Ibid.*, pp. 5-6.

interview Vattimo once stressed that tradition is not a foundation[16]. In itself, tradition is not an argument in a discussion. The fact that a certain community has always done something in a particular way is no reason the members of that community should go on doing what they have always done. Tradition is not unchangeable, but rather it is open and living. Vattimo gives the example of the thousands of American nuns who want to become priests. According to Vattimo, such a fact may not be ignored[17]. Tradition can thus develop on the basis of a consensus within the community of faith. Although it is important to note that, according to Vattimo, this community does not coincide with the ecclesiastical hierarchy. In the thought of Vattimo truth thus turns out to be a process. Truth is "produced again and again through the 'authentication' that occurs in dialogue with history" and in the case of the community of faith this process is "assisted by the Holy Spirit"[18].

The end of the belief in an objective order of Being also implies that the distinction between ordinary, so-called objective language and poetic, metaphorical language has become impossible. In this regard, Vattimo refers to a fragment of the young Nietzsche, known as *Truth and Lies in an Extra-moral sense*. In this fragment Nietzsche states that all language is metaphorical and that, as a result, truth only means that we use the metaphors that have been imposed on us by a master. So, the distinction between objective and metaphorical language was only called into being when masters degraded other languages "to the realm of the poetic, namely to the status of purely metaphorical languages". Nowadays, however, this distinction between objective and poetic language has been unmasked as "a pure effect of social power's unequal distribution"[19]. As a result, it is possible to take seriously again the fact "that there are many languages, many 'language games' for experiencing the world, each of which has legitimacy"[20] and, consequently, truth is no longer restricted to what can be verified and tested with the help of a scientific experiment.

16. G. GROOT, *Traditie is geen fundament: Gesprek met G. Vattimo*, in G. GROOT (ed.), *Een zwak geloof: Christendom voorbij de metafysica*, Kampen, Agora, 2000, 31-38. This interview with as title 'Tradition is not a foundation' is part of a little book that appeared as a result of a lecture Vattimo held for the 'Thomas More Academie' in Amsterdam (The Netherlands). It contains an introduction to G. Vattimo, the text of his lecture, an interview with him and several articles in which his views are discussed (in Dutch).

17. GROOT, *Traditie is geen fundament* (n. 16), pp. 36-37.

18. VATTIMO, *Belief* (n. 1), pp. 59 and 60.

19. VATTIMO, *After Christianity* (n. 9), p. 16. See also: G. VATTIMO, *After Onto-Theology: Philosophy between Science and Religion*, in M.A. WRATHALL, *Religion after Metaphysics*, Cambridge, Cambridge University Press, 2003, 29-36, esp. p. 31.

20. VATTIMO, *After Onto-Theology* (n. 19), p. 31.

The "liberation of metaphor", "the new legitimacy granted to metaphorical discourse by the end of metaphysics"[21], also makes it possible to take seriously again religious discourse. For, due to the loss of objective reality, modern atheism can also no longer be held. According to Vattimo, modern atheism was based on "belief in objective truth and faith in the progress of Reason towards full transparency". Modern atheism rejected God because God's existence could not be established with the help of scientific experiments and was considered as an impediment to the full emancipation of the human race. Nowadays, however, we have experienced, in the words of Vattimo, "a radical disenchantment with the idea of disenchantment itself". Or to put it differently, the ideal of the end of all myths and ideologies turned out to be just another myth, only another ideology[22].

However, does this 'end of the end of all myths and ideologies' mean that we can as well "return to placing our faith in myths and ideologies"? According to Vattimo, this return is in fact taking place in contemporary culture and is, moreover, often legitimized by many self-proclaimed post-metaphysical philosophies, which limit themselves only "to the defence of pluralism for its own sake or to the legitimization of proliferating narratives without hierarchy or centre". In this way, these philosophies are merely "preaching a pure and simple return to myth and ideology without setting up any critical principle, apart from the important principle of tolerance". This, however, is highly problematic. Is this kind of relativism not inaugurating a new normative meta-narrative, namely that of pluralism and tolerance[23]? Or, to put it differently, how can philosophy become truly post-metaphysical, without sneakily having recourse on a new metaphysical stance?

II. Is a Truly Post-Metaphysical Philosophy Possible?

According to Vattimo, a truly post-metaphysical philosophy is only possible when we reconsider the view that hermeneutic philosophers have developed, in the line of Gadamer, on the relationship between the natural sciences and philosophy. Gadamer developed his hermeneutics mainly on the basis of Heidegger's *Being and Time*. In that book, Heidegger makes a distinction between particular truths and the horizon in

---

21. VATTIMO, *Belief* (n. 1), p. 30 and ID., *After Onto-Theology* (n. 19), p. 31 respectively.
22. VATTIMO, *Belief* (n. 1), pp. 28-29. See also: ID., *After Christianity* (n. 9), p. 17.
23. VATTIMO, *After Christianity* (n. 9), p. 20.

which these truths appear. Vattimo links this distinction with Kuhn's distinction between the daily enterprise of the natural sciences (concrete verifications and falsifications based on a particular paradigm) and that paradigm itself. Vattimo formulates this as follows: "According to Heidegger, the *truth may be thought in terms of correspondence* between proposition and thing, *but only within a preliminary opening (Offenheit, Weltoffenheit)*, which in turn is not guaranteed by any verifiable correspondence (which would require another opening, and so on ad infinitum)"[24].

Given this distinction between truth as correspondence and a, seemingly, more fundamental truth as opening, the question arises as to how the relationship between both kinds of truth should be thought. To elaborate further, we now turn to the essay *The Truth of Hermeneutics*, added as an appendix to *Beyond Interpretation*, in which Vattimo deals with the question of the relationship between truth as correspondence and truth as opening, or – to put it differently – the relationship between the natural sciences on the one hand and (hermeneutic) philosophy and the interpretative sciences (the humanities) on the other. He refers to his teacher Gadamer, stating that he has merely aimed at restricting the scope of the natural sciences: "To avoid both inauthenticity and the careless and forgetful distortions of metaphysics, it would seem, therefore, that one must simply resist this unwarranted extension of the model of the simple presence of entities and objects [= the model of the natural sciences] to Being itself"[25]. In other words, Gadamer subjects the natural sciences to the humanities: the natural sciences "must be 'legitimized' by a thinking which relates them back to the *logos*, to the common consciousness expressed in the natural-historic language of a society and in its shared culture, whose continuity [...] is assured precisely by the human sciences and philosophy in particular"[26]. As a result, the truth of the natural sciences is only a secondary truth and should always be related back to the horizon in which these truths appear and which cannot be thematized by the natural sciences but only by (hermeneutic) philosophy and the humanities (in so far as these are interpretative sciences).

This is the stance hermeneutics has traditionally taken towards the natural sciences. To understand why hermeneutic thinkers have adopted this position, we should take a look at the origins of the hermeneutic movement. As Vattimo mentions in *Beyond Interpretation*, hermeneutics originated as a reaction against the increasing impact of technology and sci-

24. VATTIMO, *After Onto-Theology* (n. 19), p. 32 (my italics).
25. VATTIMO, *Beyond Interpretation* (n. 8), pp. 78-79.
26. *Ibid.*, p. 80.

ence on the daily life of human beings in the modern world, which is characterized by the primacy of scientific and technological rationality. In this sense, it can be considered as an heir to the Romantic Movement. Ever since the Enlightenment gave rise to Romanticism, there have been reactions against the colonization of the daily life world by science and technology. Heidegger, who may be designated as the founding father of contemporary hermeneutic philosophy, reacted against the primacy of science and technology. According to Vattimo, Heidegger's criticism of metaphysics was mainly dictated by an ethically inspired resistance against a society completely organized by science and technology in which human existence would "be reduced to pure presence, calculability and manipulability" and in which real freedom would become impossible[27].

However, as Vattimo stresses, the view developed by traditional hermeneutics in order to save the daily life world from the impact of science and technology, can easily lead to a new kind of foundationalism in which the particular tradition of a local community, the "historico-cultural horizon shared by a community that speaks the same language"[28], is installed as a new *Grund*, a new ultimate foundation[29]. Moreover, as has already been indicated above, post-metaphysical, hermeneutic philosophy runs the risk of becoming a new kind of metaphysics, by pretending to be able to formulate an objective view on reality, namely that there are no facts, but only interpretations. Yet, is such a statement itself not also pretending to present a fact? Is hermeneutics in this way not merely offering a new true and objective description of the world, namely in terms of an unsolvable conflict of interpretations? Thus, the challenge posed to hermeneutics should be formulated as follows: How can hermeneutic philosophy avoid turning into a new kind of objectivism?

This, according to Vattimo, is only possible when we situate the rise of hermeneutics firmly in the history of Being. This also implies that we recognize the nihilistic vocation of Being and the role played by science and technology in the realization of that destiny. In order to do this, we should not restrict us, according to Vattimo, to the Heidegger of *Being and Time* (as Gadamer has usually done). Vattimo, drawing inspiration from Heidegger's essay *The Age of the World Picture*, interprets science

---

27. *Ibid.*, pp. 30-31. See also: ID., *After Christianity* (n. 9), p. 14.
28. VATTIMO, *Beyond Interpretation* (n. 8), p. 80.
29. See e.g.: VATTIMO, *Beyond Interpretation* (n. 8), p. 87, where Vattimo speaks about "an even more monumental foundationalism, one that could express itself in the pure and simple identification of the opening with the brute factuality of a certain form of life not open to discussion, and which shows itself only in its holding as the horizon of every possible judgement".

and technology as both the end and the culmination of metaphysics. On the one hand, modern science brings metaphysics to an end. Thanks to modern science, the metaphysical "belief in the ideal world order – in a kingdom of essences that lay beyond empirical realities" has been unmasked as useless. Modern scientists do not need essences or Platonic ideas in order to explain reality. Or as Vattimo puts it, "the ideal order [of metaphysics], [...] has become the *de facto* order of the rationalized world of modern technological society". On the other hand, precisely in this way, modern science realizes the metaphysical project, namely by culminating in a complete objectification and rationalization of the world[30].

When hermeneutic philosophy is merely an enterprise in "defence of the *Lebenswelt* against colonization by specialist branches of knowledge and the applications of technology", it runs, as has already been indicated, the risk of merely replacing one description of truth by another one and, in this way, of remaining firmly within the horizon of metaphysics, objectivism and foundationalism. According to Vattimo, this can be avoided when hermeneutics interprets modern science, in contrast, "as the principal agent in a nihilistic transformation of the meaning of Being". In other words, it is modern science that has brought forth nihilism, because it is by modern science that reality has disintegrated in a plurality of representations of the world (a plurality of world pictures). Moreover, natural science itself has left the traditional conception of truth as correspondence behind in the course of its development. For, as Vattimo also indicates, there is an increasing difference between the scientific description of our world and our intuitive experience of that same world[31].

All this brings Vattimo to the following conclusion:

> The world as a conflict of interpretations and nothing more is not an image of the world that has to be defended against the realism and positivism of science. It is modern science, heir and completion of metaphysics, that turns the world into a place where there are no (longer) facts, only interpretations. It is not a matter, for hermeneutics, of setting limits to scientism, of resisting the triumph of science and technology in the name of a humanist culture, of standing up for the 'lifeworld' against calculation, planning and total organization. The critique that hermeneutics can and must move against the

---

30. VATTIMO, *After Christianity* (n. 9), p. 14.

31. VATTIMO, *Beyond Interpretation* (n. 8), p. 89: "[...] technical science as it is set out in the world of *Ge-stell*, in totally organized society, is possible only on the condition of no longer thinking truth on the model of the evidence proper to consciousness. The modern scientific project itself heralds the consummation of that model, ultimately the ever more emphatic divarication between the real – as that which is given in the immediacy of a compelling intuition – and the true, as that which is established only by virtue of its being situated within an unfounding horizon".

techno-scientific world is aimed, if anything, to aid it in a recognition of its own nihilistic meaning [...][32].

Put differently, the metaphysical pursuit of objectification, culminating in modern science, has ultimately resulted in its opposite, namely a complete loss of objective reality. To make this abstract argument a bit more concrete, we can turn to Vattimo's *The Transparent Society* in which he discusses the role of the mass media in the emergence of our post-modern society. The mass media, an important technology in contemporary society, have led to a proliferation of views and perspectives (*Weltanschauungen*), making any unificatory meta-narrative, pretending to offer an objective description of the world, impossible.

In summary, hermeneutics cannot avoid becoming a new objectivism when it considers itself as merely a correction of a previous, false understanding of truth. In that case, the statement 'there are no facts, only interpretations' is presented as a new fact, the fact that there are no facts anymore, which is of course self-defeating. As a result, hermeneutics is only possible when it considers itself as an interpretation. This is Vattimo's aim when he speaks about hermeneutics as an interpretation of Being as an event and as a history of nihilism and weakening of strong structures. This also enables Vattimo to argue that a hermeneutic stance does not have to lead to relativism. For, the interpretation of the event of Being as a history of "reduction and dissolution of strong characteristics [...] presents itself as a possible guiding thread for interpretations, choices, and even moral options, far beyond the pure and simple affirmation of the plurality of paradigms"[33].

Vattimo describes this history of Being, interpreted as an event of the weakening of strong structures, also with the term 'secularization' and with the biblical notion of 'kenosis' (Phil 2,7). This process of secularization has, according to Vattimo, only one limit, and that is *caritas* or charity. In *After Christianity* Vattimo describes love as the core of the biblical revelation and as the aim, criterion and limit of a spiritual reading of Scripture. This love is "an active commitment to diminish violence in all its forms"[34]. In *Belief* Vattimo elucidates this with the help of a phrase from the work of Augustine, namely "Dilige, et quod vis fac" ("Love, and do what you will")[35]. Furthermore, Vattimo describes the commandment of love as a categorical imperative. It is a formal commandment, "which does not command something specific once and for all, but

32. VATTIMO, *Beyond Interpretation* (n. 8), pp. 24-27.
33. *Ibid.*, p. 94.
34. VATTIMO, *After Christianity* (n. 9), pp. 49, 51-52.
35. VATTIMO, *Belief* (n. 1), p. 64.

rather applications that must be 'invented' in dialogue with specific situations and in light of what the holy Scriptures have revealed". According to Vattimo, it is precisely because the commandment of love is purely
formal that it cannot be secularized[36].

III. WHAT CAN CHRISTIANS LEARN FROM VATTIMO?

As has been indicated in section one above, according to Vattimo, a
return of religion has become possible by the so-called liberation of
metaphor, resulting from the end of metaphysics. The end of the belief
in an objective order of Being implies that it is no longer possible to
distinguish between objective and metaphorical language. Consequently,
it is also no longer possible to consider the experimental method of the
natural sciences as the sole way to truth. On the contrary, there are many
language games, many ways for experiencing the world and each of
them has legitimacy. Since natural science is no longer the sole way to
truth, an atheistic stance has become impossible (for it was based on scientism, on making absolute the method of the natural sciences). As a
result, it is possible to take religious language seriously again in its own
right.

Vattimo, however, as we have already said, does not plead for a mere
return to the old myths and ideologies. That would be merely restoring
the violence of the old metaphysical beliefs. Moreover, Vattimo wants to
avoid the ethical relativism that characterizes many contemporary philosophies that defend pluralism for its own sake without any critical principle. He rejects such a relativism as the installation of a new normative
meta-narrative, namely the one of pluralism and tolerance. In this way,
this relativism pretends to be able to objectively describe reality (as plural)
and is thus merely a new kind of metaphysics, foundationalism in dis-
guise. Therefore, as we have discussed in section two above, Vattimo
cannot consider his philosophical stance as a correction of a previous,
false philosophy. For, in that case, he would pretend to describe reality
objectively, which is, in his view, a return to metaphysics. As a result, his
philosophy can only be an interpretative answer to the event of Being,
which, according to Vattimo, reveals itself in our era as a history of the
weakening of the strong structures that were the source of (metaphysical)
violence. As has already been indicated above, this process of secularization has only one limit, namely the principle of caritas.

36. *Ibid.*, p. 66.

We shall now make clear that Vattimo's undertaking, as it has been presented in the preceding pages, can be criticized from three different perspectives, namely from nihilism, natural science and the Bible. These three perspectives can be summarized as three questions: (1) Is Vattimo a consequent nihilist? (2) Can Vattimo take the natural sciences seriously? (3) Does Vattimo fulfil his promise (mentioned at the beginning of this contribution) to take seriously again the God of the Bible? In what follows, we shall discuss these three questions separately, before turning to a conclusion.

(1) Is Vattimo a consequent nihilist? In order to answer this question, we can start from the role played by the caritas in Vattimo's thought. As we have already seen, the role of the caritas is to be a kind of categorical imperative, which directs and limits the process of secularization. With the help of the caritas, Vattimo avoids complete relativism. For, after objective reality has disappeared, only a never ending 'battle of interpretations' seems to be left. The caritas is then a criterion on the basis of which one can judge conflicting interpretations and actions. Only those interpretations and actions that are in correspondence with it are valid. The others should be rejected. The caritas can thus be described as a principle that steers the conflict of interpretations in the right direction. In this way, however, it turns out to be something absolute, something transcendent, namely a principle that is valid always and everywhere and, as a consequence, is not bound to time or space. In Vattimo's weak thought, however, there is actually no place for such an absolute principle, because – as indicated by Peter Jonkers in his *In the World, but not of the World* – "weak thinking dissolves every fixed meaning of humanity and the world into a thoroughly contingent, historical and local occurrence. In such a world, everything is hypothetical, i.e. subject to circumstance, place and time". Jonkers concludes as follows:

> Consequently, the limiting of secularization by the commandment of love is nothing but *an arbitrary decision on the part of Vattimo as an individual*. Once thinking begins to unmask every representation of the sacral, as well as the sacral itself, [...] it cannot stop short at the commandment of love as something sacrosanct anymore. If one wants to do this nevertheless, then such a decision appears from the perspective of radical nihilism as *an expression of violent arbitrariness*[37].

This remark is appropriate, as Vattimo is rejecting the belief in objective reality, how can he then still hold an objective principle? Moreover,

37. P. JONKERS, *In the World, but not of the World: The Prospects of Christianity in the Modern World*, in *Bijdragen* 61 (2000) 370-389, esp. p. 386.

why should we choose the caritas to guide us when we have to decide between conflicting interpretations? Vattimo defends his choice by stating that love is the core of the biblical message (see above). This, however, cannot be called a real justification. Is he not merely choosing for the *caritas* as principle, because he has already chosen for Christianity? The problem is thus not that Vattimo's weak thought is too radical, but that it is not radical enough. Or, phrased differently, his nihilism is not nihilistic enough. He still holds to a principle that is considered as being objective (in the sense that it is considered as not being postulated by the subject). But why would the principle of caritas escape the criticism of Nietzsche? If all reality is posited by the human subject, as nihilism states and Vattimo defends (see above), why would the principle of caritas not also be a construction of the Will to Power?

(2) *Can Vattimo take the natural sciences seriously?* As we have seen above, Vattimo rejects the animosity often found among hermeneutic philosophers towards natural science and he even gives natural science a pivotal role in the bringing about of the nihilistic vocation of Being. The question should be asked, however, whether the natural sciences can still be taken seriously once this nihilistic destiny of Being has been reached. Does the end of objective reality not imply that we can/should no longer distinguish between, for instance, a scientific account on the origins of the cosmos and the creation myth we find in the first chapter of Genesis? Should we from now on accept that the scientific account is also just a myth, merely one myth among others? It seems unlikely that Vattimo would give an affirmative answer to these questions. On the other hand, however, he also does not reject the conclusion that science has become merely another myth.

(3) *Does Vattimo fulfil his promise to take seriously again the God of the Bible?* Vattimo links Christianity and nihilism by considering the Heidegerrian depiction of the history of Being (as an event of weakening of strong structures) to be a "transcription" of the Christian doctrine of the Incarnation. He also puts it the other way round: the doctrine of the Incarnation is "an announcement of an ontology of weakening"[38]. So, according to Vattimo, secularization is the essence of Christianity and, as a result, Christians should not fear increasing secularization. By saying so, Vattimo seems to adopt a strategy already developed by a number of modern theologians who made a sharp distinction between Christian faith and religiosity (Karl Barth) and who evaluated secularization as

---

38. VATTIMO, *Belief* (n. 1), p. 36. See also: ID., *After Christianity* (n. 9), p. 113: "Christianity is the condition that paved the way for the dissolution of metaphysics".

a positive phenomenon (Arend Theodoor van Leeuwen and Edward Schillebeeckx). As far back as the 1960s, both van Leeuwen and Schillebeeckx interpreted secularization as a consequence of the biblical message and stated that secularization already commences in the book of Genesis[39]. Although Vattimo is arguing on the basis of Nietzsche and Heidegger, he seems to be making basically the same point as these modern theologians. So, the question rises whether Vattimo is not offering old wine in new wineskins. Is he not using a strategy that has already been seriously discredited by the criticism of many contemporary theologians who have rejected the so-called 'modern correlation method' as unfruitful? Or does Vattimo's analysis of the post-modern situation, on the contrary, demonstrate that we should rehabilitate this discredited method?

Modern theology came into being when a number of Christian theologians wanted to value the achievements of modernity positively. As Lieven Boeve indicates in his *Interrupting Tradition: An Essay on Christian Faith in a Post-modern Context*, in order to do this, these theologians adopted the modern critique of religion and legitimated modernity as the outcome of Christianity, by stating that the secularizing tendencies of modernity were already inherent in the biblical message[40]. In order to relate modernity and Christianity, modern theologians used the already mentioned 'modern correlation method', which consists in the attempt to reconcile modern experience and the Christian message. For instance, by stating that it is by participating in the modern attempts to create a just and good society that Christians are doing their part in realizing God's dream with humanity. In his article *Zeg nooit meer correlatie: Over christelijke traditie, hedendaagse context en onderbreking* (never say 'correlation' again: on Christian tradition, contemporary context and interruption), Boeve enumerates three presuppositions of the modern correlation method.

(1) The correlation method is based on an analysis of the contemporary situation in terms of secularization.

(2) The modern theologians using this method have great faith in the modern project of progress and emancipation.

(3) They are convinced that there is no contradiction between modernity and the essence of Christianity.

39. See e.g. A.T. VAN LEEUWEN, *Christianity in World History: The Meeting of the Faiths of East and West*, London, Edingburgh House Press, 1964 and E. SCHILLEBEECKX, *Secularization and Christian Belief in God*, in ID., *God the Future of Man*, London – Sydney, Sheed and Ward, 1969, 51-90.

40. L. BOEVE, *Interrupting Tradition: An Essay on Christian Faith in a Post-modern Context* (Louvain Theological and Pastoral Monographs, 30), Leuven – Dudley, MA, Peeters – W.B. Eerdmans, 2003, pp. 45-46.

Moreover, it is important to keep in mind the context in which the correlation method came into being: it has been developed in a society which was still largely Christian or which was at least still familiar with the Christian tradition[41]. These three presuppositions can also be found in the thought of Vattimo. First, he offers an analysis in terms of secularization. Second, as did the enlightened thinkers, he wants to defend freedom and emancipation against the violence of old metaphysical beliefs, myths and ideologies. And third, he understands modernization, interpreted in terms of secularization and as the weakening of strong structures, as the outcome and realization of Christianity.

More recently, however, the modern correlation method has been severely criticized. As Boeve makes clear, its presuppositions have been put into question.

(1) First, it is no longer certain whether an analysis in terms of secularization is still the most appropriate way to understand the contemporary situation. Many sociologists of religion have questioned the classic paradigm of secularization and stated that religion has changed rather than disappeared. As Boeve mentions, there is no longer a monolithic secular culture challenging Christianity. Rather, Christians are confronted with a wide multiplicity of religions and ideologies.

(2) Second, the modern project of progress and emancipation, in which the modern theologians had such a great faith, has been put into question. Post-modern philosophers have criticized the modern master-narratives as hegemonic, violent and totalitarian.

(3) Third, the compatibility of Christianity and modernity has been put into question. Anti-modern theologians state that their modern colleagues are merely conforming Christianity to a sinful and arrogant modernity; while those inspired by post-modern sensibilities evaluate the modern correlation method as an unjustified theological recuperation, attempting to render Christian again things that are not or no longer Christian.

Moreover, we should take into account that the still largely Christian society in which the correlation method has been developed has disappeared. As a result, interpreting human experiences, such as the desire for fulfilment and liberation, immediately as Christian experiences is probably no longer accepted by those having these experiences[42]; which amounts to saying that the correlation method has simply lost its starting point.

The most important problem of the modern correlation method is that it ultimately leads to a relativization of the narrative particularity of Chris-

---

41. L. BOEVE, *Zeg nooit meer correlatie: Over christelijke traditie, hedendaagse context en onderbreking*, in *Collationes* 34 (2004) 193-219, esp. pp. 202-203.
42. BOEVE, *Zeg nooit meer correlatie* (n. 41), pp. 202-204.

tianity. To demonstrate this, we can refer to another aspect of modern theology, namely the way it often dealt with the Bible. Confronted with the fact that the natural sciences seemed to refute many details of the Gospel narratives, modern theologians often reacted by making a distinction between the message of the Gospels and its narrative expression. In this regard we can refer to Rudolf Bultmann's project of demythologization. Bultmann stated that the biblical world view is thoroughly mythological and can, as such, no longer be adopted by us, modern humans living in an age of science. It is, however, according to Bultmann, possible to extract a timeless and eternal message from the Gospels. Unfortunately, when Bultmann formulated this unchanging basic message, it proved to be by and large his very particular Heideggerian, existentialist philosophy. This is the deadlock of any attempt to deduce a timeless basic message from the Gospel narratives: it always tends to end up reading back a particular contemporary philosophy into the Gospel. In this way, the Gospel narratives become only a 'narrative doubling' of that philosophy and, as a result, the question very quickly rises why we should hold on to these often difficult and obscure narratives, when we can read the same philosophy in all clarity in the philosophy text books.

The same question should be asked to Vattimo. He pleads for a spiritual reading of Scripture[43] and even for a drastic secularization of the doctrine of the Church. He even speaks about a "demythification" of dogma and morality, which he describes as "the removal of all the transcendent, incomprehensible, mysterious and even bizarre features" from the doctrine of faith[44]. The question certainly should be asked whether in this way Vattimo is not reducing Christianity to some vague doctrine, in which, in the end, the biblical God completely disappears from view and is replaced by an abstract and formal principle, that of the caritas? Would that not be the logical outcome of Vattimo's undertaking? And, as a result, do we not have to conclude that he does not fulfil his promise, namely that of taking seriously again the God of the Bible?

In summary, we can state that Vattimo is not a consequent nihilist. In order to be so, he would have to admit and even stress that also his principle of the caritas is arbitrary. Yet, his ethically inspired rejection of relativism prevents him from doing this. *On the other hand, he is too nihilistic to be able to really take seriously the natural sciences.* For, in order to do so, he would have to admit that, though also natural scientists

43. VATTIMO, *After Christianity* (n. 9), p. 45.
44. VATTIMO, *Belief* (n. 1), pp. 54-55.

approach reality with the help of paradigms and theoretical schemes, natural science has nevertheless a privileged access to that reality. His nihilism, however, prevents him from doing so. *Finally, he is also not able to take seriously the God of the Bible.* For, that God is much too metaphysical and Vattimo is much too modern to return to such a God. He cannot and does not want to return to the old beliefs because they have been, and still are, a source of intolerance and violence. So, when dealing with the Bible, he is repeating the strategy of many modern theologians. As they have done before him, he tries to deduce a basic message from the biblical text and finds that core in the ideas of kenosis and caritas. In this way, however, is he not ultimately, as we have seen, reducing the narrative particularity of the Bible to a vague and soft message on friendliness? And is he not reducing the biblical story on God's kenosis in Christ to a narrative double of his own nihilistic philosophy? Moreover, why attempting a return to the Bible in the first place? Is it not because he wants to avoid the relativist consequences of his philosophy and is in need of something to supplement that philosophy?

In this way, Vattimo seems to appear as the prototypical post-modern believer, struggling as he is to reconcile the several influences also experienced by every Christian in our post-modern situation:

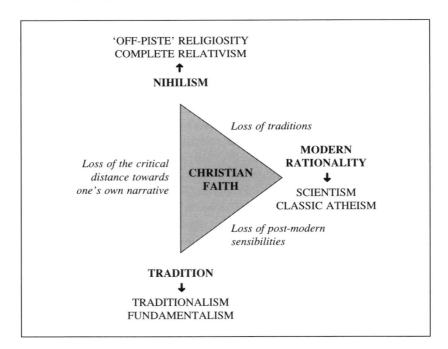

Today Christian faith always exists in an area of tension constituted by three poles (the three angular points of the triangle in the scheme above), namely (1) consequent nihilism, (2) modern (scientific) rationality and (3) Bible and tradition. Each of these poles is a constitutive element of a Christian faith that wants to be alive and contemporary, and not merely a relict from a long gone past: (1) consequent nihilism means that we take seriously post-modern sensibilities such as the awareness of radical plurality and the unfounded character of particular positions, (2) modern rationality implies the critical distance towards our own tradition as condition for freedom, and (3) without some link to the Christian tradition, there simply is no Christian faith anymore.

When we try to escape from the area of tension by taking recourse to one of the poles, we fall back in an undesirable position (indicated by the arrows): (1) withdrawing in consequent nihilism leads to complete relativism, (2) making modern rationality absolute leads to scientism and reductionism, and (3) taking refuge in tradition leads to traditionalism.

Each of these undesirable positions is also linked with a certain position on the religious field that implies that two of the three elements constitutive of a living Christian faith are lost. (1) Relativism is linked to the "autonomous, diffused, 'off-piste' religiosity" identified by sociologist Yves Lambert and which "is illustrated mainly through variables which are less typically Christian"[45]. Such post-modern religiosity often turns religion into life-style, reducing it to a product in the religious market place. This relativism implies both the loss of the integrity of the Christian tradition, which is reduced to merely material for the construction of the own religious identity and the loss of the critical distance towards the own narrative. This means that two sources of interruption by a transcendent instance (tradition, rationality) are eliminated. (2) Scientism is linked to classic atheism. It implies both the loss of traditions (which are left behind in so far as they are irrational or an obstacle for emancipation) and the loss of post-modern sensibilities. Science is posited as the sole way to truth. All language games are subjected to scientific language. God is rejected because God's existence cannot be established by scientific experiment. (3) Traditionalism is linked with fundamentalism. It implies both the loss of modern critical rationality and the loss of post-modern sensibilities.

Also when we try to reduce the tension by eliminating one of the poles (when we posit ourselves on one of the sides of the triangle), we loose a

---

45. Y. LAMBERT, *A Turning Point in Religious Evolution in Europe*, in *Journal of Contemporary Religion* 19/1 (2004) 29-45, esp. p. 38.

constitutive element of a living Christian faith: (1) when we eliminate nihilism, we loose post-modern sensibility, (2) when we eliminate modern rationality, we loose the critical distance towards our own narrative and (3) when we eliminate tradition we loose, of course, tradition.

To conclude, what we can learn from Vattimo is that it would seem that the only way to have a living and contemporary Christian faith is by remaining in the tension area sketched above. Any attempt to escape from it will result in the loss of one or more elements that are necessary for a Christian faith that wants to be more than a fossil from the past.

frederiek.depoortere@theo.kuleuven.be   Frederiek DEPOORTERE

'AND THERE SHALL BE NO MORE BOREDOM'

METAPHYSICS AND PARTICULARITY IN CONTEMPORARY PHILOSOPHY (HEIDEGGER, LEVINAS AND MARION)

Wir müssen vorraussetzen, daß es Wahrheit gibt
Martin Heidegger, *Sein und Zeit*, p. 227

Ours is not the first time that philosophy has entered the theological domain. Nowadays one witnesses a turn to religion in leading philosophical circles. There is Jean-Luc Marion who points to the phenomenological possibility of revelation, there is Emmanuel Levinas who speaks of God only in the encounter with the other person. And there is Heidegger, who probably more than any other thinker, influenced theological questioning. 'The end of metaphysics' indeed has become a slogan, and one often supposes it to be overcome by the simple fact of saying these words. As if, however burdened we were with the troubling message issuing from Nietzsche and Heidegger, we were – suddenly – able to tear off the shadows of the metaphysical God, and free ourselves from that terrible metaphysics that has caused us to mis-represent the relation with God. Thereto we embrace particularity, we are hiding in stories – albeit most often in negative theological clothing. We are eager to grant our narrative its limits, and thereby, we like to believe, its openness to otherness. In this essay, I want to question this tendency to overcome metaphysics, by pointing to the limits of its enterprise.

In the wake of Nietzsche, 'metaphysics' has been interpreted as a flight into otherworldliness, opposing to the sensible and material world a realm of supersensible entities, be it 'God' as in Christianity or 'ideas', as in Platonism. The appraisal of history and historicity that in the aftermath of Nietzsche's groundbreaking work has had the upperhand – consider, for instance, Marx' utopia – could not break the spell of the 'critical reserve' that reached us through Nietzsche's philosophy. Ironically, quite the opposite seemed to be the case and despite the laughing and dancing of Nietzsche's mad men struggling against the will to power, it seems that we are witnessing the appearance of a haunting nihilism. We find ourselves in a world without god(s), without any orienting guidelines – a world for which there is no manual. It is from this perspective that the GOA-project, aiming at some sort of reconciliation between history, particularity and truth, is a tantalising endeavour. Do we not hear in this pro-

ject once again the troubling question Lessing posed to his contemporaries as to how to reconcile history and contingent materiality with the
concept of eternal truth?

This essay portrays the way in which particularity makes it appearance
in contemporary philosophy. Heidegger, Levinas, and Marion are called
upon to seize this turn to particularity and singularity. Marion, Heidegger and Levinas frame their thought around that which might counter the
prevailing reckoning with beings and objects. Philosophy, they argue, has
preferred controllable, foreseeable and 'present-at-hand' objects[1]. Heidegger's *Sein und Zeit* was concerned precisely with showing how our
particular being-in-the-world hardly encounters objects at all. In its stead,
it is our dealings with things ready-to-hand that Heidegger sought to
describe. It is, in this way, that one can interpret the critique of metaphysics as a critique of the tendency to regard 'objects' and 'objectivity'
as the sole way to acquire truth. The critique of metaphysics can therefore also be seen as a critique of the scientific worldview, that is, as a critique of science as the sole path to truth about the supposedly external
world, as a critique of the thought that science is able to provide an adequate and transparent account of the world 'as it is in itself'. It is in this
sense that all these thinkers are querying for an other account of our particular and historical encounter with world than the one that, in philosophy, came to be known as the correspondence theory of truth, truth is
'*adaequatio rei et intellectus*', the correspondence between the thing in
itself and the thing as it is thought or represented.

My aim is twofold. On the one hand, I will depict the manner in which
Heidegger, Levinas and Marion try to surpass this narrow view of attain-
ing truth, by respectively 'being', 'the Other' and 'givenness', but, on the
other hand, I hope to provide some evidence as to why these attempts
seem not to succeed. Indeed, I will show how in all three of these thinkers
the thought of an adequate and transparent view on particularity can, after
all, be obtained. It, therefore, appears that we can surpass metaphysics
only by presupposing it, that is, by never being able to surpass it. It is this
paradox, I will contend, that needs to be thought through, and which
forces one to handle the phrase 'overcoming metaphysics' not only with

---

1. One can think here, respectively, of the idol in Jean-Luc Marion's works, which is
measured by the subject's gaze, the derived nature of *Vorhandenheit* or present-at-hand
objects in Heidegger's *Sein und Zeit*, and the category of the Same in Levinas, that functions precisely as an expression of a foreseeable, powerful and 'totalitarian' gaze of the
subject. For a fuller discussion of this matter, and the question whether what these authors
oppose to these 'objects' *really* is opposed to it, see J. SCHRIJVERS, *Ontotheological Turn-
ings? Marion, Lacoste, and Levinas on the Decentring of Modern Subjectivity*, in *Modern
Theology* 22 (2006) 221-253.

the greatest care, but also with suspicion. Hence the title of this paper which somewhat stretches Levinas' contention in *Otherwise than Being* that the encounter with the other liberates one from boredom[2]. It is, indeed, in theses like this that a return of metaphysics might be suspected. I would like to gain an understanding for the view that 'overcoming metaphysics' might itself be yet another metaphysical convulsion, another way to retreat in "illusion, intoxication and artificial paradises"[3]. Thus, one must question metaphysics as much as its supposed overcoming.

The paper closes with the consequences this 'overcoming' of metaphysics might have for theology. It is indeed barely noticed that Heidegger and Levinas *share* a similar disdain for the theological enterprise. Therefore, my question is simply does the turn to the particularity of being in a world necessarily entail a reluctance towards theology? Or, can particularity, on the other hand, serve as an impetus to rephrase theological questioning? Is the existential analytic of Heidegger, as much as it re-opens the question of being, not equally important to re-open the question of God, that is, of God's Incarnation?

I. MARTIN HEIDEGGER: *DASEIN*, METAPHYSICS, AND *DASEIN*'S METAPHYSICS

In *Sein und Zeit*, Heidegger launched an attack on the idea of *truth as adaequatio* or as contemporary thought has it, truth as representation. This correspondence between the thing in itself and the thing-as-it-is-thought is said to have as its presupposition being-in-the-world[4]. Truth as correspondence, according to Heidegger, rests upon something like a condition of possibility that Heidegger calls "'true' in a still more primordial sense"[5].

Truth as correspondence tends to forget that, for something to be true in this way, this something must first *appear* or *show itself* – phenomenologically – to be true. Phenomenology investigates, not primarily the

2. E. LEVINAS, *Otherwise than Being, or Beyond Essence*, Pittsburgh, PA, Duquesne University Press, 2002, p. 124, "Substitution frees the subject from *ennui*, that is, from the enchainment to itself".

3. LEVINAS, *Otherwise than Being* (n. 2), p. 192, n. 21.

4. M. HEIDEGGER, *Sein und Zeit*, Tübingen, Niemeyer, 2001, pp. 219 ff; ID., *Being and Time*, trans. J. Macquarrie and E. Robinson, San Francisco, CA, Harper and Row, 1962, pp. 262 ff.

5. HEIDEGGER, *Sein und Zeit* (n. 4), p. 220; ID., *Being and Time* (n. 4), p. 263. Compare however HEIDEGGER, *Sein und Zeit*, p. 145; ID., *Being and Time*, p. 184, where Heidegger asks *why* beings would be understood, "if they are disclosed in accordance with their condition of possibility"?

judgement, but the appearing of a particular appearance of which we, then, can predicate something of something. For instance, for a judgement, say, 'the table is brown', to be able to correspond to a certain state of affairs, it is first necessary that this table shows and reveals itself as brown. For something to reveal itself, however, it has to occur within *Dasein's* comprehension of being-in-the-world. Truth, thus, presupposes *Dasein*; it is only as and to *Dasein* that something can show itself as true or that something, i.c. the table, is uncovered as brown. This 'discovery' is possible only since to-be *Dasein* is essentially 'uncovering' (*Entdecken*), since to-be *Dasein* is already dwelling amongs beings (*Entdecktheit,* uncoveredness). However, this 'uncovering' is not at *Dasein's* disposal. As such, it is possible only on the basis of a more primordial disclosedness of the world that gives a particular existence (*Dasein*) to itself in the modus of being-uncovering. *Dasein*, thus, presupposes truth. *Dasein* is already "in the truth", it is thrown – *Geworfen* – into truth, that is, I, and every individual existence, is thrown into being-disclosing, always and already disclosing a certain world.

Heidegger is quick to point out that the 'truth' of this being-thrown into a world does not mean that *Dasein* is, or has, from time immemorial, been "introduced to all the truth"[6]. Rather, Heidegger tries to convey that this being-thrown into the disclosedness of world is always and already twofold, not only do I understand my own being-uncovering in terms of the world, and from out of (an imitation of) the behaviour of others, but also from out of my own most disclosing of world which time and again is mine and mine alone. It is important to note that Heidegger does not *oppose* – in a dialectical fashion – 'Eigentlichkeit' and 'Uneigenlichkeit' as unconcealment over against concealment. The first is not, and can never be, a permanent state of *Dasein*, since being proper with respect to, for instance, this table necessarily entails that one is improper towards other beings in the room. The second, inauthenticity, is not the total absence of unconcealment. To be sure, the inauthenticity of 'the They' is a concealment, but it is a concealment that does not notice its own concealment. On the contrary, it regards to be this comportment toward being*s* as the only way to relate to being-in-the world, "idle talk [...] develops an undifferentiated kind of intelligibility, for which nothing is closed off any longer"[7]. The fallenness of 'the They', therefore, seems to consist in a certain temptation to conceive of its comportment towards beings as a total and transparent unconcealment[8]. The conclusion seems to be that, for Heidegger,

6. HEIDEGGER, *Sein und Zeit* (n. 4), p. 221; ID., *Being and Time* (n. 4), p. 263.
7. HEIDEGGER, *Sein und Zeit* (n. 4), p. 169; ID., *Being and Time* (n. 4), p. 213.
8. Compare HEIDEGGER, *Sein und Zeit* (n. 4), p. 173; ID., *Being and Time* (n. 4), p. 217,

'authenticity' or a proper comportment towards the being of beings cannot be conceived of as the total absence or the privation of everything improper, whereas the simple and plain 'Verfallen' (fallen-ness), out of which the proper comportment emerges, *does* not notice its own concealment and regards therefore its comportment to beings, as for instance, the table, as the total absence of anything that would be a concealment.

For example suppose I look at this table, and then say to you 'this table is brown'. What is happening? I convey something about something to you. You look at the table, shrug your shoulders, and agree. But the very fact that you agree, Heidegger is implying, is dependent upon two things. First, it is dependent upon the fact, that in and through the assertion 'the table is brown', I communicate myself as being a *Dasein* that always and already dwells among beings that are ready-to-hand, and second, that in and through my communication of this assertion you as well can bring yourself into your awareness of a being as being-uncovering of entities within-the-world. The conclusion seems to be that, for Heidegger, truth does not so much reside in the judgement or in the assertion, taken by itself, but in speech, in our speaking together of being always and already thrown into a world, that is, both in that its "being-with is limited to a determinate circle of others" and "alongside a definite range of entities within-the-world"[9]. This is so because, at the moment of the assertion and our agreement, the uncoveredness of the table is still preserved. It is this preservation of the uncoveredness of this individual table as a brown table that accounts for the fact that the judgement or the assertion relates and corresponds to the entity about which it is an assertion.

And yet, Heidegger stresses that, for the judgement 'the table is brown' to be true, it is not necessary that one brings oneself face to face with the table, that one, as Husserl would say, has to experience the table 'in person'. After all, it is possible to speak about this table (or, of course anything else) in a proper manner while not being near to the table. What matters to Heidegger seems to be a certain modification in the understanding of the relation between the assertion and the entity being spoken of. That there is this relation, one will recall, stems from the uncoveredness of the table which is preserved in the assertion. However, once asserted the judgement, becomes "as it were ready-to-hand which can be

"Curiosity, for which nothing is closed off, and idle talk, for which there is nothing not understood, provide themselves [...] with the guarantee of a 'life' which, supposedly, is genuinely 'lively'".

9. Respectively M. HEIDEGGER, *Einleitung in die Philosophie* (Gesamtausgabe, 27), ed. O. SAAME – I. SAAME-SPEIDEL, Frankfurt-am-Main, Klostermann, 1996, p. 334, "Mitsein mit Anderen ist eingeschränkt auf einen bestimmten Umkreis", my translation, and HEIDEGGER, *Sein und Zeit* (n. 4), p. 221; ID., *Being and Time* (n. 4), p. 264.

taken up and spoken [of] again"[10]. It is here that the tendency to fall as
a peculiar relation to the uncoveredness of a being comes into play. As
one will recall, 'the They' is portrayed by Heidegger as doing what everyone does, speaking about that which everyone speaks about, reading what
others have read and so on[11]. In paragraph 44 of *Sein und Zeit*, Heidegger understands the being-uncovering of the They as "the absorption in
something that has been said", that is, "that which has been expressed as
such takes over Being-towards those entities which have been uncovered
in the assertion"[12]. Thus, in the idle talk of the They the relation between
the assertion and that which is spoken of changes, no longer is the assertion 'the table is brown' something that occurs within in a world and in
our speaking of entities within-the-world, in its stead 'the table is brown',
and the relation between the assertion and that which it speaks of,
becomes present-at-hand. The uncoveredness that was preserved in the
utterance is substituted for a, as it were, scientific and logical, understanding of the utterance: "Uncoveredness of something becomes the
present-at-hand conformity of *one* thing which is present-at-hand – the
assertion expressed – *to* something else which is present-at-hand – the
entity under discussion"[13]. In this way, "the uncoveredness (truth)
becomes, for its part, a relationship between things that are present-at-
hand (*intellectus et res*) – a relationship that is present-at-hand itself"[14],
or as it is stated in *Einführung in die Metaphysik,* "truth loosens itself,
as it were, from beings, this can go so far that saying again becomes mere
hearsay"[15]. What worries Heidegger here is that philosophy, instead of
reflecting upon being in a particular world, returns to the Cartesian and
thus mathematical understanding of world as, say, a collection of things
present-at-hand, a collection of objects that can be adequately defined
and, above all, correctly represented by a subject. Philosophy, again,
reflects upon present-at-hand beings, and does not even ask what Being,
that is, what being-in-a-world might mean. Philosophy, turning to Heidegger's critique of Descartes at the beginning of *Sein und Zeit,* "pre-
scribes for the world its 'real' Being"[16].

10. HEIDEGGER, *Sein und Zeit* (n. 4), p. 224; ID., *Being and Time* (n. 4), p. 266.
11. HEIDEGGER, *Sein und Zeit* (n. 4), pp. 117-129, and 167-179; ID., *Being and Time*
(n. 4), pp. 153-168, and pp. 210-224.
12. HEIDEGGER, *Sein und Zeit* (n. 4), p. 224; ID., *Being and Time* (n. 4), p. 267.
13. HEIDEGGER, *Sein und Zeit* (n. 4), p. 224; ID., *Being and Time* (n. 4), p. 267.
14. HEIDEGGER, *Sein und Zeit* (n. 4), p. 225; ID., *Being and Time* (n. 4), p. 267.
15. M. HEIDEGGER, *Einführung in die Metaphysik*, Tübingen, Niemeyer, 1958, pp. 141-
142; ID., *Introduction to Metaphysics*, trans. G. Fried and R. Polt, New Haven, CT, Yale
University Press, 2000, p. 198.
16. HEIDEGGER, *Sein und Zeit* (n. 4), p. 96; ID., *Being and Time* (n. 4), p. 129. For this
critique, see also F. RAFFOUL, *A chaque fois mien. Heidegger et la question du sujet*, Paris,

In his later works, as is well-known, Heidegger pondered upon the experience of being that the Greeks entertained. For this, he returned to the understanding of 'physis', as "a manner and mode of becoming present"[17]. But how then do beings become present and how are they uncovered? Beings come into the open (or they withhold themselves). If they appear, this simultaneously entails that they have a certain look (idea), which is both how a being "presents itself to us, re-presents itself and as such stands before us" and *that* something that comes to presence indeed is coming to presence[18]. The table, for instance, presents itself, but both in the sense *that* there 'is' this table and in the sense *what* the table is, i.e. as brown or as a plateau with four legs. The look – idea –, whàt a being shows itself to be like, is equated with the being(ness) of a being, *that* there is (this) being in this or that way is substituted for "that which comes to presence in the whatness of the look"[19]. A being thereby is determined from out of its lying present as *a* being for a subject, a table is what it is because it shows itself most often as a brown plateau with four legs. The being of the being table is that it 'is' as being a plateau with four legs; the 'real' being of a being is held in thought, rather than encountered from out of a particular event. The 'idea' or essence determines how the being of the table will come into presence, namely, as a being that lies present for a subject. The consequence is that the very fact *that* a being is able to lie present for a subject is considered to be secondary. Herein lies the birth of the so-called modern subject. A being is if and only if it a) shows itself *to* a subject, and b) if this subject can determine both that a being shows itself at all and what this being shows itself to be like, that is, if the subject can re-present the thing *for itself* the being of a being as if it was an object.

Thus, metaphysics loosens this second sense of becoming-present from the first sense, and detaches the 'look' that a being gives 'to us' from the

---

Galilée, 2004, p. 58 and 65, where Raffoul relates the everyday interpretation of the Self to 'the category of the subject' which the everyday understanding 'continues to produce' and p. 77-83. Raffoul refers us to M. HEIDEGGER, *Sein und Zeit* (n. 4), p. 318; ID., *Being and Time* (n. 4), p. 366.

17. HEIDEGGER, *On the Being and Conception of Physis in Aristotle's Physics B, 1*, in *Man and World* 9 (1976) 219-270, esp. 239. Contrary to many commentators, I do not support the view that there is a major difference between the Heidegger of *Sein und Zeit*, and the later works. For this view, see not only the book by Raffoul, but also L.P. HEMMING, *Heidegger's Atheism: The Refusal of a Theological Voice*, Notre Dame, IN, University of Notre Dame Press, 2002.

18. Concerning what follows, see HEIDEGGER, *Einführung* (n. 15), p. 136ff; ID., *Introduction* (n. 15), pp. 190ff. The citation is from HEIDEGGER, *Einführung*, p. 138; ID., *Introduction*, p. 192.

19. HEIDEGGER, *Einführung* (n. 15), p. 138; ID., *Introduction* (n. 15), p. 193.

becoming-present of a being itself. In metaphysics, this what-ness – *essentia, hupokeimenon, subiectum* – becomes the norm and the criterion for anything to show up. That the table is brown, for instance, is no longer inferred from the fact that the table presents itself from out of a world, but it is because the table has this or that essence – chemical elements that produce a certain pigment – that this table *must* be brown. Metaphysics retains of the becoming-present of being(s) merely the 'whatness' of a being and understands the very appearing of a particular being, its 'that-ness', always and already from out of its 'whatness'. Therefore, this what-ness or essence comes to determine also how beings in particular appear, that is, they will always and already appear as a privation, a fall and defect over against the whatness that "is most in being about beings"[20]. It is, according to Heidegger, Plato who develops this metaphysical pattern for the first time, now "beings themselves, which previously hold sway sink to the level of that what Plato calls 'me on' – that which really should not be and really *is* not either – because beings always deform the idea, the pure look, by actualising it, insofar as they incorporate in matter"[21]. It is for Plato the pure abstracted look that matters, the material being is only a deformed, inferior copy of the being as it is hold in thought. Thus, now that which appears, that which makes an appearance is but a seeming and a defect, in short, a fall over against the "whatness" of the particular being which, "is now what *really* is"[22] – Derrida *avant la lettre*!

How does all this relate to Christianity? Not only do we have here the means to grapple with that which Heidegger understood as ontotheology – 'God' as the uncaused cause and unmoved mover who founds or holds together the (immaterial) essences of the diverse material (but imperfect) beings[23] –, but also one can understand Heidegger here as a thinker who

20. HEIDEGGER, *Einführung* (n. 15), p. 140, 'das Seiendste am Seienden'; ID., *Introduction* (n. 15), p. 196.
21. HEIDEGGER, *Einführung* (n. 15), p. 140; ID., *Introduction* (n. 15), p. 196.
22. HEIDEGGER, *Einführung* (n. 15), p. 140; ID., *Introduction* (n. 15), p. 196.
23. For a good introduction to Heidegger's thinking on ontotheology, see I. THOMSON, *Ontotheology? Understanding Heidegger's* Destruktion *of Metaphysics*, in *International Journal of Philosophical Studies* 8 (2000) 297-327. It is important to note that this thinking of being as ground (*Grund*) works both ways. A being is what it is, because its being *corresponds* to, and thereby is grounded by, the essence of the being. However, this essence of a being needs itself to be grounded, since the essence of a being, in one way or another, is dependent on the (material) existence of the being of which it is supposed to be the essence (in the same way as one abstracts from the diverse, empirical tables a unified essence of them). Therefore, ontotheology has recourse to God, as the one who, supposedly un-founded or founded in and through Godself, grounds the essence of beings, by just thinking them or, which is structurally the same, by creating these (imperfect) beings of which God is said to have the perfect idea eternally. But, precisely, 'God' can only appear

is careful not to think of our particular being-in-the-world as a defect, or, to use theology's terminology, as a fallen or sinful creature that has to deplore its own status. Rather Heidegger is concerned to retrieve from this conception of a being's appearing and appearance as a defect a more original openness toward being. This new conception would no longer regard the becoming-present of a being merely to be a defect. The seeming of every appearance of a being is not something that really should not be, but the appearance of such a seeming necessarily belongs to the way in which being itself makes itself known to human beings. This seeming, then, need not be understood in a privative manner, as something that should not be. It is part and parcel of this more original truth – aletheia as the event of being – that tries to think through that which, according to Heidegger, Aristotle already understood, namely, that 'the being of *Dasein* can be concealing *and* unconcealing' at the same time, and that this double possibility is distinctive of the truthfulness of *Dasein*'s existence[24]. To return to our example, it is not that the seeming and the appearance of the table must be opposed to an adequate judgement, to, let's say, a scientific and 'correct' understanding of the table. It is, rather, the other way around, such a scientific understanding is only possible since (un)concealment is already in play. It is not that the judgement unconceals the 'essence' of the table, and is 'more true' than all the rest we would like to say about tables, for instance in poetry. Both are possible only on the basis of authentic and inauthentic (un)concealment, which, in turn, is possible on the basis of *Dasein*'s being-thrown-in-the-world as concealing and unconcealing. What happens in the distinction between ready-to-hand and present-at-hand judgements is that in the latter the reference to this particular being, and to *Dasein*'s relation toward this being, is interpreted in a metaphysical way. When the judgement becomes the locus of truth, this judgement is always and already an utterance about something that lies present (as objects lie present) for someone – the subject – for which this object already lies present and to which this object presents itself. What is overlooked is that the 'truth of the truth of the judgement' lies in *Dasein*'s appropriating it in its own way –which always is both concealing *and* unconcealing, improper and proper. In short, that *Dasein* has to be – or, rather *is* – its own 'Entdecken' from out of a particular world is no longer 'in the picture'.

here in the light of a correspondence theory, as that being, be it the highest, who assures a perfect fit between the essence, the 'being', of a being and that being itself. On this vice versa of ground and grounding, see also J.-L. MARION, *The Idol and Distance: Five Studies*, trans. T.A. Carlson, New York, Fordham University Press, 2001, pp. 9-19, esp. pp. 14-15.
    24. See HEIDEGGER, *Sein und Zeit* (n. 4), p. 226; ID., *Being and Time* (n. 4), p. 268.

But can it be? Heidegger's own account of overcoming metaphysics is a complex one. He seems to be sure, though, that one can only surmise what this 'overcoming' might be, if one understands metaphysics *from within*. The famous 'Schritt zurück' tells us precisely that, the step back out of metaphysics occurs only when metaphysics is properly understood[25]. On the other hand, whether this 'overcoming' can ever succeed is not clear. Not only is the appearance of 'ground', the movement which seeks to found finitude in an infinite and unfounded instance, portrayed as a "perhaps necessary illusion of foundation"[26], but it is also confirmed that "fallenness is a natural condition of *Dasein*"[27]. Throwness and falling are constitutive for *Dasein*'s being-in-the world. As such, they account for what Heidegger has called the inauthentic manner of being-in-the-world. We have already noted that this inauthenticity deals only with beings in their presence rather than with their becoming-present, and that it therefore has lost sight of the being of this or that being. In other words, the openness towards being is closed off in favour of a disclosing of beings which, in turn, is regarded to be as the only possible way of relating to being. It is, at least in *Sein und Zeit*, not sure whether this inauthentic manner is something that can be overcome. Indeed, authenticity is not a permanent state of *Dasein* opposed to the metaphysical nature of inauthenticity and throwness. Rather, it 'has its moments' for instance, angst, sickness, boredom and death[28]. In these moments – similar to Kierkegaard's 'kairos' – the tendency of fallenness to understand itself out of the world and out of beings disappears, but only to show, or to make appear that *Dasein* already has to be its world, that is has to be its openness toward the world and toward being, in short and more familiar terms, what is revealed is that this *Dasein* is the being that has to be its

25. Heidegger's *Die onto-theo-logische Verfassung der Metaphysik*, in his *Identität und Differenz*, Pfullingen, Günther Neske, 1976, p. 41, "Der Schritt zurück bewegt sich daher aus der Metaphysik in das Wesen der Metaphysik".

26. HEIDEGGER, *Einführung* (n. 15), p. 2; ID., *Introduction* (n. 15), p. 3. Iain Thomson seems to prefer an affirmative answer to this question of 'overcoming', see his *Ontotheology?* (n. 23), pp. 317-320. For an answer in the opposite direction, consult J. ROBBINS, *Between Faith and Thought: An Essay on the Ontotheological Condition*, Charlottesville, VA, University of Virginia Press, 2003, p. 3, who develops an understanding of ontotheology as an "inevitability, if not a necessity, of thought".

27. See M. HEIDEGGER, *Vier Seminäre*, Frankfurt am Main, Vittorio Klosterman, 1977, p. 100, "Das ontologisch verstandene 'Verfallen' ist sogar der Naturzustand des Daseins…". My translation.

28. It is barely noticed that Heidegger, at least at one place in *Sein und Zeit*, regarded sickness to play a similar role than that of death. See HEIDEGGER, *Sein und Zeit* (n. 4), p. 247; ID., *Being and Time* (n. 4), p. 291. On boredom, see, of course, M. HEIDEGGER, *Die Grundbegriffe der Metaphysik: Welt – Endlichkeit – Einsamkeit*, Frankfurt am Main, Vittorio Klostermann, 2004.

own being as a being-with others and entities within-the-world. The inauthentic tendency is not brought to halt, but what now appears is that its
unconcealing is, in fact, at the same time, concealing – a comportment
toward being*s*. Angst and death, one could say, make appear *Dasein*'s
openness – it's *Entdecken, Entwurf, Erschlossenheit* – as such, that is, as
entailing the double possibility of concealing and unconcealing, its relation to (its own) being. But since this authentic way is not a permanent
Zustand of *Dasein*, some have argued that angst and death only show the
inevitable character of fallenness[29]. However, to look at in this way,
already presupposes that this fallenness has to be conceived of as a defect
to be overcome which, as we have shown above, is not at all what Heidegger intended. Rather, and instead of deploring the inevitability of fallenness as such, one should ponder whether the tendency to regard the
appearance of beings to be a defect, that is, the tendency to regard fallenness and throwness to be a *privatio*, as "that which really should not
be" is inevitable[30].

It is not sure whether Heidegger, at least in 1927, succeeded in doing
this. Indeed, if one can maintain that Heidegger was seeking to disclose
another way of comporting toward being, it is highly disturbing precisely
how he reached to this conclusion. Throwness is part and parcel of
being-in-the-world, and it is characteristic of throwness that it is disclosed "more or less plainly and impressively"[31]. Thus, the disclosing of
throwness admits of degrees: It is either disclosed totally or in a lesser
manner. This point needs, of course, to be proven. It is Heidegger himself who, though through a single occurrence, delivers this proof. Those
instances that make appear our being-in-the-world seem like a sort of
maximum of disclosed-ness. So, for instance, angst is accompanied by the
selfsame of "the disclosure and the disclosed"[32] which is, in both cases,

29. As R. VISKER does in his *Truth and Singularity: Taking Foucault into Phenomenology*, Dordrecht, Kluwer Academic Publishers, 1999, pp. 23-46, and pp. 55ff.

30. One should not here that the 'opposition' between the inauthenticity of the 'They'
and authentic Dasein might point to the persisiting influence of his early lectures on the
phenomenology of religion. See M. HEIDEGGER, *Phänomenologie des Religiösen Lebens*
(Gesamtausgabe, 60), Frankfurt-am-Main, Vittorio Klostermann, 1995, for instance, p.
103.

31. HEIDEGGER, *Sein und Zeit* (n. 4), p. 270; ID., *Being and Time* (n. 4), p. 315.

32. HEIDEGGER, *Sein und Zeit* (n. 4), p. 188, "die existenziale Selbigkeit des
Erschließens mit dem Erschlossenen"; ID., *Being and Time* (n. 4), p. 233. Heidegger is concerned with the difference between fear and anxiety, respectively ID., *Being and Time*
(n. 4), pp. 179-182 and pp. 228-235. Whereas fear is fear for an object of any kind, anxiety, according to Heidegger, is not determined by any object whatsoever. 'Das Wovor der
Furcht', 'that, in the face of which one is fearful', can be anything (fear for snakes, heights,
water etc.). The point is that anxiety does not have such a determinate object: "that in face
of which one has anxiety is being-in-the-world as such"; "what oppresses us is not this

the (possibility of) being-in-the-world as such. Indeed, that which is disclosed is the same as that what which discloses, i.e. being-in-the-world or *Dasein* as such. However, is such a maximum not the recurrence of truth as correspondence?

Before pondering upon the question what this recurrence might mean for metaphysics, and more importantly, faith, we shall now turn briefly to the accounts of Levinas and Marion. Indeed, if one wants to overcome metaphysics, and if this means to overcome, first of all, the theory of truth as adaequatio, one should be wary of yet another occurrence of this theory. In Levinas, we will show, it is the Other who coincides with him- or her-self and who, therefore, is able to tear the subject out of its situatedness – Levinas' term for *Geworfenheit* –, in Marion, on the other hand, the gifted is, time and again, defined as the sum of his or her responses toward givenness.

II. EMMANUEL LEVINAS: ANOTHER METAPHYSICS?
THE METAPHYSICS OF THE OTHER

This section sketches how Levinas undertakes a similar enquiry than Heidegger. I will focus on two main issues: first, Levinas' insistence that all knowledge entails the correspondence theory of truth, that is, in his terms, the reduction of the other to the same, and second, Levinas' concern that this primacy of the theoretical attitude devalues both men and God.

For Levinas, all knowledge – especially that of being – exposes a will to power or a reduction of the Other to the same. To return once again to our example as to how the table appears to consciousness. Strictly speaking, I only perceive two or at times three legs of it. That I still refer to the table as a table arises from the fact that I, according to Husserl, constitute its fourth leg. But, precisely, this constitution is a mental act that already presupposes what a table in general has to look like, for instance, as a plateau with four legs. Thus, constitution presupposes an essence of

---

or that ... it is rather the possibility ... of the world itself". Similarly, Heidegger thinks about [that] which anxiety is anxious ('Das, *worum* die Angst sich ängstigt'): whereas fear fears about the very being or object it fears about, the 'why' of anxiety coincides with its 'Wovor'. I am not only anxious *for* the fact of being-in-the-world, this being-in-the-world is also *why* I am fearful. But this being-in-the world is not an object or a being. On the contrary, "The pure 'that it is' shows itself, but the "whence" and the "whither" remain in darkness", see ID., *Being and Time* (n. 4), p. 173. Thus, when 'being-in-the-world' shows itself, nothing really appears, except the fact that I have to be this being in face of which I am anxious.

the table, and this essence, in turn, functions as the horizon which secures the unity or univocity of tables in general. However, this essence of the table already precludes certain tables to appear – one need only think of certain designer tables. Of course, this is rather innocent an example, but one can think of other instances in which this reduction occurs. When, for instance, human beings came to be defined as 'animal rationale', this idea of the essence of men could not prevent that *certain* men and women were excluded from this definition. One need only think of the 15th century debate whether or not Indians had a soul. Herein also lies Levinas' critique of the Husserlian account of intersubjectivity of the alter ego. According to Husserl, it is on the basis of my own experiences, my own context and history that I determine the existence and the signification of the other. For example, if I see someone crying, I infer from seeing his or her tears, that he or she must be sad, since I know that when I cry, I am sad. For Husserl, the other is an other ego, the other is *like* me. But, Levinas would add, such a conception presupposes that between the other and me there is room for comparison, or at least a common horizon from which to judge our different experiences. Moreover, the commonality of such a common horizon, would, according to Levinas, already presuppose the postulate of a transcendental but solipsistic subject from which the signification of the other's tears emanate and to which the precise signification of these tears would also return[33].

For Levinas however, there is one instance that always escapes this violent reduction. That instance, of course, is *the face of the other*. The face of the other questions consciousness' mode of procedure. Consciousness proceeds through reducing otherness to the same, that is, through an operation of knowledge that reduces a phenomenon to that which it can adequately describe and define or represent of the phenomenon. In the face to face with the other, Levinas contends, consciousness is put into question. It cannot make sense of the other, since this otherness of the other, the transcendence of the human person, resists all identification or adequation. The other's face is not reducible to some com-

---

33. See E. HUSSERL, *Cartesianische Meditationen: Eine Einleitung in die Phänomenologie*, ed. E. STRÖKER, Hamburg, Felix Meiner Verlag, 1995, pp. 120-123 and pp. 125-127, but also the concept of 'empathy' in E. HUSSERL, *Ideas Pertaining to a Pure Phenomenology and to a Phenomenological Philosophy. Second Book: Studies in the Phenomenology of Constitution*, trans. R. Rojcewicz and A. Schuwer, Dordrecht, Kluwer, 1989, pp. 99-102 and pp. 171-178. For Levinas' critique, see E. LEVINAS, *Totality and Infinity: An Essay on Exteriority*, trans. A. Lingis, Pittsburgh, PA, Duquesne University Press, 2002, pp. 67 ff and p. 210. LEVINAS, *Otherwise than Being* (n. 2), seems to abandon the critique of the alter ego, but not the critique of 'empathy', if the latter is taken as presupposing some sort of shared horizon "common to several souls", see on this non-commonality between the Other and I, pp. 126-128.

mon characteristics, or 'form', that this particular other would share with others[34]. Hence what would be Levinas' account of racism[35], reducing black persons to their being black, his or her form or visible attributes, is to commit an injustice towards the black person's face, his or her being a unique individual. Indeed, a (white) racist seems to reduce the other, but black, person to precisely his or being black, his or visible attributes. The black person is reduced to being 'nothing other' than his or her blackness. Note that, if racism proceeds thus, it almost automatically extends to all black men and women, since you, as a black person, are nothing other than your blackness, all other black persons are merely instantiations and instances of this essence 'blackness', and thus you will be racist against these others as well. For, if one black person can be reduced to his or her participation in 'being black', the racist will also reduce all the other black persons to what they share with or have in common with this one particular other to whom he or she's being racist. In a Levinasian vein, one could therefore portray the 'end' of metaphysics as the end of thinking about anything or anyone *in general*, since the dignity of a human being precisely, for Levinas, does not lie in being a member of a particular community, a determinate context, but precisely in being irreducible to that context[36]. Thus, Levinas sets out an opposition between the (invisible) face and the (visible) form of the human person, between the manifestation, the revelation and the epiphany of the face, and the ordinary phenomenality of objects and beings, between the "pure signification"[37] of the encounter with the other and the 'impure' appearance of a form, already contaminated with the phenomenality essential to being. While the former is an inadequation par excellence, the appearance of the latter is conditioned by the correspondence between the concept and the phenomenon in question. While the former manifests itself "independently of every position we would have taken in this regard"[38], the latter is dependent precisely on the position that the subject assumes over and against the objective phenomenon (like the table can only appear to a subject over and against the horizon of a table in general).

34. See, for instance, LEVINAS, *Totality and Infinity* (n. 33), p. 66, "[T]he manifestation of a face over and beyond form. Form – incessantly betraying its own manifestation, congealing into a plastic form, for it is adequate to the same – alienates the exteriority of the other".
35. For this example, see: VISKER, *Truth and Singularity* (n. 29), pp. 328-329 and p. 349.
36. LEVINAS, *Totality and Infinity* (n. 33), p. 23, "signification without a context".
37. LEVINAS, *Otherwise than Being* (n. 2), p. 143. But note that, on this very page, this 'pure signification' seems to stand in need of something that, at the very least, resembles racism: at the opposite of this 'pure' signification, one will find "the babbling language, like […] the discourse of a stranger shut up in his maternal language".
38. LEVINAS, *Totality and Infinity* (n. 33), p. 65.

However, we need to question how Levinas maintains this distinction. It might be that the inadequation of the face with the form in turn is dependent on the correspondence theory of truth, since after all the manifestation of a face entails "a coinciding of the expressed with him who expresses"[39]. Thus, it seems that one can escape the (metaphysical) correspondence theory of truth only be presupposing it. But what does Levinas mean? The face to face with the other originates in language. In the expression, that which is manifested coincides with the one manifesting him- or herself. On one condition, however, that the one manifesting him- or herself attends to its own manifestation, that is, is able to correct its own manifestation. According to Levinas, the Saying always differs from the said[40]. For instance, it is not me who has to decide on the meaning of the tears of the other, the truth of these tears has to be communicated by him or her. It is only in discourse that the transcendence of the Other makes its appearance. But only to disappear, to leave its trace. The Other can tell me that the tears are faked, since he or she is rehearsing for a play, but he or she can just as well retrieve even this statement on a later occasion. Thus, it is not what the Other says that is the trace of transcendence, but the fact that he or she speaks and that he or she, in this way, is always able to retrieve *what* he or she has said, in short, able to *teach*[41] me. Thus, the transcendence of the other lies in his or being always other, always more or less different from that which is said, in its irreducibility to the form of the said[42]. However, this difference is, in one way or another, subordinated to the possibility that the one speaking coincides with that which is said. Thus, if there is a difference between the face – the Saying – and the form – the said –, it can only be so because the one instance that makes a difference, i.c. the other, is excepted from this difference, the other can coincide with him- or herself, and is, therefore, able to point me to the difference between his or her saying and his or her said. It seems, therefore, that the difference between the Saying and the said can only be maintained if this difference is measured by the possible adequation between the one manifesting and the manifested. This raises some important questions. First, it indicates that the difference between the face

---

39. LEVINAS, *Totality and Infinity* (n. 33), p. 66, with parallels on p. 296, "in expression the manifestation and the manifested coincide", and p. 262 "an essential coinciding of the existent and the signifier".

40. LEVINAS, *Otherwise than Being* (n. 2), pp. 45-51, 153-162.

41. For instance, LEVINAS, *Totality and Infinity* (n. 33), p. 51. In expression, the Other is supposed to 'break through all the [...] generalities of Being, to spread out in its 'form' the totality of its 'content', finally abolishing the distinction between form and content".

42. The frequent recurrence, for instance, in quarrels of formulas as 'Did I say that?' or 'I did not say that!' might be elucidated thus.

and the form might be not that clear-cut as Levinas would have wanted it[43]. Second, this might entail that the encounter with the other is not so much "without context" as Levinas contends, and that, if one wants to take particularity seriously, one best not dreams of a "total transparence"[44] in these matters. One might surmise that it is, perhaps, not me who is the modern subject, but the Other. Here is not the place to tackle all these questions, but suffice it to say that the return of truth as mere more 'adequate to the same' might point to the fact that 'overcoming metaphysics' may not be as easy a task as it nowadays sometimes seems.

One must note, however, that the encounter with the other in Levinas' thought does not allow one to speak of God any more than the *causa sui* of metaphysics did. God, for Levinas, is not the "first other", but "other than the other" and "transcendent to the point of absence"[45]. One can understand Levinas here trying to avoid an ontotheological interpretation of his thought. God is not the first other that bestows upon the human other the power to make an appeal to my responsibility. Such a line of reasoning would correspond to ontotheology in this sense that it would inappropriately transpose the encounter with the other to an experience of God, as ontotheology interprets the encounter with beings in the light of a first being which, supposedly, renders the encounter with beings reasonable and justified. There is, at least in *Otherwise than Being*, no immediate linkage between the other and God. One can argue, though, that

43. One wonders whether the 'application' of Levinas' thought in the circles of psychotherapy does not entail a serious risk. Indeed, what if the other cannot speak, or has lost the ability to speak, and speaks perhaps only a sort of "babbling language, like the expression of a mute", see LEVINAS, *Otherwise than Being* (n. 33), p. 143. This is another example as to how Levinas' attending to the other might lead into terror. Another, but similar, objection comes from Finkielkraut who has stated that "such is the task of the doctor without frontiers; he is too busy filling the hungry mouth with rice, to still have time to listen to what it is [it is] trying to say". The citation comes from A. FINKIELKRAUT, *La humanité perdue: essai sur le XXe siècle*, Paris, Seuil, 1996, p. 128, and I take it as cited in R. VISKER, *Is Ethics Fundamental? Questioning Levinas on Irresponsibility*, in *Continental Philosophy Review* 36 (2003) 263-302, esp. 276-277. For another critique of the sharp distinction between face and form, see J.-L. MARION, *From the Other to the Individual*, in R. SCHWARTZ (ed.), *Transcendence: Philosophy, Literature, and Theology approach the Beyond*, New York, Routledge, 2004, 43-59. The few instances in which Levinas gives a positive meaning to non-verbal language may not be able to counter these objections. For Levinas on non-verbal language (and thus certainly a nuance on the strict distinction between face and form), importantly, in both Levinas' *Totality and Infinity* and *Otherwise than Being*: respectively p. 262, "the whole body – a hand or a curve of the shoulder – can express as a face", and p. 85 "skin [...] is always a modification of the face. See also p. 192 n. 27, "the unity of the face and the skin".

44. See LEVINAS, *Totality and Infinity* (n. 33), p. 182.

45. LEVINAS, *God and Philosophy*, in ID., *Of God who Comes to Mind*, trans. B. Bergo, Stanford, CA, Stanford University Press, 1998, p. 69. Compare LEVINAS, *Otherwise than Being* (n. 2), p. 123.

Levinas tried to make the concept of creation acceptable in philosophical circles. The encounter with the other is a signification without context; the other signifies "prior to all civilization"[46]. The other's ability to utter an appeal, to appeal to my responsibility towards him or her is not dependent on certain qualities he or she would have. The Other appeals, is a face, regardless whether his or her form is black or white, regardless whether his or her *Geworfenheit* in a particular world[47]. Thus, the appeal is *ex nihilo*. Furthermore, since the appeal ties me to the other before I can even choose this fraternal responsibility toward him or her, and since this appeal is at the same time, in this appeal of one other, an appeal of *all* the others, it opens to the thought of one single humanity. The appeal, therefore, is the awakening in me of the trace of *creation*[48]. God is and must be 'absent' from this encounter. It concerns a responsibility to-the-other, and not primarily to God, and every mention of the word 'God' in this context can always be another way of fleeing my responsibility for-the-other. Therefore, God is not and cannot be the explanation of what happens between the other and I. This responsibility is unique – no one can be responsible in my place –, and every reason one comes up with to explain the for-the-other, be it 'for the love of God', or the more common love of one's self, *already* has acknowledged the diachronic appeal that has come towards the self in and through the uttered Sayings of the Other. Levinas' describes the responsible subject in an account close to the Heideggerian *Jemeinigkeit*, as "a recurrence to oneself out of an irrecusable exigency of the other"[49]. According to Levinas indeed, the passivity towards the other, therefore, inevitably has recourse to activity

---

46. LEVINAS, *Otherwise than Being* (n. 2), p. 198 n. 6.

47. On this topic, see Levinas' insistence on the "desituating of the subject", in *Ibid.*, e.g. p. 48 and p. 146. On the other hand, Levinas' *Totality and Infinity* interprets the Heideggerian Geworfenheit in an existentialist fashion as being born in an absurd world, see e.g. p. 140.

48. LEVINAS, *Totality and Infinity* (n. 33), pp. 104-105, and ID., *Otherwise than Being* (n. 2), p. 105. But is not Levinas, by pointing to creation as the fundamental connection between the other and I, resolving yet again the professed irreducibility and non-commonality between the Other and me? What the other and I have in common is, according to Levinas, perhaps not that we both are finite (see LEVINAS, *Otherwise than Being* [n. 2], p. 83), nor the visible attributes we might share, it is that we both are created beings and therefore connected as liturgical and 'theological' beings.

49. See for this LEVINAS, *Otherwise than Being* (n. 2), pp. 102-114, esp. 109 and esp. p. 148, "this reverting of heteronomy in autonomy"; E. LEVINAS, *Un Dieu Homme*, in ID., *Entre Nous: Essais sur le penser-à-l'autre*, Paris, Grasset, 1991, 69-76, esp. p. 76, and also Levinas' study *Énigme et phénomène*, in ID., *En découvrant l'existence avec Husserl et Heidegger*, Paris, Vrin, 2001, 283-302 in which it is asserted that "subjectivity becomes the locus of truth"; see p. 291 and pp. 296 ff. Levinas himself, however, is quite ambiguous on the relation of this singular responsibility to the Heideggerian *Jemeinigkeit*, compare for instance E. LEVINAS, *Otherwise than Being* (n. 2), pp. 126-127.

and autonomy. But this 'recurrence of the self' is not the return of transcendental subjectivity, it is the fate of men of flesh and blood that precisely because already woven into the web of creation and responsibility are unable to flee the decisions one('s self) has to take regarding the other and to God. It is with this recurring of self as Marion wrote of the gifted or the *adonné* in his *In Excess*: "the *ego* keeps, indeed, all the privileges of subjectivity, save the transcendental claim to origin"[50]. One of these privileges, at least in phenomenology, is indeed that nothing comes to pass – appears, presents itself – save through the subject[51]. That is why the 'God' professed in Levinas can equally be a God 'otherwise than being' or "a cry [...] of a sick subjectivity"[52]. Therefore, there is nothing that incites one to speak of God when confronted with the other but, on the other hand, since human beings are always already tied to the other, precisely to the other as an invisible, incomprehensible and unrepresentable face, the question of God can be re-opened, but as a question the self poses. "It is up to us, or more precisely, to me to hold fast or to discharge this God without courage, exiled since bound up with the defeated, the persecuted, thus, ab-solute, disarticulating in this way the moment itself in which he offers and proffers himself, un-representable"[53]. Before meditating upon the consequences of this for theology, we will now turn briefly to the thought of Jean-Luc Marion who develops an account very similar to that of Levinas.

III. JEAN-LUC MARION: RESPONDING AD INFINITUM?

Marion shares with Levinas the concern of thinking through, after metaphysics, the death of God[54]. The death of the metaphysical God is

50. J.-L. MARION, *In Excess. Studies of Saturated Phenomena*, trans. R. Horner and V. Berraud, New York, Fordham University Press, 2002, p. 45.

51. One can recognise this "recurrence" to some extent already in *Totality and Infinity*. See Levinas' remark on Descartes at pp. 54ff, "[God] subtends the evidence of the *cogito*, according to the *Third Meditation*. But the discovery of this metaphysical relation in the *cogito* constitutes chronologically only the second move of the philosopher". The first one is, of course, the evidence of the cogito itself.

52. LEVINAS, *Otherwise than Being* (n. 2), p. 152.

53. LEVINAS, *Énigme et phénomène* (n. 49), p. 291. My translation.

54. For Marion on metaphysics, see MARION, *The Idol and Distance* (n. 23), pp. 9-19; ID., *God without Being. Hors-texte*, trans. T.A. Carlson, Chicago, IL, The University of Chicago Press, 1991, pp. 25-52; ID., *La fin de la fin de la métaphysique*, in *Laval théologique et philosophique* 42 (1986) 23-33; ID., *Métaphysique et phénoménologie: une relève pour la théologie*, in *Bulletin de littérature ecclésiastique* 94 (1993) 189-206; ID., *La science toujours recherchée et toujours manquante*, in J.-M. NARBONNE – L. LANGLOIS

for both the opportunity for a renewed consideration of whether and how 'God' can appear in philosophy. Both will maintain, as Heidegger has done before, a strict distinction between philosophical and theological discourse. However, one can argue that Marion presents a radicalised version of Levinas' philosophy: "one should generalize to each being given the status of beyond beingness"[55]. This is, in fact, what his magnum opus, *Étant Donné*, has accomplished. Givenness gives itself in every phenomenon as a non-metaphysical present (gift). Phenomena come into being, but without that being determining essentially this or that particular being. Phenomena always exceed the gaze of the subject that tries to constitute it as an object, that is, that tries to describe it adequately. Take for example, the saturated phenomenon of the event. No one has seen the battle of Waterloo[56]. The event cannot be described adequately, but appeals to a multiplication of views that altogether forbid constituting it as one single object. Saturated phenomena have no essence, no constant presence to which one can constantly and confidently refer, but appeal to the subject to align itself to its appearance. This appearance is a gift and therefore, it cannot be, as was the case with the correspondence theory of truth, foreseen – the presence of this or that chemical element predicts that the table must be brown –, its invisible present arrives a surprise, unforeseen – as when one suddenly notices that the brown of this particular table here resembles the table in my parent's house. This non-essential character of the gift extends to all phenomena. Though to some extent everything that happens to the subject is considered to be an object, this never suffices to explain the object as it gives itself, an echography makes the birth of a child to a certain extent foreseeable, at least for the doctors, but this anticipation of its birth cannot annul the fact that this birth will be lived, at least by the parents, as unforeseeable[57]. The birth of the child, and for that matter all phenomena, give themselves as an event and summon the subject to receive itself from that which it receives. Hence Marion's thought that, for phenomena to appear, they require an individua-

(eds.), *La métaphysique: Son histoire, sa critique, ses enjeux*, Paris, Vrin, 1999, 13-36 and, ID., *The 'End of Metaphysics' as a Possibility*, in M.A. WRATHALL (ed.), *Religion after Metaphysics*, Cambridge, Cambridge University Press, 2003, 166-189.

55. MARION, *Métaphysique et phénoménologie* (n. 54), p. 198, "il faudrait généraliser à chaque étant-donné le statut d'un au-delà de l'étantité (epekeina tes ousias)".

56. For this example, see J.-L. MARION, *Étant Donné. Essai d'une phénoménologie de la donation*, Paris, PUF, 1998, pp. 318-319; ID., *Being Given. Toward a Phenomenology of Givenness* (Cultural Memory in the Present), trans. J.L. Kosky, Stanford, CA, Stanford University Press, 2002, pp. 228-229.

57. See for this also MARION, *Étant Donné* (n. 56), p. 261; ID., *Being Given* (n. 56), p. 186, and MARION, *In Excess* (n. 51), pp. 35-36. This example is taken from E. FALQUE, *Phénoménologie de l'extraordinaire*, in *Philosophie* 78 (2003) 52-76, esp. 62.

tion[58], the phenomena give their selves when giving themselves. The birth of my child is, at least for me, a *singular* event. Moreover, this event singularises me as the gifted, its happening happens to give me to myself as the one who is given, in and through the reception of the birth, to the child. I am now given to the child as a father, and this is what individualises me. Therefore, the gifted plays a secondary role toward givenness in that it is already a response to an appeal. However, it pertains to the gifted to show or to make appear what is given to him, that is, the appeal shows itself in the response of him or her to whom it is given. Marion will gladly admit that he borrows this thought from Levinas. However, the generalisation of the '*epekeina tes ousias*' requires one to consider the appeal anew. Herein lies Marion's critique of Levinas[59]. It is, according to Marion, not clear whether the appeal of the face in Levinas comes from the other or from God. This 'à Dieu' even risks to name that which cannot be named, to suppress the anonymity and ambiguity of the appeal, in short, "to dissolve the very thing [it was] to protect"[60]. Hence Marion's insistence on the pure form of the appeal, that cannot be identified, that is, thus, radically anonymous, and that, if it was to be identified, can only be named inappropriately, since pertaining to the gifted's limited and finite response[61].

What concerns us here is, however, that there is an appeal, and one cannot not respond to this "always already there interpellation"[62]. This is why Marion can determine human beings as follows: "the history of the gifted is due to the *sum* of its responses"[63]. But, precisely, *what is*

---

58. MARION, *Étant Donné* (n. 56), p. 197, 225, and esp. p. 363; ID., *Being Given*, p. 139, 159, and esp. p. 264.

59. For this critique, see J.-L. MARION, *The Voice without Name: Homage to Levinas*, in J. BLOECHL (ed.), *The Face of the Other and the Trace of God: Essays on the Philosophy of Emmanuel Levinas*, New York, Fordham University Press, 2000, 224-242, esp. pp. 226-228.

60. MARION, *The Voice without Name* (n. 59), p. 227. It is worth noting that Marion deploys a similar critique towards Heidegger. By baptising the 'Es' of 'Es gibt' as 'Ereignis', Heidegger is supposed to have withdrawn from the radical anonimity of the appeal and risks bringing into phenomenology an indeterminate force, a foundation, the shadow of a being, in short, a Giver. For this critique of Heidegger, see MARION, *Étant Donné* (n. 56), pp. 54-60; ID., *Being Given* (n. 56), pp. 34-39, and also MARION, *The 'End of Metaphysics' as a Possibility* (n. 54), pp. 182-183.

61. In fact, "seul l'amour pourrait s'y risquer", that is, "only love could risk it", see MARION, *Étant Donné* (n. 56), p. 146; ID., *Being Given* (n. 56), p. 101. Interestingly, the 'à Dieu' indeed recurs in Marion's *Le phénomène érotique*. See J.-L. MARION, *Le phénomène érotique: Six méditations*, Paris, Grasset, 2003, pp. 318ff. For a summary and a critique of this book, see my review in *Louvain Studies* 28 (2003) 167-171.

62. See MARION, *Étant Donné* (n. 56), p. 303. The translation has "an always already there interpretation", see ID., *Being Given* (n. 56), p. 217.

63. See MARION, *Étant Donné* (n. 56), p. 407; ID., *Being Given* (n. 56), p. 295. Italics

this sum and who or what is going to determine it? In any case, that such a sum of responses is possible shows that the overcoming of the metaphysical adaequatio may not have succeeded. Indeed, simply the fact stating that such a sum could be envisaged, seems to imply the recurrence of a God's eye point of view, that is, the thought that someone or something can oversee the totality of my responses. One could agree that this sum of my responses is obtained at the occasion of my death. However, since it is considered to be a hermeneutics without an end, the responses of those that respond to my death would have to be included in the sum of my responses. This sum of responses is therefore, in this world, always to be deferred and postponed. Therefore, one can surmise whether an instance 'not of this world', distant from the world[64], could oversee the sum of my responses. A god's eye point of view indeed!

IV. Toward a Theology of Incarnation
The Consequences of Overcoming Metaphysics for Faith and Theology

We have seen that Heidegger, although keen to keep our openness, *Dasein*'s openness, to *aletheia* – openness –, open, has recourse to the concept of adequatio to define this 'proper' openness. There are moments when that which is disclosed is the same as that what is disclosing itself, it's self. Levinas responds that this openness is already filled in through the other, and that this other coincides with him (or her) self, that which is spoken is the same as the one speaking. And, if it is not the same, the being that speaks can at least correct itself. Thus, point to an eventual, a 'possible', adaequatio. Marion, in turn, responds to Levinas, that this filling-in is filling in too much, and that therefore there is no reason to prefer the other, instead of something without name. It is well-known that Heidegger had a somewhat peculiar relation to Christianity, and that he

mine. Such an almost mathematical understanding of phenomena (be it human beings or other) is by no means a single occurrence, see MARION, *Étant Donné* (n. 56), p. 319; ID., *Being Given* (n. 56), p. 229: "knowledge of the historical event becomes itself historical, like the sum of the agreements and disagreements among subjects partially constituting a nonobject always to be re-constituted", and also MARION, *In Excess* (n. 50), p. 72, where the painting is said to "expos[e] itself as the potential sum of all that which all have seen, see, and will see there".

64. For this, consult J.-L. MARION, *God without Being: Hors-Texte*, trans. T.A. Carlson, Chicago, IL, University of Chicago Press, 1995, pp. 83-84, where the 'without being' can only occur through "a view instituted at and in a certain distance".

more often than not, claimed philosophy to be thoroughly atheistic. In *Metaphysische Anfangsgründe der Logik*, for instance, Heidegger deals with the accusation in a way that is at least ambiguous: on the hand he concedes the atheistic character of his thinking insofar it intends the ontic involvement of his fundamental ontology, but on the other hand, he asks "might not be the presumably ontic faith in God be at bottom godlessness? And might not the genuine metaphysician be more religious than the usual faithful, than the members of a 'church' or even the 'theologians' of every confession?"[65]. This conclusion hopes therefore to show that, 'after' metaphysics, the link between faith and atheism in all three thinkers is tightened to such an extent that one might even ask whether atheism does not genuinely belong to faith of any kind. In the later *Einführung in die Metaphysik*, Heidegger develops a similar mode of procedure towards the question of faith. "Anyone for whom the Bible is divine revelation and truth has the answer to the question 'Why are there beings at all instead of nothing?' before it is even asked"[66]. However, even here Heidegger kept open the possibility of an authentic questioning, even in matters of faith. For faith, of course, has no answer, only faith. For faith to be a mode of questioning, it must, according to Heidegger, rid itself not only of the answer that God as Creator answers for the existence of beings, not only of the agreement to adhere to a doctrine somehow handed down, but, most importantly, "continually expose itself to the possibility of unfaith"[67]. Surprisingly, we find Levinas saying the very same thing. For instance, in his *Entre nous*, he writes: "The ambiguity of transcendence – and thus the interplay of the soul going from atheism to faith and from faith to atheism – [is] the original mode of God's presence"[68]. One might even surmise in Marion's phenomenology a similar critical stance toward dogmatics. It is indeed difficult to see how the emphasis on God's incomprehensibility can be reconciled with the Church as the guarantee of truth. Here we agree with Robyn Horner who states that (Marion's) phenomenology does open onto theology, but that the theology "that

65. See M. HEIDEGGER, *Metaphysische Anfangsgründe der Logik im Ausgang von Leibniz* (Gesamtausgabe, 26), Frankfurt-am-Main, Klostermann, 1978, pp. 177 and 211. The citation is taken from M. HEIDEGGER, *The Metaphysical Foundations of Logic*, trans. M. Heim, Bloomington, IN, Indiana University Press, 1984, p. 165, and I take it as cited by R. BERNASCONI, *Heidegger in Question: The Art of Existing*, New Jersey, NJ, Humanities Press International, 1993, p. 37. For a good account of Heidegger's stance in these matters, see L.P. HEMMING, *Heidegger's Atheism: The Refusal of a Theological Voice*, Notre Dame, IN, University of Notre Dame Press, 2002.
66. HEIDEGGER, *Einführung* (n. 15), p. 5; ID., *Introduction* (n. 15), p. 7.
67. HEIDEGGER, *Einführung* (n. 15), p. 5; ID., *Introduction* (n. 15), pp. 7-8.
68. LEVINAS, *Un Dieu Homme* (n. 49), p. 72.

emerges from this opening cannot rest secure in dogma", since "the hardening of dogma betrays transcendence"[69].

The overcoming of metaphysics thus not only means that we cannot consider faith to be an object that is freely at our disposal, or as Marion would put it, an "idiomatic prolepsis of a blunt certitude"[70]. It might also mean that we, when and if theologians, have to lose our faith in order to, in one way or another, gain it. It is worth noting that this supposedly overcoming of metaphysics also entails not only the end rational theology, as explained above, but also that of natural theology. This is obvious in for instance Levinas' rejection of theodicy. 'God' cannot be invoked to explain (or to justify) the suffering of human beings. God is no longer to be viewed as the 'reason' or 'cause' of humanity's violence and miseries, since God is transcendent to history. Every attempt to explain history on the basis of the will of God is, according to Levinas, an infliction towards precisely the victims of that history and, most often, such an attempt cannot prevent this God of becoming "a protector of all the egoisms"[71]. Heidegger would argue that developing a theology on the basis of, for example, the natural sciences disregards the fact that these sciences are already indebted to the metaphysical theory of truth as correspondence. These sciences are therefore ontic, and deal with being only in terms of beings. Therefore, they cannot instruct us on what is means to be, and even less on how God might come into being.

This means that faith is not primarily dogmatical, but ethical (Levinas) and pragmatic (Marion), a faith moreover "in which it is no longer a matter of naming or attributing something to something, but of aiming in the direction of..., of relating to..., of comporting oneself toward..., of reckoning with..."[72]. It is not that this faith would become purely and solely pragmatic, it is the admission of the fact that the debate of whether or not a referent applies to this faith can only begin in and through precisely such a pragmatic stance, in which faith first and foremost has become a question. This is the reversal. Theology can no longer start with the assertion that "God is...", it can only start in prayer or in ethics, as if a *fides qua* without the blunt beforehand certitude of *fides quae*. This, therefore, seems to be the lessons to be learned from Heidegger, Levinas and Marion.

69. R. HORNER, *The Betrayal of Transcendence*, in SCHWARTZ (ed.) *Transcendence* (n. 43), 61-79, esp. p. 75.

70. MARION, *God without Being* (n. 54), p. 71.

71. LEVINAS, *Otherwise than Being* (n. 2), p. 161.

72. J.-L. MARION, *In the Name: How to Avoid Speaking of 'Negative Theology'*, in J.D. CAPUTO – M.J. SCANLON (eds.), *God, the Gift, and Postmodernism*, Bloomington, IN, Indiania University Press, 1999, 20-42, esp. p. 30.

But, then again, is it? Have we not shown how all three of them have recourse to the concept of a (possible) *adaequatio* to make acceptable their respective accounts of overcoming metaphysics? Indeed, matters are more complicated still. We have seen how both Levinas and Marion try to institute an invisible instance that accounts for our being-in-the-world. For Levinas, the other does not and cannot appear 'in' the world. For Marion, that which is shown of givenness through the gifted, is not 'of' the world. For both then, a certain distance from the world and its history is the condition of the correct interpretation of this world. That there is no metaphysical 'otherworldliness' involved, does not mean, however, that the metaphysical mode of procedure has been surpassed. Indeed, both have recourse to the metaphysical theory of truth as correspondence to justify such an instance distinct and distance from the world. This might mean that we, philosophers and theologians alike, have not yet succeeded in thinking particularity otherwise than as a fall. For Marion, givenness 'arrives' in the world from a distance which is not of this world, but which could only be given. This again seemed to imply that there is an instance that could obtain an adequate sight of the gifted, that could oversee the sum of my responses, as if I was only an object, transparent to whatever kind of subject. One can argue that the same goes for Levinas. If the other is a subject that possibly can coincide with him- or herself, what else could I be then his or her object? What, in the end, would the difference be between the "extraversion of the interiority of the subject [...] visible before making himself a seer" that, moreover, leaves me "without secrets", and the object "of which everything is exposed, even its unknown"[73]? Is not the attempt to signify particularity and facticity fully by an otherwise than being in se a metaphysical endeavour? Does not the attempt to make facticity 'in general' signify fully through an *'epekeina tes ousias' already* presuppose that the signification of particularity is given in an incomplete and imperfect manner? Trying to think facticity otherwise than as a fall, that, thus, is the way to overcome metaphysics. However, the lessons learned from these philosophers seem equally to instruct us that we lack the means to do so. It is possible, on the other hand, that these means come to us from theology. Indeed, "an incarnational paradigm operates on the basis of an affirmation of finitude"[74]. However, we need to be wary to interpret this incarnation in a

---

73. Respectively LEVINAS, *God and Philosophy* (n. 45), p. 75; ID., *Otherwise than Being* (n. 2), p. 138, and, ID., *Humanisme de l'autre homme*, La Flèche, Brodard et Taupin, 2000, p. 68.

74. In this we agree with J.K.A. SMITH, *Speech and Theology: Language and the Logic of Incarnation*, London, Routledge, 2002, p. 156.

symbolic manner. After Levinas, and his devastating critique of symbolism, an account as that of James Smith's somehow just seems to beg the question. An incarnational paradigm does not ask whether "there is any way to 'say' that which *exceeds* and resists language?"[75], it asks, rather, whether, from the part of finitude, it can still be maintained that there *is* something *exterior* to language. Only then, the question of incarnation really becomes the question of God, even when it is already a question posed to God. This entails, of course, that the distinction between a pure and an impure encounter disappears as well[76]. However, is this a lesson for which one is in need of philosophy – is it really up to us to make such a distinction? It is equally a lesson that Christ has taught us.

As for Lessing's question regarding truth, which, of course, also *already* presupposed that history is marked by a fall, we would advice to follow the lead of Heidegger: "We do not want to get this scruple out of the way. Let us, for the meanwhile, permit it to stand on the way on which it comes to meet us. For it could be that this way is no longer a way"[77].

joeri.schrijvers@theo.kuleuven.be   Joeri SCHRIJVERS

---

75. *Ibid.*, p. 9 *et passim*. My italics.
76. *Ibid.*, p. 169.
77. M. HEIDEGGER, *Was heisst Denken?*, Tübingen, Max Niemeyer Verlag, 1971, p. 156; ID., *What is Called Thinking?*, trans. J.G. Gray, New York, Harper and Row, 1968, p. 137.

THEOLOGY AND THE QUEST FOR TRUTH
SOME CONCLUDING REMARKS

Quid est veritas? Pilate's question to Jesus[1] reflects humankind's age-old search and longing for 'the truth'. This collection of essays treats this same quest for truth, be it in the context of theology. Orthodoxy – theological truth – and how to determine and articulate it, constitutes the core question of this volume and the underlying interdisciplinary research project. Interdisciplinary, while it wants to bring together two differing, even often conflicting methodologies – that of church history and of systematic theology – when it comes to the study of orthodoxy and its definition.

As already has been stated in the introduction to this collection of research-based essays, the core hypothesis of the underlying interdisciplinary research project on theology and the question of truth, is formulated as the (postmodern) rediscovery of the importance of (radical) particularity being a possible key to examine the nature of, and to determine (theological) truth[2], as well as its impact on re-formulating both historical and systematic conceptualisations of that same truth through tradition.

As the project involves church-historical as well as systematic-theological research into the nature and the determination of theological truth, both disciplines are 'present' in the different essays, and this along the lines of three major avenues of research, being the study of Augustine, theology in confrontation with (post-) modernity and a confrontation of contemporary theological epistemologies with the above-mentioned role of particularity.

Studying the nature and determination of theological truth claims both in an historical and systematic context, implies asking a fundamental methodological (meta-)question concerning the possibility of (methodological) interdisciplinary cooperation. Following the research hypothesis, both disciplines are in some way united in their attention to the particular and the contingent, and in spite of apparent and seemingly irreconcileable methodological differences, this might contribute to a renewed encounter between them, acknowledging rediscovered particularity to be the major hermeneutical key in this context.

---

1. John 18,38.
2. Cf. Introduction, pp. 1-2.

It lies far beyond the scope of these concluding remarks to come – based upon the presented essays – to a complete and elaborate answer to the research question, its focus, concept and hypothesis. However, since these contributions are the results of a first 'exercise' in the elaborate project's process – the different research projects belonging to the three main lines of research are presented in light of the research question and its hypothesis –, the main emphasis is put on the description of truth's nature and the process of its determination, starting from specific historical-theological cases, as well as from a systematic approach to this question in different – often postmodern – contexts.

Especially the meta-question on a fruitful encounter of both methodologies, will be the subject of further investigation in the course of the project, were the boundaries between both disciplines' methods in particular, will be exceeded by specifically posing the meta-question in light of particular historical and systematic contexts.

But first, with the contributions at hand, we will draw some conclusions, especially with regard to the research hypothesis: (re-discovered) particularity in relation to truth-determination.

I. THE PREDOMINANT ROLE OF PARTICULARITY IN CLAIMING THE TRUTH: CONTEXT, COMMUNITY AND TEXT

It probably goes without saying that research in the discipline of history of church and theology stresses the – often somewhat disturbing – role of contingent particularities in the process of truth-determination. As Wim François expressed it adequately in the closing remarks of his essay[3], historians are most reluctant to make claims of universality, especially when, in light of shifting, particular, highly contingent, often violent and contradicting contexts in which truth-claims apparently emerge, systematic theologians present the same facts and factors from the perspective of transcendency – often with a hint of universal truth in it – being mediated in history[4]. Hence, it is not difficult to understand François' concluding remark on the clammy hands of the church historian, who is forced into an ambiguous position: that of preserving (universal) truth-claims in light of a 'particularising' historical-critical methodological approach.

---

3. W. FRANÇOIS, *The Louvain Theologian John Driedo versus the German Reformer Martin Luther: And Who Could Impose Their Truth...*, p. 59.
4. Cf. Introduction, pp. 1, 3-7.

As strange as it may seem, also systematic theologians, describing the human search for truth through issues rooted in a postmodern context, foster the angle of particularity as well. Since the postmodern unmasking of Grand Narratives, systematicians have been engaged in a quest to define theological truth (or what is left of it) by relativising and questioning universal standards and transcendental schemes, resulting in positions taken, on a spectrum varying between either a – very particular – return-to-premodernity strategy producing exclusivist truth claims grounded in 'tradition', or, the acknowledgment that no other than particular (i.e. non-universal) theological truth-claims (in a pluralistic context) can be made, based on nothing more than the personal acceptance of them being-true. Whether, in this case, one can still talk of 'truth', remains – in the writings of several authors – a debatable matter[5].

Particularity thus presents a possible (hermeneutical) key to re-read historical reality and its systematic interpretation, when the question of determination of theological truth arises. Throughout the presented essays, three major issues seem to return when speaking of the role of particularity in this context. They can be grasped in three summarising catchwords: context, community and text.

1. *Context*

The notion of context covers a variety of – historical as well as personal – facts that influenced the way in which people and institutions have discovered and determined theological truth. Attention will especially be paid to the notions of 'biography' and 'ecclesiastical-political context'.

Biographical contextual data – as an expression of radical particularity – played a most important role in this respect. This becomes especially clear when reading the church-historical essays. Without on the one hand walking into the trap of what can be named 'historical conditionality' (e.g.: 'if Luther would not have received his training in Erfurt, he might have drawn different conclusions', etc.), one can, on the other hand, hardly deny the fact that very contingent, particular facts have exerted great influence on this matter. To present just two examples: Augustine and Luther.

As J. Yates has adequately demonstrated, Augustine's preoccupation with manichaeism clearly played a role in the way he offered ways to

---

5. Compare the concluding remarks of F. Glorieux, when evaluating what he calls "Hick's soft reductionism'. See F. GLORIEUX, *Hick's Pluralistic Hypothesis: An Intrasystemic Reading of the Evidence?*, p. 227.

determine the christian biblical canon, being the ultimate source for truth and theological authority. Augustine struggled with the fact that he had been a manichean[6] – apparently even more than having been a rationalist sceptic afterwards –, a 'demon' that had to be squelched on the personal level, and had to be engaged in the public domain[7]. A mixture of what Yates calls 'radically particular'[8] psychological, historical and ecclesiastical factors – summarised in the growing importance of Augustine's position in the North-African church – forced him to react, and led Augustine to engage the manichaeans on three levels – reflecting these contingent factors –: a 'hidden' confrontation with manichaean ideas in not overtly polemic writings, of which the *Confessiones* is the most known example; direct confrontation in polemic anti-manichaean writings; and, later on when the conflict escalated more openly, the definition of the catholic scriptural canon by condamning its manichaean counterpart.

In François' analysis of the conflict between Luther and the Louvain theologians, headed by Driedo, a similar 'particular trinity' can be found: Luther was clearly influenced by three contingent, contextual elements. His training at Erfurt university, a *via moderna* stronghold, introduced Luther to both nominalism or 'terminism'[9], and a humanist reading of Scripture[10], causing his aversion for scholastic conceptual constructions and his particular notion of Scripture being the sole valid way leading us to divine truth. Luther's entrance in the Augustinian order in Erfurt revealed a particular psychological attitude and personality, and stimulated – through the person of his spiritual advisor, vicar-general von Staupitz – enforced Bible-reading and the study of Augustine's works. The same goes for his main opponent in Louvain, Johannes Driedo. Having received his training in Louvain, a typical *via antiqua* school, at the time only slightly and indirectly influenced by humanist methodologies – at least in the faculty of theology –, and in spite of feeling some sympathy for Luther's theories, Driedo vigorously defended the notion of 'tradition' as well as the role of the hierarchy and the pope in defining (theological) truth.

6. Even here, the contingent fact that manichaeans in Asia Minor held different ideas than their North-African – Western – fellow believers, seemed to have played a role. See J.P. YATES, *Augustine and the Manichaeans on Scripture, the Canon, and Truth*, p. 21: "Unlike (at least) some of their co-religionists in other parts of the world, western Manichaeans passed over the entire collection of Jewish sacred texts...".

7. YATES, *Augustine and the Manichaeans* (n. 6), p. 13.

8. *Ibid.*, p. 11.

9. FRANÇOIS, *The Louvain Theologian John Driedo* (n. 3), p. 35.

10. *Ibid.*, p. 36.

In both examples, the influence of the political and ecclesiastical context is clearly shown as well. Augustine's gradual ascent in the context of the North-African Church made him confront the Manichaeans, and ultimately led him to define the Scriptural canon. In the case of Luther, ecclesiastical and political factors – just to mention the initiatives taken by the German princes supporting Luther, the emperor Charles V and pope Adrian VI[11] – played a most important role in the promotion and countering of Luther's movement as well as in the further development of his ideas. The adage *cuius regio, huius religio* does shed a specific light on our research question.

The influence exerted by the notion of context, as expressed in the (discussed) philosopher's/theologian's subjective condition, is also present in the systematic theologian's contributions.

When, for instance, Schillebeeckx developped his criteria for orthodoxy, being the proportional norm, orthopraxis and the decisive role of the experience of the local christian communities, he was clearly influenced by the theological climate of the 1960s, in which Vatican II's openness for the 'secular', the modern world, drew the attention to the incarnated reality of theology. The refining of Tillich's correlation theory can therefore be observed as a logical next step[12].

The same observation can be made concerning the position of F.X. von Baader, the German idealist philosopher who felt himself compelled to react against a Cartesian-Kantian defining of truth as reflected in 'modern sciences' and its "admiration of the *mathesis universalis*"[13]. Baader, who as a mining-engineer stood inside this 'modern' tradition, did not identify truth with an in his eyes too narrow a definition of 'matters being scientifically correct'. Most probably, other backgrounds also played a role in Baader's reaction to the then predominant paradigm. The fact that he had been a product of the early nineteenth century's German *Bildungsideal*, where universities not only trained students with a view to certain professions, but also educated them as human beings in a much broader sense, together with a strong self-consciousness of being a catholic and a religious person, may have influenced him as well in his confrontation with modernity.

The development of Milbank's theory of a tradition-dependant, radical christian 'orthodox' (counter-)narrative, can be explained to have

11. Cf. the second part of *ibid.*, pp. 44-59.
12. A. DEPOORTER, *Orthopraxis as a Criterion for Orthodoxy?*, pp. 172-173.
13. J. GELDHOF, *'Truth' according to the Later Schelling and Baader: An Attempt at Transcending Modernity*, p. 109.

taken shape as a reaction against nihilism, a result of the (post-)modernist slaughterhouse-of-transcendent-ideas.

2. *Community*

In numerous discussions on orthodoxy, the different parties involved refer to the/a community as bearer and guardian of the disputed truth (the true Church); and/or to explanatory or defensive mechanisms inherent to this community (tradition).

This was particularly the case in the first centuries, the ecclesiogenetic age, in which orthodoxy – in light of different challengers – not only became a notion to be defined by referring to the role of the true community of believers, but at the same time, also a notion defining the boundaries of this community, the Church, itself.

As was to be expected, this was clearly the case with Augustine when giving a delineation of the Biblical canon: those adhering different canonical contents (*in casu* the manichaeans[14]) place themselves – through pride and prejudice – outside the *Catholica*. Augustine presented a catholic canon, and corroborated his main argument – the importance of these texts as authoritative sources upon which faith is based – by referring to the role of the Church in the process of preserving and establishing authority, as well as presenting rules for interpretation to its members[15].

Throughout the history of the Church, and especially in moments of crisis, the 'ecclesiastical' argument has been used rather frequently. Driedo, when reacting against Luther's *sola Scriptura*, stressed the importance of the Church, in existence already before Scripture was actually written down, and having received the authority directly from Christ[16]; and of tradition – both through the apostles and the early fathers, and, along the line of the apostolic succession, through the *magisterium* as exerted by pope and bishops – in analysing and interpreting Scripture as the major source for theological truth[17]. In the so-called neo-modernist crisis emerging between two Roman exegetical schools at the end of the 1950s, one can notice a similar process taking place. When disputing the notion of revelation in light of Biblical exegesis, the speculative neo-scholastic party defended a 'propositional view' that can be found in Scripture and tradition, and, is explained by the (ecclesiastical) *magis-*

14. The Manichaean canon existed of four major parts, being the letters of Mani, edited gospels, edited letters of Paul and a collection of 'apocryphal' acts and gospels. See YATES, *Augustine and the Manichaeans* (n. 6), pp. 21-23.
15. *Ibid.*, pp. 26-28.
16. Reference to the gospel of Matthew, 16,18-19.
17. FRANÇOIS, *The Louvain Theologian John Driedo* (n. 3), pp. 38-44.

terium. In this context, the ecclesiology that has been developped, is rather 'conservative', in the sense that it sticks to historical continuity and unchangeable interpretations of truth in the history of the Church[18]. The other party, representing the historiographical approach, refused to attach the same weight to the interpretative role played by the *magisterium* and more easily accepted the possibility of discontinuity and change in the historical context. They also referred to the historicity of the event of revelation, and accepted the authoritative character and powers of the Church; only now the contextual input, the fact that in different contexts, the Church could bring forward varying interpretations, became more or less acceptable; it had no impact on the core of the revealed truth as such[19].

A very specific role for the community in defining and articulating theological truth, can be found in the writings of Schillebeeckx. In his criteria for orthodoxy, the local community of the faithfull plays a decisive role. In Schillebeeckx' view, the experience of accepting theological interpretation of doctrine by local christian communities, and this weighed against experiences and interpretations of other local churches, can be seen as an indication of the working of the Holy Spirit, indicating whether given theological interpretations must be understood to be orthodox or not[20].

Presenting the Church or a community of faithfull being a corroborative argument in defining and articulating orthodoxy has become rather problematic in a postmodern context. At least insofar as the argument is presented as having 'universal' validity. In postmodern theological thinking, however, the notion of 'tradition' has firmly (re-)gained its grounds, since all particular theological rationalities depart from the acceptance of a constitutive tradition that constructs – also in an historical sense – the different narratives.

---

18. See K. SCHELKENS, *Perceiving Orthodoxy: A Comparative Analysis of the Roman Controversy in Catholic Exegesis (1960-1961)*, pp. 156-160.

19. A fine example of this position is a famous article on the *Magnificat* (1903), written by the Louvain Biblical scholar Paulin Ladeuze (P. LADEUZE, *De l'origine du Magnificat et de son attribution dans le troisième évangile à Marie ou à Élisabeth*, in *RHE* 4 [1903] 633-644). In it, Ladeuze meticulously applied historical-critical methodologies to analyse the pericope and to study the songtext's alleged authorship of Maria or Elisabeth. In the end, by way of scientific conclusion, the traditional vision on the authorship is abandoned, but Ladeuze finishes by adding that in spite of the differing scientific reading, in Marian spirituality (or, in faith), the text can still be read as *ipsissima verba Mariae*, a hymn of praise sung by Maria. Ladeuze's position lies remarkably close to the one defended by J. Milbank. See T. JACOBS, *The Problem of a Postmodern (Theological) Epistemology*, p. 69, esp. n. 19, referring to Milbank's *Theology and Social Theory*.

20. DEPOORTER, *Orthopraxis* (n. 12), p.172.

3. *Text*

Within the quest for orthodoxy, authoritative text has played a most important role in delineating and articulating truth. The question particularly regarded Scripture: its canon had to be defined, and, once the borderlines were drawn, proper rules for interpretation had to be presented.

As we have mentioned already, in his confrontation with the manichaeans, Augustine contributed significantly to the delineation of the catholic contents of Scripture. In fact, as J. Yates has put it in his concluding remarks, "at least one avenue for the establishment of truth has been smoothly paved once and for all"[21]. It is interesting to note that Augustine not only defended his canon, but also the immutability of Scripture and its rules for interpretation as established and preserved by the Church[22].

Staying in the tradition of the *inerrantia* and immutability of Scripture, being written under divine inspiration, was the major issue at stake in the modernist crisis and its post-war offshoots. In the eyes of the classical, tradionalist view on Scripture, the implementation of historical- and text-critical methodologies in exegesis that had come into existence in the wake of modern science's development, would endanger the authoritative character of the Bible. Due to the very sharp reaction of the Church, exegesis developed in two mainstream schools of interpretation; on the one hand it retreated completely from theology by becoming a technical study of Biblical literature, while on the other hand, a more theological (or even spiritual) reading of Scripture based upon thorough critical study, saw the light. As the essays by K. Schelkens and J. Mettepenningen have shown, for a long period of time, the Church has been very reluctant to abandon the classical position in favour of the critical reading, for this was considered as rendering truth. This was also due to the fact that the different methodologies became connected to the ecclesiological level as well, confirming the close link between text, Church and orthodoxy: attacking the 'right way of reading the Bible', also meant an attack on the Church itself.

In the postmodernist context, tradition-depending radical epistemologies can be seen as 'texts' as well: one's own narrative as the ground for a – modest – truth-claim.

---

21. YATES, *Augustine and the Manichaeans* (n. 6), p. 30. See esp. n. 54.
22. *Ibid.*, p. 27.

II. BEYOND PARTICULARITY
SUMMARISING REMARKS AND FUTURE RESEARCH SCOPES

Thinking orthodoxy in an historical context, makes it clear that the discovery, determination and articulation of truth was and is highly influenced by contingent, often very radically particular facts and factors. In light of the quest for orthodoxy, (historical) particularity clearly is susceptible to the danger of relativism: facts can never claim universality when everything could have happened differently. Without having to resort to some kind of historical conditionality (or 'if'-ism), it can hardly be denied that certain facts could (contingently) have turned out differently in their historical contexts, thus possibly resulting in a different view on orthodoxy[23].

Thinking truth in a postmodern context, however, remains equally problematic. In order also to avoid the pitfall of relativism on the one hand, and to preserve a minimum of 'universal' validity in a particular truth-claim (if possible at all) on the other hand, thinkers seem to resort to – often tacit and covert – pre-modern style absolute and powerful narratives presented as the only possibility to surpass the omnipresent threat of relativism; or, precisely to very 'particular' presentations of truth-claims inside a specific narrative, being one of numerous possible and different narratives.

By completely 'accepting' a particular narrative, one can avoid the relativist *condition post-moderne* but only within the boundaries of the particular narrative itself; and even, while referring to faith, return to ontotheology, but the question remains whether this does (sufficient) justice to truth in claiming 'universal' validity[24]. In either case however, it remains possible, to articulate something about truth.

---

23. An interesting example in this perspective is that of the 'poverty-movements' in the high middle ages. To some extent the influential order of the franciscans owes – at least in its early days – its continued existence to – the contingent presence of – powerful ecclesiastical protectors, even in spite of the franciscans openly displaying adherence to – already convicted – Waldensian thought and principles (such as Bible-translations in the vernacular, preaching not restricted to the religious or clerics). Other, similar movements did not survive the initially reticent attitude of the catholic Church towards their programs of reform, or – like the *humiliate* –became absorbed in already existing forms of monastic life, thus loosing their original impetus for reform.

24. E.g., in the works of MacIntyre and Milbank, to name just two important authors, the former can be reproved to introduce an unwanted (in the sense of un-coincidable) element of transcendency in order to avoid a relativist stand; while the latter stresses the need for christianity to be a strong, ultimate counter-narrative. Milbank on his turn, can hardly avoid some sort of *retour au pré-modernité*, where the particular, christian tradition-based narrative, not only opens the way to (transcendent) ontotheology, but also exposes the intrinsic violent nature of the exclusive narrative.

Beyond particularity lies the meta-question: whether methodological interdisciplinary cooperation is possible, or not. Both disciplines are more or less united in their attention to the particular and the contingent as a major hermeneutical key in this context. Now, it will be the matter to apply the same key to similar contexts. This application will be a next step in the underlying research-project. Whether or not we will have answered Pilate's question, remains open for debate; but we will have come closer to an answer, having explored mechanisms and contexts through which theological truth-claims are defined and articulated.

dirk.claes@theo.kuleuven.be   Dirk CLAES

LIST OF ABBREVIATIONS

AAS	*Acta Apostolicae Sedis: Commentarium Officiale*, Vatican City.
BETL	Bibliotheca Ephemeridum Theologicarum Lovaniensium, Leuven.
CCSL	Corpus Christianorum, Series Latina, Turnhout.
CSEL	*Corpus Scriptorum Ecclesiasticorum Latinorum*, Vienna.
ETL	*Ephemerides Theoligicae Lovanienses*, Leuven.
HTR	*Harvard Theological Review*, Chico (CA).
NPNF	A select library of the Nicene and post-Nicene fathers of the christian Church, Grand Rapids (MI).
RHE	*Revue d'histoire ecclésiastique*, Leuven – Louvain-la-Neuve.
RTAM	*Revue de théologie anciènne et médiévale*, Leuven.
SC	Sources chrétiennes, Paris.
WSA	The Works of Saint Augustine: a Translation for the 21st Century, New York (NY).

INDEX OF NAMES

BIBLIOTHECA EPHEMERIDUM THEOLOGICARUM LOVANIENSIUM

SERIES III

131. C.M. TUCKETT (ed.), *The Scriptures in the Gospels*, 1997. XXIV-721 p.
60 €

132. J. VAN RUITEN & M. VERVENNE (eds.), *Studies in the Book of Isaiah. Festschrift Willem A.M. Beuken*, 1997. XX-540 p. 75 €

133. M. VERVENNE & J. LUST (eds.), *Deuteronomy and Deuteronomic Literature. Festschrift C.H.W. Brekelmans*, 1997. XI-637 p. 75 €

134. G. VAN BELLE (ed.), *Index Generalis ETL / BETL 1982-1997*, 1999. IX-337 p. 40 €

135. G. DE SCHRIJVER, *Liberation Theologies on Shifting Grounds. A Clash of Socio-Economic and Cultural Paradigms*, 1998. XI-453 p. 53 €

136. A. SCHOORS (ed.), *Qohelet in the Context of Wisdom*, 1998. XI-528 p.
60 €

137. W.A. BIENERT & U. KÜHNEWEG (eds.), *Origeniana Septima. Origenes in den Auseinandersetzungen des 4. Jahrhunderts*, 1999. XXV-848 p. 95 €

138. É. GAZIAUX, *L'autonomie en morale: au croisement de la philosophie et de la théologie*, 1998. XVI-760 p. 75 €

139. J. GROOTAERS, *Actes et acteurs à Vatican II*, 1998. XXIV-602 p. 75 €

140. F. NEIRYNCK, J. VERHEYDEN & R. CORSTJENS, *The Gospel of Matthew and the Sayings Source Q: A Cumulative Bibliography 1950-1995*, 1998. 2 vols., VII-1000-420* p. 95 €

141. E. BRITO, *Heidegger et l'hymne du sacré*, 1999. XV-800 p. 90 €

142. J. VERHEYDEN (ed.), *The Unity of Luke-Acts*, 1999. XXV-828 p. 60 €

143. N. CALDUCH-BENAGES & J. VERMEYLEN (eds.), *Treasures of Wisdom. Studies in Ben Sira and the Book of Wisdom. Festschrift M. Gilbert*, 1999. XXVII-463 p. 75 €

144. J.-M. AUWERS & A. WÉNIN (eds.), *Lectures et relectures de la Bible. Festschrift P.-M. Bogaert*, 1999. XLII-482 p. 75 €

145. C. BEGG, *Josephus' Story of the Later Monarchy (AJ 9,1–10,185)*, 2000. X-650 p. 75 €

146. J.M. ASGEIRSSON, K. DE TROYER & M.W. MEYER (eds.), *From Quest to Q. Festschrift James M. Robinson*, 2000. XLIV-346 p. 60 €

147. T. RÖMER (ed.), *The Future of the Deuteronomistic History*, 2000. XII-265 p. 75 €

148. F.D. VANSINA, *Paul Ricœur: Bibliographie primaire et secondaire - Primary and Secondary Bibliography 1935-2000*, 2000. XXVI-544 p. 75 €

149. G.J. BROOKE & J.D. KAESTLI (eds.), *Narrativity in Biblical and Related Texts*, 2000. XXI-307 p. 75 €

150. F. NEIRYNCK, *Evangelica III: 1992-2000. Collected Essays*, 2001. XVII-666 p.
60 €

151. B. Doyle, *The Apocalypse of Isaiah Metaphorically Speaking. A Study of the Use, Function and Significance of Metaphors in Isaiah 24-27*, 2000. xii-453 p.   75 €

152. T. Merrigan & J. Haers (eds.), *The Myriad Christ. Plurality and the Quest for Unity in Contemporary Christology*, 2000. xiv-593 p.   75 €

153. M. Simon, *Le catéchisme de Jean-Paul II. Genèse et évaluation de son commentaire du Symbole des apôtres*, 2000. xvi-688 p.   75 €

154. J. Vermeylen, *La loi du plus fort. Histoire de la rédaction des récits davidiques de 1 Samuel 8 à 1 Rois 2*, 2000. xiii-746 p.   80 €

155. A. Wénin (ed.), *Studies in the Book of Genesis. Literature, Redaction and History*, 2001. xxx-643 p.   60 €

156. F. Ledegang, *Mysterium Ecclesiae. Images of the Church and its Members in Origen*, 2001. xvii-848 p.   84 €

157. J.S. Boswell, F.P. McHugh & J. Verstraeten (eds.), *Catholic Social Thought: Twilight of Renaissance*, 2000. xxii-307 p.   60 €

158. A. Lindemann (ed.), *The Sayings Source Q and the Historical Jesus*, 2001. xxii-776 p.   60 €

159. C. Hempel, A. Lange & H. Lichtenberger (eds.), *The Wisdom Texts from Qumran and the Development of Sapiential Thought*, 2002. xii-502 p.
                                                                                                                                            80 €

160. L. Boeve & L. Leijssen (eds.), *Sacramental Presence in a Postmodern Context*, 2001. xvi-382 p.   60 €

161. A. Denaux (ed.), *New Testament Textual Criticism and Exegesis. Festschrift J. Delobel*, 2002. xviii-391 p.   60 €

162. U. Busse, *Das Johannesevangelium. Bildlichkeit, Diskurs und Ritual. Mit einer Bibliographie über den Zeitraum 1986-1998*, 2002. xiii-572 p.
                                                                                                                                            70 €

163. J.-M. Auwers & H.J. de Jonge (eds.), *The Biblical Canons*, 2003. lxxxviii-718 p.   60 €

164. L. Perrone (ed.), *Origeniana Octava. Origen and the Alexandrian Tradition*, 2003. xxv-x-1406 p.   180 €

165. R. Bieringer, V. Koperski & B. Lataire (eds.), *Resurrection in the New Testament. Festschrift J. Lambrecht*, 2002. xxxi-551 p.   70 €

166. M. Lamberigts & L. Kenis (eds.), *Vatican II and Its Legacy*, 2002. xii-512 p.   65 €

167. P. Dieudonné, *La Paix clémentine. Défaite et victoire du premier jansénisme français sous le pontificat de Clément IX (1667-1669)*, 2003. xxxix-302 p.   70 €

168. F. García Martínez, *Wisdom and Apocalypticism in the Dead Sea Scrolls and in the Biblical Tradition*, 2003. xxxiv-491 p.   60 €

169. D. Ogliari, *Gratia et Certamen: The Relationship between Grace and Free Will in the Discussion of Augustine with the So-Called Semipelagians*, 2003. lvii-468 p.   75 €

170. G. Cooman, M. van Stiphout & B. Wauters (eds.), *Zeger-Bernard Van Espen at the Crossroads of Canon Law, History, Theology and Church-State Relations*, 2003. xx-530 p.   80 €

171. B. Bourgine, *L'herméneutique théologique de Karl Barth. Exégèse et dogmatique dans le quatrième volume de la Kirchliche Dogmatik*, 2003. xxii-548 p.   75 €

172. J. HAERS & P. DE MEY (eds.), *Theology and Conversation: Towards a Relational Theology*, 2003. XIII-923 p. 90 €
173. M.J.J. MENKEN, *Matthew's Bible: The Old Testament Text of the Evangelist*, 2004. XII-336 p. 60 €
174. J.-P. DELVILLE, *L'Europe de l'exégèse au XVIᵉ siècle. Interprétations de la parabole des ouvriers à la vigne (Matthieu 20,1-16)*, 2004. XLII-775 p. 70 €
175. E. BRITO, *J.G. Fichte et la transformation du Christianisme*, 2004. XVI-808 p. 90 €
176. J. SCHLOSSER (ed.), *The Catholic Epistles and the Tradition*, 2004. XXIV-569 p. 60 €
177. R. FAESEN (ed.), *Albert Deblaere, S.J. (1916-1994): Essays on Mystical Literature – Essais sur la littérature mystique – Saggi sulla letteratura mistica*, 2004. XX-473 p. 70 €
178. J. LUST, *Messianism and the Septuagint: Collected Essays*. Edited by K. HAUSPIE, 2004. XIV-247 p. 60 €
179. H. GIESEN, *Jesu Heilsbotschaft und die Kirche. Studien zur Eschatologie und Ekklesiologie bei den Synoptikern und im ersten Petrusbrief*, 2004. XX-578 p. 70 €
180. H. LOMBAERTS & D. POLLEFEYT (eds.), *Hermeneutics and Religious Education*, 2004. XIII-427 p. 70 €
181. D. DONNELLY, A. DENAUX & J. FAMERÉE (eds.), *The Holy Spirit, the Church, and Christian Unity. Proceedings of the Consultation Held at the Monastery of Bose, Italy (14-20 October 2002)*, 2005. XII-417 p. 70 €
182. R. BIERINGER, G. VAN BELLE & J. VERHEYDEN (eds.), *Luke and His Readers. Festschrift A. Denaux*, 2005. XXVIII-470 p. 65 €
183. D.F. PILARIO, *Back to the Rough Grounds of Praxis: Exploring Theological Method with Pierre Bourdieu*, 2005. XXXII-584 p. 80 €
184. G. VAN BELLE, J.G. VAN DER WATT & P. MARITZ (eds.), *Theology and Christology in the Fourth Gospel: Essays by the Members of the SNTS Johannine Writings Seminar*, 2005. XII-561 p. 70 €
185. D. LUCIANI, *Sainteté et pardon. Vol. 1: Structure littéraire du Lévitique. Vol. 2: Guide technique*, 2005. XIV-VII-656 p. 120 €
186. R.A. DERRENBACKER, JR., *Ancient Compositional Practices and the Synoptic Problem*, 2005. XXVIII-290 p. 80 €
187. P. VAN HECKE (ed.), *Metaphor in the Hebrew Bible*, 2005. X-308 p. 65 €
188. L. BOEVE, Y. DEMAESENEER & S. VAN DEN BOSSCHE (eds.), *Religious Experience and Contemporary Theological Epistemology*, 2005. X-335 p. 50 €
189. J.M. ROBINSON, *The Sayings Gospel Q. Collected Essays*, 2005. XVIII-888 p. 90 €
190. C.W. STRÜDER, *Paulus und die Gesinnung Christi. Identität und Entscheidungsfindung aus der Mitte von 1Kor 1-4*, 2005. LII-522 p. 80 €
191. C. FOCANT & A. WÉNIN (eds.), *Analyse narrative et Bible. Deuxième colloque international du RRENAB, Louvain-la-Neuve, avril 2004*, 2005. XVI-593 p. 75 €
192. F. GARCÍA MARTÍNEZ & M. VERVENNE (eds.), in collaboration with B. DOYLE, *Interpreting Translation: Studies on the LXX and Ezekiel in Honour of Johan Lust*, 2005. XVI-464 p. 70 €

193. F. Mies, *L'espérance de Job*, 2006. XXII-636 p.   87 €
194. C. Focant, *Marc, un évangile étonnant*, 2006. XV-402 p.   60 €
195. M.A. Knibb (ed.), *The Septuagint and Messianism*, 2006. XXXI-560 p. 60 €
196. M. Simon, *La célébration du mystère chrétien dans le catéchisme de Jean-Paul II*, 2006. XIV-638 p.   85 €
197. A.Y. Thomasset, *L'ecclésiologie de John Henry Newman Anglican*. Forthcoming.
198. M. Lamberigts – A.A. den Hollander (eds.), *Lay Bibles in Europe 1450-1800*. Forthcoming.
199. J.Z. Skira – M.S. Attridge, *In God's Hands. Essays on the Church and Ecumenism in Honour of Michael A. Fahey S.J.*,2006. XXX-314 p.   90 €
200. G. Van Belle (ed.), *The Death of Jesus in the Fourth Gospel*. Forthcoming.
201. D. Pollefeyt (ed.), *Interreligious Learning*. Forthcoming.

PRINTED ON PERMANENT PAPER • IMPRIME SUR PAPIER PERMANENT • GEDRUKT OP DUURZAAM PAPIER - ISO 9706

N.V. PEETERS S.A., WAROTSTRAAT 50, B-3020 HERENT